Pierre Lanfrey

The History of Napoleon the First

Vol. 1 (1769 - 1800), Second Edition

Pierre Lanfrey

The History of Napoleon the First
Vol. 1 (1769 - 1800), Second Edition

ISBN/EAN: 9783337350062

Printed in Europe, USA, Canada, Australia, Japan

Cover: Foto ©ninafisch / pixelio.de

More available books at **www.hansebooks.com**

THE HISTORY

OF

NAPOLEON THE FIRST

BY

P. LANFREY

IN FOUR VOLUMES.—VOL. I.

1769–1800

SECOND EDITION

London

MACMILLAN AND CO.

AND NEW YORK

1886

CONTENTS

CHAP.		PAGE
I.	Childhood and Youth of Napoleon, 1769–1793	1
II.	The Siege of Toulon and the 13th Vendémiaire, 1793–1796	25
III.	Submission of Piedmont and the Conquest of Lombardy, 1796	60
IV.	Violation of the Neutrality of Venice—Defeat of Würmser, 1796	95
V.	Creation of the Cispadane Republic—Arcola, 1796	117
VI.	Rivoli and Tolentino, 1797	143
VII.	The Preliminaries of Léoben, 1797	159
VIII.	The Occupation of Venice—The 18th Fructidor, 1797	190
IX.	Campo-Formio, 1797	233
X.	The Expedition to Egypt, 1797, 1798	253
XI.	Campaign in Syria, 1798, 1799	286

CHAP.	PAGE
XII. THE 18TH BRUMAIRE, 1799	307
XIII. THE CONSTITUTION OF THE YEAR VIII, 1799	354
XIV. ORGANISATION OF THE CONSULAR GOVERNMENT — ITS POLICY, INTERNAL AND EXTERNAL, 1799, 1800	386
XV. SESSION OF THE YEAR VIII — CENTRALISATION, 1800	426

This Translation has been made with the sanction of the Author.

THE HISTORY OF NAPOLEON

CHAPTER I

CHILDHOOD AND YOUTH OF NAPOLEON

1769–1793

NAPOLEON has for the most part had no judgment passed upon him but that either of profound hatred or of profound attachment. After his death, as during his life, it has been his fate to stir the hearts of men to their depths, and the battles to which his policy gave rise have been fought again over his memory. To popular deification and the interested encomiums of party spirit, to the complaisant eulogy of historians, the dupes or accomplices of vulgar prejudice, others have retorted by violent invectives, in which we have often seen Truth wounded by her own weapons. Napoleon's glory has always found more flatterers than detractors, for the incense of which there is no more to spare for the idol is still lavished on the worshippers. History is made for neither of these parts, for neither is compatible with the dignity of the judge, nor with the calm of perfect equity.

Now that detraction and apology have, while exhausting themselves, prepared all the elements of complete information, the time seems to have come for a more clear-sighted estimate. If, after so many eminent politicians, philosophers, historians, and poets, I venture in my turn to examine a figure that so few of them have been able to touch without damage, my single claim is that I am able to take advantage of the lapse of time. Information abounds, motives are better known, facts are clearer, and false prestige is gradually vanishing. As for the passions awakened in us by the recollection of the influence of Napoleon's memory in the defeats which liberty has suffered in our times, it is now tolerably easy to be on our guard against these. The present having become less unendurable, no longer allows us to despair for the future. I feel myself free alike from the prepossessions of hatred and the superstition of enthusiasm, and I should repulse as an ignoble servitude any opinion which could withhold me from paying reverence to true greatness.

There is, besides, in history itself a pacifying force, which shields the mind from the fanaticism of party spirit. If, on the one hand, it presents a spectacle of discouraging failures and endless contradictions, it shows us, on the other, that there is a constant tendency in civilisation at once to recover and to raise its level. It shows us especially that we are the authors of our own destinies, and that a nation is always responsible for the creation of a yoke under which it has afterwards been obliged to bow. In spite of certain appearances wrongly understood, history is not a school of fatalism; it is one long pleading in favour of liberty.

This lesson, which is common to all epochs, comes out with striking force in the progressive movement of the century in which Napoleon was born, down to the dawn of the French Revolution; and the deviation which took place later is no contradiction to its teaching. Never has activity been more free notwithstanding its extravagances, more rational notwithstanding its illusions; never have men sought truth with more generous or more sincere ardour. The success of their efforts may have been compromised by passion, by error, by the power of old prejudices and the difficulties inherent in circumstances, but their efforts have not been lost. A host of great men sprang up, who brought new life into every part of the domain of science and thought; they introduced a higher idea of human dignity, a wider conception of the rights of nations and individuals; they fought against every kind of servitude, and they reconciled policy with justice and liberty. They softened their temper to such a point as even to tolerate abuses, so as to give them time to die a natural death.

Was the eighteenth century an exception in this? Did it pursue an Utopia? Nay; it carried on the work of its forerunners,—the sixteenth which saw the birth of the Reformation, and the seventeenth which saw the triumph of English institutions; it was in communion with all the stirring spirits of the past; it marched along the great highway of the human mind, and knew this, and it was this confidence that threw over its decline an air of serene majesty. The thinkers who had shed a lustre over its course were followed by great practical men who carried their plans into execution. After Locke, Montesquieu, Voltaire, and Rousseau, rose Turgot, Franklin, Mirabeau, and Washington. The American Republic, child of experiment, irreproachable as a creation of pure reason, was on the point of rising up beyond the seas to serve as a beacon to all future societies. The future appeared so assured, and the course of events so irresistible, that even the wisest among them were not proof against a certain intoxication, and in their too scornful impatience of facts they pushed impetuously out to the very verge and final limits of the possible. Not content with proclaiming the end of religious and political despotism, they went on to predict the end of superstition, the end of misery, the end of slavery, the end of conquest, the end of war. It was towards this time that there was born in a small island, obscure and nearly without history, a child who was to be called NAPOLEON BONAPARTE.

There is little need to point out the contrast between this extraordinary man and the general spirit of his epoch; it strikes the eye instantly. From his character and his ideas, and especially from the aim he had in view, Napoleon seems to belong to another age. Again, the more closely we study his life, the more plainly we shall see that the only part of his work which has survived him is precisely that which he borrowed from the genius of his time. The rest is purely phenomenal. The part played by Napoleon, then, presents nothing which it is beyond the power of history to explain.

His country, like Poland, seemed a living refutation of the dreams of philosophers. Corsica formed in this cosmopolitan century a country apart in Europe; it was isolated by its misfortunes, as well as by the character and manners of its inhabitants. Their intercourse with the mainland, which had never been frequent, had become still rarer during their long struggle with Genoa. The result of this isolation was, that, in spite of a certain polish of civilisation, which the young men acquired in the universities of Italy, they had lost none of the energy and wild originality of their character. 'Corsica,' wrote Livy, 'is a rugged, mountainous, and almost uninhabitable island. The people resemble their country, being as ungovernable as wild beasts. Servitude in no way softens the Corsicans; if they are made prisoners, they become unbearable to their masters, or else give up life from sheer impatience of the yoke.'

This was still true to a certain extent, in spite of the changes which a mixture of races and the progress of time had wrought. Successive invasions and the influence of general civilisation had softened the primitive type, but had not destroyed its principal features. To their indomitable wildness had been united a certain suppleness borrowed from the Italians, and to the energy of their character a subtle and shrewd intelligence. Sober, courageous, and hospitable, but deceitful, superstitious, and vindictive, such were, and such still are, the people of Corsica. Like their climate, which is burning on the plain and freezing on the heights, their passions are violent and their heads cool. They are capable of excelling both in diplomacy and war. They shared none of the ideas of their time, except through the scraps of classical learning which they brought back from the Italian universities. Hence the antique simplicity of their political ideas, which, we may admit, was hardly discountenanced by any of the institutions still existing at that time in the rest of Europe. Paoli was able seriously to dream of playing in his country the part of Solon or Lycurgus, and, as far as circumstances permitted him, he did so, without meeting any of the resistance he would inevitably have found everywhere else. What in France was matter for speculation became in Corsica the programme of the statesman, and could be realised on the spot. It was for this reason that Corsica attracted the attention of Jean-Jacques Rousseau, absorbed as he then was in his reminiscences of antiquity. In his *Contrat Social* he calls Corsica 'the only country left in Europe capable of legislation,' a remark which suggested to Paoli the idea of asking him, through Buttafuoco, for the scheme of a constitution. Corsica was in a situation only to be conceived as possible in any other country, on condition that everything existing should be swept utterly away. This social state and the spirit which was its consequence explain in a certain measure what of the antique there is about Napoleon's political ideal, as well as in that of Paoli; for a Cæsar was just as incompatible as a Lycurgus with the fine complications of modern societies.

After long years of obstinate struggle, during which this little country astonished Europe by its indomitable courage, the Genoese, seeing all their efforts to reconquer it fail, sold it to France. Choiseul, who first undertook the office of mediator, and in this capacity occupied all the principal ports of the island, did not scruple to turn all the strength of a powerful nation against the weak people who had placed confidence in his protection. Paoli, the hero of the war against the Genoese, tried in vain to resist the French invasion; he was obliged to yield. Despair in his heart, he exiled himself from a country that he had only delivered from its old oppressors to see it succumb under a new despotism. But the same year in which the patriots were put down by our arms, Corsica gave birth to one whom its conquerors were soon to acknowledge as their master. Napoleon was born on the 15th of August 1769, just two months after the conquest of the island.

The childhood and youth of great men necessarily elude history; fiction, for this reason, usually takes possession of them. Youth, with its secret transformations and psychological mysteries, is a difficult study, and one on which very few certain ideas can be formed even by the most attentive observer. It is an age of growth, in which the whole mind is changing and unsettled. We fail to find either that firm contexture and those marked lines, or the guarantees and precise information, which alone constitute historical reality. It is still rarer to meet with actions in childhood which are worthy of record, and the constant efforts which have been made to throw some light on the early years of Napoleon have only ended in the creation of legends, whose puerility matches their improbability. Between the two improprieties of being too brief, and giving the record of trifles which are neither serious nor true, I shall choose the less, and, putting aside hypothetical stories, shall pass rapidly through facts and observations, which from the concurrence of the evidence deserve to be accepted for certain.

Among the foremost of the companions of Paoli stands Charles de Bonaparte, father of Napoleon. His family had originally come from Italy, and they had still relatives in that country. They had acquired a certain reputation, both in politics and literature, under the Italian Republics. They took refuge in Corsica after the civil war which rent Florence, but they had always kept up an intercourse with the country which had given them birth, and remained as much Italian as they were Corsican. They had the marks of the subtle and resolute race from which a Machiavelli had sprung. When Paoli left the island, Charles Bonaparte, who had only a short time before married Lætitia Ramolino, a woman of great beauty, and the companion of his perils even when she was pregnant of Napoleon, was obliged to submit like the majority of his fellow-citizens. He had the art of obtaining, with an ease that is surprising, the favour of the French administration, while for several years a handful of patriots, who were hunted down in the mountains of the interior, kept up the struggle, and whose punishment stained our conquest.

It was among this people, overthrown though not mastered, in the midst of passions sometimes controlled and at others bursting loose with all the savage violence of the Corsican temperament, that the young Napoleon grew up. He witnessed as a child the last struggle for the independence of his country. 'I was born when my country was sinking,' he wrote to Paoli in 1789; 'the cries of the dying, the groans of the oppressed, and the tears of despair surrounded my cradle from my birth.' Born in the midst of storms, he early became familiar with their commotion, and it is to this he partly owed the self-possession which he showed in later life in the midst of the revolutionary chaos. Like the infant Achilles, he had been dipped in the Styx.

The recollections of the war of independence, the tales of those who had taken part in it, the curses of oppressed patriots, and, above all, the legendary exploits of the great Paoli, the warrior legislator, an ancient figure straying into the eighteenth century, were all food for his young and ardent imagination. These impressions were strongly engraven in the depths of his soul, and ruled over all the feelings of his youth. They made him serious with extraordinary precocity. While still a child, he shared high and patriotic emotions, to which he surrendered himself by instinct before he could grasp them by intelligence; he witnessed sights which lighted up for him all the extremes of human life. He was acquainted with political passions at an age at which ordinarily the only passions are for playthings; it was, perhaps, from having been initiated into them too early that he so quickly freed himself from them. Hardly arrived at Brienne, this child, eleven years old, perceived in one of the apartments the portrait of Choiseul, the author of the wrongs of his country; he apostrophised it with fury, and was full of rage that they should keep at Brienne the portrait of such a man. A little later, speaking of his father, who was dead, he declared that he could never forgive him for not following even into exile the fortunes of Paoli.

Charles Bonaparte, whose family was large, and his patrimony most moderate, solicited and obtained, thanks to the protection of Count Marbœuf, governor of the island, scholarships for his children in some of the principal schools in France. It was thus that young Napoleon was sent to Brienne. Putting aside all doubtful anecdotes which abound on this part of his life, and only taking into account the general impression of those who knew him at this epoch, we discover in him even at that time a concentrated and resolute character, a quarrelsome temper, and, notwithstanding momentary flashes of gaiety, a singularly gloomy disposition for so young a child. The hardness of his lot had stifled in him all the charms of childhood. He lived alone, seldom seeking the companionship of his schoolfellows, not much liked by them, and scarcely ever joining in their games. This inclination for solitude, experienced by all who do not find in those around them the sympathy of which they have need, often attends superior minds even at an age when they are unconscious of superiority, and children find this as hard to forgive as men find it.

Napoleon was a laborious scholar; he showed great application, and, what is somewhat remarkable, was extremely tractable with his masters. We have a positive proof of this in the certificate of Chevalier de Kéralio, Inspector of Military Schools, who was struck with the intelligence and character of the youth. Napoleon Bonaparte knew even then, when he chose, how to make his natural abruptness give way to circumstances, and could be insinuating and yielding. In a short time, he got to be head of his school in mathematics, for which he had great talent. He displayed the same ardour in the study of history, but showed a decided preference for that of the ancient Republics, in which he found a picture of the struggles to which his own country had just been a victim. Plutarch and the Commentaries of Cæsar were from an early period his favourite books. In the one he found that mixture of reality and romance which had always a strong attraction for him, while the other aided him in his military studies, and at the same time gave him the grandest model that he could dream of. He paid but little attention to other subjects; it was not till much later that he took to perfecting himself in French, some of the most essential elements of which he never mastered thoroughly, though he more than once showed in it the skill of a superior writer.

At the Military College in Paris, where he went to complete his studies on leaving Brienne in 1785, and where the discipline was much less strict, his individuality began to reveal itself, and he appeared in a new light. He there found himself in a sort of comparative freedom, or as one lost in the midst of a crowd. His docility was gradually replaced by a kind of surly independence; he was stubborn, bitter, imperious, and dissatisfied; even his masters complained of the change. His character took a marked tinge of misanthropy. His prospects were of the gloomiest. His father had died, leaving his family in difficulties that were worse than absolute poverty; his brothers and sisters were scattered about in different schools, where they were brought up, as the phrase was, at the King's expense; he had nothing to reckon on but the precarious support of his protectors, whose kindness would, he knew, soon be exhausted.

The contrast of his position with that of his companions, who were mostly the younger sons of wealthy families, made him keenly alive to the bitterness of the privations which he was obliged to impose on himself, and which he knew how to bear without complaint. Discontented, soured, and already tormented by that restless activity which was the first manifestation of his genius, he lived alone and acquired a character for being thoroughly unsociable. He was constantly criticising the old *régime*, and, though only sixteen years of age, he adopted the language and tone of a moralist, censuring on all occasions the abuses of a society in which, according to all appearance, he was destined to vegetate obscurely in the lower ranks of the army. Bourrienne has preserved some curious fragments of a manuscript, written by Bonaparte at the École Militaire, against the extravagant habits in which, owing to the lax discipline, the students were able to indulge. The incredible incorrectness of his letters at this time forbids the supposition that the composition of the paper was his own, but the ideas bear the impress of his practical and organising mind. He rightly considered that living in such luxury was a miserable preparation for the privations of military life; but the severity of the system that he proposed to substitute betrays too visibly the secret rancour which inspired the young reformer's zeal for equality.

At the end of a year, Bonaparte left the École Militaire to enter the regiment La Fère as second lieutenant, and was sent to the garrison of Valence (1786). He was then rather more than sixteen. There, through the influence of a kind and distinguished lady, who gave him a warm reception in her own house and introduced him into society, that reserved nature, till now a stranger to a single gleam of sunshine, for the first time began to expand. A striking change took place in the character, habits, and manners of the young lieutenant. It was then that he first revealed that insinuating and seductive charm which he at times threw into his conversation, ordinarily so blunt and downright when it was not actually imperious. His mind grew more refined, and he acquired more ease of manner, by contact with this society of the old *régime*, made by women and for women. At the same time he increased his knowledge and enlarged the circle of his ideas by extensive reading. The voluminous extracts, which remain in his own handwriting, prove that no soldier in garrison ever employed his leisure hours more laboriously.

Passion does not appear to have had much dominion over him, if we may judge from a *Dialogue on Love*, which remains among his papers, and which contains a passage quite in keeping with his later opinions on this subject. 'Love,' he says, 'produces more evil than good, and, if a protecting divinity could deliver us from its influence, it would confer a benefit on humanity.' No amusement could make him forget his native island, his poor Ithaca, which he had not seen for so many long years, and which was then his only true love. But in what state would he find it on his return? Reflections of this kind produced a sadness which would almost seem to have suggested thoughts of suicide, if we may interpret literally the confidences of a young imagination :—

'How depraved men are! What cowardly, cringing wretches they are! What a spectacle my country presents!

The trembling inhabitants clasp the hand that oppresses them. They are no longer the brave Corsicans whom a hero inspired with his love of virtue and his hatred of tyranny, of luxury, of base courtiers. . . . Frenchmen, not satisfied with depriving us of all we most prize, you have also corrupted our manners. . . . Life is a burden to me, for I enter into none of its pleasures, and everything is a toil, because the men with whom I live, and probably shall always have to live, have tastes which differ as much from mine as the light of the moon does from that of the sun. I cannot live in such a manner as alone would make existence endurable; so I am full of disgust for everything.'[1]

It was, in all probability, at Valence that Bonaparte felt the first awakening of ambition. It was there, at any rate, that he began to write the *History of Corsica*, which appears to have engrossed his mind during his youth, and of which only fragments were published.[2] He sent the first two chapters of it, in 1786, to Abbé Raynal, accompanied by a most flattering letter, in which he solicits advice and protection. The Abbé, who was then at the height of his glory, willingly granted his request. The choice of this subject, and everything we know of Bonaparte at this period of his life, indicate that his native island was still the object on which all his thoughts centred, and the sphere in which he hoped to carry out his future plans. His brightest dreams showed him no more inviting scene for action than Corsica. He only cared for literary success in Paris, in order to present himself in a more dazzling light

---

[1] Libri, *Souvenirs de la Jeunesse de Bonaparte*. Among the numerous books which have been written on this epoch of Napoleon's life, none contains more correct information than this little work. See also, on the same subject, *Mémoires de M. Nasica*, on the childhood and youth of Napoleon; *l'Histoire des premières années de Bonaparte*, by Baron de Coston; *Mémoires de Bourrienne*, and *Mémoires de la Duchesse d'Abrantès*, etc.—all of which ought to be read with caution.

[2] According to M. Libri (*Souvenirs de la Jeunesse de Bonaparte*) the manuscript of this history is still in existence, and forms part of the collection of papers, which were originally confided to the care of Cardinal Fesch, by the First Consul.

before his countrymen. Corsica was the refuge of his imagination; there he found consolation under the meanness of his present fortunes, and there he shaped a destiny after his own fancy. To play the part of Paoli, and realise one day by the recovery of the independence of his country the projects which his hero had conceived, appeared to him the loftiest prospect to which he could aspire.

It was in this temper that the opening of the French Revolution found him. He did not hesitate for an instant to declare himself in its favour, for his situation made him one of its natural partisans. But though he adopted the ideas and language of the Revolution, he in no way shared its enthusiasms or its antipathies. He recognised in it a power rather than a principle. And, notwithstanding that he was a professed partisan of the new ideas, he was still for a long time after much more absorbed in the affairs of Corsica than in those of France, a country in which he had always regarded himself as a stranger; and this patriotic preference was kept up by ever more and more frequent visits to the island. The effect of the great crisis of 1789 was only superficially felt in Corsica, because there were no privileged classes to destroy. The inhabitants, who at first only demanded that their island should be on the same footing as the French provinces, afterwards hoped for a moment to obtain its complete independence. But the National Assembly declared Corsica united to France, before Paoli, who had started to plead his country's cause, had arrived in Paris. He was received with great honours a few days later, but the decree was maintained.

The year following (July 1790), Paoli went back to Corsica, and his return excited the greatest enthusiasm among his countrymen. Bonaparte was there also, full of agitation. He and his brother Joseph had just been taking an active part in the little municipal revolution of Ajaccio, and he was entrusted by the authorities of the town with the drawing up of a congratulatory address to the General. He was delighted to undertake a work which would afford him an opportunity of knowing his hero tolerably closely. Paoli gave the son of his old friend a distinguished and cordial reception. He was greatly struck by the originality of this young man of twenty-one; by the energy with which he expressed his opinions; by his impetuosity; and by the strong and singular temper of his character. He admired too the military genius he displayed in his plans of fortifications for the defence of the island. He predicted for him a brilliant career.

Nor did Bonaparte, on his side, feel any diminution of his admiration for the General, the simple dignity of whose manners sustained the high opinion which his virtues had inspired. Ambition alone could alienate Bonaparte from Paoli. It was about this epoch, that is in 1791, that Bonaparte published his first political manifesto, under the title of a *Letter to Matteo Buttafuoco.* This pamphlet is the passionate expression of his opinions and feelings at that time. It shows that, in spite of his French education, Bonaparte had remained thoroughly Corsican, and was still inconsolable for the fall of his country. It breathes the rancour of a patriotism which could not pardon the French conquest, notwithstanding the change of 1789. The object of the piece is to defend Paoli against the unjust attacks of Buttafuoco. It was published contrary to the express wish of Paoli, who wrote to Bonaparte, with all the simplicity and abnegation of a great mind: 'I only wish to be spoken of as a man with none but right intentions.'

Buttafuoco had been the principal instrument of Choiseul at the time of the union of the island to France, and had received from him the reward of his services. When he was afterwards sent as Deputy of the Corsican nobility to the National Assembly, instead of trying to wipe out the remembrance of the odious part he had played in this intrigue, he proved himself the inveterate enemy of all reform. All his past political life was unmasked, and described in language in which the bitterest irony is mingled with the most burning and declamatory eloquence. Bonaparte, who was then an indefatigable and most popular speaker at public meetings, had his pamphlet read in the Club of Ajaccio, where it was greatly applauded, and a resolution was passed for its publication. The letter, though intended for Corsica, did not lose sight of France, and, with a view to the public opinion then reigning there, contained invocations marked by an exaltation peculiarly southern :—

'Oh, Lameth! oh, Robespierre! oh, Pétion! oh, Volney! oh, Mirabeau! oh, Barnave! oh, Bailly! oh, Lafayette! this is the man who dares to take a seat by your side! Dripping with the blood of his brothers, polluted by every kind of crime, he presents himself in the uniform of a General, the iniquitous reward of his guilty deeds! He dares to call himself the representative of the nation—he who sold it, and you suffer him to do so! He dares to raise his eyes, and listen to your speeches, and you allow it! As for the votes of the people, he never had more than those of a dozen nobles! Ajaccio, Bastia, and the greater part of the cantons have treated his effigy as they would fain have treated his person.'

The *Letter to Buttafuoco* is by far the best of Napoleon Bonaparte's early writings. Inspired by sincere and patriotic indignation, and written under the sway of strong emotion, it bears, in spite of a declamatory style that spoils it, traces of genuine feeling, which cannot be said of the *Discours* written at the same time for the Academy of Lyons, nor of the *Souper de Beaucaire*, which belongs to the year 1793.

Bonaparte, like almost all young men of his generation, was a warm disciple of Jean-Jacques Rousseau; and, like many others, it was the faults of his model that he imitated by preference, for they were easier to reproduce than his excellences. His hour of excitement and enthusiasm was due entirely to this influence. When he was quartered at Auxonne, his want of fortune obliging him to make a virtue of necessity, he lived with great sobriety and economy. He employed all his leisure time in educating his brother Louis, and he made a rule never to join any of the pleasure-parties of his companions, always assuming the manners and appearance of a Stoic, and dressing with a plainness that was almost sordid. It was while in this virtuous mood that he wrote his *Discours sur les Vérités et les Sentiments qu'il importe le plus d'inculquer aux Hommes pour leur Bonheur*, a subject proposed for competition by the Academy at Lyons.

Judging from the manner in which he treated the subject, and notwithstanding the energy he displayed, we may safely conclude that he had no vocation for the profession of moralist. His style, which was one day to attain such admirable precision, and which even in his first pamphlet was remarkably vigorous, is in this diffuse and declamatory; he had not yet acquired that laconic style after the fashion of St. Just, which may be termed his second manner. We must read the *Discours* to be able to conceive the extent to which a great mind, led away in a direction contrary to its natural bent, may fall below itself. It is impossible not to believe the work to be Napoleon's; he betrays himself by many characteristic marks, especially in the address to his protector Raynal, and in the enthusiastic eulogy of Paoli. It is well known, too, that this essay, found at Lyons—thanks to a piece of complaisance on the part of Talleyrand that looks very like a piece of sly malice—was preserved in spite of Napoleon, who threw the original manuscript into the fire, little suspecting that a copy had been made by M. de Hauterive. But for these positive proofs of authenticity, who would discover in this schoolboy's diffuseness, in this wordy and sentimental rhetoric, in the trite phrases and commonplace philanthropy, in this pathos as of Florian, in this emphasis sometimes verging on burlesque, the man of action, the mighty sword that was so soon to perform so terrible a work? It was not for nothing that he thus belied his genius by parodying feelings that had never been in his heart. The *Discours* instead of gaining the prize, as is wrongly stated in the *Mémorial de Sainte-Hélène*, received from M. Vasselier, the examiner of the papers, this curious mention: 'This essay may have been written by a man of feeling; but it is too incongruous, too desultory, and the style and arrangement too bad, to fix the attention.'

Bonaparte was not the only man who at the close of the eighteenth century mistook his vocation for the dreams of humanitarianism. It was just before this that Robespierre had composed his madrigals for the Academy of the *Rosati*. Bonaparte's true character comes out more clearly in a circumstance hitherto very little known. This episode, which is the key to his whole life, proves that none of a man's good or bad qualities reveal themselves without first having in some manner betrayed that they were there. Characters are not made by sudden explosions, though many aspects may remain unperceived till opportunity draws them out of the shade. Historians make a great mistake when they arbitrarily represent in the same man several successive characters.

The law concerning the National Guard produced more lively agitation in Corsica than anywhere else,—a result that might have been expected from a country only half subject. The arming of all citizens gave to local forces a kind of preponderance over those of the metropolis. This fact made the Corsicans attach great importance to the election of chiefs for their Militia. Bonaparte, though an officer in the army, taking advantage of the many irregularities which the Revolution had introduced into the service, spent one of his furloughs in seeking the place of major in the National Guard of Ajaccio,—a sure pledge of popularity, and consequently of promotion, popularity being at that time the source of all power. This appointment, which was the highest in the Ajaccio Militia, was sought by several rich and influential men, whose chances of obtaining it appeared much better than Bonaparte's. Marius Peraldi and Pozzo di Borgo were the heads of the opposite party, and they had all the principal inhabitants of the town on their side. But Bonaparte more than matched these advantages by his activity. In enlisting new votes in his favour, and inflaming the enthusiasm of those who were already his partisans, he displayed an amount of address, energy, and stern pertinacity, that were quite extraordinary in a man so young. He bought the votes of corrupt electors, and tried to frighten those whom he could not buy; money, promises, threats, family influence, private friendship, were all set to work to win the election.

Before long, the number of young Bonaparte's partisans

was nearly equal to that of his adversaries, and the town was divided into two hostile bands, both ready to come to blows. But it was not enough to have gained the people; he must obtain the suffrage of the Commissioners appointed by the Constituent Assembly to organise the battalions. Representing as they did the central power, the dissensions which had broken out at Ajaccio gave them a decisive influence over the elections, in placing them as arbitrators between the two parties. If they were hostile, all was lost. Each party seemed resolved to submit to them its complaints against the other and to choose them as umpires, and their arrival was awaited with impatience in order to proceed to the ballot. They came at last, and Murati, the most important of them, proceeded at once to the house of Marius Peraldi, Bonaparte's principal competitor. This was clearly to pronounce for his candidature, without, however, openly taking a side or exerting any undue influence on public opinion. Bonaparte had not anticipated this blow, which overthrew his plans, as it were, without attacking them. It affected him deeply. He showed himself by turns moody, dejected, irresolute. To let things take their chance was to give his adversaries a certain victory; to resist was no less dangerous. He passed a considerable part of the day in consultation with his most confidential friends, disturbed, harassed, not daring to take a decided step, only throwing out vague hints, and hoping to be spared the responsibility of a hazardous resolution. At last, as no one took the initiative, he decided to act.

Towards evening as the Peraldis were seated at table, a loud knocking was heard at the door of the house. A servant having opened it, a body of armed men instantly made their way in, and burst upon the terrified party. Murati had made his escape; he was overtaken, seized, and forcibly conducted to the house of Bonaparte, who was anxiously awaiting the result of the expedition. Mastering his emotion and composing his features, he received his prisoner with an assumed affability. 'I wished you to be free,' he said, 'perfectly free; you were not so at Peraldi's house.' Dumb at this audacious stroke and at all that was implied by it in case of opposition, the Commissioner thought it was no time to protest, and did not venture to return whence he had come. The next day the votes were taken, and Bonaparte appointed head of the battalion.

Pozzo di Borgo attempting to protest at the tribunal of the section against the violence offered to the Commissioner and the intimidations which had impaired the integrity of the vote, was immediately seized, thrown to the ground, trampled on, and only saved by the intervention of Bonaparte himself. The affair was overlooked in the headlong march of events in Paris, and Bonaparte retained his position. But if on the eve of the Eighteenth Brumaire the Five Hundred had known this episode in his life, it is hardly probable that they would have assembled at Saint-Cloud.

In the meantime the Revolution held its stormy course. The Girondists had seized the helm of government after the fall of the Constitutionalists, but everything seemed to show that it would soon slip from their failing grasp. An insurrection broke out at Ajaccio. When order was re-established, Bonaparte, who had been deprived by the Minister of War, Lajard, of his rank in the artillery of which he had made a sinecure, appeared at Paris to justify himself both for his prolonged absence, and for the part he had taken as Major of the National Guard in the repression of their tumults. Thanks to the influence of powerful protectors, he was soon reinstated in the army. To this he owed the opportunity of watching the events of some of the most famous days of the Revolution; amongst others, those of the Twentieth of June, the Tenth of August, and the Second of September.

One may imagine the effect produced on a practical mind like his by the sight of all this mad and unbridled passion. His faith was now for ever destroyed in principles which he had never thoroughly believed in; but instead of hastening to join the opposite side, as is the ordinary course, he remained a more decided supporter than ever of the ideas which he no longer had faith in, and was ready to act if need be with men whom he despised. The contradiction is only an apparent one. With his innate love of order and authority he could not see the tumults and excesses of the victorious populace without repugnance; and we know the regret he expressed on the Twentieth of June to his friend Bourrienne, that 'he could not see all this rabble swept away.'

But the influence of power on his mind was none the less for this; and from the day that he recognised the invincible strength of the movement, he followed it to the end notwithstanding his aversion, and without questioning its course or its incidents.

Behind the extreme opinions which he began to profess, until the moment when they should be no longer useful to him, we perceive one who contemplates the Revolution simply as a spectator, and France itself almost as a foreigner; who is as free from the passions of his age as he is preoccupied with his own interests; who would never compromise himself for the sake of a lost or waning cause; whose one only policy, in short, is to follow the current and to embrace the conclusions of the majority, so as to secure from circumstances the utmost advantage for himself. Once only he found himself compromised, and then not for the side which most attracted his sympathies, but for that which had shown the greatest determination and rigour in the exercise of power, and which seemed destined to fix the destinies of the Revolution.

Bonaparte's visit to Paris at such a time was well calculated to set him thinking, and it brought about a genuine transformation of his ideas. Nothing could have instructed him to the same extent in knowledge of human nature, in the science of revolutions, and in the art of making men's passions subservient to his own interests while pretending to be subservient to them. At a glance he took in all the advantage he might derive for his own advancement from these changes, sudden as they were irresistible.

As more than three-fourths of the officers of the army had emigrated, those who remained and had espoused the cause of the Revolution were sure of a rapid and brilliant fortune. He compared the almost boundless field opened to him by the Revolution with the circumscribed sphere which was all that his own country offered. From that time he attached himself to the fortunes of France, which he had only served hitherto because unable to devote himself to his own country. He allied himself the more closely to this cause in proportion as his fellow-countrymen, terrified by the excesses committed at Paris, became more and more alienated from it. The breach widened with time, and the day drew near when he was under the necessity of choosing between his old and his new country.

The Corsicans having scarcely known, except by name, the privileges and the abuses which had long pressed so heavily on France, could see nothing but unjustifiable barbarity in the bloody reprisals which accompanied their downfall. Transferred to Corsica, the revolutionary legislation, with its category of suspected persons and its wholesale executions, was only the delirium of a cruelty for which there was no excuse. They desired to escape from it at whatever cost. Already they foresaw that their priests, who had never given them the slightest grounds of complaint, were soon to be included in the proscription which had been levelled against their colleagues in France, and this apprehension caused mingled alarm and irritation amongst a people sincerely attached to their faith.

Paoli, with the modest title of President of the Directory of the Department, had the actual government of Corsica, and was its absolute master. His popularity had gained for him an informal sovereignty a thousand times more real than that of the French authorities. Judging from these circumstances that the time was not far off when his fellow-countrymen should again seize the independence for which they had made so many useless sacrifices, he prepared their minds by degrees in the direction of such a resolution. He openly declared his indignation at the news of the massacres of September and the death of the king. Bonaparte, who had returned to Corsica thoroughly impressed with French ideas, associated himself neither with the views nor the plans of Paoli, who was not long in perceiving the change which had come over the mind of his young favourite. Already his regard for him had considerably cooled in consequence of the ambitious instincts he had observed in him. For his own part, Bonaparte resented Paoli's persistent opposition to a pressure that was too unmeasured. This national movement, in which Paoli was followed by the immense majority of his countrymen, completed their mutual alienation. The rupture, which caused France the temporary loss of Corsica, took place while Bonaparte was absent.

On his return from an expedition to the Sardinian coast, in which the French fleet under Admiral Truguet made an unsuccessful attack on that island, Bonaparte found his country in arms. The Convention had sent commissioners to Corsica with instructions to depose Paoli, who was also summoned to appear at their bar. These measures proving too difficult of execution, he was appointed Commander-in-Chief of the army of Italy, an ill-contrived scheme for drawing him to France; but the successive arrests of Biron, Anselm, and Brunet warned him only too plainly of the fate which awaited him. He refused an honour that was intended only to lead to his destruction, and soon after was declared an outlaw. Corsica rose as one man to defend its great citizen.

Forced to seek a powerful ally for his country, Paoli solicited the protection of England, as her fleet could easily cut off all our communications and shelter the island from a descent. Those who still adhered to France soon found themselves utterly powerless before the unanimity of the patriots. They did not attempt any decided opposition. Bonaparte appears to have had a momentary hesitation, when obliged to choose between the cause of his country's freedom and the advantages to be gained by his fidelity to France. A half-formed scheme for defending Paoli before the Convention was discovered among his early writings; but this project remained a fragment. The author of the *Letter to Buttafuoco* became the opponent of the patriotic movement which he had extolled with so much ardour, and he organised a secret conspiracy at Ajaccio, with a view to the surprise of the citadel and its surrender to the French Republic. But, notwithstanding the assiduity and remarkable pertinacity that he brought to the execution of this plot, the only result was to involve his family in his own peril. He was proscribed, denounced as a traitor, and only effected his escape with great difficulty. His house was pillaged, his mother and her children compelled to take flight, and, like him, found refuge on the continent, and in a short time not a single open adherent of France was to be found on the island.

After establishing his family at Marseilles, where they lived for some time in an almost destitute condition, Bonaparte rejoined the army of Italy, in which he held the rank of Captain of Artillery. He found France a prey to the violent convulsions of that horrible crisis which ended in the downfall of the Girondists and with them of liberty. He took part with his regiment in the suppression of the insurrection in the south, and probably figured for a short time at the siege of Lyons. It is certain that with his own hands he pointed the cannons with which Carteaux cleared Avignon of the Marseilles Federates. It was just after this exploit, otherwise unimportant, that is, towards the end of July 1793, that he wrote and published his *Souper de Beaucaire*. This little work, written with an affected impartiality which belied itself in every page, is moderate enough in style, though far from being so as to intention, and is an evident apology for the *coup d'état* of the Mountain. Its obvious aim was to convert irresolute and wavering spirits, or rather to give them a plausible pretext for rallying round their party. It made, however, no sensation, nor did it merit success. It was wanting in the vehemence, the real fervour and the cutting irony of the *Letter to Buttafuoco*. It is obvious that it was written without enthusiasm and that it is an interested piece of work. In reality Bonaparte often acknowledges that as long as the struggle lasted, all his sympathies were on the side of the Girondists. Unable to repudiate his connection with their opponents, a connection which nearly cost him his life, he imagined it a sufficient excuse to treat it as a mere matter of policy on his part. In the *Souper de Beaucaire* we find ideas, commonplace enough, expressed in a style remarkable only for the frequent occurrence of Italian expressions, but which becomes singularly expressive and exact when the author propounds his military theories. It displays, under an apparent frankness, an extraordinary degree of caution, leaving nothing which might compromise the writer even should the current of events be changed. His principal argument, that which had evidently made a deep impression on his own mind, shows us that what seemed to him to settle the question in favour of the Mountain was its indisputable success. This argument is nothing but the vulgar sophism by the aid of which the most violent measures have always been justified, by veiling them under the inviolability of the country itself.

'I do not enquire,' said he, speaking of the Girondists, 'if these men, who on so many occasions had proved themselves worthy of the confidence of the nation, really had conspired against it. It is enough for me to know, that on the Mountain, whether from public spirit or from party spirit, proceeding to the furthest extremities against them, proscribing, imprisoning,—I will even grant this to you— calumniating them, the Brissotins were lost without a civil war that should have put them in a position to dictate terms to their enemies. . . . If they had deserved their earlier reputation, they would have thrown down their arms at the sight of the Constitution; they would have sacrificed their own interests to the public good; but it is easier to cite Decius than to follow his example; they became guilty of the greatest of all crimes,' etc.

We see by this passage, that the theory of accomplished facts is far from being an invention of our time. In this doctrine there is at bottom a total absence of all rule and principle; for if the arguments here employed against the Girondists were admissible, by how much more ought they to have protected these men, who were the representatives of lawful authority, against proceedings so dishonourable to the Convention as the days of the 31st of May and the 2d of June. And if the civil war were so great a crime, on whom ought the responsibility to fall if not on the first aggressors? The argument, in short, is reduced to this, that it was an act of good citizenship to join the party of the Mountain, because the Mountain had proved itself to be the strongest. This idea is worked out in a hundred ways in the *Souper de Beaucaire*. The author strives to give it all the clearness of an axiom—but only succeeds in showing with what force it had taken possession of his own mind. This accounts for the extraordinarily practical and direct tone which pervades the production. We perceive a dispassionate calmness and precocious ingenuity in the way in which difficulties are turned aside. Extreme care is displayed by the writer to avoid identifying himself irrevocably even with the party whose cause he adopts; he states the arguments of his opponents; he preserves an appearance of impartiality. Let us add, as a last trait, that Bonaparte drags through the mire Paoli, the idol of his youth. He accuses him of having 'deceived the people; crushed the true friends of liberty; involved his countrymen in his cruel and ambitious projects; pillaged the public stores by selling their contents at depreciated prices, in order to obtain money to sustain his insurrectionary movements,' etc.

In a word, when Bonaparte begins to belong to history, calculating self-interest and ambition had already gained the ascendency over every other motive. We behold him freed from every scruple, proof against any political impetuosity, on the best terms with the conquerors, without being irreconcilable towards the conquered; unburdened of all his generous illusions of other days, and measuring with his glance the unbounded field that lies stretched out before him. This predestined favourite of glory even now has no adviser but his insatiable genius, and no rule but a certain ideal of greatness, and what he himself styles 'circumstances;' in other words, accomplished facts, success, fortune. Only let opportunity come, he will not allow it to escape. It was not slow in offering itself with a brightness most unhoped for.

CHAPTER II

THE SIEGE OF TOULON AND THE THIRTEENTH VENDÉMIAIRE

In September 1793 the Republican army was besieging Toulon. This town, following the example of Lyons, Marseilles, Caen, and Bordeaux, had revolted against the dictatorship of the Jacobins, become all powerful since the day on which the mob of the Sections had laid hands on the representatives of the people. Soon after, terror-struck by the frightful means employed to put down this insurrection, and carried away by Royalists, who were not long in getting the mastery of a movement begun in the name of the heroic and unfortunate Girondists, the inhabitants of Toulon opened the gates of their town to the allies, and it thus became the arsenal and advanced post of the invasion. A numerous garrison, composed of men of every race and every variety of antecedents, hastily formed out of this great medley of nations, defended the place. Fugitives who had escaped the massacres of Lyons and Marseilles, exiles who counted among them as many shades of opinion as there were vanquished parties in the Revolution, misguided Frenchmen who did not perceive that in thus combating a party they were rending their country asunder, found themselves side by side with soldiers of every nation, whom the allies had thrown on our Southern shores, to help, by creating a diversion, the insurrection of La Vendée and the attack on our Provinces in the North. In its eagerness to seize this rich spoil, the English squadron had hastily assembled and landed at Toulon troops from almost every country bordering on the Mediterranean; Spaniards, Sardinians, Neapolitans—a cosmopolitan collection, whose only bond was a common hatred. The Pope himself had been anxious to contribute his part, by despatching to the allied army a band of priests and monks.

The troops of the Convention consisted of two divisions separated by the inaccessible barrier of Mount Pharon, and there was scarcely any communication between them. Composed partly of fugitives from Marseilles after the chastisement inflicted on that town, partly of detachments from the army of the Alps, swollen every hour by contributions from that overflow of twelve hundred thousand men which the Revolution, assailed from every side, poured on its enemies like lava from a volcano, these troops presented a mixture, unparalleled in history, of inexperience, disorder, and wild grandeur. There were in them all the contrasts and all the confusion of the formidable chaos out of which they had sprung; impetuousness, ignorant enthusiasm, popular ardour, and extreme courage united to extreme arrogance. These troops, the nucleus of the army of Italy, who were very early mixed up with our civil dissensions, possessed in the highest degree the fanaticism of the Revolution, but they had neither the purity nor the disinterestedness of those who had never consented to be the instruments of party retaliation. Without chiefs, without the material of war, without organisation, without discipline, the cannon of the enemy in front, and the scaffold behind, their sole sustaining force lay in the sombre and inflexible resolution that had taken possession of every mind; but this was enough to prevent any doubts of success. The greater part of the officers of the old army having been mowed down by war or proscription, a certain amount of daring or patriotism was all that was needed in order to obtain a commission, and the highest ranks had thus been filled by men full of energy, but almost strangers to the first elements of military science.

Common soldiers were made generals, artillery sergeants superintended the firing of the batteries, an ex-artist, Carteaux the painter, was Commander-in-Chief of the principal *corps d'armée* charged with operations on the right side of the place, and he was soon to have for successor a doctor, the Savoyard Doppet. An ex-Marquis, General Lapoype, who had escaped suspicion by his extreme opinions, directed the attack on the left; above them, and invested with almost unlimited authority, were the Convention Commissioners, Salicetti, Albitte, Gasparin, Fréron, and Barras, who, in spite of the increasing importance which the army had acquired since its intervention in our civil struggles, still represented the sovereignty, too absolute not to be in peril, of the civil over the military powers.

Notwithstanding the ardour of the Republican troops, the siege made but little progress. They had seized, with their usual bravery, the defile of Ollioules and the other passes which defended the approach to the place; but their impetuosity had died away at the foot of the ramparts of Toulon, and they made no way against the formidable works in front of them. In conducting a siege, warlike passion can never supply the place of skilful dispositions; these alone can insure success. Carteaux, the General-in-Command, did not know even approximatively the range of a piece of artillery; the whole service was in a state of disorganisation; the army stood in need of the most indispensable implements for the erection of a battery, and as every one had his own particular plan for the taking of Toulon, which had been a subject of debate in the popular societies, the operations went forward at random, without uniformity of action and without superintendence. In the midst of the boundless disorder of these confused and tumultuous preparations, Bonaparte arrived at the camp.

He was on his way from Avignon to Nice, the headquarters of the Italian army, and passing through Toulon, he stopped to see his countryman Salicetti, who, as one of the Convention Commissioners, was watching the operations of the siege.[1] Salicetti introduced him to Carteaux, who

---

[1] Napoleon relates in his *Mémoires* dictated at Saint Helena, that he was sent to Toulon by the Committee of Public Safety, to command the Artillery, and nearly all his historians have said the same. But the fact is contradicted, not only by his brother Joseph and Marmont, who both took part in the siege of Toulon, but by Napoleon himself

immediately showed him the batteries he had just had erected to cannonade the English fleet. They were placed at thrice the carrying distance from the nearest vessels; Bonaparte could scarcely restrain his contempt for so much ignorance and presumption, but he had not much difficulty in convincing Carteaux of his error. The balls scarcely reached the shore; Carteaux, in confusion, declared the powder was bad. The observations of the young officer and the arrangements which he advised, showed so much skill and so great a knowledge of military affairs, that the Commissioners, who were present at the interview, were greatly struck and immediately put him in requisition for the service of his own particular arm.

From that time Major Bonaparte had the command of the Artillery, and consequently conducted the principal part of the operations of the siege. He soon showed himself worthy of the favours which fortune had conferred on him by the skill with which he profited by them. In a few days the various services were reorganised. He sent to Lyons, Grenoble, Marseilles, and all neighbouring places for officers, cannon and ammunition; several new batteries were erected in situations where they inflicted great damage on the enemy. He became indispensable. So great was the ascendency which he soon acquired over every one, that when General Duteil came to Toulon to command the Artillery, he did not for an instant dream of disputing the kind of dictatorship which Bonaparte had assumed by necessity, and of which he made such good use.

in his Correspondence: 'When the Representatives of the people, he writes, *kept me at Toulon, and gave me the command of the Artillery.* . . .' He altered the circumstance in his *Mémoires*, because he did not wish to admit that he had been under any obligation to Salicetti, who afterwards became his enemy. Napoleon's *Mémoires* are full of errors and omissions, some of which were accidental, but by far the greater number were designed. With regard to the *Mémorial* of M. de Las Cases, which states that Napoleon was chosen for the siege of Toulon, on account of certain papers written by him and found in the *bureau de l'Artillerie*, he scarcely ever gives either the precise account, or, what is worse, the true colour of events. We find much more of his own language and character in his book, than of his hero's.

Shortly afterwards, the General-in-Chief called a Council of War to determine definitely the plan of attack. The instructions sent from Paris by the Committee of Public Safety were read. These instructions, drawn up in the War Office, remote from the scene of action, contained the plan of a regular siege, which, from the nature and strength of the fortifications, must inevitably be both long and difficult. The investment alone would have required sixty thousand men, and they had scarcely twenty-five thousand. The chiefs of the army who had any military knowledge could not shut their eyes to the difficulties of such a project, but numerous recent examples had shown them how perilous it was for a General to question the plans of the terrible Committee. They also knew by the same experience that failure was as unpardonable as disobedience, and that misfortune had more than once been punished as a crime. Divided between duty and fear, they contented themselves with criticisms which only showed their embarrassment. One voice, however, was raised in the Council against it; it was that of the young Major of Artillery.

He maintained that a regular siege was by no means necessary. In his opinion, the whole strength of the garrison lay in the squadron; for it was the squadron which brought them reinforcements and insured their retreat. If then they should succeed in cutting off the squadron from Toulon, the garrison, seeing themselves blockaded and certain sooner or later to be made prisoners of war, would prefer the destruction of all the stores and the evacuation of the place, to a prolonged defence of which the issue had become inevitable. The only thing needed to drive away the squadron was to get possession of a point commanding the two harbours, at the bottom of which Toulon is situated. Now there was such a point; it was situated at the extremity of Cape l'Eguillette, which separates the two harbours. As he finished this striking demonstration, Bonaparte put his finger on the map at the spot he had mentioned and said, 'Toulon is there!'

This inspiration of genius is the finer, because it is founded, not only on a simple calculation of material forces, but on a profound insight into the motives that would be likely to actuate the enemy. It was the first conception of this great captain, and the detailed Report is still preserved in which, a month before the fall of the place, he laid this plan before the Minister of War, the points of which were to be realised one by one in every particular.

The views of the Artillery Major having been at length adopted in a second Council of War called together by Dugommier, an intrepid and experienced soldier, whom the Committee of Public Safety had sent as successor to the painter Carteaux and the doctor Doppet, affairs soon began to take a new turn. All the efforts of the besieging army were directed towards Fort Mulgrave, which defended the approach to Point l'Eguillette. The English on their side had also perceived the importance of this position; they had raised several very strong redoubts on it, and named it Little Gibraltar. In order to create a diversion they made a fierce attack on another point, which was at first successful but was afterwards energetically repelled by Bonaparte himself, who was wounded in the skirmish. The English General O'Hara remained among the prisoners.

After this incident they drew still closer the circle of fire which girdled the place, and for several consecutive days Fort Mulgrave was covered with ball and shell. By the eighteenth of December the breach appeared sufficient, and the word was given to storm the English redoubt. After several unsuccessful assaults, a battalion under the command of Muiron, the future Aide-de-Camp, penetrated into the fort, cut down the artillerymen at their guns, and turned the cannon against the Anglo-Spanish squadron. Fort l'Eguillette, no longer defensible, was evacuated during the night. As Bonaparte had said, Toulon was taken.

Still the town appeared secure. Its fortifications were intact; not one of the great fortresses which protected it was seriously threatened, and judging from the distance at which the Republican batteries still remained from the walls, the inhabitants of Toulon might have believed in the indefinite duration of the siege. Already, however, Bonaparte's prediction was coming true; the English fleet began to withdraw, involving the evacuation of the place. The inhabitants of Toulon learned with inexpressible dismay that the squadron was on the point of leaving, and that vessels were offered for those who wished to fly. A multitude, struck with despair and beside themselves with terror, rushed to the ships to escape from Republican vengeance. More than fifteen thousand inhabitants thus abandoned their homes. The town was soon deserted and given up to the convicts, who had broken their chains. Night came on and increased the confusion of the scenes of which the port was the theatre. All at once a flame rose from the Arsenal, and soon after a sudden blaze shot into the air from the middle of the harbour; it was our magazines and vessels which the enemy set fire to before leaving. On the other hand the Republicans had taken possession of the evacuated forts, and their balls sank the boats into which the fugitive families were crowding.

The next day the troops of the Convention entered the mute and terror-stricken town. Many hundreds of the inhabitants, who had not supposed it needful to take to flight, were publicly shot without any other form of trial than the simple denunciation of their fellow-citizens, and their execution completed an expiation, already out of proportion to the crime of this unfortunate city. Fouché, afterwards one of the great dignities of the empire, who had hastened from Lyons to witness the triumph of our army, wrote to Collot d'Herbois on the twenty-third of December: 'We have only one way of celebrating victory. This evening we shoot two hundred and thirteen rebels. Adieu my friend; tears of joy run down my cheeks, and my heart is overflowing.' Such was this strange and sombre epoch in our history, in which we come at once upon the basest infamy and the most exalted virtue.

It is from the siege of Toulon that we may date the time of Napoleon Bonaparte's name beginning to engrave itself in the recollection of men. Surrounded by such terrible pictures, the figure of this extraordinary man first appears on the stage of history. Although not then more than twenty-four years of age, he had been brought into contact with so many different men that his mind had acquired a maturity, an experience, and a self-possession, such as the ordinary conditions of life are scarcely capable of developing. 'One ages quickly on the battlefield,' he said one day, speaking of himself. This is still more true of revolutions. The private and public vicissitudes through which he had passed had turned his heart into bronze. As often happens in similar cases, this sudden and premature check to youth, while giving an immense vigour to the mind, had dried up the sources of some of the best and noblest portions of the man. An ambition, as yet without any definite aim, but active, tenacious, impatient, irritated by the obstacles it had hitherto encountered, and still more by the misfortunes it had brought on the innocent, subjugated every other motive and reigned alone over his soul. To what might not such ambition aspire, in the midst of such a chaos, and armed with weapons so tempered, the genius of a great captain, the art of striking men's imagination, an eye of marvellous penetration, knowledge of men and contempt for them, the subtlety of the Italian, the indomitable and rugged self-will of the Corsican?

After the siege of Toulon, Bonaparte was raised to the rank of General of Artillery, and was sent to defend the coast of Provence which had been left perfectly unprotected. He took to this mission all his accustomed activity, re-organised the defence on a new plan which simplified the old methods, and which he carried into execution undisturbed by the objections of ignorance and routine. In consequence of one of his operations he was even summoned to the bar of the Convention, on the charge of having tried to restore a Bastille in Marseilles, but men of wealth and influence gave security for him and spared him this perilous journey. In a short time he had completely protected the Mediterranean coast from the attacks of the English fleet, which he kept at such a distance that it could no longer damage our coasting trade. That done, he rejoined the head-quarters of the army of Italy at Nice (March 1794).

This army, under the command of General Dumerbion, an officer of merit but past service, had been exhausting its strength for several months, in useless attacks on the almost impregnable position in which the Piedmontese troops were intrenched at the foot of the Maritime Alps, on the Mediterranean slope. The soldiers, discouraged by this monotonous warfare, in which they saw no progress nor any hope of an end, showed an unwonted indifference; and the officers, in whom all the fire and spirit of enterprise had been stifled by the chastisement for failure inflicted on their predecessors, dared attempt nothing, and contented themselves with holding their position and executing slow and methodical operations like those of a siege, which could bring them neither glory nor peril.

But Bonaparte was not a man to flinch from the responsibility that frightened them, especially since his enterprise at Toulon had turned out so excellently well. He had obtained a great ascendency over the minds of the General-in-Chief and the Convention Commissioners, particularly over the younger Robespierre, at that time his most intimate friend; he used it to induce them to attack the Piedmontese troops and drive them over the Alps. After having studied the difficult geography of this mountainous district and the position occupied by the enemy, he explained his plans first in a memorandum addressed to Dumerbion, and afterwards in a Council of War, where they were discussed and adopted.

The sixth of April 1794 the army began its march. The Piedmontese camps were firmly supported on Saorgio, a very strong place, defending the approaches to the Col di Tenda, which is on this side the key of the Alps. Instead of attacking these formidable positions in front, as they had hitherto repeatedly done at the cost of great and useless sacrifices, Bonaparte resolved to turn them. To this end, a part of the army, divided into three columns, ascended the Roya, the Nervia and the Taggio, to commence operations on the left of the Piedmontese camp so as to invest and command it. During this time a fourth corps, reserved for the decisive stroke, under the command of Masséna, filed along the Corniche, beat the Austrians and Piedmontese at Saint Agatha, and took possession of Oneglia and

Loano. From thence, continuing this bold course, Masséna crossed the Alps at Ponte-di-Nave, not far from the source of the Tanaro, won a new victory there, entered Piedmont, seized the castle of Ormea, and Garessio, and then suddenly falling back again upon the Alps, began to threaten the Col di Tenda from the opposite slope to that occupied by the Piedmontese army. The enemy whose positions had thus been turned, and who were on the point of having all communication with Piedmont cut off, hastily evacuated the camp of Saorgio, and thus without a battle surrendered this long-disputed position. They effected a retreat by the Col di Tenda, which shortly after fell into the hands of our troops (May 7). This brief and brilliant campaign of one month gave the French army command of the whole range of the Alps, of which we occupied all the defiles from the Col di Tenda to Bardinetto.

This success carried Bonaparte's influence with the younger Robespierre to the highest point. The latter shared the dictatorship of his brother Maximilian; he was master of the army of Italy, as his brother was master of France. His colleagues Ricord and Salicetti were bound to yield to him or else quit the army. After this victory he was entirely guided by the General of Artillery. It is only just to Bonaparte to state here, that if, from interested motives, he allied himself to a party whose opinions he did not share, and whose excesses were repugnant to his feelings, he in no wise used this influence to serve his own ambition, but employed it to good purpose in protecting the Italian army from the proscriptions and dismissals which were of every-day occurrence in the armies of the North. He even saved the lives of some *émigrés*, who had been seized on board a Spanish vessel, and against whom the law against returned *émigrés* was on the point of being enforced. Nevertheless the two Robespierres considered him to be entirely devoted to their cause, as the Report published against him after the Ninth Thermidor proves, in which he is spoken of as '*their man.*' Notwithstanding the extreme discretion with which he habitually passed over this period of his life, he has himself related a circumstance which shows to what extent he had gained their friendship and confidence. When they were about to engage in the struggle with the Committees, knowing that they should need the assistance of a skilful and resolute officer, they offered him the place of Henriot, then in command of the armed forces of Paris, and whose want of ability they both were aware of. The younger Robespierre was recalled to Paris by his brother, just before the Ninth Thermidor, and he tried to induce the General to accompany him. Bonaparte, however, in spite of the extreme opinions he had seen fit to proclaim, really entertained nothing but repugnance for the cruelties that had been committed, and felt all the more averse to identify himself with them, because even then it was possible to foresee a coming reaction in favour of humanity. He was willing to make use of the two Robespierres, but not to compromise himself irrevocably with them. He therefore refused his friend's offers, preferring to remain in a career which promised more lasting successes; but this refusal did not obviate the danger of finding himself implicated in a catastrophe which he had not believed to be so near.

Bonaparte, who was already meditating a new campaign in Italy, undertook a journey towards the middle of July 1794, the object of which was for a long time unknown, and which gave rise to many contradictory suppositions. The ostensible motive for his visit to Genoa was to press for the delivery of certain stores for the army, which though paid for had never-been forwarded. The real object was, as Marmont who was one of the party says, 'to ascertain what obstacles a *coup de main* on the town might meet with.' The taking of Genoa formed a part of Bonaparte's new schemes. The Republic had given a kind of pretext for this violence by allowing the English, in spite of the laws of neutrality, to seize the frigate *La Modeste;* but her greatest wrong in the eyes of the future conqueror of Italy was her weakness, and the inconvenience of having to respect her rights when it would have been so useful to have her territory for the base of operations.

Bonaparte had no sooner returned from his journey to

Genoa than he was placed under arrest, and summoned to appear at Paris before the Committee of Public Safety, a summons which at that time was considered a death warrant. The Revolution of the Ninth Thermidor was just over, and the General paid the penalty of his connection with the Robespierres. His arrest, over which a certain mystery still hangs, was signed by two Convention Commissioners, first to the army of the Alps, and afterwards to that of Italy. Salicetti, who had left it shortly before this after a dispute with the younger Robespierre, hastened back after the victory, and joined Albitte and Laporte in the imprisonment of his young countryman.

Salicetti, all the hotter Thermidorian as he had to earn a pardon for the notorious extravagance of his former opinions, was on this occasion the most active instrument in Bonaparte's disgrace. At first his protector, he had gradually grown to be his enemy, as the General's fortunes had improved. This antipathy, which had all the intensity of Corsican vindictiveness, was increased by a rivalry which we are assured was not a rivalry in ambition only. What is certain is that all the charges brought against Bonaparte in the Report addressed to the Committee of Public Safety dated the 19th Thermidor, were furnished by Salicetti, who alone had followed all the operations of the army, and Albitte and Laporte knew nothing of them.

In this indictment his connection with the Robespierres is only made a secondary matter; the chief charge against him is his journey to Genoa. By the most outrageous of all possible theories, only to be explained either by panic or else by wilful perfidy, this journey associated itself in their minds with a vast scheme of treason concerted between Robespierre and Ricord, for giving up to the enemy the whole plan of our military operations. Once the truth of this fable admitted, everything was clear; there was no need of seeking a further motive for the journey to Genoa: 'Bonaparte was *their man*, the framer of their plans, whom we were to obey.' The Report goes on to show how this fine idea first arose; it was Salicetti who disclosed all these machinations. 'Salicetti came and told us that Ricord had authorised Bonaparte to go to Genoa. What had the General got to do in a foreign country? All our suspicions centre on his head.' This expression, which at that time was no mere rhetorical figure, proves by what danger that head was for a moment threatened.

However, Bonaparte's arrest, and above all the order for his speedy departure for Paris to appear before the Committee of Public Safety, caused a lively excitement among all the young officers of the army, who had already united their own fortunes with his. They devised a plan for delivering him by main force, and passing with him into the States of Genoa. Of this number were Junot and Marmont. The General had some difficulty in restraining and calming them. 'I have a clear conscience,' he wrote to Junot; 'do nothing, you would only compromise me.' It would, in fact, have been very difficult to prove an accusation of treason before an impartial and clear-sighted judge; but in those times of trouble and agitation everything was possible.

In the meantime he addresses his accusers, recalling the services he had rendered the Republic at Toulon and at Saorgio; he reproaches them for declaring him suspect, before examining the acts imputed to him. If he went to Paris with this suspicion hanging over him, the Committee would be influenced in its judgment, and his fate was settled beforehand; would it not be better to reverse the order, and examine first the grounds of suspicion? 'Salicetti, you know me; have you seen anything in my conduct during the last five years which is suspicious towards the Revolution? Albitte, you do not know me; nothing has been proved against me, you have not heard me, but you know how artful sometimes is the breath of calumny. . . . Listen to me, remove the oppression which surrounds me; give me back the esteem of patriots. An hour afterwards, if bad men wish for my life, I care so little for it, I have so often counted it for nothing. . . . Yes, nothing but the idea that it may yet be of use to the country gives me courage to bear its weight.'[1]

[1] This letter, though perfectly genuine, like many others of the same period is not published in Napoleon's *Correspondence*.

The General's papers were sealed up. Among them was found the order relative to his mission to Genoa, signed by Ricord and containing full instructions; there was nothing in it to justify the strange suspicions of which he had been the object. In consequence of this, the Commissioners issued a decree (the Third Fructidor) by virtue of which he was set at liberty *provisionally*, and at the same time they wrote to the Committee, that having no positive proof of his guilt they had released him principally in consideration 'of the great use the talents of such an officer might be, necessary as he is to an army which he knows better than any one else, and where men of this kind were extremely difficult to find.'.

Such is the true account of an incident which has been confused and misrepresented at will, whether by Bonaparte himself, or by historians to whom history is only a servile commentary on the testimony which he chose to leave about his own life. He was, he says, 'put under arrest, *for a few moments, by the Commissioner Laporte, whose authority he would not acknowledge.*' In the first place, the few moments were ten days, which were days of anguish and anxiety for himself as well as his friends, and secondly, Laporte was absent during the whole time and took no part in the affair. It would be difficult to understand the object of a statement so ridiculous, did we not know how diligent Bonaparte was in obliterating all trace of his connection with the Robespierres—a connection which has latterly been so clearly established. The recollection of his opinions at that time was afterwards troublesome to him, and all the more so, because he treated that party with extreme severity; and he did all in his power to make his connection with it forgotten, for the same reasons which induced him to destroy the copies of the *Souper de Beaucaire*, and to have his speeches at the Club ascribed to his brother Lucien, then too young to have spoken them.

Bonaparte was soon reconciled with Salicetti, for each had powerful motives for keeping on good terms with the other, but the reconciliation was only formal. They rendered each other mutual services, but the old friendship was never revived. At the time of the First Prairial, Bonaparte could have destroyed Salicetti, and he refrained from making use of his power. He was capable of anger, but as entire a stranger to hatred as to sympathy; he was governed only by calculation.

The assertion contained in the *Mémoires* of Robespierre's sister, whom Bonaparte knew at Nice and to whom he granted a pension under the Consulate, that on the news of the Ninth Thermidor the General instantly proposed to the Commissioners to march upon Paris and overthrow the Thermidorians, has often been repeated; but in this story we must only look at the idea that was then entertained about his character and opinions, and if we admit it without further proof, we should misunderstand the irresistible force of the reaction of Thermidor, and the stupor with which it struck its enemies. Besides, we have positive evidence of the impression produced on the mind of Bonaparte by the news of the fate of Robespierre, in a letter which he wrote at the time. In this letter, in which one cannot help tracing the hidden notion of procuring a certificate of Republican orthodoxy, he briefly relates what had taken place and its results, and then, alluding to the tragical end of him who had been his friend, by way of funeral oration he adds: 'I was *somewhat affected* at the fate of the younger Robespierre, whom I liked and whom I believed pure, but I would have poniarded my own father with my own hand if he had aspired after despotism.'[1]

It was thus that Bonaparte shook off the patronage of the extreme Democratic party, as soon as he found in it more risk than profit. He separated from it as he had done from Paoli, and from similar motives; but the Terrorist Democrats were not entirely defeated on the Ninth Thermidor; they preserved for some time longer active influence and persistent hopes, and Bonaparte did not definitely break with them till much later. Although his connection with them arose mainly from interested motives, it would be a mistake not to recognise in it also

[1] This letter is dated Thermidor 20th, year ii. It is addressed to citizen Tilly, Minister at Genoa. It is wanting in the *Correspondence*.

an effect of his strong natural leaning towards force and authority. There is a connection between all systems of absolute power, and as his own was historically speaking the child of that of the Committee of Public Safety, it is plain that he would at first be drawn by instinct towards the men whose heir he was one day to be. In the same way Cromwell was the most ardent of levellers before he became the most absolute of masters.

The difficulties of communication in the elevated regions which the French troops occupied from Bardinetto to the Col di Tenda, and much further up the Higher Alps, a vast semicircle of which the enemy had only the diameter to defend, made the Committee desirous to see the army resume the offensive. Dumerbion received orders to recommence hostilities. The movement, too, was hastened by the approach of a considerable body of Austrians, who were proceeding to the Bormida. At the same time they learned that an English division was going to land at Vado and occupy Savona, in order to compel the Genoese Republic to abandon its neutrality. Dumerbion again applied to Bonaparte, whose plan, only partially carried out, was a kind of rough sketch of one which he soon afterwards executed in his capacity of General-in-Chief (20th September 1794). The French army debouched upon Piedmont by the plain of Carcara, not far from the place where the Alps join the Apennines. From thence they proceeded rapidly to Cairo; here they found themselves in sight of the Austrian army, which immediately beat a retreat. They overtook it at Dego, where they attacked and defeated it. But instead of following up this success by a campaign in Piedmont, where they could not have encountered many obstacles, the French fell back upon Savona and Vado by way of Montenotte, and undertook nothing more that year.

It is easy to imagine with what dissatisfaction General Bonaparte saw the army thus fall back, when it was just on the point of effecting operations from which he expected such great results. But this short campaign, notwithstanding the bitter disappointment which its sudden interruption caused him, was not wasted either for his genius or his glory, for it was at this point that he entered Piedmont in his memorable campaign of 1796; and it is possible that he might not have achieved so many prodigious successes in the same theatre, if he had not beforehand so thoroughly studied the topography of his field of battle.

When the army of Italy returned to take up its winter quarters in its former position, it was decided to employ a part of the forces in a naval expedition. This expedition was organised at Toulon in a great measure by Bonaparte himself. Its first object was to recover Corsica from the English, but this idea was soon given up; then to punish the Grand Duke of Tuscany for his timid complicity with the allies—a chastisement which he brought upon himself more by his weakness than any wrong he had done; and lastly, to effect a descent on the Papal States, and avenge the assassination of Basseville. But Admiral Martin, then in command of our fleet, having measured its force against the English squadron and seeing his own inferiority, abandoned an expedition from which nothing but disaster could be expected (January 1795).

It was shortly after the miscarriage of this enterprise that Bonaparte, to his great astonishment, received the appointment of Artillery General in the army of the West. This change was part of a general measure, of a political rather than a military character, and affected several other officers in the army of Italy. As this army was considered the hot-bed of Jacobinism, it was thought advisable to disperse its principal elements as widely as possible. The measure had been passed by the Committee of Public Safety, on the report of Dubois de Crancé. It took Bonaparte away from an army where he had grown up, had done brilliant service, and had won high renown, to send him among troops exclusively employed in putting down civil dissensions, a duty of a hateful kind even when most honourably discharged. Thus his name was scarcely known, and were he to distinguish himself by the brilliance of his achievements, the only recompense he could look for was the dangerous one of an equivocal and compromising glory.

It needed all the patriotic abnegation of a Hoche to accept without a murmur this post of sacrifice.

This unexpected blow gave Bonaparte mortal displeasure. He started immediately for Paris, there to counteract its effect and get a hearing for his complaints. He was accompanied by his two aides-de-camp, Junot and Marmont, both of them completely subjugated by his ascendency, warmly attached to his person, and already full of a boundless confidence in his star. On his arrival at Paris, he learned that he was sent to the army in La Vendée, not as an artillery general, but only in command of a simple brigade of infantry.

During his journey, Aubrey, the deputy, Carnot's successor, had been examining more closely Dubois de Crancé's Report, and had made this further change. Aubrey, who had been a captain in the artillery before he was a deputy to the Convention, was Bonaparte's senior in the army, and he saw with bitter envy, it is said, the rapid promotion of officers much younger than himself. To this motive of animosity, which is hardly consistent with the high position Aubrey then occupied as Member of the Committee of Public Safety, may be added another, which is more likely to have influenced him, and this was Bonaparte's antecedents and the antagonism of their political opinions. Aubrey was a Girondist; he had courageously signed the protest against the events of the 31st of May, he had been imprisoned with the seventy-three, and he was still one of the most zealous chiefs of the Thermidorian reactionary party.

To any one who knows the envenomed passions of this bloody period of our history, there is no need to account for Aubrey's hatred of Bonaparte by motives of personal jealousy. Each party in turn committed acts of such atrocious vengeance, that the measure of which the young general was a victim might almost pass for a mark of moderation on the part of an all-powerful adversary. Bonaparte employed the zeal of his most influential friends. Barras, Fréron, and the Bishop of Marboz interceded by turns, but without success. Aubrey replied to all their entreaties by dwelling on the restless ambition of the general, his premature promotion, due to the good terms on which he had been with the Jacobin tyrants, while to one of them, who pleaded the most powerfully, he asked, 'How he could espouse the cause of a terrorist with so much warmth?' Bonaparte tried to maintain his rights in person, and presented himself before the Members of the Committee of Public Safety. Aubrey listened to his complaints, but persisted in his refusal. 'You are too young to be commander-in-chief of the artillery,' he said, by way of conclusion. 'Men age fast on a field of battle, and I am no exception,' replied Bonaparte warmly. This reply, in which Aubrey could clearly perceive a criticism on his own military services, which had always been of the most pacific kind, was not likely to induce him to change his resolution. He remained inflexible. Bonaparte had the littleness to remember this afterwards, when a word from him would have sufficed to save Aubrey from his unjust punishment at Cayenne, and he thus lost an opportunity of avenging himself in the only way worthy of a lofty character (June 1795).

After this repulse Bonaparte, unable to make up his mind to serve in the troops of the line, remained for some time in Paris, unoccupied and irresolute. It has been not unjustly remarked as to this that the *esprit de corps*, then very strong among the artillery officers, by reason of the value set by the general ignorance on their special service, had the effect of making Bonaparte greatly exaggerate the consequence of his disgrace; for if it be true that in the rank of the subalterns a command in the artillery is more important than the corresponding command in any other part of the service, the difference disappears in the higher ranks. A general of infantry very often plays a far more conspicuous part in battle than a general of artillery. It was so in the first two campaigns of the Italian army, in which Bonaparte had, as it were, done everything, and in which all the plans were his, yet he was, notwithstanding his post as Commander-in-Chief of the Artillery, much less conspicuous than many other generals, Masséna for instance, whose name figured in the first line of all the bulletins. We must not however accuse him of being the dupe of a military superstition, for he was changing an independent command for that of a brigade, relatively a subordinate post, and, as he wrote to Sucy, he might believe that 'many officers would lead a brigade better than himself, whilst few had been more successful in command of artillery' (August 17, 1795).

However this may be, he had fallen into a momentary state of depression and disgust, a mood not likely to last long with him, and he alleged bad health as a reason for not accepting the appointment which had been assigned to him. It was not just then but a little later, that his name was struck off the army list for having refused to proceed to his post, and the statement made in the *Mémorial* that he sent in his resignation is incorrect. In his letters to his brother Joseph, Bonaparte only speaks of two or three months' leave of absence, and he explicitly and repeatedly says that he had never ceased to be employed as 'general in the army of the West, but that he was kept at Paris by illness' (July 25, 1795). At the same time what is admitted is that his situation, which was much more like the position of one waiting for an appointment than taking a regular leave of absence, was just then most precarious. France was suffering from the effects of a fearful financial crisis, produced by the increasing discredit of the assignats, and there was a famine, with all its attendant horrors, in Paris. The future master of the continent was more than once reduced to live from hand to mouth, and to accept help from his friends Junot and Bourrienne. Rich and poor alike were in want of bread; the louis was at seven hundred and fifty francs, and there came a day when Bonaparte saw that he must sell his books to live. But this misery was only accidental and temporary. His brother Joseph, who had married a lady of fortune, and who was warmly attached to him, would never have left him in destitution, as has been said. His imagination, for a moment depressed by his changed circumstances, got back more activity, movement, and fire than it had before. Every day it conceived some new project, coloured by his passion for the marvellous and gigantic. When the inevitable disappointment came and chilled him, he would think of nothing but a comfortable retreat in the country, with all the quietness of middle-class existence. He busied himself in finding good investments for his brother Joseph's capital, and the choice of a suitable career for his younger brothers. Especially he studied with an attentive and scrutinising eye the society in which he was trying to make himself a place —that Parisian society reviving after its long oppression, intoxicated with joy at the renewal of pleasure, luxury, enjoyments; and he drew pictures of it which were not without a trace of envy, for though ambition gave him thoughts beyond his years, he still had the feelings of a young man.

'The carriages and the fine people are all coming to light again, or rather it seems only a long dream to them, during which they ever ceased to glitter. . . . Everything is got up in this country to amuse and make life agreeable. People tear themselves away from reflection, and how is it possible to look at the dark side of this busy vortex? Women are everywhere, in the theatres, promenades, libraries; in the closets of the learned you meet pretty women. This is the only place in the world where they deserve to hold the helm, and men are mad about them; they think of nothing else, and live by and for nothing else. A woman only needs six months of Paris life to find out what is due to her, and what power she has' (Napoleon to Joseph, July 12, 1795).

It was about this time that he conceived the idea of asking the Committee of Public Safety to send him to Turkey, to increase the military resources of that country, to improve its means of defence, to construct new fortifications, and to reorganise its artillery. The motive he urged in support of his demand was the possible event of an approaching war between this, the natural ally of France, and either Austria or Russia; but the real attraction which this mission had for Bonaparte was the indefinite prospects it opened up to his ambition. Already he had in these regions and their future revolutions those grandiose and chimerical views which he delighted in developing in later years, when, anxious at all cost to dazzle his fellow-citizens, he threw in their eyes the gold-dust of the East.

But before he had even submitted his project for the approbation of the Committee, the army of Italy, having met with some serious checks, Doulcet de Pontécoulant, Aubrey's successor in the direction of military operations, asked for Bonaparte's services in the topographical office, in which the plans for the campaign to be sent to the various armies were being drawn up. When the General applied for permission to set off with the officers whom he had chosen to accompany him, the Committee, on the representation of Jean Debry, one of its members, refused to grant it, alleging as a reason in the most flattering terms the usefulness of his services to the Republic. It was by a similar chance that Cromwell, when on the point of sailing for America, was in spite of himself retained in England.

During the short time he spent in the topographical office, Bonaparte drew up for Kellermann, then Commander-in-Chief of the army of Italy, and afterwards for his successor, Schérer, a series of instructions which it is impossible to read without admiration. They contain a clear exposition from point to point, based upon political as well as strategic considerations, of all the principal combinations which made the first campaign in Italy the most brilliant conception of his genius and the masterpiece of military art. He even calculates the exact time necessary for the execution of each part of his plan. He points out the precise spot at which the first blow will have to be struck, in order to separate the armies of Piedmont from those of Austria. He foresees with unfailing accuracy that when once these two armies had been beaten, they would be easily induced to separate on account of the different interests they had to defend—the one having to cover Piedmont, and the other to protect Lombardy—a separation that would allow of their being crushed singly, and of peace being imposed on the king of Piedmont, but by giving him some compensation in Lombardy for Nice and Savoy, and so having him for an ally instead of a secret enemy, as happened in 1796. If after this campaign the Empire does not demand peace, our troops are to penetrate by the Tyrol into the Hereditary States, and support the army of the Rhine. Such is the plan, which has this inestimable advantage over that afterwards carried into execution, that although it contains the first idea of violating the Venetian neutrality, since the Adige is fixed upon for the line of operations, at any rate we see nothing of conquest disguised under the name of emancipation of peoples, nor of war alternately carried on and abandoned from motives of personal ambition, nor of the baseness of Campo-Formio.

It is hardly necessary to say that a creation of genius like this could only be successfully realised by the man who had conceived it. These plans, although they had received the sanction of the new Committee, exercised no influence over the operations of Kellermann and Schérer. Kellermann replied, that 'the author was a fit inmate for a lunatic asylum.'[1] Schérer, 'that it was for him who had drawn them up to come and carry them out.' It is easy to perceive by the slight importance attached to the instructions, that they did not bear the formidable signature of the Committee of Public Safety. The armies were beginning to free themselves from its yoke, before in their turn imposing it on others. But this system of sending from Paris, far from the theatre of operations, the plans of a campaign all ready drawn up, was eminently vicious; and he who then devised them with so much skill was the first to revolt against it, when he had in his turn to receive them from others. And this function, however suited to the special aptitudes of Bonaparte's mind, which dealt with military operations with mathematical precision, was too obscure and unsatisfactory to please him. He was not of a temper to leave to others the honour of ideas where the merit was his own. Besides he was devoured by an almost feverish need of action, as much the effect of physical temperament as of reason. He had by no means given up his projects in the East, but his first impatience had somewhat cooled in face of the threatening circumstances which were beginning to show themselves in the political theatre.

[1] Life and Correspondence of Pontécoulant.

Why should not the crisis, which every one felt to be imminent, present to him in Paris itself that opportunity he was willing to go so far in search of? In the midst of all his trials he had ever preserved an unshaken confidence in himself and his future. To this he added that fatalism which belongs to all great adventurers, and living from day to day always on the alert, he was sufficiently weaned from life unhesitatingly to stake his own when the moment seemed propitious.

'I am constantly,' he wrote to his brother Joseph, 'in that mood in which men find themselves on the eve of a great battle, being fully convinced in my sentiments that when death is flying in the midst to put an end to everything, to be disturbed about it is madness. I can meet fate and destiny with courage, and unless I change, I shall very soon not move out of the way when a carriage passes' (August 12, 1795).

His name had been struck off the list of officers in active service for having displeased Letourneur, Pontécoulant's successor,[1] when the 13th Vendémiaire (October 5, 1795) brought him the occasion he was waiting for. It presented itself in even a finer and more decisive form than at the siege of Toulon, with that opportuneness and splendour which Fortune reserves for her favourites. She seemed to have permitted his temporary disgrace only to render his elevation more dazzling and more sudden.

The Convention had just brought its long and stormy career to a close by giving France the constitution of the year III. Its last days had been made honourable by the firmness it had shown against the tyranny of the multitude, more difficult to repress than that of the losers at the day of Thermidor. After having closed the Jacobin clubs, disarmed the faubourgs, repealed that work of frenzy and delirium, the Constitution of '93, subdued and muzzled the populace at the risk of ruining its principal support, struck without pity its own members as if to punish itself for having been their accomplice and instrument, this assembly,

[1] This took place September 25, 1795. Bourrienne, who made an entry of it, made a mistake in the date.

great notwithstanding its faults and mutilated by its own hands, was anxious to preserve its successors from the painful trials of its own experience. It left the fruit of its long experience and tardy wisdom in institutions which are still, in spite of their imperfections, the most liberal that France has ever possessed. But having finished its work, seeing itself irrevocably committed to the animosity of the extreme democratic party, and leaving the Republic to the mercy of a generation who, though by no means hostile to the Revolution, knew nothing of its passions, detested its excesses, and from impatience to act in their turn only looked upon the Convention as an obstacle to their own accession, this assembly failed in confidence in the future.

From this distrust of the Convention in the nation arose the principal defeat of the Constitution of the year III, I mean the almost inevitable antagonism which it created between the legislative and executive powers, by allowing the second to withdraw itself from under the control of the first, and providing no mediatorial power to spare them the alternative of an open rupture or entire submission. This dread of seeing its work fall into hostile or inexperienced hands caused the Convention to commit another fault, of which the consequences were much more immediate. Under the sway of these conservative feelings, which were so much the stronger within it while they were new, the Convention remembered with fear the fate which had befallen the Constitution of '91 from not having been protected by its authors. The dupes of an exaggerated scrupulosity and a mistaken disinterestedness, the members of the Constituent had excluded themselves from the Legislative Assembly which was to succeed them. The members of the Convention fell into the contrary extreme of forcing themselves on the electors. The decree of the 5th Fructidor decided that two-thirds of the Convention should form part of the legislative body which was about to assemble, and that of the 13th Fructidor that the electors should nominate the remaining third. These decrees, which were an insult to the nation, produced a great irritation among men who were disposed fairly to accept the new institutions : they saw in them, and not without reason, an encroachment on their own rights. They proceeded, however, notwithstanding the complaints, and the Constitution of the year III, with the two decrees, was submitted to the Primary Assemblies; a hollow ratification, extorted by fear, for any nation finding itself under the necessity of choosing between known and unknown evils, would infallibly embrace the former as the safer of the two.

Paris, however, ventured to reject the two decrees, though it accepted the Constitution ; but the provinces, following a method which it seems impossible for them to break through, voted all that was proposed, by a very large majority. This somewhat disconcerted the enemies of the Convention, who had believed their success certain. They made an appeal against the validity of the vote, but failed to establish the truth of their allegations. They soon proceeded from complaint to menace, and the tribunes of the forty-eight sections of Paris resounded with the most vehement attacks. Then, finding their appeal to public opinion did not produce the result they expected, they resolved to appeal to arms.

The party with which the Convention had just broken was the same that had acted as its auxiliary against the extreme democrats. It included the richest and most enlightened portion of the population of Paris, almost all the national guard, nearly the entire electoral body, in short the whole of that brilliant bourgeoisie, that illustrious third estate, which, after having given so many eminent men to France, and done the work of '89, had so long been trampled under foot by the populace of the faubourgs. Just when they were seeking to blot out the recollection of so many humiliations by the recovery of an influence which was justly theirs, they all at once perceived themselves to be struck by a measure of distrust, stopped in their course, and defrauded so to speak of the fruits of their most rightful conquest. In the liveliness of their anger they greatly exaggerated the effects of the decrees of Fructidor, and they exaggerated still more extravagantly their own strength. The ferment, which was rapidly gaining in Paris, was adroitly increased by the agents of the royalist party, who had become very bold since the encouragement given them by Pichegru. On the 11th Vendémiaire the electors of the different sections assembled in the Odéon, to count their adherents and try their strength. On the 12th the Section Le Peletier, situated in the centre of Paris, and the best known from the number and boldness of its members, declared itself in insurrection.

At the first noise of the revolt, the Convention, not much troubled by a spectacle which was by no means new, announced that it was in permanent session. The small number of troops which were in Paris at the time were concentrated in one place, and the two or three thousand patriots who had been disarmed only a few months before were now ordered to take up their arms again. As the numerical weakness of the defenders only increased the arrogance of its enemies, General Menou was ordered to proceed by force to disarm the Section Le Peletier. Menou, a fair officer, but wanting self-possession, and acting reluctantly in the embarrassment of having for adversaries the very men who had helped him to put down the insurrection in the faubourgs, crowded his troops pell-mell into a narrow space where they found their action completely paralysed. He then entered the Convent of Les Filles Saint Thomas, where the Section held its meetings; a building situated on the spot on which the Bourse now stands. There disturbed and alarmed by the salutations which followed one another in quick succession from the irritated crowd, instead of commanding he parleyed. The result of this interview, as encouraging for the rioters as it was unworthy of the dignity of the Convention, was a sort of capitulation, by virtue of which it was agreed that the troops should withdraw, and that the members of the Section should evacuate the hall of their meetings. But, as might have been expected, the troops alone fulfilled their agreement. The Sections hastened to proclaim their victory to all Paris. The danger became imminent. It was now half-past eight in the evening.

Bonaparte was at the Feydeau theatre that night. As

soon as he was informed of what was taking place, he hastened to the spot, and witnessed the close of this singular scene; from thence he proceeded to the assembly, to watch what was to be the issue. They had just decreed the arrest of Menou, and were discussing upon whom of the different generals it would be best to confer his command. The extreme peril of the situation made their choice exceptionally momentous, and the small number of officers in Paris at the time made it very difficult. Bonaparte, hidden in the audience, heard, he assures us in his *Mémoires*, his own name put forward, and he deliberated for 'nearly half an hour' what he should do. It is certain that the name of Barras drew the greatest number of votes, for the remembrance of his energetic conduct on the 9th Thermidor had placed him in the position of an arbitrator. Barras asked that he might have Bonaparte for a colleague. Napoleon has given us three different versions of this important event, and in all three he carefully omits to mention the recommendation of Barras, which was however the real means of his appointment. The version given by Las Cases, and which was corrected by Bonaparte himself, differs in several important particulars from the one recorded by Montholon; and we here get an insight into the reflections which made him hesitate for half an hour about espousing the cause of the Convention.

'Was it wise to declare himself? Victory itself would have something odious in it, while defeat would devote him to the execration of future generations. Why should he be the scapegoat of so many crimes, in which he had taken no part? Why gratuitously expose himself by the work of a few hours, to swell the number of names which were never pronounced but with horror?

'On the other hand, if the Convention falls, what is to become of the great truths of our Revolution? Our numerous victories and our blood so often shed will be henceforth only actions to be ashamed of. The foreigner whom we have so often conquered will triumph and overwhelm us with contempt; a weak race with an insolent and a perverse court will come back exulting, will upbraid us with our crimes, will wreak their vengeance on us, and will govern us like helots, with foreign help. Yes, the defeat of the Convention would crown our enemies, and set the seal of bondage and shame on the country.

'These feelings, with youth and confidence in his strength and his destiny, decided him.'

The only point of any value to the historian in these bombastic phrases, evidently written long after the event, is the very clear fact that Bonaparte did not lean to one side more than another; and that cold calculation and not principle guided his choice. If he felt any scruples, they arose not from the cause in itself, but from the uncertainty of success. As soon as his resolution was taken, he presented himself before the Committee, and on the recommendation of Barras received his command. Barras had known Bonaparte at the siege of Toulon, and had formed a hearty friendship for him, he tells us in his unpublished *Mémoires*, on account of his likeness to Marat, to whom he had been warmly attached. The parts were divided thus: Barras was to be Commander-in-Chief, and Bonaparte was to be his lieutenant, and to execute his orders.

The army of the Convention did not number more than eight thousand men, including the patriots to whom they had given back their arms; but it was well disciplined and full of confidence, and it possessed forty pieces of artillery, which had been brought from the camp of Sablons, giving them a precious advantage over their adversaries, who counted less on strategy than on their mass. Bonaparte passed the night in preparation. He turned the Louvre and the Tuileries into a sort of intrenched camp, with artillery posted at all the outlets. He secured his communications in such a way as to enable him to throw all his strength at any time on the point most seriously threatened; at the last moment he armed the members as a reserve in case of extreme peril, and took care to keep open for his little army a retreat to St. Cloud if necessary. This done, he waited, and gave orders to his troops not to fire till they were attacked.

The following morning, the 13th Vendémiaire, when the

troops of the Sections entered from all the surrounding streets to storm the Tuileries, they came into collision at every point with the posts of the Convention, and found all the approaches guarded. The National Guard, which consisted of about forty thousand soldiers, men full of ardour, but wanting in experience and stability, shouldered their guns, and took up their position in front of the army of the Convention. Their two chiefs had been chosen at random: General Danican, a cashiered officer without ability, and a returned emigrant named Lafond, a young man of the most brilliant courage.

The two armies spent the greater part of the day within fifteen paces of each other, threatening but not moving, as though after so much bloody dissension both shrank from again rending the bosom of their country. At one time there seemed some hope that this extremity, so fatal to liberty, would be avoided; but the blind animosity of both parties caused the attempted reconciliation to fail. At half-past four in the afternoon Danican gave the signal, and Napoleon mounted his horse. The fighting began at several points at once. The struggle was not so long, nor was it marked by the same tragic fury which the walls of this city have witnessed so often since. Public places had not yet served for fields of battle, and the strategy of street warfare was not yet become a science. The issue of the combat was never for an instant doubtful. Lafond, who directed the attack on the side of the Quays, threw his column through the Rue Dauphine, along the Quay Voltaire, on to the Pont Royal; but overwhelmed in front and flank by the cannon, it stopped short and rapidly dispersed. Thrice he rallied the scattered remnants under the fire which was decimating them; but he did not succeed in storming the bridge. At the church of St. Roche, the resistance offered was not more serious. A few cannon-shot sufficed to sweep clear all the adjoining streets. The members of the Sections, in the ardour of their first attack, did not seem to have foreseen that their opponents might meet them with cannon-ball. They held no ground before artillery, which drove them successively from all their posts. At six o'clock it was all over; the Convention had carried the day. They were afraid to exult over their victory, for they had more than one kind of enemies; and in destroying the one, they placed themselves at the mercy of the others. The vanquished were treated with diplomatic and generous indulgence by their conquerors, who contented themselves with disarming and disbanding their battalions. Lafond alone could not be saved, from the fact of his being an emigrant, which at whatever cost he refused to disown. The Convention declared that their defenders had deserved well of the country; it confirmed Barras and Bonaparte in their appointments, and, as the former lost no time in sending in his resignation, Bonaparte was left in single possession of the title of General of the Interior. This day, so profitable for the young general whose fortunes it advanced to a prodigious degree, was a fatal one for France. It strengthened and embittered the antagonism, which the Convention by its unfortunate decrees had created, between public opinion and the Government. Instead of conciliating that part of the nation, eminent as it was, which creates public opinion, and on whom it had thrown suspicion by the decrees, depriving them of their legitimate hope of influencing the Government, it had wounded and irrevocably alienated them. It was easy to foresee that from that time a spirit of hostility to the Convention would pervade all the elections, and that thus driven from the Legislative Body it would take refuge in the executive body and make that its stronghold. This is exactly what actually happened. The third of the Deputies to be added to the members of the Convention who were to be retained were all chosen from a hostile party; and the Convention which still formed a majority in the Councils replied to this manifestation of the wishes of the nation by calling to the Directory five regicides: Barras, Carnot, Rewbell, Letourneur, and Lareveillère-Lépaux. Now, as in the Legislative Body a third of the members were changed every year, whilst in the Directory it was only a fifth, it is evident that at a given moment the Government composed of regicides would find itself at open war with the Councils composed of Moderates.

And as neither of these bodies had any legal authority over the other, it followed as a matter of course that force would remain the only judge left between them. Unfortunately the 13th Vendémiaire had shown all the world what weight the sword of the soldier had in the scale. So this inauspicious day taught authority to reckon on the army, and the army to dispose of authority. It made ready from afar off the paths to military government.

Bonaparte employed the few months which elapsed between the 13th of Vendémiaire and his appointment to the army of Italy in assuring the victory he had won, and getting rid of the elements of trouble and disorder, in reorganising the National Guard, in forming a guard for the Directory and another for the Legislative Body, and finally in busying himself with great activity about his own fortunes. Like every essentially ambitious man, he only saw in his new position the means it offered him of gaining one still higher. The part he had played in the late events, the importance of the post he held, his connection with powerful personages, the formation of a government still new and uncertain in its steps, were all circumstances that enabled him to mix himself up in all that went on, to interfere when he wished in the affairs of his colleagues, and to reign uncontrolled in his own department. He took advantage of this latitude with his accustomed decision, acting without consulting any one, and paying very little attention to any representations that were made to him. He was not less indefatigable all this time with the heads of the Government, whose good will he was interested in winning. At the same time he protected the old nobility, in order to efface from their recollection the cannonades of Vendémiaire; he recalled the banished generals, and filled the governmental guard with men who were his 'creatures,' and whom he was glad, he assures us in his memoir, to find again on the 18th Brumaire; he distributed appointments to his relations and friends, many of whom he sent for from the remotest corners of the country to establish them in Paris; and he despatched large sums of money to his family (Letters to Joseph, from October 1795 to February 1796).

A man of this restless character was not likely either to find scope for his mind in such a place, or to remain long without giving great offence. To confine himself strictly within his own functions was misery to him, to go beyond them was to plunge into the most dangerous of all undertakings. Yet in the midst of the incessant activity of parties, it was difficult not to feel the temptation. The Directory soon began to regard Bonaparte with a certain uneasiness, which had something to do with his nomination as commander of the army of Italy. Rather than make an enemy of him by recalling him within the limits of ordinary law, they preferred the expedient of getting rid of him by granting him some special favour; not reflecting that under pretence of averting the danger they were only rendering it more inevitable for the future. This cowardice, which was repeated several times, and at last punished by a cruel and memorable lesson, was the only policy the Directory had skill enough to employ to protect itself against the designs which it imputed to Bonaparte. However, it is not certain that on this first occasion the suspicion which the General inspired would have been worth such promotion, if his marriage with Joséphine de Beauharnais had not happened to crown and consummate his fortune.

Bonaparte has himself related how he made the acquaintance of Madame de Beauharnais. A few days after the disarming of the Sections, a child between ten and twelve years old came to Bonaparte to claim the sword of his father, once a general of the Republic, who had perished on the scaffold. This child was Eugène de Beauharnais. The General, touched by his tears, ordered the sword to be given him, and the next day he received a visit from Madame de Beauharnais, whom he only knew by name, although she was the 'intimate' friend of his protector Barras. The silence which Bonaparte has kept with regard to this connection, and the share that Barras had in the ultimate resolution of Madame de Beauharnais, is easier to explain than his forgetfulness of the service done him the night before the 13th Vendémiaire. But the fact is none the less incontestable; it is certified by all trustworthy authority, and confirmed by Joséphine herself, who, with her creole apathy, would perhaps never have made up her mind to the marriage, if Barras had not added to her marriage-settlement the promise that Bonaparte should be made Commander-in-Chief of the army of Italy. 'Barras assures me,' she wrote a short time previous to her marriage, 'that if I marry the General, he will obtain for him the appointment of Commander-in-Chief of the army of Italy. Yesterday, Bonaparte, speaking to me of this favour, which has already caused some jealousy among his companions in arms, although it is not yet granted, said, "Do they think I need patronage to insure my success? Some day they will be only too happy if I grant them mine. My sword is at my side, and that will carry me a long way."'

Bonaparte had a burning and violent passion for Madame de Beauharnais, which was still further inflamed by his ambition; for he knew that the marriage would not only give him the position which he most coveted, but also an entrance into a society which till then had only responded to his overtures with excessive mistrust. To this affection, the only one it is said by which his heart was ever moved, he brought all the passion and fire of his impetuous nature. As for Madame de Beauharnais, she felt even in his presence far more trouble and amazement than love. The genius which she saw sparkling in his piercing and imperious glance exercised over this amiable but indolent nature a kind of fascination which she yielded to with a secret terror, and before surrendering herself entirely to its influence, she asked herself more than once if the extraordinary assurance evinced in every word of the General was not the effect of a young man's presumption, destined to meet with bitter disappointment. Her irresolution increased when she reflected on the difference of age between them, for Joséphine's beauty was already declining, and the General was still a long way from the maturity of life. However, she succeeded in overcoming her scruples. The twenty-third of February 1796 Bonaparte was named General-in-Chief of the Italian army, and on the ninth of March the marriage took place. Carnot seconded his nomination in opposition to Rewbell, the patron of Schérer; but it was by no means he who proposed him, as is pretended in his *Mémoire of the 18th Fructidor*. In the marriage register Bonaparte put himself down as one year older than he really was, which has given rise to doubts as to the exact date of his birth; and Joséphine made herself four years younger, a double fiction suggested probably by a little feminine vanity on the one hand, and acquiesced in on the other from a wish to restore some parity of age between them in the eyes of the public by means of an obliging falsehood. In the first line in the list of witnesses of the marriage figured the name of Paul Barras.

CHAPTER III

SUBMISSION OF PIEDMONT AND THE CONQUEST OF LOMBARDY

A FEW days after his marriage, Bonaparte set out to join the army of Italy, and arrived at the head-quarters at Nice on the 26th of March. Some days before his departure the Directory sent him detailed instructions for the campaign which was about to open. These instructions were only partly conformable to the plan which had been previously suggested more than once by the General himself. He was ordered it is true to cross the Apennines, and open the campaign by separating the Piedmontese and Austrian armies; but this object once attained, instead of forcing Piedmont into peace, as he had always designed, the General was to content himself with taking Ceva and Tortona, with obtaining Gavi from the Genoese voluntarily or by force, and with leaving a corps of observation before Coni, after which, taking no account of the Piedmontese army, he would pour down into the Milanese, in order to drive the Austrian army across the Adige; a monstrous plan, condemning him to leave in his rear Piedmont in arms, as well as Genoa hostile and ready to break out on the first occasion, besides exposing him to the inevitable risk of having his communications cut off. In addition to this, the Directory deprived him of the power of conceding a suspension of hostilities, while they reserved exclusively to themselves that of treating for peace. They adopted the General's ideas upon the necessity of making the enemy's country support the army. Finally they recommended him to 'use every means in his power to excite the malcontents of Piedmont against the court of Turin.' The Milanese once overrun, what was to be done with it? The Directory let it be seen that it might, in accordance with his own plan, be offered as an indemnity to Piedmont for the two provinces of Nice and Savoy, which France had taken from her; but they did not settle the question, for they had some thoughts of giving it back to Austria in exchange for the Low Countries; a proposition which shows at once how much ground the generous principles of the Revolution had already lost; not the France of 1792 would thus have disposed of nations without their consent. These instructions, all the consequences of which had no doubt not been foreseen by the Directory, as their first result were calculated to change the character of the war. The struggle between France and Europe had hitherto been a defensive war; for the reasons which had led to our occupation of Savoy and Belgium were not only identity of race, and the almost unanimous wish of the inhabitants of the two countries, but also the enormous increase of territory which Russia and Germany had acquired by the partition of Poland. We had only invaded Holland when compelled to do so in self-defence, and without any intention of encroaching in any respect on the rights and possessions of that country. In entering Italy with the hidden notion of disposing of territories wrested from the enemy, not by any rule of right but merely to serve our own purposes, in giving authority to their General to excite the people against their sovereign, not to insure their independence, but on false pretences to make use of them, the Directory not only commenced a policy of offensive warfare, of which it was impossible to foresee the subsequent development, but they substituted interest for principles, and force for right; they returned to the old routine of wars of aggrandisement, and by an inevitable consequence, they were giving a preponderating force in the Republic to the military element.

Nor was Bonaparte's proclamation on taking the field less opposed to the spirit which had hitherto animated the Republican armies. It was an appeal to their ambition, and no longer to their patriotism; it was a war of conquest and not a war of liberty that his words announced.

'Soldiers,' he said, 'you are hungry and nearly naked. The Government owes you much; it can do nothing for you. Your patience and courage do you honour, but cannot procure you either profit or glory. I am come to lead you into the most fertile plains in the world. There you will find rich provinces and great towns. There you will find glory, honour and *riches*. Soldiers of Italy, can your courage fail you?'

These seductive promises, so often afterwards repeated in Bonaparte's proclamations, of fortune and abundance, of victory for conquest and no longer for liberty, were then heard for the first time. The Republican soldiers had often listened to addresses about tyranny to destroy, of liberty to avenge, of chains to break—and if this was a worn-out phraseology, at least the virtues it hallowed had not grown old; but no one had ever yet spoken to them of riches to acquire; none had ever yet thought of inflaming their valour by kindling their cupidity; till then it was only by their disinterestedness and their courage that they had been known. In reading these first words addressed to the army of democrats by this powerful tempter, we think with sadness of the subsequent mad and gigantic adventures into which he was destined to draw them by the false allurement of grandeur. Not in a day did the soldiers of the Republic become the soldiers of the Empire; but the commencement of the change dates from this proclamation, in which Bonaparte pointed to Italy—Italy, not as a nation to deliver, but as a prey to seize.

It is easy to imagine the effect which such summonses, relieved now and again by appeals to nobler passions, would have on an impatient, famishing and squalid host, composed for the most part of men who were young, ardent, adventurous, and all of them with their fortunes to make. They produced instantly in the common soldiers a thirst for pillage, of which modern warfare offers no other example; in their leaders a spirit of ambition and insatiable cupidity, of which we shall have to speak only too often. But it was by no means the immediate consequences of this transformation of our military spirit which were either the most serious or the most dangerous.

When Bonaparte arrived at head-quarters, he found that the army had not changed its position since the battle of Loano, a brilliant but useless victory for General Schérer, who was skilful enough to gain a battle, but not to profit by the issue. Our troops were ranged in échelons along the Corniche road from Nice to Savona, occupying the Col di Tenda and along with Sérurier's division watching from Garessio the intrenched camp at Ceva, on the other side of the Apennines.

Our forces have generally been estimated at no more than thirty thousand men, according to the number given by Napoleon, who however is not always consistent on this point. It is more natural to refer on such a matter to his correspondence, written as it was from the dictation of events, than on his *Mémoires*, composed long afterwards for posterity, and in which so many circumstances have been either distorted or else passed over in silence. The figures vary even in the correspondence itself; if however we may trust to the number given in a letter to Carnot, dated from Cherasco, April 29th, a fortnight after the opening of the campaign, and before the arrival of reinforcements from the army of the Alps, a letter in which he earnestly begged for aid, and was therefore interested in keeping down the number of troops, we find that they amounted to thirty-five thousand men.[1] At the same time he announces his intention of entering Lombardy with twenty-eight thousand men; a figure it is impossible to admit on the supposition that he had commenced the campaign with only thirty thousand men, for since that he had fought six bloody battles, and left considerable garrisons in several fortified places.

Allowing then for exaggerations in both directions, we may safely estimate the French army at thirty-six or thirty-

[1] Elsewhere he says thirty-four thousand infantry, and three thousand five hundred cavalry; and in the same letter he estimates the enemy's forces at the fanciful number of a hundred thousand men.— *To the Directory, Carrù,* April 24th.

eight thousand men; but it was composed of excellent troops, now for long inured to the fatigues of mountain warfare in the Alps and Pyrenees, consumed with an ardent impatience to exchange for new fields of battle the barren rocks, where they were wasting their strength in unprofitable and inglorious combats. At the head of this army Generals already celebrated were to be seen; such as Masséna, Augereau, Sérurier, Laharpe, Cervoni, and Kilmaine; in its ranks were the greater part of the men who were destined to make the fortune of the Empire:—Junot, Murat, Marmont, Lannes, Victor, Suchet, Berthier, Rampon; others who were to fall without seeing the fruits of victory confiscated for the profit of a single man, Joubert, Muiron, Stengel, Lanusse.

Bonaparte's appointment to the chief command had been viewed with some disgust by several of these generals whose services had been both longer and more conspicuous, if not more real, than his own; but their murmurs were lost in the midst of the acclamations of their young companions, who saw in Bonaparte's rapid promotion a certain pledge of their own advancement. The young General was quite aware of the existence of this feeling of dissatisfaction, but full of confidence in himself, he assumed from the first towards the malcontents, as he did towards everybody, that tone of authority and determination which was so natural to him. Masséna and Augereau, who were supposed to be the two most hostile to him, wrote him letters of congratulation, and very soon their secret rancour no longer ventured to disclose itself in face of the dazzling splendour of his victories.

The Piedmontese army numbered about twenty thousand men, commanded by General Colli, an officer of high repute; the Austrian army amounted to thirty-eight or forty thousand men. It was under the command of Beaulieu, an experienced general, but old and badly served. These two armies, which had agreed to act in concert, occupied the slope of the Apennines away from the sea, but each obeyed a private motive of its own, very little calculated to keep up that unity of movement which was so indispensable. The first was especially interested in covering Piedmont, the second in closing Lombardy against us. This diversity of object, unfavourable as it was to unanimous action, was further complicated by dull misunderstandings and mutual distrust. Piedmont, connected with Austria by a treaty of alliance since 1794, was extremely dissatisfied with the way in which this power had fulfilled its engagements, and though making common cause with her, it submitted to the necessity with regret. The first object in the campaign then was to separate Piedmont from her ally, an undertaking easy to begin by military tactics and to finish by diplomacy.

In accordance with his first plan of the campaign, Bonaparte resolved to cross the Alps at the lowest point, that is to say at their junction with the Apennines above Savona. By taking this road he not only greatly facilitated transport, which was an immense advantage considering the still backward season of the year, but also, instead of encountering either the fortresses which defended the approaches to Piedmont on the side of the Col di Tenda, or the intrenched camp at Ceva which protected it on the side of the Col di Bardinetto, he entered Piedmont at the point where the two armies were encamped, and he could thus attack either one or the other as he pleased. He therefore fixed his head-quarters at Albenga, about sixty miles from Nice on the Corniche road. He expected to surprise the Austrians, but the movement of one of his divisions on Genoa gave them warning, and he was the first to be attacked.

Beaulieu, mistaking Bonaparte's design, crossed the Apennines with a part of his army at Bochetta above Genoa, in order to cover this town. D'Argenteau, his lieutenant, had orders to cross the mountains at the Col di Montenotte, above Savona, that is to say by the same road which the French had chosen to enter Piedmont. If this movement had succeeded all that part of the French army which was found in the line of the coast between Savona and Genoa would have been cut off and taken prisoners. But whilst Beaulieu was driving before him Laharpe's division, which occupied our forward outposts on the side of Genoa, D'Argenteau encountered an obstacle on his way to Montelegino which stopped his advance. It was a simple redoubt defended by twelve hundred men under the command of Colonel Rampon. At that moment the issue of the whole campaign depended on this ill-guarded redoubt; both sides understood this. The soldiers swore that as long as one was left they would not yield. Rampon repelled three furious attacks, and his resistance saved the army.

When Bonaparte, who was at Savona, heard of the danger from which by a kind of miracle he had just escaped, he spent that night in stealing a march on the enemy, in order to strike one of those unexpected blows which were the favourite peculiarity of his military genius. The following morning, April 12, Beaulieu who had remained on the Corniche road found nothing in front of him, whilst D'Argenteau who had fallen back on Montenotte from Montelegino found himself confronted by Laharpe's and Augereau's divisions, posted in advance of the fort, and behind him was Masséna's division which had arrived by by-paths. Thus surrounded by superior forces, he was compelled to beat a retreat upon Dego, where the rest of the Austrian army was stationed, and he left two thousand prisoners in the hands of the French.

This first feat of war, known under the name of the battle of Montenotte, not only recovered all lost ground, but it also threw into disorder the Austrian army, whose different corps dispersed between Genoa and Dego no longer had numbers or compactness enough to resume the offensive. Bonaparte, who was impatient to consummate the victory, proceeded to his attack the next day, April 13. But this time he found himself in presence of both the Piedmontese and Austrian armies, the former at Millesimo, covering the road to Piedmont, the latter trying to rally their scattered forces at Dego, on the road to Acqui and Milan. He first directed his main efforts against the Piedmontese, hitherto unbroken. He succeeded in driving them back upon Ceva, over the gorges of Millesimo, after having cut off one of their divisions commanded by Provera, which was reduced to take refuge in the castle of Cossaria, where after twenty-four hours' resistance it was forced to surrender. The following day, April 14, leaving Augereau only and his division to keep the pass of Millesimo against the Piedmontese, who failed to perceive the necessity of effecting a coalition with Beaulieu at any cost, Bonaparte concentrated all the rest of his forces against the Austrian army; after several attacks he drove them from Dego, capturing four thousand prisoners. This number happened to be nearly doubled some hours after by a mistake of one of Beaulieu's divisions, which having left Genoa to rejoin the Austrians came full upon the French army, and only regained Dego to be themselves taken prisoners almost at the same moment.

Thus after four days' fighting, owing to the rapidity of his movements and that method of acting by surprises by which he contrived on every battlefield to have forces superior to any that his adversary could oppose to him, Bonaparte had obtained the most important result of the campaign, the separation of the allied armies. The Piedmontese were in full retreat for Ceva and Mondovi, the Austrians for Acqui, while the French army found itself master of both roads, certain of its superiority in force over either army separately, and able to throw itself at its own choice upon either one or the other. The greatness of these results created a striking impression that was felt everywhere; and when the soldiers in the march towards Ceva reached the heights of Monte Zemoto, and beheld the splendid plains which lay stretched before them, surrounded by the magnificent amphitheatre of the Alps, they were seized with such admiration that they halted and saluted their young chief with universal acclamations.

The separation of the allied armies once effected, the instructions of the Directory required Bonaparte to leave Piedmont, and to bear down on the Milanese. This was not however a positive order, for he had authority to bombard Turin 'if circumstances rendered it necessary;' but still with as little delay in Piedmont as possible. The General, on the other hand, was fully resolved to do nothing in Lombardy till he had absolutely reduced this power. So he left Laharpe's division at San Benedetto, to protect himself against any renewal of attack by the Austrian army; and reinforced with Sérurier's division which had been posted for purposes of observation at Garessio before Ceva, he threw himself with all his forces upon the weak Piedmontese army. This force, compelled to retreat before an enemy of such superiority, scarcely made any attempt to defend the intrenched camp at Ceva, and contented themselves with falling back step by step, taking advantage of every obstacle the country offered, to impede the march of the French and to give time for the Austrians to re-form and come to their assistance. The 21st of April, after a series of desultory combats, they met at Mondovi. They fought with gallantry but without success, and lost three thousand men, killed or taken prisoners. The 23d of April Colli demanded an amnesty in order to gain time; they would not even listen to him. On the 25th Bonaparte arrived at Cherasco, which was only ten leagues from Turin.

Dismay reigned in the Sardinian court. The king wished to continue the war; but nearly everybody about him was so alarmed at the thought of a revolutionary irruption triumphant in Turin, that they were urgent with him to make peace. The situation was not however desperate, for a protracted resistance must increase the chances of the conquered as it diminished those of the conquerors. The geographical position of Piedmont, its passes, its numerous fortresses, the brave, energetic, and tenacious character of the population, all gave it great advantages in an irregular warfare. Turin of itself could have offered a long resistance to the French, who had neither artillery nor material for a siege. It had only to consult its own history to find the glorious example it had to follow and that might deliver it. Their army had still the valuable resources of a considerable artillery, and of excellent cavalry, far superior to ours; and Beaulieu was already marching to their relief. But what power have considerations like these over minds demoralised by fear? The king yielded to the supplications of his court and to the terrors of an opulent and luxurious *bourgeoisie*, and delivered himself up to his enemy.

By his order Marshal de la Tour repaired to the French camp. Bonaparte, to whom these overtures were an unlooked-for surprise, received him with that air of conqueror and master which he knew to be so likely to impose on men; and when the marshal pronounced the word terms, 'Terms,' cried Bonaparte, 'it is I who name the terms; accept them at once, or Turin is mine to-morrow.' The Directory had explicitly denied to the General the right of suspending hostilities. He did not however hesitate to exceed his instructions, confident that victory would insure pardon. But he did not in reality feel all the assurance he thought it right to affect; it was at bottom so far from being genuine, that he proceeded to stir up a revolutionary demonstration at Asti, in order to hasten negotiations which were proceeding too slowly to please him (Letter to Ballet, April 26). The armistice was signed on the 28th of April. Piedmont withdrew from the coalition and gave up as pledges of submission till a declaration of peace the fortified places of Coni, Ceva, and Tortona, or else Alessandria; she surrendered to the French all the military routes leading to France, and lastly she dispersed her army and disbanded her militia. Bonaparte, desirous of deceiving the Austrians as to his projects, added another clause to the treaty, by virtue of which the town of Valenza was to be surrendered, in order to secure his passage across the Po.

By this armistice Bonaparte had done better than if he had conquered Piedmont; for the conquest would have necessitated a protracted, burdensome, and exceedingly dangerous occupation of the country; as it was, he held it at his mercy, his means of communication were assured, and he could safely attack Lombardy.

Even before the armistice was signed, he hastened to make it known to the Directory, taking care to shield himself under the approbation of the generals and the Government Commissioners, 'who, as well as myself,' he wrote, 'regard this event as the most fortunate that could possibly have happened' (April 27). The next day he informed the Directory of the suspension of hostilities; and while he declared himself ready to bow to their decision if they refused to sign the treaty of peace, he in a measure compelled them to do so by informing them that he was going in pursuit of Beaulieu, and by advising them 'not to count on a revolution in Piedmont, because,' he wrote, 'the people are not ripe for it;' thus overthrowing beforehand their favourite chimera. He hoped within a month to be in the Tyrol, co-operating with the armies of the Rhine, and carrying war into Bavaria. 'If, however,' he wrote on the 29th of April, 'you do not accept peace with the king of Sardinia; if your plan is to dethrone him, you must occupy his attention for a time, and let me know at once. I will take possession of Valenza and then march upon Turin. I shall levy,' he added, 'some millions on the duke of Parma; he will propose terms of peace; do not be in any hurry to accept them, so as to give me time to make him pay the expenses of the campaign.'

As regards the Republic of Genoa, where the old claim of indemnity for losses sustained by the frigate *La Modeste* was still pending, claims made more by way of intimidation than for any other reason, Bonaparte had written at the commencement of the campaign to Faypoult, our Minister at Genoa, that they ought to think themselves fortunate if they got *three millions*. After the armistice, he advised him to demand *fifteen* millions; to such an extent had victory swollen the claims. This spirit of cupidity, this thirst for gain which he had so imprudently roused in the army in order to create in it a taste for great enterprises, expressed itself in acts of spoliation, pillage, and violence, with such unbridled passion that he was at first appalled at his own work. At Ceva, at Saint Michel, and at Mondovi, the soldiers committed such excesses, that, to use Bonaparte's own expression, 'they made him blush to be a man·' (Letter to the Directory, Carrù, April 24).

'I am going to make some signal examples,' he added, 'I will re-establish order, or I will give up the command of these brigands.' He published an order of the day at

Lesegno, the 22d of April, in which he said that 'he saw with horror the frightful pillage which some abandoned men were indulging in;' and he commanded the heads of the army to make their reports 'on the morality of the Commissaries, the adjutant generals, and superior officers,' and gave authority to all generals of division to have any soldier or officer shot who should be convicted of pillage. A few days after a second order was issued, proving that the first had been ill executed. 'If pillage continues,' he said, 'all is lost, even glory and honour;' and he announced in order to appease their cupidity his intention of levying heavy contributions on the conquered country, in such a way as to enable him to discharge half their pay in cash. He did in fact make some examples; several officers were degraded, and several common soldiers shot; but with the system of spoliation which he thought it perfectly legitimate in himself to apply to the nations we were supposed to have come to free, he was not likely to obtain any very thorough reformation. All that he could do was to put an end to open disorder and scenes of public violence. It was, in a word, to regulate pillage, not to abolish it; disinterestedness was impossible in the common soldier, when it was not to be found in the chiefs. Bonaparte was the first to find excuses for those whom he was obliged to punish. 'These wretches,' he said, 'are excusable; they have sighed for three years after the promised land from the summit of the Alps, and now they have entered it, they wish to enjoy it' (Cherasco, April 26, to the Directory). The promised land! it was in the same phrase that he had first designated Italy to his troops. Was it wonderful that they understood him literally, and claimed their share of the booty? What right had he to the sole disposal of a common conquest? Did it suffice that the spoliation should be carried on under regular forms and in the name of the Government, to make the act equitable? Such was evidently his opinion, for in the same letter in which he speaks of 'the horrors which made him shudder,' he said, 'if this splendid country can be saved from pillage, we may obtain considerable advantages from it; the province of Mondovi alone will give us a million.' From pillage to this kind of spoliation there was evidently an immense distance, so far as regards the behaviour and discipline of the army, but in a moral point of view the two circumstances flowed from the same source, and were sure to lead to the same effect.

In a fresh proclamation from Cherasco, dated April 26, in which Bonaparte addresses the army as the *Conquering Army of Italy*, he summed up the results of this crushing campaign; he enumerates the past exploits of his soldiers, and those they were soon to achieve; he reminds them 'that the ashes of the conquerors of Tarquin were still trodden on by the assassins of Basseville.' But with the promise of what reward did he stimulate them? The promise was still Italy. 'Friends,' he said, 'I promise it to you, this conquest!' And by the strangest of contradictions, he styled them 'the liberators of the people.' He concludes by an address to the Italians themselves: 'Natives of Italy, the French army has come to *break your chains;* the French people is the friend of all the peoples; come with confidence before her.' To plunder those they were come to save from oppression was a sorry way of beginning this scheme of redemption.

The effect produced in Paris by the news of these successes was immense. Never were the wings of victory so swift, never were triumphs better adapted to strike men's imagination by simplicity of process and grandeur of result. The fever of excitement which had taken possession of the army spread through France. Each morning the *Moniteur* published one after another Bonaparte's reports to the Directory, his proclamations, the value of the *spolia opima* which he had taken from the enemy. Men's imaginations became violently heated. The new men who formed the majority in the Directory, obscure yesterday, to-day invested with the power of disposing of conquered kingdoms, were dazzled by the prospects opened out by the General before their eyes, and failing to see the inevitable term to which the spirit of conquest would soon lead them, forgetting that their strength lay in fidelity to the new ideas, they only followed Bonaparte with intoxicated enthusiasm in the path along which he was drawing them. They gave the warmest reception to his aide-de-camp, Murat, who brought them the standards taken from the enemy; they lavished the most flattering marks of approbation on the General; they passed a decree declaring that the army of Italy had deserved well of the country; they established a festival in honour of the victory; they confirmed, by a treaty of peace, the policy which Bonaparte had pursued towards the court of Sardinia, thenceforward at the mercy of France; in short, blinded by his representations of the inexhaustible wealth of Italy, and by the advantages which they hoped to derive from it for their ruined finances, they encouraged him in the system of plunder which he designed to follow towards the Italians, and like those sovereigns by the grace of God, whom they so often reviled in their manifestoes, they looked upon Italy as a rich farm to make money from, and upon its inhabitants as a class of subjects liable to taxation at pleasure.

The new instructions to Bonaparte issued by the Directory, May 7, had an immense influence on the manner in which the war was subsequently carried on. It is in these documents that we must look for the true spirit of our occupation of Italy, for it is impossible in this matter to trust to the conventional commonplaces that have been uniformly repeated by historians without principle or without penetration. The great error in the first instructions of the Directory lay especially in the want of explicitness on certain points which ought never to have been matters of doubt to a government that had sprung from the French Revolution; in the second, they entered without power of return upon a path which had hitherto been only indicated, and they entered it in the most deplorable way, for there is something graver than the policy of conquest, there is the policy of rapine and depredation.

What instantly strikes and revolts the reader of these documents is the incredible intensity acquired in so short a time by this thirst for the wealth of a friendly people, and the shamelessness with which they display a greed that is usually artful enough to hide itself under the semblance of policy. They do not renounce the idea of plundering Genoa, only it would be safer to temporise for a while, because it may become dangerous. Without any pretext for attacking Tuscany, since the French Republic was on good terms with her, they were to enter Leghorn, seize the English and Neapolitan vessels, confiscate the property of strangers, and leave a garrison to protect the town. The Duchy of Parma, which had joined the allies, was to be spared out of consideration for Spain with whom we had made peace; but at the same time they were to take care that a heavy ransom was paid.

The Milanese, possibly, will find favour in our eyes, for it is this we are going to deliver from the yoke of Austria. 'It is the Milanese especially that *you are not to spare*,' wrote the Directors to Bonaparte; 'levy heavy contributions there in cash, and during the first moment of terror that the approach of our army will produce, let the eye of economy superintend its expenditure. If Rome makes any advances, the first thing to require is that the Pope should at once order public prayers to be offered up for the success of the French arms. Some of their fine monuments, statues, pictures, medals, libraries, silver madonnas, and even bells, will pay the expenses of your visit to him;' and so on.

This last kind of plunder, unknown in the history of the world since the famous taking of Corinth by the Romans, is perhaps that which has most contributed to rouse the nations against us, and with justice; for to rob the Italians of their works of genius was in some sort to despoil them of their past and their glory. Every previous conqueror had respected these memorials of their history, the only titles to honour with which they could then adorn themselves in the eyes of the stranger: it was reserved for their liberators to ravish them of these.

That the corrupt Barras should have signed such instructions is not astonishing; but that the rigid probity of Carnot should not have revolted against lending his name and authority to a policy so antagonistic to the principles of the Revolution, is incomprehensible. What was not to be expected, when the man who passed for the personification of ancient virtue felt no scruple in ratifying such designs? It is very difficult to know accurately whether the first idea of confiscating the pictures and statues of Italy, a measure perfectly at variance with modern manners, but which had unfortunately been attempted the preceding year in Holland and Belgium, though not in the wholesale fashion afterwards adopted, arose with Bonaparte or the Directory; it is probable that this disgraceful expedient was discussed and recognised verbally and as a possible contingency before the departure of the General. It could only have been adopted and reduced to a law by the man who contributed so largely to the revival of the old right of conquest and its most iniquitous abuses; but the Directory must share with him the miserable honour and the responsibility.[1] All that can be said in defence of the Directory is that the instructions only proposed this measure for the Papal States, whilst Bonaparte, even as early as the 1st of May, wrote to Faypoult, our minister at Genoa:—

'Send me some information about the dukes of Parma, Piacenza, and Modena; let me know the numerical force of their armies, and in what the wealth of the country consists. Especially send me a list of the *paintings, statues,* and *objets de curiosité* which are to be found in Milan, Parma, Piacenza, and Bologna, etc.'

And on the 6th of May, the day before the instructions were sent off from Paris, he alluded to the subject in writing to the Directory without any introduction, as if it were a thing quite understood and already agreed upon: 'It

---

[1] Thibeaudeau, one of the men who best personifies this epoch, relates with indignation in his *Mémoires sur le Directoire*, that some French artists dared to petition the Government against this removal of *chefs-d'œuvre* of art. He forgets to mention the courageous protestation of Quatremère de Quincy. The adversaries of this measure appeared to him enemies of our glory, 'morose and unpatriotic fanatics.' He alludes, in support of his opinion, to what was done in Greece and in Egypt, and he is astonished that any one should think of disputing 'our right to pictures which our soldiers *might have burned*, or marbles which they *might have broken to pieces*.' It was thus that this tribune understood justice.

would be as well for you to send me three or four good artists, to make a choice of the best things to send to Paris.'

National pride has generally led us to throw a veil over the motives of shameless cupidity which directed our first occupation of Italy, and which from the first tarnished the glory of our victories and compromised their results. People prefer to dwell upon the artificial phrases and rhetorical commonplaces which were meant to amuse the crowd; the picture is more flattering and more pleasing to popular vanity; but in this way the true spirit of events escapes us, and their subsequent turns are so many riddles. People are astonished to see so much heroism and virtue end in the negotiation of Campo Formio; the rapidity with which our work in Italy falls to pieces is wholly inexplicable; they cannot make out how the Republic perishes at the hands of Republican soldiers. To him who has followed step by step the progress of the spirit which perverted our political and military institutions, these events are clear; he is neither astonished at the coolness with which these apostles of Republican virtue trafficked in the rights of nations, as if the bargain related to cattle, nor at the slight durability of those vain phantoms of republics which we left in Italy after our conquest; it is easy for him to understand how soldiers accustomed to recognise no other law than the right of war, to look upon power as the price of victory, to hold all from their chief, did not hesitate on the Eighteenth Brumaire to throw one last conquest at his feet.

With regard to military operations the Directory communicated to the General a conclusion at which they had arrived of the utmost gravity, and which would have had as one of its consequences the division of the command, and a complete change in Bonaparte's plan of the campaign. They informed him that the army of Italy was to be made into two separate corps; one under the command of Kellermann was to protect the Milanese against the ulterior designs of Austria; the other under Bonaparte was to file along the coast to Leghorn, Rome, and Naples. The Directory attached great importance to the expedition to Rome, either because they hoped to strike a weightier blow against the old superstition by exposing to all eyes the infirmity of the idol, or else their zeal may have been stimulated by the jealous fervour of the theophilanthropic Lareveillère who saw in the Pope a personal enemy. They repeated their former injunctions to Bonaparte to do nothing without consulting the Commissioners, and since they could not blame him for the armistice of Cherasco, they congratulated him with the transparently hollow assumption that he had consulted them before treating. 'These kinds of negotiations,' they wrote, 'are especially the province of the Government Commissioners with the army.'

These instructions followed the old routine of French invasions, which had all failed successively by taking possession of the centre of Italy before the approaches had been secured. They were completely subversive of Bonaparte's plan, who with his sure glance had seen that Austria was the only enemy we had to fear, and wished to concentrate all his strength against her, and make the Adige an impassable barrier, feeling certain that when once this was done the weak states of Italy would fall one by one into our hands. The rapidity of his onward march, his promptitude in engaging the Government in his own course by his first brilliant success, preserved him from having to choose between a useless remonstrance and a perilous acceptance of their plan, and strengthened his representations sufficiently to make them prevail.

The same day on which the Directory signed the despatches that gave him such an unpleasant surprise, that is to say the 7th of May, Bonaparte, who had already reopened the campaign, after reinforcing his army and securing his communications, presented himself unexpectedly before Piacenza, intending to cross the Po there. Deceived by skilfully spread reports and false manœuvres, Beaulieu was expecting him at Valenza. Here he had covered with increased defences not only the approaches to the Po, but those to the Ticino also, which presented a second line and offered him a strong position at Pavia, the scene of one of our former disasters. In marching on

Piacenza with some thousand troops, at about twenty-four miles below the place where the Ticino falls into the Po, Bonaparte turned both Pavia and the Ticino, and was able besides to effect the passage over the Po, always dangerous in itself, without serious disturbance from the enemy. He was not attacked till the next day at Fombio near Pizzighettone, and then only by a single division of the Austrian army, of which he made two thousand prisoners.

Beaulieu, who was not strong enough to keep the field against the French army, could do nothing but take advantage of the natural lines of defence formed by the numerous tributaries of the Po which run through Italy from north to south, the Ticino, the Adda, the Oglio, the Mincio, and the Adige. The line of the Ticino having been forced, he fell back on the Adda, evacuating the whole of that part of Lombardy comprised between these two rivers, after having left a garrison in the castle of Milan. On May 9 Bonaparte overtook him at Lodi, a town situated on the Adda on the bank occupied by the French army. The town was easily taken, but to cross the stream it was necessary to storm the bridge, which was defended by artillery and twelve thousand men. This was an obstacle which most generals would have hesitated to encounter for the sake of the soldiers' lives; but Bonaparte in forcing the bridge hoped to cut off two divisions of Austrians which he supposed to be on the other side of the Adda. He did not hesitate in attempting this bold blow. He formed a column composed of the best troops in the army, which he placed for shelter behind the ramparts of the town, after having given orders to the cavalry to ford the river a few hundred paces above the bridge. This done, he covered the bridge with showers of grape-shot and ball. The enemy's line fell back and took shelter behind a rise in the ground. Our cavalry soon shows itself on their flank. Then the column unmasks, rushes on to the bridge, and though bending for an instant before a storm of shot, crosses it at quick pace, killing the enemy's gunners at their pieces.

Such was the battle of Lodi, of less importance from its material results than from the profound demoralisation it produced among the Austrian troops by giving them an exaggerated idea of their own inferiority. We only lost two hundred men, and we took two thousand prisoners. This extraordinary stroke gave us the whole of Lombardy. Beaulieu was forced to beat a retreat upon Mantua and the Mincio.

It was at the head-quarters at Lodi, May 14, four days after his victory, that Bonaparte received the despatches from the Directory which overthrew his plan of campaign by informing him that he was henceforth to share the command of the army with Kellermann. Nothing could have been more galling to a man of his pride and ambition; but with the decision of one who knows that he is indispensable, he did not hesitate to send in his resignation, fully convinced in the bottom of his heart that it would not be accepted. His letter to the Directory was firm but full of deference and courtesy. He began by announcing the conquest of Lombardy, which was certainly the best introduction he could have chosen to give weight to his words. Then passing on to the projected expedition upon Leghorn, Rome, and Naples, he assured them that a simple military demonstration would suffice, provided he were left free from embarrassment. 'If I have to refer everything to the Government Commissioners, if they have the right to change my movements, to send me troops or withdraw them at their pleasure, do not expect any further success.' But what was more important still in his eyes was, that the unity of the military idea should not be broken. 'In the present state of affairs, it is indispensable that you should have one general who has your entire confidence. If it is not I, I shall not complain; I shall only redouble my zeal in order to deserve your esteem in whatever post you may appoint me to. Every man has his own way of making war. General Kellermann has had more experience, and will make war better than I; but both together we shall make it ill.'

He addressed his letter to Carnot, with whom he had kept up a close correspondence and who undertook to be his champion with the Directory. Bonaparte, relying on his prudence and warm attachment, gave him authority to make whatever use of it he chose. 'I swear to you,' he wrote, 'that I have had the good of the country only in view. You will always find me in the straight path. I am ready to sacrifice my own ideas to the Republic. If any one tries to lower me in your estimation, my answer is in my heart and my conscience. . . . I believe one bad general is better than two good ones. War like politics is an affair of tact. . . . I will not be fettered,' he wrote in conclusion, 'I have begun with some glory; I desire to continue to be worthy of you.'

Bonaparte knew that this skilful mixture of dignity and flattery would insure him Carnot's support, but that of the rest of the Directory was more uncertain. Many of its members were notoriously hostile to him. Besides, the situation was serious and was worth the trouble of mature meditation. What the General demanded in his letter was not only the disavowal of two false ideas, the expedition to Naples and the division of the command: there was also visible in it a strong desire to free himself from all control. This they saw was the point of his recriminations against the Government Commissioners. He indirectly asked to be invested with a kind of dictatorship. Nor was this all; yielding to his demands involved a retreat from a step that had actually been taken, for Kellermann had received his appointment, and it was making a bad precedent to withdraw a decree of which all had approved, simply on the demand of a general who had before this given proofs of his uncompromising and imperious spirit. It was an error to concede to him by artifice what they had not granted to the force of his arguments. Possibly it would have been better to gain less brilliant successes, and not encourage the usurpation of the military over the civil power. They might also remind Bonaparte that his views on the necessity of unity of command had been quite different at one time, when another and not himself was concerned. When the proposal was made to unite under a single command the two armies of the Sambre and Meuse and of the Rhine, he had offered a lively opposition to the measure, alleging that it would be to give too much power to one general.

These arguments were discussed in the Directory; and it is certain that the Government had at least for a time a secret desire to accept Bonaparte's resignation, and that under any other circumstances they would not have hesitated to sacrifice him. But the General had already learned how to fetter the Directory, as much by the services of all sorts that he rendered them, as by the popularity he had acquired. Every day and every hour he became more indispensable to them. They were in no hurry either to confirm or to dissipate his doubts, for they did not reply to his offer of resignation till the 28th of May; but in the interval between the sending off of their first despatch and this day they received accounts of his brilliant success, one upon another, so that their hands were to some extent forced. It was not only the bulletins of Bonaparte's rapid triumphs—the Po crossed, Lombardy conquered, our troops marching into Milan amidst the acclamations of the people,—it was the more tangible benefits to which the Directory attached so much importance, under the pressure, we may add not by way of justification but as an excuse, of a fearful and almost unexampled state of financial distress.

In a communication addressed to the General by the Directory, May 16th, their intentions are as clear as possible. 'The resources which you will procure,' they wrote to the General, 'are to be despatched towards France. And,' they added, in words which well express the cynical thought that inspired them, 'leave nothing in Italy which our political situation will allow you to carry away, and which can be useful to us.' Bonaparte had at once anticipated and surpassed their wishes. Before the end of a month, he had caused a very shower of gold to fall upon them; he knew that this was the best way to plead his cause successfully with them. By the suspension of arms imposed on the duke of Parma, he stipulated that the duke of Parma should hand to France the sum of two millions of francs, twelve hundred horses with equipments, twenty paintings, *Saint Jerome* among the number, which the duke tried in vain to ransom for a million of francs, and supplies of every kind for his army. By another suspension of arms, he levied on the duke of Modena contributions in money to the amount of ten millions of francs, and twenty pictures to be chosen by the Commissioners. By a decree, issued the day after his entrance into Milan, he levied contributions on Lombardy of twenty millions of francs, besides paintings and works of art. His promises were not made in vain; as early as the 22d of May he informed them that six or eight millions of francs in gold, and a quantity of ornaments, were on the road; he offered to send a million of francs to the army of the Rhine, where the soldiers had received no pay; and he sent one million two hundred thousand to Kellermann.

And all these sums, which, seeing the state of our finances, were inestimable treasures, had been realised by the same man who less than a month before had already given France the spoils of the conquered kingdom of Sardinia; by the same man to whom the Directory at the time of his departure for the army of Italy had only been able to give three hundred thousand francs to distribute among his famishing troops. How could they deprive themselves of the services of a man so precious, just at the moment when they were most needed; when no one could finish the work he had begun, and when he was adding new lustre to our arms abroad and increasing our prosperity at home?

The 28th of May the Directory replied: 'You appear to wish, citizen-general, to command alone the military operations of the present campaign in Italy. The Directory has given your demand mature consideration, and the confidence it has in your talents and Republican zeal has decided the question in your favour.' They no longer insisted on the expedition to Rome and Naples; they only recommended a *coup-de-main* upon Leghorn; and, as for the General's proposals with regard to Germany, they left him in this respect perfect latitude, while urging on him to be extremely prudent.

The General availed himself of this latitude, which was in reality almost a discretionary power, to obtain still more. The Directory had, in fact, just surrendered to him the entire control of everything not only in war but in politics, in exchange for the advantages derived from his conquests. Bonaparte knew from this time forth how to silence the scruples of the Directory. A tacit compact existed between them. It is thus that men become little by little slaves of the necessities which they themselves have created.

A deputation headed by Count Melzi, one of the most important and highly-esteemed men in Italy, came to Bonaparte at head-quarters to offer him the submission of Milan. He immediately sent Masséna to take possession of that opulent city. The following day, May 15th, he made his public entry under a triumphal arch amid the enthusiastic cries of this intelligent population, who hailed in him a son of Italy and the natural defender of her independence.

Every one in Milan was weary of the Austrian yoke. Ideas of liberty had spread throughout all classes, and the Milanese could not believe that this French Revolution, which had just delivered them from it in the name of the noble principles that were to regenerate the world, would one day leave them to fall under the sword of their enemy. They crowded eagerly to catch sight of the young man who in one short campaign of two months had done as much as the greatest captains. His short stature, his pale face, the sickly thinness of his frail body which seemed consumed by the fire of genius, and which was in reality made of muscles of steel, seized their imaginations by the contrast it presented to such dazzling feats of arms. His direct and penetrating glance, his abrupt, imperious gesture, his Cæsarean profile, his laconic speech, and his peremptory and absolute tone, all bespoke in him the man born to command; and from the first day he so identified himself with his situation, that it was impossible to distinguish in his manner what was studied from what was not so.

When he was first sent to the army of Italy and raised above generals who were mostly his superiors in age and reputation, he saw that in order to have power over them he must command their respect, not only by the brilliancy of his achievements, but by firmness, gravity, and character. Hence the severe watch he kept over himself, the studied simplicity of his habits, and the surprising austerity of his life in the midst of a licence which he willingly tolerated in others; for those who knew him intimately both before and after this epoch, this austerity was neither the effect of natural inclination, nor homage rendered to principles which had no place in his heart. It was a means of power, and nothing more. He felt that genius alone was not sufficient to gain him an ascendency over his companions in arms, unless he added to it that moral authority which is the prize of a pure life. For the same reason he rather encouraged others to indulge in pleasures from which he himself so carefully abstained, sure as he was of keeping them subordinate to his will when once they had given him this hold over them.

Although he was opposed to the wasteful spoliation which endangered the resources of the army or tarnished its reputation, he systematically shut his eyes to it when it was done with sufficient tact to save appearances, but he always let the perpetrators know that, if he thought proper to be silent, he was not their dupe, and from that time he was their master: these men became all the more submissive in proportion as they felt themselves in his power. The scandalous fortunes which most of the generals and French agents made in Italy, were only additional guarantees for his absolute empire over them. He often offered them opportunities of making their fortune, by giving them a mission in which large sums of money passed through their hands without any supervision, and if they took no advantage of these he laughed at their scruples. Marmont mentions many instances of this concerning himself only, which bear all the marks of truthfulness and which at any rate agree with what is known from other sources. But, if Bonaparte chose to remain incorruptible among so many venal souls, he did so from superiority of pride and ambition and not of virtue. We cannot better describe the motives by which he was actuated than he has done himself. The *Mémorial de Sainte-Hélène* assures us that when Bonaparte was negotiating with the duke of Modena, Salicetti came into his room: 'Commander d'Este, the duke's brother, is here,' he said, 'with four coffers of gold; they contain four millions of francs; he comes in his brother's name to beg you to accept them, and I advise you to do so. I am your fellow-countryman, and know the affairs of your family; neither the Directory nor the Corps Legislatif will recognise your services; this money is yours; accept it without scruple and without publicity.' 'Thank you,' replied Bonaparte coldly; 'for such a sum as that I am not going to put myself in the power of the duke of Modena.'

Nor, he might have added, into the power of Salicetti. There is here, as we see, neither indignation nor reproach; it is a simple calculation and nothing more. The pious Las Cases remarks on this circumstance with his peculiarly expressive and precious trustfulness: 'The emperor dwelt with a certain complaisance on the details of this disinterestedness, *concluding, however, that he had been wrong* and wanting in foresight; for whether he thought of making himself the leader of a party and an agitator, or of remaining a simple citizen in the crowd, it was the same; on his return, said he, he was left almost in misery, and might have continued in poverty, whilst the lowest of his subordinates and generals brought back large fortunes. But, he adds, if my subordinate had seen me accept it, what might not he have done? My refusal checked him.'

It was the 15th of May when Bonaparte entered Milan amid the acclamations of the Lombards, and the day but one after, May 17th, he wrote to the Directory,—'We shall levy contributions in money to the amount of twenty millions of francs on this country; it is one of the richest in the world, *but entirely exhausted by five years of war.*' He further stated that Milan was in favour of liberty, and much more patriotic than Piedmont, which, however, did not exempt the people from our exactions, any more than the exhausted state of the country to which the General had previously referred. Milan, which had spontaneously made advances to us, was treated with much greater severity than Parma, whose sovereign had joined the allies, but had been spared on account of his relationship with the king of Spain. Bonaparte, referring to a contingency which had already been foreseen, but not knowing whether the intentions of the

Directory had changed, asked again, 'If this people wishes to organise itself in a republic, is it to be allowed to do so?'

The Directory did not immediately give a final answer to this question; for the chiefs of the Revolution, the liberators of nations, were thinking more seriously than ever of giving Lombardy back to her oppressors in exchange for the surrender of the Low Countries; and this hesitation hindered the conclusion of a treaty of alliance with Piedmont, which would have given us twenty thousand more soldiers in Italy.

In the meantime Bonaparte organised a provisional government in Lombardy of an almost exclusively municipal character, composed of a consultative committee, which already existed under the name of State Congress, and which he only interfered with to the extent of changing its members. He also formed a National Guard, partly to act as the police of the country, but still more with the idea of persuading the inhabitants that they were henceforth to govern themselves—an illusion which was soon to be belied. He endeavoured to render himself popular by flattering men of eminence, and receiving with marks of distinction the artists and savants of the country, an idea for which he has often got all the honour, but which was not a mere suggestion, but a strict injunction of the Directory; and the same may be said of his fine letter to the astronomer Oriani, which has been so often quoted.

It was, however, necessary to notify to the Lombards, at the risk of chilling their enthusiasm, the sacrifices they were to make in payment for their freedom. The General did this on the 19th of May, in a proclamation addressed to the people of Lombardy. He begins by reminding them 'that the Republic, which had sworn hatred to tyrants, had also sworn the fraternity of peoples. . . . The victorious army of an insolent monarch must spread terror in the nation over which it is victorious; a Republican army, forced to undertake a war to the death against the kings that it combats, vows friendship for the peoples whom its victories free from tyranny. But,' added he, 'if the French conquerors look upon the Lombards as their brothers, these latter owe them some return. They ought then to aid in supporting the army which protects their independence; the right of war secures this assistance, but friendship ought to prompt the eager offering of it.' He goes on to announce a tax of twenty millions of francs, '*a small contribution* for a country so fertile, especially when we reflect on the advantages it is to obtain.'

These last words, which were hardly consistent with what he had written on the subject of the exhaustion of the country, contained a formal promise, and of this promise we know in what degree the General and the Directory intended to keep it. But the vagueness and obscurity in which Bonaparte designedly covered himself in his conversations with influential Milanese allowed them to guess only too well the aim of his policy. With the view to a very uncertain advantage, they were asked to load themselves with the too certain disadvantages which accompany conquest and foreign occupation, and at the same time to expose themselves to the reprisals of their former masters. Bonaparte himself pointed out the method in which the contribution ought to be raised. It ought 'to be levied on the rich, on the people who were really well off, on the church corporations,' and to spare the indigent class.

A decree of the same day contained the nomination of 'an agent to follow the French army in Italy, to seek out and transfer to the territory of the Republic all the objects of art, science, and so forth that are in the *conquered towns;*' and this independently of the works of art surrendered by the Italian powers in execution of the treaties and suspensions of arms concluded with the armies of the Republic. In virtue of the fifth article of this decree, if the French authority could not procure for this agent 'the means of conveyance,' he was empowered himself 'to make requisition for horses or carriages in the town where the removal was taking place.'

The works of art and science were partly enumerated in the decree: they comprehended not only 'pictures, statues, manuscripts, but machines, mathematical instruments, maps,' and the decree added an *et cetera*, which implied a sufficiently great variety of other objects, especially considering the hearty goodwill of those who were charged with its interpretation. A short time afterwards, in fact, Bonaparte himself informed the Directory that Monge and Berthollet were busy at Pavia 'in enriching our Jardin des Plantes and our cabinet of natural history,' and were shortly to fulfil the same mission at Bologna. Even horses kept for pleasure were not long in being considered as objects of art. A large number of them were carried off from Lombardy, and of this quantity the General sent a hundred of the finest as a present to the Directors, 'to replace,' he wrote to them, 'the middling horses now harnessed in your carriages.' But this term of objects of art, however wide was the interpretation given to it by the conquerors of Italy, was still further extended in the imagination of the Directory, for at this very moment they commended to Bonaparte's serious attention some observations that had been addressed to them by Truguet, the Minister of Marine. In the Romagna, in the States of Naples, they would, according to the minister, find in abundance wood ready for embarkation; in other parts of Italy hemp of the finest quality, sail-canvas, etc. All this was considered as being among objects of art. 'Would it not be as well,' said Truguet, 'for each of these states to furnish and transport to Toulon with as little delay as possible such quantities as they can produce and as they have already in store? *Let us make Italy proud of contributing to the splendour of our marine.* It is, as I think, to second the views of the numerous patriots of these countries, which enjoy the *noble and proud satisfaction* of having helped on the equipment and the success of the armies of the Republic.'

Strange epoch, when such was the confusion of all ideas that rapacity spoke the language of patriotism and patriotism that of rapacity, each entangling itself so with the other, that it is sometimes hard for us to tell which of the two sentiments is uppermost. Thus money, means of equipment, monuments of science and art, products of industry and agriculture,—nothing escaped a system of spoliation hitherto without a precedent in the history of modern nations. To measure the precise effect that such exactions must have produced on the minds of an intelligent and cultivated population, to whom we were presenting ourselves as brothers and whom Austria had always treated with much mildness and conciliation, it is right to add to these the calamities occasioned by the frightful fever of robbery, pillage, and greedy extortion which had seized the army, and of which we find evidence in so many orders of the day, in the almost daily executions, and the innumerable complaints of general officers, powerless to repress an evil of which they had generally been the first to set an example. Along with our soldiers a swarm of jobbers, contractors, commissaries, speculators of every sort threw themselves on this unhappy country to gorge themselves on the prey, so that the army devoured everything in its passage.

It is undoubtedly painful for a historian, jealous of the honour of his country, to have to place this sombre picture by the side of so many brilliant exploits, but the omission would involve not only the suppression of truth, but a complete misunderstanding of events,—a misunderstanding of a crisis at once decisive and fatal for our national character and our political liberties.

At the same time there appeared a new proclamation from Bonaparte to his soldiers (May 22): 'You have rushed,' he said, 'like a torrent from the height of the Apennines,' an image only too true of our devastating march through Italy. No barrier, no army had been able to stop them, and their success was a joy to their country and the pride of their families. 'Yes, soldiers, you have done much; but is there nothing more to do? Shall it be said of us that we knew how to conquer, but not how to profit by victory? Shall posterity reproach us with having found Capua in Lombardy? No: I see you already fly to arms; a slothful repose wearies you; every day lost for glory is lost, too, for your happiness. Let us be stirring, then! We have still forced marches to make, enemies to subdue, laurels to win, and wrongs to avenge.

'Let those who sharpened the steel of civil war in France, basely assassinated our ministers, burned our vessels at Toulon, tremble! The hour of vengeance has struck.

'But the peoples have nothing to fear. We are the friends of them all; we are especially friendly towards the descendants of the Brutuses, the Scipios, and those great men whom we have taken for models. To rebuild the Capitol, and place there with all honour the statues of heroes of renown, to rouse the Roman people, whom so many centuries of bondage have enthralled, such will be the fruit of your victories. They will mark an epoch for all time to come. You will have the immortal glory of having changed the face of the most beautiful country in Europe.'

These proclamations, which electrified the soldiers, have since been pronounced to have an excess of emphasis. It is impossible, however, to deny the breath of poetic life which animates them. Bonaparte, so inferior to Cæsar in good sense, in practical temper, in that keen sense of proportion and of the possible which alone constitutes a great political genius, possessed to a far higher degree than Cæsar the gift of seizing and striking the imaginations of men. But while doing him this justice, we cannot but recognise the fact that these warlike appeals appear more and more declamatory, the further we are removed from the time when they were written; this is never the case with writings inspired by deep and sincere feeling. If we look for the reason of the growing impression that these proclamations of Bonaparte are cold, we shall find it in the fact that they are the work of his imagination only, instead of being the product of his inmost emotion. They were composed like rhetorical exercises, and they were not the outburst of sentiments which stirred them; he feigned an enthusiasm which he did not really feel. He only employed these invocations of the great men of ancient Rome, because he knew that they were likely to act upon the minds of his contemporaries; and if, in spite of what was artificial about them, they really did produce an immense effect, it was because from the beginning of the Revolution his contemporaries may be almost said to have lived on nothing else but the recollections of antiquity. But if he made this use of oratorical artifice as a means to an end, he was by no means its dupe himself; hence what we find in it that is factitious and affected. This artifice and this search after effect, which his contemporaries did not see because they were warmed by their own emotions, are now perceptible under every word. This is why they leave us cold and unmoved. With the great orators of the Revolution, on the lips of Mirabeau or of Vergniaud, these images, though drawn from the same source, are still stirring and have preserved a real grandeur, because they are the sincere and tragic expression of their sentiments as well as of their situation. In Bonaparte's proclamations they are only theatrical, because we see the manufacture too plainly. He has, in fact, himself taken the trouble to tell his secret about this in some curious and significant instructions, addressed by him to one of his agents, General Gentili: 'If the inhabitants of the country,' he wrote (he was speaking of Corfu), 'are inclined for independence, flatter their taste, and *do not fail in the different proclamations which you issue to make allusions to Greece, Athens, and Rome*' (Letter to Gen. Gentili of the 26th of May 1797). In this phrase the writer of the proclamations stands undisguised. Where he was more sincere and more fully expressed real feeling, was when he spoke to his soldiers of glory and tried to inspire them with passion for it. Bonaparte in truth loved glory ardently, and by it his ambition, selfish as it was, rose far above the vulgar level. On this side at least it was disinterested, and, though insatiably greedy for power, he was not the man to be content with power without grandeur. But the glory that he proposed to his soldiers was not glory in the sense which the modern world, and especially the French Revolution, had attached to the word: it was glory as understood by the great conquerors of antiquity, which consisted in vanquishing, subjugating, and dazzling men, and not in raising and ennobling them; glory which has in view victories of the sword, and not the conquests of civilisation; which proceeds by repression, craft, and intimidation, instead of acting by the moral forces and with the spontaneous aid of the noblest passions of the human soul. Between these two conceptions of glory lies all the difference which exists between a Bonaparte and a Washington.

The effect of the fiscal measures announced to the Lombards by the proclamation of the 19th of May, and still more of the depredations and excesses of every kind committed by our army, soon made itself felt. Five days later, the 24th of May, just as the troops were making preparations to begin their march and resume operations against the Austrian army, the tocsin was heard ringing violently in all the villages between Pavia and Milan. The peasants in armed bands flocking in from the country threw themselves on our detachments. It was the uprising of distress, and not, as some have ridiculously asserted, a conspiracy of the monkish party. The slight support it found among the clergy only proves the unanimity of the population, and Bonaparte himself never dreamed of attributing this revolt to them. In his proclamation he involves in it the 'priests and the nobles,' using the formula of the times, but he could never have so completely deluded himself about the true causes of the insurrection as to attribute it to clerical influence.

The next day Pavia rose. The inhabitants disarmed the guards and surrounded the French garrison in the Town Hall, which was soon forced to surrender, principally owing to want of firmness in their commander. There was no actual revolt at Milan, but the inhabitants assumed a threatening and hostile attitude, and appeared only to be waiting a signal to declare themselves more openly.

Bonaparte was at Lodi, where he was finishing his preparations for the campaign on the Mincio and the Adige. He started immediately for Milan with two thousand infantry, three hundred cavalry, and six pieces of artillery. Milan murmured hoarsely, but committed no act of insurrection. Things had been confined to a sally of the Austrian garrison, which still held the castle and had judged the moment favourable for extricating itself. Bonaparte had several hundred persons arrested by way of precaution, and then proceeded towards Pavia, sending on before him the archbishop of Milan, an old man of eighty, suddenly and by violence made into a peacemaker, from whose mission there could come no success. The insurgents had pushed their advance-guard as far as Binasco. Lannes drives them back after a short resistance, and Bonaparte sets fire to the town, in order to strike terror into the revolters. From eight to ten thousand peasants had shut themselves up in Pavia, and manned the ramparts, when the French column came in sight. The summons of the General producing no effect, the ramparts were swept by successive volleys which rapidly cleared them. Then the grenadiers forced the gates of the town by blows of their axes. The peasants dispersed precipitately into the country, where they perished in large numbers by the sabres of our cavalry. The soldiers, finding themselves masters of the town, loudly demanded permission to pillage, and Bonaparte granted it, thus yielding to a barbarous tradition long proscribed by the code of civilised nations, and one scarcely likely to cure his troops of the propensity with which he was always so ostentatiously reproaching them. He also gave orders that the municipal authorities should be shot, but, fortunately for his memory, the order was not immediately executed, and the General was glad enough a few days later to show them a mercy which was no more than justice. As for the commander who had quailed before the rising, he was shot. Bonaparte completed this pitiless repression by different precautions for security. Four hundred hostages chosen from among the most important families in Lombardy were sent to Paris as pledges for the future docility of their countrymen. Every man taken with arms in his hands was shot. The 28th of May Bonaparte addressed to the people of Lombardy a fresh proclamation. How different the tone of this second address from that in which only a week before he had introduced himself by invoking the fraternity of nations! This time he painted his army as 'terrible as the fire from heaven' against all insurgents. He warned them that his generals had orders to march against the rebel villages, 'with sufficient force to crush them, to burn them to the ground, to shoot down all whom they should find with arms in their hands. All the priests, all the nobles who remained in the rebellious communes would be seized and sent as hostages to France. All villages where the tocsin was rung would be instantly set fire to; every house in which guns were discovered would also be burned,' etc.

Thus, thanks to the iniquitous system of plunder which had been practised in Lombardy, a week had sufficed to change a friendly people, remarkable for the gentleness of their disposition, and whose gratitude and sympathy amounted almost to enthusiasm for us, before they had learned the real value of our services, into a suspicious, hostile, and irritated population, whom nothing but terror kept from openly manifesting their true feelings; and we were pretending to restore to them the noble pride of liberty, while we were treating them with more brutality and contempt than their ancient masters.

While these things were occurring in Lombardy, the Directory was occupied in Paris in celebrating the festival in honour of Victory, which had been instituted in commemoration of the triumph of the army of Italy. At the moment when all Lombardy was on fire, by one of those frequent contrasts which sometimes appear like the sport of an ironical chance, Carnot delivered a pompous and sentimental speech in the Champ de Mars, in which he mixed up eulogy of our armies with that of filial love, paternal love, sensibility, gratitude, and above all *humanity*. 'O humanity!' he exclaimed, 'how delightful is thy practice, and how much to be pitied the selfish soul that knows nothing of thee!' These philanthropic effusions were followed by dances and a banquet, and then a hymn composed for the occasion by Lebrun-Pindare, with the following chorus:—

> ' Enivrons, mes amis, la coupe de la gloire;
> Sous des lauriers que Bacchus a d'attraits!
> Buvons, buvons à la victoire,
> Fidèle amante des Francais.'
> (*Moniteur of the* 29*th of May and* 2*d of June* 1796.)

Slight details, which may seem beneath the dignity of a historian; but they have the merit of showing how little seriousness there was at this epoch in a nation whose principal fault has ever been want of seriousness.

CHAPTER IV

VIOLATION OF THE NEUTRALITY OF VENICE—DEFEAT OF WÜRMSER

On the 27th of May the French army resumed its march towards the Mincio. All that General Bonaparte could attempt for the moment was to hurl the Austrians across the Adige, drive them out of Italy, and then return to the Italian States, and subdue them one after another by violence or by the fear of it. As for his projected campaign in Bavaria, with a view to co-operating with the army of the Rhine, he was obliged to postpone it by the armistice which had suspended hostilities during the negotiations for peace. Notice of the armistice had been given on the 20th of May, but as this left a delay of ten days to the belligerent forces, the armies of the Rhine were still stationary in their cantonments, unable for want of money and supplies to make use of this delay in furthering any common operations.

Instead of at once marching against the Austrian army, Bonaparte removed his head-quarters to Brescia, threatening the Tyrol with an advance-guard at Salo on his left, and keeping watch over the Mincio with his right. This was to violate the territory of the Venetian Republic, one of the few Italian states which had refused to join the coalition against France. Bonaparte had long before determined on this violation in his own mind, for his plan of the campaign had always pointed to the Adige as the only possible base of operations against the Austrian army. Nevertheless his instructions were to treat Venice, if not as a friendly, at least as a neutral power. But the General also knew that the Directory was ill disposed towards this republic, and would not be sorry for any ill turn which he might do it, if there was advantage to be gained. He took his measures accordingly.

Venice, enervated by the repose of a long peace, half-ruined by the discoveries which had transferred the sceptre of navigation and commerce from her hands into those of the western nations, governed by a worn-out aristocracy, the only aim of whose policy seemed to be that their city should form a centre for all the voluptuaries of Europe, presented at the end of the eighteenth century no more than a blurred shadow of its former self; but, still imposing by so many glorious memories, the Republic, thanks to its traditions of freedom, possessed the most robust and intelligent population of Italy. The institutions of Venice preserved their renown for mystery and terror, but the gentleness of the people tempered the absolutism of the law; never was tyranny more inoffensive, and these antique forms subsisted rather through the patriotism and tolerance of the subjects than through the omnipotence of the masters. Yet Venice had what was under the present circumstances one capital defect; she was no longer formidable. When the war which threatened to overrun her frontiers first broke out, she had adopted the policy which was most in accordance with her own weak state, but also most perilous to her independence—that of unarmed neutrality. As soon as the French entered Brescia, she protested against this invasion of her territory. The General replied by a manifesto couched in language which, though vague, was apparently the most reassuring possible. 'The French army *passed on to* the Venetian territory in pursuit of the enemy, but would not forget that the two republics were bound together by a *long friendship*.' This was followed by warm expressions of our respect for 'religion, government, usage, and property;' of the respect to neutral powers not a word. The General appealed to the rights and duties of friendship, but it was only that he might dispense with speaking about those of neutrality which he was trampling under foot.

The Austrians had hitherto respected the neutrality of Venice. They had the right of way through her territory, and possessed a military road which was indispensable for their communications with the Tyrol, but they had never touched any place in the Venetian states, and it was evidently to their interest that Venetian neutrality should be maintained, since it gave them but a short line of frontier to defend. Some fugitive bands had crossed the frontier by the side of Bergamo after the battle of Lodi, but this fact did not constitute a violation of the right of neutrals. If we had observed this right on our side, we should either have reduced them to powerlessness, or else have obliged them to break with Venice. The Mincio flows out of the Lake of Garda at Peschiera, and falls into the Po not far from Mantua, following almost a direct course from north to south. The first of these two places belonged to the Venetians, and was left by them perfectly unprotected, notwithstanding the strength of its position; the second was the only point of Lombard territory which the Austrians had retained, and the remnant of Beaulieu's army was encamped at some distance thence, half on one side of the Mincio, and half on the other.

As soon as Beaulieu saw Bonaparte occupying Brescia in violation of neutrality, he no longer felt any scruples about violating it in his turn, and he planted his right wing at Peschiera, where he could more easily defend the passage of the river.[1] His centre was at Borghetto and at Valeggio, two towns separated from each other by the Mincio, and connected by a bridge. His left wing rested on Mantua. He thus guarded the whole line of the river. Bonaparte feigned a design to turn the Lake of Garda, in order to cut off the Austrians from the road to the Tyrol, and at the same time to force a passage over the Mincio at Peschiera. By this double feint he drew the greater part of the Austrian forces to Peschiera, and after one of those night marches as rapid as lightning, which were among his favourite

[1] The fact that Brescia was occupied first has been denied by some historians and passed over in silence by others; but Bonaparte himself establishes the fact that it was in his correspondence with the Directory. 'The Austrians entered it (Peschiera) when I had reached Brescia' (June 7th, 1796). The *Storia documentata di Venezia* of Romanin leaves no doubt upon the subject.

VOL. I.   H

stratagems, he attacked the Austrian centre at Borghetto on the morning of May 30th. His cavalry had done comparatively nothing up to this time. They were badly mounted, were very inferior to the enemy's, and could not be depended upon. 'It is impossible to give you an idea of the want of courage of our cavalry,' wrote Marmont to his father after the battle of Lodi. At Borghetto, Bonaparte put them in front, and under the command of Murat they did wonders. The Austrians were driven back upon Valeggio. As they retired they blew up the bridge which united the two villages; but the grenadiers of Gardanne threw themselves into the river which was fordable at that point, and the Austrians no longer attempted to dispute the passage. They beat a retreat upon Peschiera, and from thence made towards the Tyrol.

Bonaparte was thus at length able to make himself master of that line of the Adige which he had so long coveted. But how was he to take up his position without breaking openly with the Venetian Republic, to whom all the places commanding the river from Verona to Legnago belonged? However much he might despise a right which was not sustained by force, he had still an interest in keeping on friendly terms with the Venetians so long as he was liable to another attack from the Austrian forces, for, unprepared as they were at the moment, they could when they chose bring as many as thirty thousand men into the field. It was necessary to use force against the Republic in order to take possession of its towns, but it was necessary to do so under a show of reason, and only to the extent in which it was absolutely indispensable for the execution of his projects. He had already perceived by the manner of the *Proveditores* who had come to his camp, what alarm the report of his rapid victories, the bloody executions at Milan, and the depredations of his army, had produced in the minds of the Venetians, and he resolved to strike such terror as would stifle even the thought of resistance.

He was not long in finding a grievance to serve as a pretext. Bonaparte had entered Peschiera after the Austrians had evacuated it. He immediately fortified the place, seized the arsenal and magazines, and disposed of it as if it had been his own. The Proveditore Foscarini was sent from Verona in the name of the seigniory of Venice, to remind the General afresh of the rights of neutrality. 'As he crossed,' he says in his Report to the Senate, 'the long columns of these wild-looking soldiers, he commended his soul to God.' Bonaparte, seeing his agitation, played before this trembling man one of those comedies of fury in which he so excelled. Venice, by allowing the Austrians to occupy Peschiera without hindrance, had made herself their accomplice and ally; and when the Proveditore explained that the place being without garrison had been occupied by a surprise, which was true, he complained in violent and irritated language of the refuge which Verona had given to the Count de Provence (afterwards Louis XVIII.), although he was perfectly aware that the Venetians had consulted the Committee of Public Safety before authorising this reception, and had only allowed him to remain after having received the formal assurance that France would not regard it as a breach of neutrality. Besides the prince had received orders to quit the Venetian states two months before. All these grievances called for startling vengeance; he should burn Verona that very night. 'After which,' he continued, 'I shall march upon Venice, and demand from the senate an explanation of treachery so glaring.' The terrified Proveditore was lost in apologies and supplications; he was even weak enough to offer to receive the French troops in Verona, to which the General was willing to consent, though he added 'that he did not know how his Government would regard it;' for he wished to reserve a fresh ground for violence against the Venetians, if he should see any advantage to be gained by it.

Masséna had received orders even before this interview took place to take possession of Verona at all cost, and he was already at the gates of the town. Almost the whole population took flight when they heard of our approach. A few days later we occupied Legnago also, which with Verona forms the key to the Adige. The Venetians were also burdened with the stipulation of furnishing provisions and munitions of war on credit. Bonaparte thus obtained his end at very little expense.

On the 7th of June he wrote a minute account to the Directory of all these circumstances, and taking credit to himself for the success of his trick, and alluding to the words by which he had taken care to preserve liberty of action for his Government, he said: '*I have purposely devised this sort of rupture, in case you may wish to obtain five or six millions from Venice. If you have more decided intentions, I think it would be well to keep up the quarrel;* let me know your wishes, and wait for the right moment, which I will take advantage of according to circumstances, for it will not do to have to deal with all the world at once.' And he finished by this incredible acknowledgment: 'the truth about the affair of Peschiera is that *Beaulieu basely deceived them;* he asked for a passage for fifty men, and then took possession of the town.'

Yet it was on this pretext, which he knew so well to be without any foundation, that he had taken from the Venetians all their strong places on the Adige. It was this that made the starting-point of all our complaints against Venice, and of that policy which ended in the preliminaries of Léoben and the treaty of Campo-Formio.

Once master of these strong positions on the Adige, holding Venice at his mercy by the seizure of its best places and the terror with which he had inspired it, free from all anxiety with regard to Austria, who for some time at any rate would not be in a state to resume the offensive, General Bonaparte was able to turn his attention uninterruptedly to the Italian states, and enforce their entire submission. He first completed the investment of Mantua by taking possession of the entrances to the roads which led to the place. By this operation he was able with eight thousand men to hold in check a garrison of more than twelve thousand. He next turned his attention to Genoa. A number of armed bands, composed chiefly of Piedmontese and Austrian fugitives, deserters, and malcontents, had been organised on the territory of this republic under the name of *Barbets*.

Taking advantage of the absence of our army, they intercepted our convoys and assassinated our stragglers. These bands had been greatly increased in numbers by the revolt in Lombardy which had followed our exactions, and they threatened to cut off our communications. The senate, which had good reasons for not contemplating our success with any pleasure, did not interfere, and the Austrian minister at Genoa, Girola, aided by certain members of the Genoese aristocracy, encouraged the Barbets almost openly.

Bonaparte did not stop at diplomatic remedies for this. Lannes set off with twelve hundred men, beat the bands, shot the prisoners, set fire to the houses of the supposed abettors of this brigandage which was really insurrection, and finished by demolishing the village of Arquata and the château of the Marquis Spinola, who was suspected of being one of the secret chiefs of the Barbets. At the same time Murat was sent with a letter from Bonaparte to the senate. It was worded in the most imperious and threatening terms: 'If the Republic did not know how to repress disorder, he would come at the head of his soldiers and do it himself. He would burn every town and village in which a single Frenchman had been killed. Girola was to be arrested, or at any rate leave Genoa.' This satisfaction was immediately granted. Bonaparte here lost an opportunity of reassuring the Genoese against their apprehensions of our supposed designs, and of gaining their friendship by a frank and generous policy; but what he cared for was being master. 'Let twenty families of the aristocracy be exiled, and some ten others who have been banished be recalled. By this means,' he wrote to the Directory, 'the government of Genoa will be composed of our friends,' which meant of our creatures. Everywhere and always his system was that of conquest.

Already the reaction of alarm and mistrust, which Bonaparte had foreseen with so much sagacity as an inevitable effect of the defeat of the Austrian arms, was beginning to be felt in Italy. Events took place exactly as he had predicted them. The Italian sovereigns, left to their own resources, trembled before the conqueror of the Empire.

Instead of our having to march upon Naples, the king came forward to offer the most humble protestations—a shameful submission after so much bravado. Prince Belmonte Pignatelli hastened to the French camp to beg for an armistice. He found favour with the General, whom it suited just then not to abuse his victory. The armistice was signed June 5th, 1796. It deprived the allies of the aid of the Neapolitan navy and a valuable body of cavalry; and what was of more importance still, it spared our troops the necessity of a march upon Naples, which in the existing state of things would have been a very hazardous operation. Bonaparte showed both skill and prudence in being content with thus much. From a simple soldier of the Republic become in so short a time the judge of sovereign princes, Bonaparte, whose claims on his own Government increased in proportion as he felt himself more and more indispensable, assumed in his negotiations with Naples the tone of a man who was acting only on his own ideas; he caressed in Prince Belmonte influences which he believed he ought henceforth to conciliate; he represented himself to him as a mediator between the Revolution and old interests, as the protector of the Italians, and as the man from whom they ought to hope everything, seeing the magnificent future which fortune promised him. 'And do you think,' he said to the prince, 'that I am fighting for those scoundrels of lawyers?'

The Pope, who knew that Bonaparte was far better disposed towards a policy of conciliation than the Directory, had already sent the Spanish minister, M. d'Azara, to him, to sound his intentions. But the grievances of the French Government against Rome were not so cheaply satisfied as our rancour towards Naples, complicated as the former were by the impunity assured to the assassin of our ambassador Basseville, by the religious war which had been kindled and kept alive among us by the Pope, and finally by the strong and very legitimate antagonism of all philosophical minds against Catholic absolutism, its implacable persecutor through so many centuries. The pontifical power, then, could not hope for such easy conditions as those granted to the king of Naples ; and, notwithstanding his perfect indifference to the just prepossessions of the Directory against the court of Rome, Bonaparte could not do otherwise than feign to a certain degree to share them.

Augereau received orders to march upon Bologna and Ferrara. He had only to make his appearance in these two states to find himself master of them, for the pontifical government was execrated. Bonaparte himself arrived at Bologna on the 19th of June, and was received with boundless acclamations. In fact, whatever system of rule our army should bring, it could not be other than a boon to a population bowed down under priestly yoke, a domination that is intolerable even when least offensive, because it enslaves both body and soul, conscience and interests, and leaves no refuge for liberty even in the mind. Bonaparte meant to frighten the Pope, but he did not wish to go to Rome. He had little trouble in producing the effect he wished, and M. d'Azara, whom he accepted as negotiator, soon received full powers from the court of Rome. The diplomatist quickly came to an understanding with a conqueror who was so willing to meet him half-way. Twenty-one millions of francs, fifteen in money and the rest in supplies, a hundred pictures, five hundred manuscripts, the provisional occupation of Ancona, Bologna, and Ferrara, and the busts of Junius and Marcus Brutus, a stipulation introduced by the General with an affectation of republicanism, to hide his secret complaisance towards the court of Rome,—such were the conditions of this new suspension of arms, which was not to be so quickly followed by a treaty of peace; for both the Directory and the Pope tried to gain time, in order to regain what had been ceded. Bonaparte knew that the Directory would not be satisfied with his armistice, and he took care, according to his custom, to anticipate their reproaches by throwing the whole blame on the two Government Commissioners. 'They had,' he said, 'fettered his action, and by their want of address prevented him from obtaining more favourable conditions : this way of negotiating by threes was very detrimental to the interests of the Republic.' He then tried to satisfy the Directory, by proving from detailed accounts that on the whole France had gained by the campaign against the Pope no less than thirty-four millions of francs, including the sum stipulated in the treaty, the contributions levied, and the money seized in the coffers of the money-lending establishments (June 26th, 1796).

Italy might now be regarded as in a state of tranquillity for the time. The grand duke of Tuscany was the only prince who had not either been attacked, or else had to pay his ransom to France. He had only nominally joined the coalition, and was the first of the sovereigns of Europe to make peace with the Republic; the mildness of his administration was proverbial, and he had not a single enemy among his subjects. But the Directory had for a long time coveted the port of Leghorn, an important entrepôt of English commerce, and supposed to contain piles of gold; Bonaparte, too, was not less anxious to seize upon this place, with a view to his projects for the recovery of Corsica. As pretexts are never wanting for the most iniquitous acts, it was resolved to consider some affrays between emigrants and French sailors, in which some English had taken part, as a breach of neutrality. To this complaint another still less sincere was added, that of the seizure of several small French trading vessels effected by the English navy, but outside of the waters of Leghorn, and for which consequently the grand duke could in no way be held responsible. Even if under the Tuscan Government some of those wrongs had been committed which were almost unavoidable in a small state lying between two such powerful antagonists as France and England, we should have demanded reparation before taking action. When Miot, our minister at Florence, a clear-sighted and moderate man, heard from Bonaparte of the projected *coup de main* upon Leghorn, he tried in vain in an interview he had with the General at Bologna to dissuade him from it; he was not long in perceiving that the object of the Directory was not to obtain reparation, but to seize upon the wealth of Leghorn. 'If I had heard all you have to say earlier,' said the General, 'I might perhaps have followed your advice, but it is too late now, the orders are given and the movement is already begun.'[1]

Thus confiscation, which until then had only attended the war, became now the sole ground for it. In the dispute got up with the grand duke, as in the 'open quarrel' with Venice, everything was fictitious and imaginary, except our own cupidity. It was very important for the success of our operations against Leghorn not to give the alarm to the English, from whom Bonaparte was anxious not only to carry off their merchandise, but also to surprise their vessels. For that it was necessary first to deceive the grand duke.

This prince was living in perfect security, when a French division crossed the Apennines, and proceeded to Pistoïa, pretending to be making for Rome by way of Florence. Bonaparte soon joined it in person. Manfredini, the grand duke's minister, came to the head-quarters at the bishop's of Pistoïa, to learn the General's intentions. Bonaparte assured him they were entirely friendly and pacific. The reason of this unexpected march of our army, he said, was simply to intimidate the court of Rome. The minister insisted that the troops should not pass through Florence, and consequently it was agreed that they should pursue their road to Rome by way of Sienna.

In accordance with the promise given, the troops set out on their march under the command of Murat. But after a certain distance, they suddenly change their direction, and swiftly throw themselves upon Leghorn. The English had already had warning, and when we entered the town, Murat and the two commissioners, Gareau and Salicetti, who had hastened hither to seize the rich prey, saw their vessels, about forty in number, sheering off. The plan had in some measure failed, to their great disappointment. They were obliged to be satisfied with the seizure of English merchandise to the value of twelve millions of francs. The grand duke only received notice of this treachery when the French column was at the gates of Leghorn. Bonaparte informed him, in a letter full of

[1] *Mémoires* of Miot de Melito.

expressions of respectful submission, of the orders which he had received from his own Government to occupy Leghorn, in order to 'maintain neutrality' against the English; he repeated his assurances of the friendship of the French Government, and concluded by promising that the flag, the garrison, and *property, should be scrupulously respected*, a promise which formed a strange contrast to the instructions he had just given to General Vaubois, who remained behind at Leghorn in the capacity of governor. 'If he discovered any plot at Leghorn, or anything else involving the safety of the French troops, he was to take all necessary measures for the suppression of tumult and riot, and the repression of the malcontents. *He was to spare neither persons nor property*' (June 27th).

On the 30th of June Bonaparte had the bad taste to visit Florence and seek hospitality from the prince whom he had just plundered. The grand duke gave him the most friendly and flattering reception. He rightly deemed it very unlikely that his claims would be listened to, and therefore kept a dignified silence about his personal wrongs. He treated the General as a great man for whom he had no other sentiments than those of the warmest admiration. The General in return showed his gratitude to his host by commending him to the attention of the Directory. 'You ought to feel,' he said, 'that it is not well to leave the duchy of Tuscany in the hands of a brother of the emperor (July 20th): a thought which was in fact politic, and which would have been more so still if it had been an answer to aspirations that we never dreamt of consulting, but at all cost it ought to have made him careful to avoid Florence.

Bonaparte only remained one day in this capital, and then proceeded to North Italy. He knew that this affair of Leghorn, which added nothing to his glory, might be turned to good account in another way. It was easy to see that with its immense wealth this unfortunate town would fall a victim to the grasping contractors and agents who followed the track of our army, beginning with the two commissioners themselves, whose character was settled from that time. Bonaparte, who had always been exceedingly jealous of the mere shadow of authority and control which these representatives of the Government exercised over his conduct, and was perpetually complaining of their encroachments on his prerogatives, determined not to lose so excellent an opportunity of ridding himself of them, by destroying them through their own weakness. At first he allowed them to do what they liked in the town, and they availed themselves of the liberty with their usual rapacity; then, taking advantage of a proclamation against the emigrants, foolishly published at their instigation by General Vaubois, he denounced them openly, including them almost directly in an accusation against the pillagers, and this completed their discredit with the Directory.

'Instead of one responsible person,' he wrote, 'commissions have been substituted in which every one commits pillage and lays the blame on his neighbour . . . *they* are treating the inhabitants of Leghorn with more harshness than you intended them to show towards the English merchants. It is alarming all Italy, and we are looked upon as Vandals.' *They* (*on*) meant the two commissioners, Gareau and Salicetti. At the same time he wrote to Vaubois, blaming him for consenting to sign their proclamation, and to Gareau, begging him henceforth to confine himself to the discharge of his duties, by which he evidently meant, not to interfere with those of the General. The two commissioners had by their unworthy conduct placed themselves in a position in which they could make no defence of their rights or their character. 'I know perfectly well,' he wrote to Gareau, 'that you will repeat the saying that I shall do like Dumouriez. It is clear that a general who has the presumption to command an army which his Government has entrusted to him, and give orders without a decree of the commissioners, can be nothing else than a conspirator.'

For some time past Bonaparte had been pressing on the Directory the necessity of allowing him to do everything of himself. He no longer wanted an uncontrolled military command of the army, but unlimited authority over all affairs whatever. In a letter dated June 21st he very clearly sets forth his pretensions in this respect: 'There ought to be,' he wrote, '*unity of military, diplomatic, and financial design.* Here we have to burn, shoot, and strike terror by making signal examples. . . . You can understand that as each power or municipality goes indiscriminately to one of the commissioners or myself, and as we each reply according to our own manner of judging, *this unity of thought* is no longer possible, nor can any one plan be carried out.' What was required in these significant words, which contain so unmistakable a warning to the Directory of what had already been nearly realised, was nothing less than a dictatorship. If the members of the Directory had had eyes to see, they would have plainly foreseen the fate which awaited them; they had only to compare the imperious tone the General now assumed with the very different manner in which less than two months before he had apologised to Letourneur for the liberty he had taken in signing the treaty of Cherasco without being authorised to do so: 'If I have taken any responsibility on myself, it has only been with the greatest reluctance, and with the firm conviction that I was carrying out your wishes' (May 6th, 1796).

From this time the power of the commissioners ceased to annoy him. During his short stay at Florence, the General received, while dining with the grand duke, a despatch informing him of the surrender of the castle of Milan, news that he lost no time in communicating to his host. After this capitulation there was nothing left to conquer in North Italy but Mantua, which still held out for Austria. After having stifled by terrible measures of repression an attempt at insurrection which broke out at Bologna, Bonaparte spent the rest of the month of July in completing and drawing closer the investment of Mantua. The operations were pushed forward with great vigour, and were powerfully aided by the sickness engendered at this season by pestilential exhalations from the swamps which surround the town. Our efforts were on the point of being crowned with success, thanks to this dreaded auxiliary, when a formidable diversion saved the place and menaced the French army.

Far from being discouraged by the late reverses, the court of Vienna threw more energy into the war than ever. Field-Marshal Würmser, recalled from the army on the Rhine which he had commanded with distinction, now at the head of thirty thousand men crossed the Tyrol, where he rallied the scattered forces of Beaulieu's army. Before long the total number of the Austrian troops rose to seventy thousand men, including the garrison of Mantua. The French army consisted of about forty-five thousand men, including the seven or eight thousand soldiers occupied in the siege.[1]

The French line extended from Brescia to Porto-Legnago, a ground cut up by hilly ridges and streams, and consequently admirably suited for a war of surprises and rapid movements. The position could be reached by three different roads; one, only practicable for light troops, led from the Tyrol down to Salo, behind the Lake of Garda, and finished at Brescia; a second ran along the left bank of the Adige up to Verona; and the third was a road which lay between the lake and the Adige and led to Peschiera. Würmser resolved to come upon our army at all three points at the same time, a fault which Beaulieu's misfortunes ought to have made him avoid; but this plan of campaign, which was especially defective on account of the marvellous power of concentration which his adversary had displayed in the previous campaign, was forced upon the old marshal by the Aulic council, which directed the military operations from Vienna.

[1] Napoleon in his dictations at St. Helena, which most of our historians have copied, gives the number at forty thousand. In his Correspondence, however, in which, as Carnot pointed out to him, he always underrates his forces, he estimates his army at forty-four thousand (Letter to the Directory, July 6th). It is worth remarking, not for the importance of the fact, but as an indication of his character, that he constantly over-estimated his enemy's forces, and undervalued his own. The figures given in the correspondence of his generals (among others in that of Joubert) nearly always differ from those given by Bonaparte himself, and especially bring down the forces of the Austrian army in a most singular manner.

His army was divided into three corps. The first had orders to follow the valley of the Adige as far as Verona; the second was to drive the French from the posts which they occupied between the Adige and the Lake of Garda, and then effect a junction with the first; as for the third, under the command of Quasdonowich, it was intended rather to take advantage of the victory than aid in winning it; it was to descend the Tyrol behind the Lake of Garda, turn the French army by Salo and Brescia, and cut off its communications with Milan.

The attack was made with so much vigour and impetuosity, that at first it succeeded. In one centre Joubert and Masséna were successively driven from the posts of La Corona and Rivoli, which they held between the lake and the Adige. On our left, Sauret was forced to evacuate Salo, where only a few hundred men remained intrenched and surrounded in an old castle, and Quasdonowich took possession of Brescia; finally, on our right, the Austrian troops debouched on Verona, and threatened the Adige at all points. Our line was broken on every side (July 29th, 30th).

The French army was in a most critical situation, but by a rapid concentration of its forces it could regain its lost advantages, for if it was a third less in number than the whole of the troops which surrounded it, it was stronger than each of Würmser's corps taken separately, and could beat them one after another before they had effected their junction. Bonaparte saw at a glance the necessity of following this plan, and he carried it out with that incomparable decision which in these difficult moments astonished the most resolute, and made people say that a god was in him. As he required all his forces, he did not hesitate to raise the siege of Mantua, a sacrifice which has undoubtedly gained him more praise than it deserved, for it was a matter of necessity; but it was a sacrifice that none but he would have made with the same promptitude. They burned the gun-carriages, threw the powder into the river, and spiked the cannon; and when this was done, the besiegers disappeared with such celerity that Würmser, who had come by forced marches to bring assistance, found no one to fight, and by this mistake was absent from a battle which decided the fate of his principal body.

As soon as Bonaparte's troops were concentrated at the south of the Lake of Garda, in a position where they could keep the three Austrian corps apart, he began by attacking Quasdonowich, who cut off his retreat upon Milan, and who was too weak to make any serious resistance (July 31st). He beat him at Lonato, recovered from him Salo and Brescia, and after having driven him back far enough to make sure of his own communications, he retraced his steps towards the Mincio to fight the other two Austrian corps who had not yet completed their junction. They had crossed the Mincio as well as the Adige, and had advanced to Lonato in the hope of co-operating with Quasdonowich, whom Bonaparte had driven out of it the day before. The Austrians were beaten again on the 3d of August, and this time they suffered great losses, owing to the short-sighted dispersion of their divisions and the useless parade of Würmser before Mantua. Instead of taking advantage of the superiority of their numbers, they had only twenty-five thousand men engaged at Lonato, and of these they lost in killed, wounded, and prisoners, nearly ten thousand.

The army was in such a state of confusion and disorder, that the day following the battle one of the divisions, already reduced to four thousand men, after a night's wandering, came upon Lonato through the corps of the French army stretching out in echelons over the environs. The General-in-Chief had remained in Lonato with only twelve hundred men, and was preparing for a fresh battle. He might easily have been made prisoner or at any rate have been stopped short in the midst of his preparations. He was summoned by the Austrian general to surrender. Bonaparte called his staff together, the messenger was introduced, the bandages taken from his eyes, and as he was beginning to read the summons, 'Go and tell your chief,' cried Bonaparte, 'that I hold him responsible for the personal insult he has offered me in daring to summon the French army to surrender, and that I give him eight minutes to lay down his arms!' This happy stroke of audacity was worth four thousand prisoners more to us.[1]

His plans were already made for the next day's battle. Würmser, who, after having revictualled Mantua, had returned from his ill-advised march, collected the rest of his divisions that were beaten at Lonato, and proceeded to take up a position in front of us at Castiglione, supporting his right on the Lake of Garda and extending it as far as possible in that direction, in the hope of enabling the scattered remnants of Quasdonowich's corps to join him; but these troops, energetically hemmed in by a French division at a short distance, gave our army nothing to fear (August 5th). Bonaparte, who had troops at his disposal now about equal in number to those of Würmser, saw at once how much advantage he could gain by this prolongation of the Austrian right, and he resolved to assist a movement which could do him no harm. Consequently, while Sérurier, who had been despatched by him on the Guidizzolo road, advanced behind the Austrian troops, he gave up to them by degrees the ground on the side of the lake, thus leading them on to lengthen their line of battle beyond rational measure. Sérurier's cannon was soon heard. The retrograde movement stopped, and the attack opened on all points at once. The enemy's line was broken in the centre; the left taken in front and flank gave way; and after a slight resistance the whole army was in retreat: only the excessive fatigue of our soldiers saved it from complete destruction. The line of the Adige was retaken, and Würmser was driven back to the Italian Tyrol with an army reduced to less than half its number. Fifteen thousand prisoners and twenty thousand killed and wounded, and seventy pieces of artillery, were the trophies of this short campaign. From the tremendous effort she had made Austria had derived one single advantage—she had revictualled Mantua.

[1] The truth of this fact has been doubted, although Bonaparte relates it in a letter to the Directory; but it is confirmed by a great quantity of evidence, especially by Marmont and Joubert (*Correspondence*).

The French army, having lost all its siege artillery, was obliged to confine its operations henceforth to a simple blockade. Bonaparte devoted the rest of the month of August to giving his army rest, to hastening the arrival of reinforcements, to reassuring the friends of France who had been shaken for an instant by the rumour of our reverses, and to making her enemies tremble. He was willing to pardon Cardinal Mattei, who had come in the Pope's name to resume possession of Ferrara, and only had him put under arrest in a convent. He threatened the king of Naples that he would march against his 'pretended army of seventy thousand men with six thousand grenadiers, four thousand cavalry, and fifty pieces of artillery.' He also wrote to the duke of Tuscany, complaining, though in very measured terms, of his indifference in securing respect for the rights of neutrality. We had taken Leghorn from the duke; by way of compensation, the English took from him Porto-Ferrajo.

It was as difficult for him to defend himself against them as against us. Nevertheless, Bonaparte ventured to reproach him for not having prevented the English from taking possession of the capital of Elba. But while he complained of this, which he could only attribute, he said, to the treachery of the governor of Porto-Ferrajo, faithful to his system of 'putting people to sleep till the proper moment for awaking' (Letter to Faypoult, July 11th), he took care to declare in the name of his Government his firm intention 'not to disturb in any way the good understanding which existed between him and his royal highness.' And yet he wrote the very same day (August 12th) to Miot, our ambassador at Florence, to tell him not to forget to inform him directly the grand duke left for Vienna, whither he was called as heir to the imperial throne, so that he might surprise and seize him on the way. He added: 'It is to the interest of the Government that nothing be done in Tuscany which might annoy the grand duke; so maintain neutrality.'

During this time some important operations had taken place on the Rhine. Our two armies, led, one by Jourdan, the other by Moreau, advanced into the heart of Germany, in order to open communications with the Italian army, driving before them the Austrians under the Archduke Charles. But their success was compromised by the defective plan which had been imposed on them by Carnot. The archduke perceived the vice of systematically adopting a strategy which might be either good or bad according to circumstances; and skilfully taking advantage of the want of unity in the operations of the French army, he only left a corps of observation in front of Moreau, concealed his march from the latter, and attacked Jourdan with all his force, a manœuvre which might seem to have been borrowed from Bonaparte's triumphant method of concentration in Italy. Jourdan, beaten each time that he endeavoured to stand firm against his young adversary, was obliged to fall back upon the Rhine, while Moreau was making a useless demonstration in Bavaria, shortly to be followed by a perilous retreat.

Bonaparte, who knew nothing of these events, wrote to Moreau from Brescia, August 31st, to inform him that the time was come for combining their forces, and named Innsbruck for the common meeting-point. But he could not venture on the German side of the Tyrol till he had completely destroyed or driven away Würmser's army. The Austrian forces, who, though scarcely recovered from their late defeat and profoundly demoralised, were still nearly equal in numbers to the French army, occupied on one hand all the passes which close the approaches to the Tyrol on the two banks of the Lake of Garda; and on the other, the posts provided by the course of the Brenta between Trent and Vicenza. Würmser was on the point of resuming the offensive on the Adige when Bonaparte forestalled him.

His plan this time was so hardy that nothing but the certainty of victory could justify it; but his superiority had been sufficiently proved to authorise its adoption. Leaving Sahuguet with Sérurier's division before Mantua, and Kilmaine at Verona and Porto-Legnago, with only four thousand men to keep the Adige, he did not hesitate to lead the rest of his army by the Adige and the two banks of the Lake of Garda into the gorges of the Tyrol. He supposed that this movement would induce Würmser to evacuate Vicentino, in order to cover Friuli and Trieste.

This supposition was not realised; but, as Bonaparte was never found at a loss under any contingency, he derived more advantage still from the resolution which his adversary did actually adopt. It was the beginning of September when the army began its march. After a series of skirmishes the divisions met at the head of the lake, and at Roveredo routed Davidowich's corps, which tried to dispute their entrance into the Tyrol. Our soldiers took all the passes by which access is found into these mountains one after another, and entered Trent, which only a few days before had been Würmser's head-quarters (September 4th).

The latter, feeling convinced that the invasion of the Tyrol was only a prelude to our entrance into Germany, instead of falling back upon Friuli, as Bonaparte had supposed he would do, resolved to push on to the Adige, force a passage, and by this turning movement shut us up in the mountains. This was a bold plan, but one for which he had not adequate strength, and which if it should fail would expose him to the risk either of being taken or cut to pieces. The bulk of his army was already at Bassano, and one of his divisions was on the march for Verona. He thus exposed Friuli, and cut off all retreat for himself if the French should follow him. This could not escape the perspicacity of his enemy, who, giving up the idea of venturing higher in the Tyrol, left Vaubois with his division there, crossed at Levico the ridge which separates Trent from the sources of the Brenta, and following the course of the stream, by forced marches came upon Würmser's rear. Würmser, beginning to perceive the fault he had committed, suspended the movement on the Adige, and despatched one of his divisions to Primolano, in an excellent position, to stop the French army, but it was overcome in a few minutes, and almost the whole body taken prisoners (September 19th).

The following day the French army arrived at Bassano,

where Würmser was, with all his troops except the division he had sent before Verona. The previous evening he would still have had time to retreat on the Piave, but he could not make up his mind to abandon this division. The battle of Bassano finally cut off his retreat on that side. The astounding rapidity of Bonaparte's movements seemed to have wrought a spell upon the Austrian army; they made scarcely any resistance, and left us six thousand more prisoners. Würmser in despair, shut in between the Adige on one side and an army in hot pursuit on the other, followed the bank of the river with his cavalry, whose strength was so far unimpaired, trying everywhere to find a passage which should enable him to gain Mantua, knowing that if he did not, the remainder of his army, to the number of fifteen thousand men, would be obliged to lay down their arms. By an unhoped-for chance, Legnago, from which Kilmaine had drawn away forces for the defence of Verona, was without garrison, and there Würmser crossed the Adige. Bonaparte, furious at seeing such a prey escape him, made vain efforts to overtake him before he could reach Mantua. Only an advance-guard was in time to reach Cerea, on the road from Legnago to Mantua, but it was not strong enough to detain him, and Würmser took four hundred prisoners and passed on. The day following he cut to pieces two other detachments which tried to dispute his passage, and at last entered Mantua. These trifling successes poured a little balm into the wounds of the old marshal, and finding himself once more at the head of an important army, owing to the reinforcements furnished by the garrison of Mantua, he again tried to take the field, but the battle of St. Georges, which he lost under the very walls of the town, forced him to shut himself up in the citadel. He had lost in all since entering Italy twenty-seven thousand men; the French had only lost seven thousand five hundred.

Such was the end of the army which was to drive us out of Italy.

CHAPTER V

CREATION OF THE CISPADANE REPUBLIC—ARCOLA

BONAPARTE, who had been recalled from the Tyrol by Würmser's unexpected descent upon the Adige, found himself obliged to put off his designs upon Trieste. The retreat, which Carnot called the 'wretched failure of Jourdan' (Letter of September 19th, 1796), had made this expedition more difficult, and the unquiet state of Italy imperatively required his presence. He therefore merely wrote to the emperor, calling on him to choose between peace or the destruction of Trieste. But so strange a proceeding was not likely to produce any effect, unless accompanied by a formidable demonstration, and Bonaparte received no reply.

He employed the truce which the exhausted state of the Austrian army left him, in organising the conquered country, in confirming French influence in Italy, and above all in consolidating his own authority. Armistices had been signed with the greater part of the Italian states, but Sardinia was the only power to which the Directory had granted a definite treaty of peace. The Directory deliberately kept the vanquished princes in this uncertain and precarious state, which was neither peace nor war, and which would allow them at any given moment to withdraw all that had been conceded. The advantage of this policy was that it kept the Italian sovereigns in a state of complete dependence on the French Government; but later on it occasioned some inconvenience,—it made them look for their own safety in our defeat. As they did not consider themselves bound by conventions of a provisional character, each of them held himself ready on the first rumour of reverses to join our enemies, so that by keeping fear alive we had made hope lawful. In spite of our brilliant exploits, the Italian princes did not believe in the duration of our success, and were desirous on the whole of prolonging negotiations. On the other hand, the Directory, hoping soon to drive Austria into a peace, flattered itself that later it would be able to make more advantageous terms with them, and became more exacting as it saw their plenipotentiaries less urgent.

Such a system was more likely to produce ruptures than reconciliation. This is what actually happened with Rome, and what was very near happening with Naples. The want of straightforwardness displayed by the Pope's legate, his sole end being to gain time, had induced the Directory to require, in addition to the stipulations of the armistice, that the pontiff should withdraw all the briefs issued against the French Republic and the civil constitution of the clergy, and that he should abolish the Roman Inquisition, an unwise interference with the spiritual power, which it would have been much better to pass over in silence and treat as non-existent. Besides, these conditions, devoid as they were of practical importance, gave the pontifical government a pretext for refusing everything. It did give an energetic refusal to them, and stopped the convoys of money which were already on the road to our head-quarters to be poured into the treasury of the army, in agreement with the terms of the armistice.

Exactions of another kind had compromised the issue of our negotiations with Naples. Not satisfied with imposing peace, the Directory demanded the payment of some millions of francs, which was refused with the invincible obstinacy of these small monarchies, at once so magnificent and so needy. Nor was anything concluded with either Genoa or Modena. Venice, too, had reason for becoming more and more discontented. This kind of diplomacy, which might have its advantages after victory, but was full of peril in a doubtful juncture, kept everything in suspense in Italy, and rendered our successes useless. All might be lost at a blow if a third Austrian army should come up before the settlement of these difficulties, for the danger we incurred at the time of raising the siege of Mantua had given warning, and shown on what the safety of our army depended.

Bonaparte was in a better position than anybody else to understand all the risks of such a policy in Italy; he surveyed them with all the rapidity of his keen imagination. He pressed urgently upon the Directory to make a peace with Rome and Naples, that our army might have nothing to fear from behind; he considered it a necessity also to enter into an alliance offensive and defensive with Genoa and Sardinia, so that there might be nothing to fear for the safety of our communications. At the same time, he called without ceasing for supplies and reinforcements. 'They count our numbers now,' he wrote; 'the prestige of our arms is vanishing.' He found fault with General Willot in bitter and angry terms, for keeping back part of the troops which were destined for Italy to put down an insurrection in the south, rightly saying 'that it was better they should come to fisticuffs at Lyons than that we should lose Italy.' He wrote, too, very bluntly to his colleague of the army of the Alps, Kellermann: 'Help us as promptly as you can, if you wish us to continue *sending you any more seven hundred thousand francs;*'—an argument whose force of persuasion he knew by experience, which was in reality, though in less coarse form, the *ultima ratio* of all his discussions with the Directory. Was it not with the same reasoning that he had silenced the scruples of the Directors and overcome their resistance?

General Bonaparte did not, however, really feel all the anxiety he expressed. He purposely exaggerated the danger, in order to prepare the Directory for his future action in creating on his own responsibility a system of alliances, of which he felt the necessity for our security in Italy. For some time previous the Directory had had no other part in Italian affairs than that of ratifying the General's plans, though they assumed an air of authority to save appearances. But Bonaparte was too penetrating to be duped, and, encouraged by their weakness, he soon ceased to trouble himself to wait for even this semblance of authority for acts that were of incalculable importance, and that must involve the policy of the country for an indefinite time. Thus he brought about against their express wish the gravest transaction since our entrance into Italy. If the Directory in lack of pride had had a little clear-sightedness when they read the summary decree by which the General on his own authority proclaimed the forfeiture of the duke of Modena and the measures which were a prelude to the foundation of the Cispadane Republic, they might have begun to suspect henceforth that, to use his own words, 'he was not fighting for those scoundrels of lawyers.'

The duke of Modena had taken refuge in Venice, leaving the government of his states in the hands of a regency. This prince, though not in any way particularly interesting, had given since the signing of the armistice no cause of serious complaint. The only accusation Bonaparte could bring against him was that the population had not refrained from expressing its joy at the success of our enemies (October 2d), and that five or six hundred thousand francs had not been paid out of the nine millions which had been levied on the country. A few days later he accused the regency of having helped the victualling of Mantua. Whatever truth there might be in these accusations, they were such as would apply to all the Italian Governments, which we had taken pains to make our natural enemies. Besides, they had nothing to do with Bonaparte's determination, and only served as pretexts. He was influenced in the matter by nothing but a desire to substitute a friendly people for a Government which was necessarily and rootedly hostile to us; and perhaps still more by the need of exercising sovereignty by creating new states, so as to render himself more indispensable than ever.

The Directory, notwithstanding its mania for revolutionising the Italian states, a mania which Bonaparte had at first skilfully resisted, had never intended to form a permanent settlement in Italy. This proselytism was intended to go as far as agitation, but not so far as responsibility for a charge of souls. This plan of stirring up the people against their rulers had been merely an expedient to give the one an opportunity of freedom, if they cared to profit by it, and to frighten the other in order to facilitate negotiations for peace. After the Government saw the possibility of accomplishing this, after they witnessed the sluggishness and apathy of populations whom they had supposed to be impatient for liberty, they had been more backward in encouraging insurrection. In their instructions to the General they had repeatedly dwelt on the prime necessity of making everything in Italy secondary to peace with the emperor, and of avoiding any engagements with the Italian patriots which he might not be able to keep, or which would render the conclusion of peace impossible. These considerations were dictated by a wise policy, seeing the state of feeling in Italy and the not very edifying part we were playing there; but they implied the speedy evacuation of Italy by our armies, and for that reason were not likely to please General Bonaparte. Not that he felt a very lively interest in the liberty of the Italians; he was the first to declare that they were unworthy of it, and to treat them as being so; his correspondence leaves no room for doubt in this respect. But he could not make up his mind to abandon so soon that incomparable theatre in which he had attracted the attention of the whole world, and associated his name with the greatest characters of history, nor to leave a country where for some months all had been at his sole disposal, and where he had reigned as absolute master. In no position in France, not even at the head of the Government, could he possess power so extensive, nor so seductive to such ambition as his.

Accordingly, after having written to the Directory as if to consult them as to his project of dethroning the duke of Modena and proffering liberty to his subjects, he hastened, according to his custom, to carry his plan rapidly into execution, without waiting for an answer which would be, and could not but be, unfavourable. So he issued this decree, which was in itself a complete revolution, entirely on his own authority. He declared the people of Modena and Reggio under the protection of the French Republic, and invited them to form their constitution freely : an act, the gravity of which lay in the measures and designs which it implied for the future. For a republic so weak as this could not live isolated in the midst of the old Italian states; it was condemned either to absorb them or be absorbed by them. Nor had he here, as in the Milanese, the only plea which can make interference legitimate, the expulsion of the foreigner. In the account which he gave of his conduct, the General did not stop to examine either the immediate or the remote consequences of his act; he spoke of his resolution in a tone of premeditated unconcern, and as a thing perfectly simple. It was 'a prepossession he gave to men's minds, in order to oppose *fanaticism to fanaticism*, and to make friends of a people who would otherwise become our implacable enemies;' nothing more. He knew better than any one how superficial was this new fanaticism which he flattered himself he could oppose to the old, but it did not suit him to remember this at the moment, and above all he reckoned that things would go too far and too fast for the French Government to draw back.

The decree appeared on the 4th of October. On the 11th of October the Directory were still in ignorance of these events of such capital importance, and were so far from desiring their realisation as to write to the General in the following terms :—' Do not forget that we shall be asked for compensation in Italy for the districts which for our future security we shall be obliged to keep on the left side of the Rhine. . . . The restoration of Lombardy or its cession may be made the guarantee of a lasting peace, and though we have as yet come to no determination on this point, we think it would be imprudent to deprive ourselves of the possibility of making peace at that price.

'What we have said about the independence of the Milanese applies to Bologna, Ferrara, *Reggio*, *Modena*, and all the other small states of Italy. We must redouble our circumspection and prudence so as not by excessive pliancy to compromise the future interests of the Republic. You must urge the duke of Modena to pay the sums that remain due to us by virtue of the armistice ; *but you must be care-*

ful not to raise up against him the populations who were subject to him before our entrance into Italy; and our wish is that you should keep them in a state of substantial dependence till our political horizon clears, and we are in a position definitely to arrange the affairs of Italy by means of a general peace.'

It would be impossible to pronounce more explicit and formal condemnation on the General's recent action at Modena. But, far from changing his plans, he merely replied by briefly expressing his regret at having received the letter from the Directory *too late*,—an excuse which was mockery from one who had asked for advice and then taken care not to wait for it. At the same time he announced that to Modena and Reggio he had joined Bologna and Ferrara, by a new decree issued on his own authority, 'uniting them all *sous un même bonnet*,' so as to increase their strength, which was a logical completion of the principle of his first act once admitted. Instead of reversing his policy, he proceeded to involve the French Government still more deeply in it, in order to become the necessary arbitrator of a situation which he himself had created, and which he alone could control. It is impossible to deny that in this case the Directory, notwithstanding its past faults, the tardiness of its scruples, and the reprehensible side of some of its calculations, displayed both wisdom and judgment. In fact, to undertake the protection of republics which were artificial structures, and had no relation to the interests and opinions of the people, which were besides incapable of defending themselves not only against the foreigner but against their own subjects, and had never either been accustomed to liberty or had any taste for it, was to condemn ourselves to constant interference, and to the necessity of taking sides in all their internal disputes; and as power by the very nature of things goes hand in hand with action and responsibility, it was inevitably making an engagement to govern them, to manage all their affairs, and to occupy their territory indefinitely. Sooner or later they must have become annexed to the French Republic, and foreign interference be kept up with all its attendant evils. We shall see how rapidly these consequences came to pass. Such a system was nothing more than conquest disguised under republican forms. Our policy was thus drifting farther and farther from the liberal spirit of the French Revolution, only to prepare the way for the imperial *régime*.

Before the inconveniences and abuses inseparable from such a policy were disclosed, for a time unquestionable advantages flowed from it. A barrier was erected capable of offering a temporary resistance in case of possible invasions from South Italy, and by organising in the Duchies and in Lombardy, in addition to the National Guard, two Italian legions which sufficed for the maintenance of order in the interior of the country, Bonaparte was able to have the whole of his forces at his disposal. Strange circumstance, that these measures, so revolutionary in appearance, went side by side in his mind with a desire to make peace with Rome and Naples; but so blinded was he by his ardent wish, not for the final liberation of Italy, but for the momentary maintenance of the exceptional position which he had created for himself in the country, that the inconsistency of wishing for two things so contradictory did not strike him. This was the real cause of his disputes with the Directory. The Government counted war subordinate to politics, the General exerted every effort to make politics subordinate to war. They were bent only on making peace with the emperor; they only looked upon the conquests in Italy as means of compensation for Belgium; they would have liked nothing better than to evacuate the country after having extracted a ransom for the principal states. It was a policy without generosity; but if it did nothing to repair the faults already committed, it did not at any rate compromise the future.

Bonaparte, on the other hand, as he tells us in his *Mémoires*, 'believed that the Republic had a right, besides extending its limits to the Rhine, to require the creation of a state in Italy which should spread French influence, and maintain in a condition of dependence the Genoese Republic, the king of Sardinia, and the Pope;' that is to say, a creation incompatible with the existence of the ancient states, which could only be erected at the price of new battles, only kept up by the presence and authority of its founder, and by inflicting on ourselves the task of dealing with difficulties without end, and which, in fine, held out to the Italians hopes of an emancipation that was not only illusory, but would be purchased by the sacrifice of the most interesting portion of the nation.

The Directory yielded on this as on every former occasion, and though increasingly dissatisfied with the man who imposed his wishes upon them, they were afraid to deprive themselves of his valuable services, and by that cowardice earned the treatment they had afterwards to undergo at his hands. And, as if this act of weakness were not sufficient, they allowed the General to resume the negotiations with Rome, and blindly left the whole matter in his hands,—an inconceivable blunder, which was to result in placing a man notorious for his ambition in the position of mediator between Catholicism and the Revolution. If he wanted to increase his power, he had only to send in his resignation and to complain of his health, assurances which were received with as much good faith as inspired them, but which nevertheless invariably succeeded. 'As soon as everything in Italy ceases to centre in your general, you will run great risks. In saying this, no one can accuse me of being actuated by ambition. I have only too many honours already; but my health is so broken that I believe I shall be obliged to ask you to find a successor.' These complaints, so often recurring in his letters, had an unfailing effect on the minds of the Directory, thanks to other arguments which he added to them, directed to the minister of finance, and he had only to express a wish to see it realised.

In his negotiations with Rome he had an immense advantage over the Directory; he was not fettered by any scruples nor by any philosophical antipathy, as he only recognised in politics forces and never principles; he looked upon the Papacy simply as an historical fact, and this fact inspired him with neither love nor hatred. But the power which he discovered in the Papacy struck him all the more in proportion as it was purely moral, and as he felt its force without being able either to measure or reach it. Accordingly he always evinced a certain deference for it, and more than once reproached the Directory for not treating it with sufficient tact and conciliatoriness.

Two events which had just taken place greatly increased the difficulties of the court of Rome. Naples and Genoa had made their peace with the French Republic, and the English, who had been driven out of Corsica by a popular insurrection, before even the expedition organised by Bonaparte had set sail, were on the point of quitting the Mediterranean. The only hope of Rome thus isolated lay in the success of the Austrian army. It was at this moment that Bonaparte reopened the negotiations. A little time before he had sent for Cardinal Mattei from the monastery in which he had confined him, and had restored him to his diocese with reassuring words. On the 21st of October he repaired to Ferrara, the city of which Mattei was archbishop, visited him at his house, and after several interviews, despatched him to Rome charged with pacific assurances. At the same time he wrote to Cacault, our agent at Rome, a skilful diplomatist notwithstanding his apparent openness, and told him that he alone was entrusted with the negotiation. At the same time he recommended him to gain time, 'in order to deceive the old fox.' He saw that nothing short of a vigorous demonstration would succeed with the court of Rome, but he was obliged to defer it for a time. 'You must feel,' he added, 'that I am only waiting for a favourable moment to rush upon Rome, and there avenge the national honour' (October 24th).

It is evident that he here expresses more than he intended, for a few days later he spoke in much more measured terms :—

'You may assure the Pope that I have always been opposed to the treaty which has been laid before him, and especially to the manner in which the affair was conducted, and that in consequence of my repeated pressure, the Directory has charged me to open the way for fresh negotiations. I covet the title of saviour far more than that of destroyer of the Holy See. You are yourself aware that we have always followed the same principles in this matter, and if they will only be wise at Rome, we will take advantage of the unlimited power given me by the Directory to confer peace on this lovely portion of the world, and quiet the alarmed consciences of many nations' (28th October 1796).

This policy was much more in keeping with his habitual attitude than the tone he assumed in his letters to the Directory, to gratify the strong philosophical passions which still had a vigorous life among its members, or than the menaces which escaped him in those moments of impatience when he saw his overtures ill received. He perceived already, from the movement of public opinion in France, that a religious reaction was inevitable, and that the support of the priests would be an all-powerful lever for his ambition. Hence there began a double game, which he played with great adroitness. Though he spoke of the court of Rome with the utmost contempt, to prove that he was neither its friend nor its dupe, he exaggerated the extent of its moral influence as an excuse for the considerateness with which he treated it. On the other hand, when talking with ecclesiastics he deplored the encroachments of the Directory upon the spiritual domain, and represented himself as their only safeguard. Owing to this intrigue they counted on him in both camps. In other matters the time was not come for the negotiation to come to an end. Austria had not been sufficiently crushed for Rome to recognise the necessity of capitulating. Alvinzi was advancing towards Italy with a new army, and the Holy See no longer thought of treating.

It was in anticipation of this third invasion that Bonaparte had made sure of having the whole of his army completely at his disposal. In addition to this he tried to obtain the alliance of Sardinia, the only Italian state that had soldiers capable of standing fire, and the only one whose support would have been effective. One of his agents was sent to Turin, to negotiate this alliance in the General's name; but as he had nothing more to offer the king of Sardinia in return for the assistance he demanded than a guarantee of his reduced states, he failed in drawing him into the enterprise. The cession of Lombardy was the only thing that would have induced him to make common cause with us, but this was kept in reserve for another object.

The Directory was not more successful in its efforts to obtain the alliance of the Republic of Venice. Our relations with Venice at that time afford the best example of the character of this war, and it is important to follow step by step all the changes which took place, in order to judge with impartiality the issue of events. It is equally indispensable fully to understand under what conditions that offer of alliance was made, with which our historians have so often armed themselves against her. First of all, we violated the neutrality of Venice by occupying Brescia, which led the Austrians to retaliate by occupying Peschiera to defend the passage of the Mincio. Then, under pretence of punishing Venice for having suffered this second violation, which was in reality the consequence of the first, and which in any case it was not in her power to hinder, we seized the greater part of her strong places on land. We drove out a part of her garrisons to make more room for our own; we pillaged her arsenals and magazines, and we exacted from her supplies of provisions for our troops. Nor was this all. By way of reparation for the harm we had done her, we gave her to understand that she would have to pay us an indemnity of several millions of francs. All this was done under pretexts which Bonaparte in his correspondence acknowledges to be devoid of all foundation; Bonaparte, who had invented them and who invoked them with so loud a voice. It was then that this unfortunate republic, crushed by our exactions, compromised with Austria, driven to the depths of despair, bethought herself a little late of an expedient which in the beginning might have saved her. She began to arm, as much to enforce respect of the laws of neutrality, as to protect herself against an insurrection which had begun stealthily to manifest itself in her inland provinces. This measure only drew upon her fresh reproaches from us. As early as the 12th of July Bonaparte denounced these warlike preparations. He fastened zealously on this new text for recriminations, and advised the Directory not to lose so excellent an opportunity for accusation and complaint. 'Perhaps,' he wrote, 'you may be inclined to commence at once some slight quarrel with the Venetian minister in Paris, so that as soon as I have driven the Austrians from the Brenta, I may more easily demand the few millions of francs which you intend me to make Venice pay.'

It is not difficult to conceive what feelings such a policy would inspire among those who were its victims; it was not likely to smooth the way for an alliance. Nevertheless, so great was the terror spread abroad by our arms, that the senate of Venice bore all, if not without complaint, at least without attempting resistance. To these proceedings was soon added the iniquity of not paying the Venetians for the supplies which they had advanced to our army. By the 20th of July they had already sent us provisions to the value of three millions of francs, and had only received in payment, and that by dint of entreaties, a bill of exchange for three hundred thousand. But our very wrongs towards them were set down as their blame, and became the occasion of new machinations against the Republic. Thus this payment of three hundred thousand francs, paltry as it was when compared with the debt, was, according to Bonaparte, a decided fault, and became the source of such vexations that the Venetians had an interest in never being paid. This payment was a fault, he said, because it had let them see that by importunity and failing in supplies they could extract money from us. 'So that,' he continued, 'I am obliged to *quarrel with the proveditore, to exaggerate the number of assassinations perpetrated against our troops*, and to complain bitterly of these warlike preparations, which they never made so long as the imperial forces were the stronger; for by this means I shall force them, for peace's sake, to furnish me with all I want. That is the way to treat these people. They will continue to furnish supplies half willingly, half by force, till Mantua is taken, and then I shall openly declare that they must pay the sum named in your instructions, which it will not be difficult to enforce.'

Such was the state of our relations with Venice when the Directory made this new attempt to induce the Republic to enter into alliance with us. They represented its difficult and perilous situation between powerful neighbours, all coveting the Venetian possessions; neighbours of which one especially, Austria, would sooner or later try to find an indemnity for the losses she had sustained, at the expense of the Republic. What guarantee had they against this danger? Public right? It no longer existed. The balance of power in Europe? Every trace of it had disappeared. Venice could only find safety in a powerful alliance, and such as France alone was in a position to offer her.

These propositions were not accepted by the senate, who gave as grounds for refusing them, not the too real reasons which they had for want of confidence in us, but a desire to spare the Venetian people the burden of a war that was desolating so many other nations. Historians have generally not hesitated to blame this determination. And yet what confidence could the Venetians have in us after the treatment they had received at our hands? What security could our conduct towards other Italian states inspire them with? Admitting the sincerity of our protestations, what serious guarantee did our position in Italy offer them? Were we not in reality encamped rather than established there? Would it have been prudent to unite the fate of Venice to that of a people whose influence arose from a success that was indisputably brilliant, but was in all probability very ephemeral? Had it not been by triumphs of a similar kind that all French armies had effected their entrance into Italy? and yet had we ever been able to consolidate our authority? And when once the hour of reverse had struck, what would be left of promises of support so magnificent and imposing? Our armies would disappear behind the Alps, their natural rampart, and Venice would remain alone at the mercy of her enemies. If it was absolutely necessary to make a choice, was it not better to break with France, so far removed from her frontiers, and with whom her only contact was by accident, than to have Austria for an enemy, her permanent neighbour, who closed in the Venetian possessions on every side?

These considerations carried the day, and the Venetians persisted in their neutrality. Although the determination was their destruction, it was not only legitimate but irreproachable. A French alliance would probably have saved them from Campo-Formio, but would neither have preserved their independence under our domination, nor protected their territory when the disasters occurred which gave Italy back to Austrian influence. There are times when weakness is an unpardonable crime.

Bonaparte had now to prepare himself to meet the new army which the Aulic council had placed under the command of Alvinzi. Notwithstanding the exaggeration of his constant complaints about the insufficiency of his forces and the negligence of the Government in not sending him reinforcements, his troops were really in the best condition. On the 1st of October, after his campaign against Würmser, he calculated their total number at forty-eight thousand men, a figure which is certainly below their true strength (Letter to the Directory, October 1st). Of this number he counted eighteen thousand sick, of whom four thousand only were wounded. After that reinforcements came up, and for a whole month no movement took place; the creation of the Cispadane and the Italian legion allowed him to dispose of nearly all his garrisons. Deducting the sick then, and the eight thousand men employed in the siege of Mantua, he had from thirty-eight to forty thousand men that he could bring into the field against Alvinzi.

During this month of October he had greatly increased the morality and discipline of the army, by the war he had made against the habits of plunder and petty theft which had become a serious danger to our occupation of Italy. As the highest functionaries in the army had been the first to set the example, the evil had assumed such frightful proportions that nothing short of inexorable severity could stop it. In the towns there was some sort of rule in the pillage, and wealth being more abundant the inhabitants were better able to bear the scourge; but the country people were completely ruined by it, and in certain provinces, such as the district of Mantua, they emigrated in a body. Bonaparte felt the necessity of employing strong and severe measures, and he struck high and low alike. The moment he began to look into all the misery thus caused, he perceived that the evil was much greater than he had suspected. 'I am surrounded by robbers,' he wrote (October 8th). Generals, commissaries, civil administrators, everybody plundered. He determined to have several executed, but the number condemned fell far short of the real number of the culprits. 'You have no doubt calculated,' he wrote to the Directory, 'that your administrators would commit a certain amount of pillage, but that they would do their work and preserve some little decency; but they plunder in such a barefaced and ridiculous manner, that if I had a month longer, there is not one who might not be shot' (October 12th). But was it not he who had said, '*Italy shall be our prey*'?

Since the first days of November Alvinzi had been on the Piave with an army of forty thousand men, composed mainly of recruits. At the same time Davidowich was advancing in the Tyrol with eighteen thousand troops, among them a good many belonging to the Tyrolese militia. These two corps were to meet under the walls of Verona, after a plan somewhat similar to that of Würmser, but more simple and less hazardous, because it divided the army into two columns instead of three. Vaubois guarded the Tyrol with twelve thousand men; he was to cover Trent on the line of the Lavis. Bonaparte advanced in person with Masséna and Augereau to meet Alvinzi. They met on the 6th of November at Carmignano, between Vicenza and Bassano. After a very sharp engagement the Austrians were driven back on the latter town, but the French did not succeed in taking it. In the night bad news arrived from the Tyrol. Vaubois, beaten by Davidowich, had been forced to evacuate Trent, and he effected his retreat by the left bank of the Adige, instead of keeping the important roads of the Corona and Rivoli, which opening behind

Verona, between the Adige and the Mincio, would allow Davidowich's corps to cut off the retreat of our army.

It was urgent that this danger should be warded off. General Bonaparte was forced on this account to give ground after his success, to the great astonishment of the Austrians. He led his troops to Vicenza and Verona, sent Joubert in all haste to take up his position at La Corona, made Vaubois recross the Adige, took him back to Rivoli, and came himself to harangue the vanquished division. He addressed the soldiers in terms of biting reproach, filled them with shame at their defeat, and then, when he saw that he had produced his effect, he consoled them by a few kind words, and left them impatient for their revenge.

All the rest of his army was concentrated at Verona, and Alvinzi had followed it step by step in its retreat. On the 11th of November Bonaparte, on his return to headquarters, judging it advisable to occupy the heights of Caldiero, which cover Verona on the side of Vicenza, found Alvinzi already intrenched there in a very formidable position. He did not hesitate, however, to attack him. Heavy rain, which poured down the whole day, had so soaked the ground, that it was impossible for our artillery to move, while that of the enemy, being already in position, gave them an immense advantage over us. At the end of several hours and after repeated attacks, we had not succeeded in breaking the enemy's line. When night came on, the two armies bivouacked in front of one another on the field of battle.

This battle, though it was not decisive, was a grave check for us. The next day our troops returned to Verona. The situation of the army was becoming extremely perilous. On one hand Vaubois' corps, considerably reduced, had great difficulty in holding its position at Rivoli, whilst at Mantua the garrison annoyed us by incessant sallies; on the other, we ran the risk of being besieged in Verona. These reverses, so new as they were for us, greatly discouraged the soldiers. They began to be weary of interminable war, and murmured aloud at the neglect in which the Directory left them. Even Bonaparte himself for an instant doubted fortune. He wrote to the Directory, and painted in the most sombre colours the unfortunate situation in which he was placed. He would, perhaps, be obliged a second time to raise the siege of Mantua; perhaps the hour of Masséna, of Augereau, perhaps his own even was come. He had, he added, only eighteen thousand men (including the seven thousand troops of Vaubois) against the fifty thousand of the enemy, an assertion of a puerile degree of exaggeration, and which will not bear investigation. Still, in spite of the well-grounded fears inspired in him by his real inferiority, and in spite of the excess of despair which he put on with the Directory, he displayed more confidence than ever with the soldiers. The very day after that on which he had given vent to these complaints and apprehensions he put into execution, with his incomparable firmness of decision, the famous manœuvre which was to give victory back to him.

At nightfall he ordered his troops to take up arms; they crossed the town in silence, and passed over to the right side of the Adige, as if to place the river between the enemy and themselves. The army marched with dumb resignation, supposing a retreat on the Mincio. But on leaving Verona, instead of taking the Peschiera road, he took his soldiers back along the banks of the Adige, which from the town makes a bend to the left towards the Adriatic. As Alvinzi had not stirred from his position on the heights of Caldiero before Verona, it was only necessary to follow the course of the river seawards to find themselves in his rear. Our troops went down as far as Ronco, and there recrossed the Adige on a bridge of boats which had been prepared by the General beforehand.

This striking manœuvre, by which they were going to turn a position that a few days before they had not been able to force, seized all imaginations, and roused the enthusiasm of the army. Our position at Ronco was almost impregnable, protected as it was on one side by the Adige, and on the other by marshes only crossed by a couple of narrow raised roads which both started from Ronco, and led, one to Verona, in front of the enemy, insuring our communications with this town, the other to Villanova, behind Alvinzi, who could thus be placed between two fires, while his communications with Vicenza were intercepted. As the battle must take place on these two roads, where the enemy's troops could not extend themselves, and everything depended on the courage displayed by the heads of the columns, their numerical superiority became useless.

Early in the morning Masséna advanced on the right embankment with his division, and Augereau on the left. Masséna reached the extremity of the marsh without meeting any one. But Augereau was stopped by an unforeseen obstacle. Midway between Ronco and Villanova is the village of Arcola. A little stream, called the Alpon, crosses the road there, and falls into the Adige just below Ronco. The Croats, who had bivouacked in the village, fortified the bridge over this, and suddenly stopped the advance of Augereau's column, who tried in vain to take it. The contest gave the alarm to Alvinzi. One of his divisions took the right road, the other the left, where it brought reinforcements to the defenders of Arcola. Masséna drove into the marsh those who opposed his passage, but both Augereau and Bonaparte himself returned to the charge in vain against the bridge of Arcola. One after the other they rushed on the bridge, standard in hand, in hopes of drawing on the soldiers, but neither could force a passage; Bonaparte was driven into the marsh, and lost in this attack a great many officers of the highest merit.

This resistance saved the Austrian army, by preventing our overtaking it at Villanova, where it had time to effect a retreat, after precipitately abandoning the heights of Caldiero. The next day the Austrians evacuated Arcola, which was no longer of any importance to them, and which Bonaparte had turned by a single brigade. The Austrians had nevertheless sustained considerable losses, and Verona was freed.

This was by no means, however, a decided success, and Alvinzi remained in front of us, having only retreated a little from his former position. Bonaparte had to cross the

Adige again at Ronco, to communicate with Vaubois, and assure himself that this general had not been forced at Rivoli. This retrograde movement resulted as successfully as the best devised stratagem. The Austrians, finding no one in front of them, advanced on the causeways in the marshes. The French recrossed the bridge at Ronco, which had remained in our possession, charged at the point of the bayonet in that narrow space, and made fearful carnage. This was the second day of Arcola.

Evening came; Bonaparte continued his movement of the day before, and recrossed to the right side of the Adige. Having received good news of Vaubois, whom Davidowich had not attacked, he returned the next morning for the third time to the field of battle in the midst of the marsh, and found it occupied once more by an enemy whom no lessons seemed to teach. This time the victory remained for a long while uncertain, but the resistance of the Austrians only served to increase their own loss, which was so great during these three days that by the end of them their numerical superiority had disappeared.

Bonaparte saw this by calculating the number of dead, wounded, and prisoners which had fallen into his hands, and no longer hesitated to leave the marsh and attack the enemy in the plain and uncovered. He assailed him with resolution on the right bank of the Alpon, and soon put him completely to the rout. Alvinzi retreated on Vicenza, and thence on the Brenta, not very closely pursued by our troops, who had to return and relieve Vaubois. The French army made a triumphal entry into Verona. Davidowich, who from ignorance of Alvinzi's movements had remained inactive, at last resolved to attack Vaubois, and drove him from Rivoli to Castel-Novo. But this exploit which, three days earlier, would have placed the French army in a most critical situation, was now of no consequence; and Davidowich, finding Masséna's division before him at Castel-Novo instead of Alvinzi's soldiers with whom he hoped to effect a junction, immediately hastened to resume the road to the Tyrol.

These new victories and the losses sustained on both

sides in this sanguinary campaign, made the conclusion of peace at once more desirable and more easy. It was universally wished for in France, and the press was not less unanimous than the Legislative Body in expressing public opinion on this point. The Directory would have preferred to put it off, in the hope of making a more favourable treaty later. But the nation was weary of supporting alone the weight of all the armies of Europe, and Europe was not less desirous of putting an end to this bloody and ruinous war.

Lord Malmesbury, a skilful diplomatist, had been in Paris since the end of October. He had been sent by England to negotiate a general peace on the basis of the *status quo ante bellum*. Each power was to make restitution of its conquests, and return to its ancient limits; a principle that was just in itself notwithstanding all that we had to lose by it, if it had been applied with perfect sincerity. But the three countries which had been the first to disturb the balance of power in Europe by partitioning Poland never meant to allow this principle of compensation to be applied to themselves; and England herself, who was the first to propose it, formally refused to restore to Holland the colony of the Cape, notwithstanding the vast possessions she had acquired in India. On the other hand, how could we abandon nations who had so loyally and faithfully given themselves to us? It might have been possible to agree to the separation of Belgium from France, but how could we suffer that she should again be forced into bondage which she had thrown off in imitation of our example? How could we suffer this, after so prolonged a community of sorrows, struggles, and triumphs?

Lord Malmesbury's terms were such as might have been offered us after a series of reverses, but were not likely to be accepted by a people who were nearly everywhere victorious; and whatever may have been said to the contrary, the Directory did not on this occasion manifest any unreasonably exacting spirit. They may be more justly reproached for having managed the negotiations with an abruptness and indiscretion of manner which were peculiarly ill fitted to make them succeed. After several interviews, seeing there was nothing to be gained from British tenacity, they flattered themselves that they should succeed better by treating separately with Austria. They chose for negotiator General Clarke, who arrived at Bonaparte's head-quarters a few days after the battle of Arcola. The instructions given to General Clarke by the Directory, dated November 14th, were not such as were likely to please the Commander-in-Chief. His mission was first to conclude an armistice, and then discuss the conditions of an arrangement with Austria.

Before the battle of Arcola there would have been more opportuneness in an armistice. There could be no object in it now but to save Fort Kehl, which, with the head of the bridge of Huningen, was the only point we should have preserved beyond the Rhine after the retreat of Jourdan and Moreau. Kehl was important rather as an entrance into Germany than as a really strong place; but it was far from being as valuable to us as Mantua was to Austria; and in order to keep Kehl we ran the risk of losing Mantua, which was then on the point of surrendering. All conditions of peace had for basis the preservation of Belgium; and Clarke was charged to proffer several different combinations to the emperor, which the Directory thought might console him for this loss. Austria was offered compensation, but it was at the expense of other powers. The first proposition was to give back to the emperor his Italian possessions, and to allow him, as indemnity for his loss of Belgium, to take several German cathedral towns, and a part of the Palatinate. The second was to leave the Milanese to France, and give him the Papal States, with the title of king of Rome for the grand duke of Tuscany. By the third, he was to have the whole kingdom of Bavaria with the ecclesiastical electorates. All these plans were drawn up with that unceremoniousness which these licensed liberators of nations had so promptly learned to adopt. The surrender of Venice was not as yet debated; but they already talked of spoiling this republic of her inland provinces for the advantage of Lombardy, if this latter republic was found likely to stand : they were ready to sacrifice a state which had endured for centuries, for a chimerical creation doomed to failure from its first hour. From this to the preliminaries of Léoben there was only a step.

Clarke's mission displeased Bonaparte extremely, and he made no secret of his dissatisfaction. Now sole master of Italy, invested with unlimited authority to destroy old states and to create new, he was not a man easily to give up such a position. All this was gone and his work annihilated if Clarke's mission succeeded. But fortunate circumstances spared him this disappointment. He hastened to explain to the Directory, as he had done to Clarke himself, the objection he had to an armistice. His reasons, we must allow, were very strong since the defeat of Alvinzi. It was evident that when once Mantua was taken—and it was on the point of falling—we should be in a much better position to treat for peace. But he was carried away by passion beyond all reason, when he added that three months' repose would ruin his army, and that the armistice would prevent the possibility of making good our claims on Rome, 'the Papal States being unapproachable in summer.'

The truth was, that what really displeased him about the armistice was that the armistice was a prelude to peace. He could not resign himself to this sudden interruption of so many dreams of glory and ambition. In his impatience he took up his pen again the same day to urge the Directory afresh to abandon their projects. 'Send me thirty thousand men,' he said, 'and I will march into Friuli, seize Trieste, carry war into the states of the emperor, raise an insurrection in Hungary, and go to Vienna. After that, citizen Directors, you have *the right to expect millions*, great success, and a solid peace.' These were doubtless prophetic visions, since he realised them all only a few months later. But was that a solid peace which left behind it the iniquities of Campo-Formio? Not more so than the solid peace he afterwards had to go in search of in all the capitals of Europe.

A few days were enough to give him a complete ascendency over Clarke. He at first give him a cold and suspicious reception, then adopted a tone of alternate roughness and familiarity, accompanied by peremptory declarations which let the negotiator see pretty plainly that he must choose between open rupture and complete submission. He chose the latter, which was most in accordance with his timid and mediocre character. He adopted the General's ideas with a good grace, and was soon completely under his influence. He wrote to the Directory that 'it was better that Bonaparte should continue to direct diplomatic operations in Italy.'

This change of tack much diminished the chance of peace: but Clarke had not even to discuss its conditions; for as he was not allowed the *entrée* at Vienna, on the pretext that the emperor did not recognise the government of the French Republic, he entered into communication at Vicenza with the Baron de Vincent, who declared that he had only power to sign the armistice for Italy—an absurd proposition, since Austria would have kept Mantua without assuring Kehl to us. The question of an armistice being thus set aside, Clarke was despatched to the Austrian ambassador at the court of Turin on the question of peace, which was equivalent to an indefinite adjournment.

But before learning this issue of Clarke's negotiations, Bonaparte did all he could in Italy to hinder his success, by involving the French Government, as he usually did, by means of *faits accomplis*. When he saw from Clarke's instructions that the Directory with some natural scruples inquired whether the Italians were or were not ripe for liberty and capable of maintaining it, he did his best to convey the illusion that they were so—an illusion in which, for his own part, he did not believe; and he pointed out, in support of his opinion, an artificial state of which he was himself the single author. He carefully repressed in the Cispadane Republic everything which had the slightest appearance of anarchy. 'I am,' he said to the inhabitants of Modena, 'a sworn enemy of thieves, rogues, and anarchists. . . . I shall shoot those who overturn social order and cause all the disgrace and misfortune in the world.'

He encouraged them in their attempts at organisation; he summoned them to unite, to arm themselves, and helped them to form a Polish legion to reinforce their militia. He led the Lombards, against the formal instructions of the Directory, to hope that they would be united to the Cispadane, and he authorised their State Congress to send deputies to the federation of Reggio, busy in cementing the union of Bologna with Modena. 'If Italy,' he said on that occasion, 'wishes to be free, who can prevent her? It is not enough for the different States to unite, the ties of fraternity must be drawn closer among the various classes of the State. You can, you ought to be free, without revolutions and without running the risks or experiencing the misfortunes which the French people have had to undergo. Protect property and person, inspire your countrymen with the love of order, of law, and of the warlike virtues, which are the security and defence of republics and liberty' (December 10th). Excellent advice, if it were the privilege of conquest to inspire civic virtues, if patriotic devotion could alternately slumber and awaken just as the convenience of the conqueror might bid.

But Bonaparte by no means aimed at the real awakening of national sentiment in Italy. Such a circumstance would have embarrassed him, perhaps, more than the armies of Austria: he only desired the outward appearance of it; and this to a certain extent he succeeded in creating. It could hardly have been otherwise with an artistic people, over whom the remembrance of the past exercises so potent a charm. Writing on this subject, he once said that 'he knew how to use the words "liberty" and "national independence" as a talisman.' No one could find a more appropriate phrase. He employed the word 'liberty' adroitly, because it was useful to his designs, but without the least concern for the thing itself; nor had he more than a verbal concern for the republic which was his creation, and hence its slight stability. He says in the same passage (*Mémoires*), 'that he not only showed great respect for religion, but he forgot nothing that could win over the clergy.' This was another talisman, handled with the same skill but with the same want of conviction. He delighted in contrasting the virtues of the Italian clergy with the vices of the ancient clergy of France (1st January 1797): 'If the French clergy,' he said, 'had been as wise, as moderate, and as warmly attached to the principles of the Gospel, the Roman Catholic religion would have undergone no change in France.' An assertion historically false, and one which he must have known better than any one to be without foundation. 'But,' he added with edifying compunction, 'the corruption of the monarchy had infected all classes, even the ministers of religion. There were not to be found men of exemplary life and pure morality such as Cardinal Mattei, the Archbishop of Bologna, the Bishops of Modena, Pavia, and Pisa. I have sometimes felt in talking with these good men as if we were back again in the first centuries of the Church.' These venerable prelates were, however, those whom the General with his intimates talked of as 'twaddling dotards.'

But his fine words did not succeed so well in this quarter as with the patriots. Rome turned as deaf an ear to his flattery as to his menaces. The Pope and his advisers already knew that a fresh effort was being prepared by Austria for the relief of Mantua ; and being ready, in case of need, to fly from Rome and take refuge in Naples, they feared no serious movement from our troops, and openly defied France. The cardinals who directed the Roman policy, and particularly their chief Albani, had opened communications with the court of Vienna, followed its inspirations, and were ready to combine operations with it, for they had an army which, though harmless in itself, could become dangerous at a critical moment. It was commanded by General Colli, who had been our adversary in Piedmont. In order to avert this peril, reinforcements were sent to the Cispadane Republic, and a French detachment pushed on as far as Bologna to frighten the court of Rome. But owing to the information which the Pontifical Government had received from Vienna, this demonstration produced no effect. News had just reached Rome that Alvinzi had again taken the field.

CHAPTER VI

RIVOLI AND TOLENTINO

1797

OUR relations with Venice had not changed. Bonaparte continued to keep up a misunderstanding with her, which was sufficient to cause the Venetians anxiety, without giving them adequate grounds for an open rupture. He harassed them with incessant reproaches, hoping by this means to drive them into losing all presence of mind, and to throw upon them the appearance of the first wrong, in case an opportunity should present itself for dealing them a blow. But if the Venetians came to complain to him in their turn of the numberless excesses committed by our soldiers, he feigned one of those fits of exaggerated passion which he knew so well how to assume. 'They were pure inventions, fairy tales, the exaggerations of a mischievous schoolboy.' Besides, if the Venetians suffered, what was to blame? Their partiality for Austria. 'They felt the warmest solicitude for Alvinzi' (Letter to Battaglia, December 8th, 1796). It was only too true that we had done everything to produce this feeling. He continued to watch the arming of the Republic with assumed anxiety, and lost no opportunity of complaining of it; at the same time, in the midst of his complaints, he kept giving them new grounds for continuing their warlike preparations more actively than ever.

For instance, he suddenly seized the castle of Bergamo, which was guarded by a weak Venetian garrison. It was impossible from its situation that this castle could be of any use in his military operations, but it belonged to 'the most disaffected province of all the Venetian States.' The people of Bergamo were, in fact, a brave and energetic race of men, who showed more impatience at the pressure of our army than the Lombards, and some few pillagers had been killed in the neighbourhood, a circumstance which Bonaparte did not fail to turn to good account, being under the necessity, as he said, 'of exaggerating the number of the assassinations that were committed.' The French not only took possession of the castle, but seized on a magazine of arms containing several thousand guns. And when the Venetian senate remonstrated with Bonaparte through M. Battaglia, he replied, 'The French troops have occupied Bergamo to forestall their enemies, who were meditating the possession of this indispensable post. I *frankly* own that I was glad of this opportunity of driving out the large number of emigrants who had taken refuge there, and inflicting some punishment on the libellous, who are also very numerous in the town. I know that a few disaffected men have for the last six months been preaching a crusade against the French; woe to them if they do anything to destroy the *good understanding and friendship which exists between the two Governments*' (January 1st, 1797).

The last words, which so ill expressed the real state of affairs, were intended to soften the evil impression produced by the occupation of the castle, and to keep up the illusions of the members of that party in Venice who were anxious to be deceived at all cost, because they had not energy enough to take a decided resolution. But such constant violation of the rights of nations, such repeated acts of vexation and insult, could not fail sooner or later to bear their fruit, and the longer the feeling of injury was pent up, the more likely it was to burst forth with violence.

When Bonaparte took possession of Bergamo, he ordered the evacuation of Leghorn, which was no longer of any use to us, since we had taken and sold all the merchandise found in it, that belonged to merchants who were subjects of belligerent powers. The possession of Leghorn obliged us to keep a garrison far removed from the centre of our operations, which could be more usefully employed elsewhere. But notwithstanding all the profit we had derived from the occupation of Leghorn, we could not evacuate it without being paid for our evacuation. Bonaparte settled with the grand duke for two millions of francs. We entered Leghorn to protect his Government against the English; we remained there as long as there was anything to seize, after which our protection became useless, and he was glad to pay a sum to be delivered from it. These exactions did not prevent the General from carrying on with more vigour than ever his war against plunderers. The evil had diminished, but was all the more difficult to deal with from being kept within bounds, as is always the case when the law is being evaded; and the General was beginning to regard it as incurable. 'There is venality everywhere,' he wrote to the Directory (6th January 1797). 'The army consumes five times as much as is necessary, because the storekeepers are in league with the commissaries and go halves with them. The principal actresses of Italy are kept by the *employés* of the French army; luxury, corruption, and embezzlement are at their height.' And he proposed as an extreme but indispensable remedy the institution of a syndicate composed of two or three persons, with power to judge of this class of offences summarily, with the right of condemning the offender to be shot, whatever his position might be.

The hour of a fresh struggle was just striking. Alvinzi had collected a new army out of the remnants of all the troops that we had successively beaten in Italy, and of a few new corps brought together from all parts of the Empire. The strength of the Austrian monarchy consisted in that singular faculty which at first sight appears impossible in a state so wanting in homogeneity; she was already the European power which could longest sustain defeat with impunity. She displayed in the midst of her reverses a most surprising vitality. No sooner had she lost one army than she created another, and launched it against us with unshaken confidence, as if the French army must be more weakened by its victories than her own by its defeats. This time, however, the effort was more visible than before. She had been obliged to appeal to the volunteers. Vienna alone had furnished several battalions, and the empress had embroidered their colours for them with her own hands.

The French had also on their side received important reinforcements. It is difficult to ascertain the exact number, on account of the extraordinary discrepancy between the estimates given by the Directory and those of Napoleon. Suffice it to say, that on the 28th of December the Directory estimated the total number of troops sent into Italy since the opening of the campaign at fifty-seven thousand men, whilst Bonaparte did not make it more than twelve thousand six hundred. With the healthy season too the state of the army was very satisfactory: Bonaparte had scarcely any sick left. His troops numbered about forty-five thousand men, so that after deducting the blockading corps that remained under Sérurier at Mantua, he had still nearly thirty-five thousand men to bring into the field against Alvinzi's army.

The plan devised by the Aulic council was this time to deceive the French by a feigned attack on the lower Adige, on the side of Legnago, to draw the bulk of their forces into this quarter, and then take advantage of their mistake to force a passage between Lake Garda and the Adige to the positions of La Corona and Rivoli which Joubert was guarding. This passage once effected, nothing could hinder the Austrians from getting as far as Mantua. If the feigned attack only succeeded the result would be almost the same, for they would be equally well able to succour Mantua and be in a position to co-operate with the Pope's army.

In accordance with this plan Alvinzi advanced by Trent and Roveredo with thirty thousand men, doing his best to hide their number, while Provera marched from Padua on the lower Adige, making as much display as possible of his entire force, which did not exceed fifteen thousand men. To add to our uncertainty one of his divisions was detached in the direction of Verona, where Masséna encountered it and took nine hundred prisoners (12th

January). The same day we were attacked both at La Corona and Legnago, but not vigorously. The stratagem partially succeeded. General Bonaparte's first idea was that the principal attack would be made upon the lower Adige, but he was too prudent to decide without some knowledge, and waited with his reserved corps behind Verona, at an equal distance from Rivoli and Legnago, ready to throw himself upon whichever point should appear most seriously threatened. He recalled Masséna's division, leaving only a weak garrison in Verona, and then passed the day of the 13th in waiting for the reports of his lieutenants.

There was no time to be lost; it was absolutely necessary to move forward in one direction or another, lest isolated corps should be exposed to the shock of the entire Austrian army; our salvation would depend on a right decision, the main elements of which were wanting to the General-in-Chief. Fortunately, towards ten o'clock in the evening, he received circumstantial information from Joubert which relieved him from this painful state of perplexity, by showing clearly that the principal attack would be between the lake and the Adige. Joubert announced that he had been forced to fall back from La Corona upon Rivoli, having been outflanked the whole day by considerable forces, and that if he did not receive prompt succour he should be obliged to evacuate this last post. Augereau, on the other hand, sent word that on the lower Adige he had only had to deal with insignificant demonstrations.

The enemy's plan was at last unmasked. Taking no notice of Provera's corps, Bonaparte instantly marched all the troops within reach, including Masséna's division, towards Rivoli. He recalled Rey's division from Desenzano, and sent it to Castel-Novo to serve as a reserve in case of need. At two o'clock in the morning he arrived on the plateau of Rivoli. He immediately recognised the enemy's positions. He saw below us in the plain and on the surrounding heights the five encampments marked by the watch-fires, their extent indicating a considerable force, the disposition of which in a semicircle round the plateau of Rivoli showed an evident intention of turning us, in order to cut off all retreat from Joubert. It was clear that Alvinzi did not expect to have to do with more than Joubert's twelve thousand men; for if he had imagined that the plateau would be occupied by a more numerous force, instead of thinking of turning us, he would doubtless have hesitated to attack in so strong a position. Though the plateau of Rivoli is accessible on several sides, there is only one point, called St. Mark's Chapel, by which the cavalry and artillery could approach, and even this was difficult, for the path was in a kind of winding staircase, a circumstance which assured the defenders of the plateau of a considerable advantage.

Bonaparte saw at a glance the conditions of the coming engagement, and by four o'clock in the morning he had reoccupied St. Mark's Chapel, which Joubert had been obliged to evacuate, by this step compelling the enemy beforehand to fight without cavalry and without artillery. The arrival of Masséna's division gave him on the plateau an army of twenty thousand men, with strong artillery. Alvinzi, who still believed that he had only Joubert's division before him, sent a column under the orders of General de Lusignan up to the heights of Monte-Baldo which border the lake. This column took up its position in our rear between Rivoli and Castel-Novo, where Rey's division was (14th January 1797).

But when Alvinzi tried to reach the plateau, he was not long in perceiving that the moment for cutting off our retreat was not yet come. His infantry had no difficulty in attaining our positions, and even for an instant threatened them by routing one of our brigades, but our cavalry charges and the fire from the batteries promptly repaired this check. On the other hand, every time the Austrian cavalry and artillery attempted to climb the winding staircase, they were repulsed in frightful disorder with enormous losses. After several useless assaults Alvinzi was forced to withdraw, having only been able to engage with half his army. Meanwhile Lusignan's corps, which had received the fire of our reserve, and had been cut off by Rey's division, laid down its arms. Joubert pursued Alvinzi with such impetuosity that he got before his rear-guard at the passage of the defiles, he retook La Corona the next day, and drove him as far as Trent.

Such was the battle of Rivoli, less striking perhaps as a brilliant victory than for the sagacity and skill displayed in the dispositions which prepared it. The same day, on the lower Adige, Provera, escaping the vigilance of Augereau, crossed the river at Anghiari near Legnago, and marched towards Mantua to force the blockade. Bonaparte received this information at Rivoli, just after the battle. Leaving Joubert to consummate the victory and pursue Alvinzi, he immediately set off with four regiments in the hope, if not of forestalling Provera before Mantua, at any rate of being in time to relieve the besieging army.

These four regiments belonged to Masséna's division; they had fought the day before at Verona, they had afterwards decided the battle of Rivoli, and now they were marching all night, and did sixteen leagues, to reach Mantua. Provera had arrived before them, but had been recognised by our soldiers before the city soon enough to prevent a surprise, and he lost precious time at St. Georges, then held by Miollis with a detachment of fifteen hundred men. He was preparing to make a fresh attack, in combination this time with a strong sally from Würmser, when Bonaparte's regiments, commanded by General Victor, arrived and took up a position between Provera and the citadel, whilst Augereau attacked him from behind, and Sérurier confronted Würmser. The latter was driven back after a keen struggle; and Provera, left to his own resources, and surrounded on all sides, was forced to surrender with all his troops. This engagement was called the battle of La Favorita, after the name of a place belonging to the dukes of Mantua, which happened to be close by. The new army thus disappeared in a few days as if it had been suddenly swallowed up by some great disaster. It had lost, with scarcely any injury to our forces, nearly thirty thousand men, of whom twenty thousand were taken prisoners. This astonishing result was due partly to the growing demoralisation of the Austrian troops, but still more to the conceptions of an incomparable military genius, and the rapidity with which he multiplied successive strokes.

Mantua had for some time been reduced to the severest extremities; the garrison had eaten all the horses, and were now on half rations. Bonaparte acquainted Würmser with Alvinzi's complete annihilation; the old general loftily replied, that he had still provisions for a twelvemonth. Nevertheless a few days later they were obliged to come to a parley: twenty-seven thousand men had died in Mantua from wounds or sickness since the beginning of the siege, and the resistance could not be prolonged. The marshal's aide-de-camp, M. de Klénau, came to the French camp to confer with Sérurier, who directed the blockade, and they began to discuss the terms of capitulation. Klénau enumerated, with the exaggeration usual in such cases, the means of defence which the garrison still possessed. While they were talking a stranger wrapped in a large cloak, to whom they paid no attention, was writing at a table without saying a word. When he had finished he rose, and extending a paper to Klénau, said: 'Here are my conditions; if Würmser had only provisions for twenty-five days and spoke of surrender, he would be unworthy of honourable terms, but I respect the age, the courage, and misfortunes of the marshal; if he opens his gates to-morrow, or if he waits a fortnight, a month, or three months, the conditions will be the same; he can wait until he comes to his last morsel of bread.' Klénau recognised the General-in-Chief, and after reading the terms, admitted that Mantua had only provisions for three days more.

Such is the dramatic account of the surrender of Mantua, which Bonaparte has left in his dictations at St. Helena. There is every reason to believe that, with a soul open to all great impressions, he on this occasion was actuated by noble feelings; but the historian, whose first duty is accuracy, is obliged to add that inclinations so magnanimous did not last. When Würmser made new efforts to obtain better conditions, Bonaparte wrote to the Directory: 'I am going to reply that I keep to my first propositions, that *if General Würmser has not accepted them before the* 15*th, I shall retract,* and agree to no other terms than those of making him a prisoner of war with all his garrison' (to the Directory, 1st February 1797, from Bologna).

After all, the conditions proposed to Würmser were characterised by a generosity that might have been expected from such youth and so much glory. The garrison were to surrender as prisoners, but the general was to go out free with his staff, his officers, two hundred of his cavalry, and fifty others whom he might choose. A large number of French emigrants had come to join the defenders of Mantua; Sérurier had orders to let them pass without paying any attention to them. Würmser wished to salute his young conqueror as he went out, and had even expressed a desire to do so, but he found Sérurier alone before the citadel, and the old marshal filed off before him. Bonaparte had started for Bologna, leaving all the honours of the triumph to his lieutenant, a piece of self-denial evidently calculated to produce a great effect, but which showed perhaps too much contempt for the vanquished to be the inspiration of true nobleness of nature.

Würmser, out of gratitude to General Bonaparte for his generous conduct, saved his life at Bologna by warning him of a plot to poison him, which in consequence of this warning miscarried.

The taking of Mantua was of immense importance in the future conduct of our military operations. The war might henceforth become offensive without danger to us, for we left behind us a rallying point and a centre of resistance of tried force, instead of a hostile army always threatening us in spite of the blockade. We were no longer forced to wait for the enemy on this line of the Adige, watered with so much blood—a perilous necessity, and entirely repugnant to our military instincts, ever readier for attack than defence; we could now go forward, and attack them on their own ground. Bonaparte had long conceived this project, but before he put it into execution he wished to finish with the court of Rome.

Alvinzi's defeat had annihilated the hopes of that court, which was now in a state of cruel embarrassment, being able neither to proceed with the smallest chance of success, nor to deny its connivance with the Austrian cabinet. Even if its extravagant preparations for war, and its inflammatory discourses to rouse the population, had not spoken so loud, it would still have been impossible to deny the testimonies against it, for they emanated from its own ministers. A letter had been intercepted, addressed to Monseigneur Albani by Cardinal Busca, Secretary of State to his Holiness, in which all the plans of the Roman Government were stated in the fullest detail, as well as the principal conditions imposed by Austria as the terms of her alliance. The letter contained such hatred towards the French that it seemed to justify any retaliation; and Bonaparte's first care was to insert it at full length in the manifesto which he published on entering the pontifical territory.

Whilst he was advancing from Bologna at the head of a detachment of his army, Rome, panic-struck, a prey to terror and infatuation, and yet trying to shut her eyes to her real perils, was proclaiming a holy war and having the tocsin rung in all the country districts. 'We shall make the Romagna a second Vendée,' cried Cardinal Busca. Bands of peasants appeared, headed by monks, crucifix in hands. Nothing was wanting for imposing effect except Vendean heroism. All this enthusiasm spent itself in words. Our soldiers met the first army of the Pope at Castel-Bolognese; they remained in front of it for the night, and attacked at daybreak; in an instant it was put to rout.

The Holy See was at General Bonaparte's mercy. What would he do with this power which seemed to fall to pieces even before he had raised his hand against it? It was not difficult to guess, judging from his previous conduct, in spite of the impatience and irritation which the discovery of the duplicity of the court of Rome had caused him. He had more than once spoken of utterly destroying the temporal power of the Pope, and had even suggested to the Directory the idea of giving up Rome to Spain (Letter of February 1st), so as to interest that power in keeping up the state of things in Italy which he dreamt of establishing; but this had only been a passing inclination. At bottom his thoughts had always been in accord with his ambition. A stranger to the hatred of the French Revolution towards the ideas which the Papacy represented, he had not failed to remark signs of a coming reaction in France in favour of the Catholic Church, and he hoped to turn it to the advantage of his own popularity.

'They are becoming Roman Catholic again in France,' wrote Clarke some weeks before; 'it may be that we have gone so far as to need the Pope himself to get the Revolution supported among us by the priests, and consequently by the country districts, which they have again got into their power.' This observation, which was no doubt suggested by a desire for peace, contained a great deal of truth, and did not, we may well believe, pass unobserved under the eyes of Bonaparte, who saw in it the confirmation of his own conviction.

This was not all. His aim was now to carry the war into the states of the emperor; it was there that he hoped to eclipse by some dazzling blow the most glorious and brilliant exploits in our military annals.

Now, to overthrow the papal power was to declare war against the kingdom of Naples, and would involve us, not in serious dangers, but in interminable difficulties which would postpone indefinitely any offensive movement against Austria. All these considerations had decided Bonaparte, and he made up his mind all the more easily, because the instructions of the Directory left him free to follow his own inclinations. After looking for a long time upon the overthrow of the papal power as the noblest part of their work, the Directory, in their impatience to give peace to France, had resigned themselves to allowing it to live, if nothing else could be done. Their instructions to the General reminded him 'that the Roman Catholic religion would always be the irreconcilable enemy of the Republic,' and expressed a desire to see destroyed 'this centre of Roman Catholic unity;' but they added, 'this is not an order given to you by the Directory as executive, it is an aspiration they entertain; they are too far removed from the scene of action to judge the real state of affairs; they trust to the zeal and prudence which have ever directed you in your glorious career, and whatever may be your determination, the Directory will never see in it anything on your part but a desire to serve your country for the best, and not lightly to compromise her interests' (3d February 1797).

The General's resolution was taken before he received this advice. He wished first to frighten the court of Rome by the rapidity of his successes, so as to enable him more easily to dictate his terms, and then to present himself as her deliverer. He devoted himself first to reassuring and calming the excited populations, and with this view a proclamation was issued at Imola, in which he announced himself as the protector of religion and the people. 'The French soldier,' he said, 'carries in one hand the bayonet, the guarantee of victory, and in the other an olive branch, the symbol of peace and pledge of his protection.' He enforced the severest discipline on his troops, and refused them the pillage of Faënza, which they demanded with loud cries, according to the barbarous habit he had allowed them to contract. He sent for the prisoners of Castel-Bolognese, who were expecting to be massacred, spoke to them with gentleness and kindness in their own Italian, told them the French were their friends, that they were come not to destroy religion, but to benefit the poor and reform the abuses of clerical government; then he sent them back to their families with copies of his proclamation, requiring from them no other ransom than the obligation to distribute it.

The second army of the Pope had taken up its position before Ancona; and it shared the same fate as the first, even more promptly. It was made prisoner before a gun was fired. Never did an armed multitude give proof of such degradation. The papal government had destroyed in its subjects even the quality of manhood. Ancona was an important place, and contained numerous arsenals. Bonaparte left a garrison there. He next proceeded to Notre Dame de Lorette, the treasure of which had been removed to Rome, but there still remained gold and silver ornaments to the value of about a million of francs (10th February). The Madonna, which was in wood and very rudely carved, was sent to Paris, where, till the signing of the Concordat, it was to be seen in the National Library.

The Papal States had been the refuge of a great number of emigrant French priests. Forced to fly before their countrymen, driven from the monasteries whose inmates were afraid of compromising themselves, and repulsed from the frontiers of Naples for a similar reason, their position was as painful as a position could be, and it would have been barbarity to add to the sorrow of these unfortunate men, 'who wept whenever they perceived a Frenchman' (Letter to the Directory). The General extended his protection to them, and relieved their sufferings. Whatever may have been his motive, calculation or generosity, he received a full reward for his conduct, for the greater part of these priests afterwards returned to France, and did not forget this act of humanity.

At length the court of Rome ended by perceiving that it must submit, and entrusted Cardinal Mattei, for whom Bonaparte had shown a kind of predilection, with the negotiation. Pius VI., the heir and victim of so many centuries of glory, bending under the burden of expiation which his predecessors had bequeathed him, was forced to write to 'his dear son, the General Bonaparte,' a letter which was the capitulation of the papacy. He presented to him the agents who were to treat in his name, and told him, 'that feeling perfectly sure of the benevolent feelings of the General, he had abstained from any disturbance of things at Rome, thus giving him a proof of the confidence he had in him.'

Bonaparte was at Tolentino, three days' march from Rome. He had cleverly calculated that it would be better for him not to appear on the scene, where the eyes of all Europe were looking for him. His reputation could not be increased by such a triumph. What glory would not be eclipsed by the recollections which the single name of Rome would call up? He received at Tolentino the four envoys of the Pope, and with them Prince Belmonte

Pignatelli, who came in the name of the king of Naples, to support them by his presence and representations. The king had declared that he was ready to interfere in favour of the threatened papacy, and had concentrated his troops on the frontier, a piece of bravado which had a reason in the fresh preparations of the court of Vienna, and which at any other time would have received a prompt chastisement. Bonaparte, who was anxious not to make useless complaints just then, acted with much more consideration than was usual with him, and all danger was removed on the side of Naples.

The negotiations could not take very long, for there were not there two belligerent parties, but a disarmed power at the mercy of an absolute master, who could impose what conditions he pleased. Those which the General was about to dictate were irrevocably settled in his own mind; it was the minimum of the chastisement which the state of public opinion in France obliged him to inflict on the court of Rome. He listened with much apparent deference to the complaints of the cardinals, Mattei and Galeppi, the two principal envoys, but remained substantially inflexible. They only obtained from him the suppression *ad referendum* of a clause relative to the Roman Inquisition, a clause to which the Directory attached great importance, because it did not know that this institution had at Rome nothing but its name in common with that bloody tribunal; the prelates, on the other hand, would not ratify it at any price, because they considered it an attempt directed against the spiritual power of the Pope.

The treaty of Tolentino contained, to begin with, all the stipulations of the armistice signed some months before. In addition to this, the cession to the French Republic of Avignon, the Legations of Bologna and Ferrara, of the Romagna, and of the town and territory of Ancona. It stipulated further for the proclamation of a general amnesty, the disavowal of the assassination of Basseville, the re-establishment of our school of fine arts at Rome, and the payment of an additional sum of fifteen million of francs.

The treaty of Tolentino was signed on the 19th of February 1797. Nothing but a shadow of the temporal power was left, but the principle was recognised, and recognised by the French Revolution. A shelter was left to it, under which it might go through stormy days and await more prosperous times. After having survived so many trials and dangers, it might hope everything from the future, and its friends already began to recognise by unmistakable signs that he who had just struck the blow would be its future restorer.

As soon as peace was signed, the aide-de-camp, Marmont, set out for Rome with a letter from the General-in-Chief for the Holy Father. It was couched in that tone of respectful deference which he invariably adopted in his relations with the Church. He informed him of the conclusion of the treaty, and expressed his hope that the French Republic would in future be '*one of the truest friends of Rome.*' The letter finished thus: 'All Europe is aware of the pacific intentions and conciliatory virtues of your Holiness. I send my aide-de-camp to express to your Holiness all the esteem and deep veneration which I entertain for your person, and I entreat your Holiness to believe that my desire is to give proof on all occasions of my respect and veneration. I have the honour to remain, etc.' (19th February).

The previous day he had written to Joubert: 'I shall return to the army, where I feel my presence is necessary, in a day or two. The army is within three days' march of Rome. *I am in treaty with these black-coats (cette prétraille),* and for this time St. Peter will again save the Capitol by giving up his finest states and money, which will put us in a way for executing the great task of the approaching campaign.'[1]

[1] The very day of the signature of the treaty he wrote to the Directory: 'My opinion is that Rome cannot exist once deprived of Bologna, Ferrara, and the Romagna, and the thirty millions which we take from her: the old machine will fall to pieces when left all alone.' And in another letter, the same day, he added: 'The commission of savants has had a good harvest at Ravenna, Rimini, Pesaro, Ancona, Loretto, and Perugia. All will be at once forwarded to Paris. When you have

This double language expresses with perfect accuracy the difference between his real feelings and those that his ambition dictated to him.

received this and what will be sent from Rome, we shall have almost every fine thing in Italy, except a few objects which are at Turin and Naples' (19th February 1797).

This is what has been called the deliverance of Italy!

CHAPTER VII

THE PRELIMINARIES OF LÉOBEN

As soon as General Bonaparte had settled all the conditions of peace with the Pope, he hastened back to the Adige. He was impatient to open his campaign with Austria, and force that haughty power to acknowledge its defeat. Until Mantua had fallen he had been compelled to await the blow of his adversaries on the Adige, a painful and perilous mode of warfare, as contrary to our military temperament as to his own genius, which could never sustain a defensive war but by transforming it into open attack. But having no longer a strong place containing a large army behind him, and Italy ready to rise, he was free to go forward, and follow his own inspirations without check. He had received considerable reinforcements, composed of veterans from the army of the Rhine, and commanded by General Bernadotte, one of the best officers. Moreau, who had picked these for his rival from his own troops, did so with remarkable care, thus displaying a disinterested and delicate courtesy which justly kindled the enthusiasm of Carnot. 'My dear Fabius, how great you were in that,' he wrote some little time after, in recalling this circumstance.[1] These reinforcements, in addition to the corps which the surrender of Mantua had rendered available, increased Bonaparte's army to seventy-five thousand men. Owing to the formation of the Lombard and Cispadane legions, almost the whole of this number could be brought into the field in the new campaign.

The Austrian army was this time very inferior, even in

[1] Carnot, *Mémoire sur le 18 Fructidor*.

numbers, to our own. The Aulic council had recalled from the Rhine the Archduke Charles, who had just saved the monarchy by his brilliant exploits against the combined armies of Jourdan and Moreau. This prince who, like Bonaparte, was still young, and like him famous from his earliest stroke, seemed the only general that Austria could henceforth bring into the field against us. The last resources of the Empire were entrusted to his skill. To the new army which they had succeeded in forming for him were added, by a transfer similar to that which we had just effected, six divisions, making forty thousand men, drawn from the troops which he had been commanding on the Rhine; but as the orders for moving them were delayed, they could not arrive for another three weeks at least.

The advantages and disadvantages of this were matter of some doubt. The arrival of the archduke's reinforcements would inevitably render General Bonaparte's task more difficult; but, on the other hand, it would in the same degree lighten that of our armies on the Rhine. These were to commence operations at the same time, co-operating in the same scheme, and they would weigh all the more heavily in the balance for only having a weakened enemy in front of them. Bonaparte knew that one of the two armies of the Rhine was commanded by Hoche, a young man full of genius and ambition, who had displayed a superior character and qualities of the first order in the obscure difficulties of the pacification of Vendée, and who, though kept back by the delays of Moreau and the Directory, was burning with impatience to throw himself upon Germany. Nor, in fine, could the fact escape his observation that after a double triumph of our two armies, the army of the Rhine and the army of Italy, such a peace as we should then dictate would be of far more irresistible urgency to the enemy, as well as far more advantageous for the Republic, than any we could impose if the successes were simply those of his own forces in an isolated campaign.

But these very reasons, instead of inducing him to wait for the co-operation of the army of the Rhine, made him decide on opening the campaign earlier than the time he had himself fixed on. By attacking the archduke before the arrival of his reinforcements, he was certain of beating him easily, and driving him before him up to the walls of Vienna; if he should be obliged to pursue him further, the situation of the conqueror would undoubtedly become more critical than that of the conquered; but Bonaparte was fully persuaded that the court of Vienna would accept peace rather than sacrifice the capital. The conditions of such a peace would doubtless be less favourable for France than a treaty obtained with the aid of Hoche and Moreau, but on the other hand it would be his own work, and he would not have to share the glory with any one.

These were the considerations which determined Bonaparte to hasten the resumption of hostilities. His reason for shortly afterwards complaining so loudly about the delay of the armies of the Rhine, and the little support they gave him, was as much to answer beforehand the just reproaches to which he had exposed himself by such unpatriotic calculations, as it was in consequence of the real embarrassment in which he for a moment found himself, from insisting on acting entirely alone. He wrote to the Directory (17th March 1797), that in order to be of any use to him, 'the armies of the Rhine ought to have commenced hostilities at the same time as himself.' This could have been arranged by the simple means of concerting operations with them instead of opening the campaign without consulting any one. The General's triumph would have been less dazzling, but the advantage gained would have been more solid, and we should not have been drawn into betraying Venice and sacrificing her as an indemnity to the emperor.

Near as it was, no one yet foresaw this deplorable issue to a war which had so long been carried on in the name of liberty and the rights of nations, or at any rate none of those who were either apprehending or preparing it dared openly avow it. Clarke had offered to the Marquis Gherardini, the Austrian ambassador at Turin, a partial cession of the Venetian states, but this proposition had remained buried in the twilight of diplomatic mysteries. The persistent neutrality of Venice had afforded Bonaparte and the Directory a good pretext for levying some millions of francs, but it was not a crime which in the eyes of the world would justify the total destruction of the Republic. It was enough to have punished her by the occupation of her strong places, and by making all the evils of war fall so heavily on her. But in spite of these just grounds of complaint, envenomed by the silent antipathy which the oldest aristocracy in Europe must have felt for our democratic ideas, Venice had invariably refused to listen to Austria's repeated attempts to draw her into an alliance. Shortly before the opening of the campaign against the archduke, she gave us a new pledge of her good intentions, by receiving coldly the advances which Prussia made her out of hatred for Austria.

She thus threw away a precious chance for fear of displeasing the two belligerent powers. But Venice had also refused our alliance; this one wrong had obliterated all claims to equity at our hands. Notwithstanding the way in which we had already turned everything to account against her, the Directory speedily began to take fresh advantage of this wrong, and magnified it into a conspiracy. They had just found out for certain that the emperor insisted on an indemnity in Italy, and would not accept it in Germany. His intimates began to whisper that this indemnity, so much desired, might be found in the states of Venice. Quirini, the Venetian ambassador at Paris, got wind of the rumour, and hastened to inform the Seigniory of it (Despatch of 25th January 1797).

It was then that the Venetian armament afforded fresh pretexts. This measure, which the excesses of our occupation and fear of Austrian cupidity had first suggested, was in the beginning only designed for the defence of the lagoons, but later the intolerable abuses that were perpetrated had led her to extend it to the territories on the mainland, which were necessarily overrun and despoiled by the hostile armies, and if this was not a sufficient reason for arming, she was thoroughly justified by the threatened revolt of several towns. We had a right to take all precautionary measures against this rising in arms, but we had no right to impute to the Republic as a crime an act of legitimate defence. The ferment, which had openly begun, was our work; it was the effect of the democratic ideas which we had spread in Lombardy and the Cispadane; it was due to our presence in Italy, which alone had permitted it to manifest itself. We had found in the Venetian states the same seeds of discontent which exist in every country, and which can only show themselves when encouraged by the presence of a foreign army to give them a force which they would never have had alone. It was vexatious to have contributed even to their manifestation; to develop them was a sovereign iniquity. Yet the Directory did not hesitate, for its own ends, to conceive the plan of secretly encouraging the revolt, and at the same time interdicting the Republic from all means of defence. As soon as Venice showed her intention of checking the attempts of her enemies, the newspaper which was the organ of the French Government published an article containing an open appeal to insurrection in the inland provinces.

It said: 'All that portion of the Venetian states which lies on this side of the Adige may at once declare themselves, without fear that Venice will try to bring them afresh under the power of aristocratic despotism. Bergamo, Brescia, Como, Peschiera, etc., may at once join the Lombard Republic; a great number of the inhabitants are in favour of this plan. The only compensation they can hope for the sufferings they have endured from the presence of foreign armies, is the recovery of their liberty. The remainder of the Venetian state will for some time be the theatre of war, and will remain undecided, but it is easy to foresee that this also will soon declare its independence. The weakness of the Venetian Government is by this time well known to its subjects; its sole strength lay in public opinion, and public opinion has changed. Whatever may happen, it is certain that this terrorist government is drawing to a close.'

The reproach of terrorism was at least singular on the part of the Directory, addressed as it was against a Government that, during the last two centuries of its existence, had been a long way from equalling the number of proscriptions which the Directory had decreed in one year. As for the article, it was intended to excite a rising among the people, which was necessary to facilitate the disposal of the provinces. These words were an exact programme of the course of events in the Venetian provinces; but General Bonaparte, who was then on the point of opening his campaign, did not think the moment had come for an open rupture with Venice. This he explained in a letter to the Directory (7th March 1797), and he contented himself with complaining to Battaglia of the persecutions to which, according to his account, the friends of France were subject from the agents of the Republic. On the eve as it were of leaving Italy to herself, he was anxious to leave in his rear a state of peace, with the assurance of being able to take his revenge later. He had, on his own responsibility, concluded a treaty with the king of Sardinia, which insured him the support of that state; but the Directory refused to ratify it. The General made a last attempt with the Venetian Republic.

He sent for the procurator, François Pesaro, who was then one of the most influential men in the Republic, and tried to win him over to his views by that mixture of menace and caress with which he had the art of subjugating his adversaries. 'Venice wished to stop what she called her enemies, in reality the friends of France; she was hastening her own ruin. She could not believe that he, Bonaparte, would allow her to do so, for he held Venice at his mercy. All her inland provinces were ready to rise; with one word he could reduce the Republic to the lagoons. Why would she not take him for an ally? All trouble would then be avoided; he would guarantee *her states against revolution*, and the Republic would get out of its difficulty without any other penalty than that of inscribing the names of the principal families in the inland provinces in the Golden Book; a condition of which he did not, for that matter, make a *sine quâ non*.' Pesaro promised to refer the matter to the senate, and set off for Venice.

These overtures met with no better reception than the previous ones; and whoever has carefully studied these events must feel convinced that an alliance would no more have saved Venice than her neutrality saved her. Strength alone would have been of any service, on whichever side it might have been employed. However this may be, Bonaparte's words as well as his acts clearly prove that, while he took every opportunity to assert his intention of not interfering in any quarrels within the Republic, he had made up his mind that those whom he termed the friends of France should be covered with complete impunity in whatever they undertook; and yet the principles and sympathies by which he pretended to be actuated had so slight a hold on him, that he himself offered to betray them for the price of an alliance 'with this perfidious aristocracy,' to employ his own expressions which our historians have adopted after him (10th March).

The day after this interview General Bonaparte opened the campaign against the Archduke Charles. The success of that campaign depended on the rapidity of operations; but for once the obstacles were rather those of nature and climate, the season and the ground, than the enemy; for if the Austrians were not prepared, the Alps were still covered with snow, and they had to be crossed before he could march on Vienna. There were three different points of approach: one through the Tyrol, a second by Carinthia, and a third by Carniola. Of these three routes, the one which led into Carinthia by the Col de Tarwis was the most direct road to Vienna. According to Bonaparte's calculations, the Archduke Charles had everything to gain by taking up his quarters in the Tyrol. The inhabitants of these mountains were warlike and warmly attached to the monarchy, the passes were easy to defend, and it was the nearest spot to the reinforcements he was expecting. As long as he was not driven from this position, nothing very serious could be attempted on any other side. But the prince, who was not, like his adversary, in the service of a republic, was obliged to conform, like any other officer, to the plans laid down by the Aulic council, which enjoined upon him to cover Trieste. He only left in the Tyrol a corps of fifteen thousand men, under the command of Laudon and Kerpen; another still smaller detachment covered the Carinthian route, under the command of Lusignan; and he himself was stationed near Pordenone, between the Piave and the Tagliamento, to protect the route which leads to Trieste and into Carniola.

Bonaparte's dispositions were both simple and bold. Leaving Kilmaine and Victor in Italy, to keep watch over Venice and the Pope, he sent into the Tyrol General Joubert, a young officer who had already distinguished himself in that part of the country, and who had become in a very short time one of the most brilliant leaders in the army. Joubert had a corps of nearly twenty thousand men under his command; he was not to commence his movement till later. His task was to drive Laudon and Kerpen over the Alps by the Brenner, after which he was to join us in Carinthia by the road which goes from Brixen to Villach, to march upon Vienna with the rest of the army.

The General-in-Chief, whose first object was to make sure of the shortest road to this capital, hastened to take advantage of the mistake with which the instructions of the Aulic council burdened his adversary, by sending Masséna on the Pontéba route which comes out on the Col de Tarwis. This operation was at once to make us master of the passes opening into Carinthia. Masséna, finding only Lusignan's corps before him, gained an easy victory, and even made the general prisoner.

This movement allowed the whole of the army to cross the Piave, almost without striking a blow; and the arch-duke, in strict obedience to his instructions, retired behind the Tagliamento, covering Trieste in preference to Pontéba. It was behind this torrent that on the morning of the 16th of March the French army found the Austrians drawn up in order of battle, at a little distance from Valvasone. The Tagliamento is fordable along the greater part of its course. The army was preparing to cross it, but Bonaparte, after a short cannonade and a few cavalry charges, finding the enemy better prepared than he had expected, gave orders to bivouac and make breakfast. The archduke, deceived by this stratagem, directed a retreating movement, and returned to his tents. This was no sooner done than the French soldiers took up arms again. Bernadotte's division rushed into the stream, and the enemy, on returning, found it drawn up in compact array on their side of the river. The second line also crossed the torrent with the same good fortune. The archduke's forces were inferior to ours; he resisted, however, for some hours, but at last, seeing himself turned by one of our divisions, he was obliged to beat a retreat, leaving in our hands a number of prisoners and eight pieces of cannon.

During this time Masséna, driving before him the remnant of Lusignan's force, had taken possession of the gorges of Pontéba, and was nearing the Col de Tarwis. The archduke, who fully understood the importance of this post, sent forward three divisions under the command of Bayalitsch, towards Tarwis, with directions to take an indirect road which follows the upward course of the Isonzo, and passes by Caporetto. But Masséna, who was several hours' march in advance of this corps, arrived at the defile before him, and as Bonaparte had already sent Guyeux's division into the valley of the Isonzo, Bayalitsch's retreat was entirely cut off. The first object then was at all cost to stop Masséna. The archduke flew to Klagenfurth, put himself at the head of a division there, rallied Lusignan's scattered troops, and took up his position in advance of the Col de Tarwis, where he had little difficulty in driving back one of Masséna's advance-guards. The latter arrived there by forced marches. The whole issue of the campaign now depended on the occupation of the Col de Tarwis, for, without Bayalitsch's division, the archduke would no longer be in a state to offer us serious resistance. Both sides understood this. A fierce contest took place on these rugged heights, covered with ice. The archduke fought with desperate courage, and was several times on the point of being made prisoner, but his troops at length gave way, and were driven back to Villach. The road to Vienna was open.

The archduke repelled, Masséna waited for Bayalitsch, who, believing his road clear for retreat, followed the valley of the Isonzo, closely pursued by General Guyeux. On nearing Tarwis, he perceived that he was between the two fires. Demoralised and beaten beforehand, he only made an insignificant defence, and then surrendered with five thousand men. The rest of the soldiers fled across the mountains.

The head-quarters of the two armies had remained in front of one another, upon the road which leads into Carniola, by Palma-Nova and Gradisca. The Austrians did not attempt to defend Palma-Nova, which was a Venetian fortress, and our troops occupied it; but they tried to make a stand at Gradisca. Bernadotte first appeared before the place with his division. His men, who had served in the army of the Rhine, had less impetuosity, fire, and revolutionary ardour than the army of Italy, who often laughed at the reserve and respectability of their manners. On the other hand, the soldiers from our northern provinces were in better discipline and order, and displayed astonishing steadiness under fire. It was in a great measure owing to their immovable firmness that Moreau was able to effect his miraculous retreat, in which the army showed itself as grand as its captain. Their self-restraint and moderation were so well known, that the Italian towns disputed who should have them for garrison.[1] This trustworthy force had already been placed in the front rank in the battle of Tagliamento, and inflamed and animated by this honour, they were no sooner before Gradisca than they resolved to take it by storm without help. But their attack met with obstacles that were insurmountable, and four or five hundred men were uselessly sacrificed before ramparts which would not have resisted a more prudently devised attempt. In fact, as soon as Sérurier led his troops and cannon to the surrounding heights, the place immediately fell and the garrison surrendered.

After this last blow, a single division sufficed to take possession of Trieste and Carniola. Bonaparte left the

[1] Carlo Botta, *Storia d' Italia.*

provisional command of the district to Bernadotte, with orders 'to turn out of Palma-Nova the governor and all the Venetian troops,' without taking the trouble this time to make a complaint or assign a reason; the fortress suited our purposes, and that sufficed. The General-in-Chief was now able, in his turn (March 28th), to go up the valley of the Isonzo, the scene of Bayalitsch's disaster, and descend into Carinthia by the Col de Tarwis, with the main body of his army. At Villach he was in Germany. The inhabitants showed themselves both gentle and hospitable in their dispositions. Bonaparte issued a proclamation, dated from Klagenfurth, in which he assured them that the French army was come among them, not as conquerors, but as friends. Far from bringing with it the calamities of war, it had no other end in view than to force the emperor to accept peace. As for this struggle, so detested by nations, it was the work of a ministry sold to England. 'But,' he added, 'in spite of England and the ministers of the court of Vienna, let us be friends. The French Republic has the right of conquest over you; let this right disappear in a contract which will bind us together reciprocally. You will have nothing more to do with a war which has never received your assent nor approbation'; on my side, I will protect your property, and will levy no contributions on you.'

Joubert was still quartered in the Tyrol. The General-in-Chief had left him orders to wait there till he gave him notice to commence his march, with instructions of which the third article ran thus: 'Thoroughly to cajole the priests, and to try to form a party among the monks' (dated March 15th). Bonaparte, who measured difficulties of a moral order like material obstacles, only left him a few days to realise this task, which was the programme of his own policy. Joubert was stationary on the Lavis, keeping his eye on the two corps of Kerpen and Laudon, when he received orders to drive them beyond the Brenner, and then effect a junction with the army by the Carinthian road. Joubert did all this with his accustomed skill. Escaping the vigilance of Laudon, he concentrated all his forces against Kerpen, whom he completely overwhelmed at St. Michel. The Austrians lost five thousand men, wounded and killed. Laudon, whom he next attacked at Neumarkt, shared the same fate. Their scattered forces rallied at Clausen, in a strong position not far from Bolzano. Here they received the reinforcement of a division from the Rhine. Nevertheless, Joubert drove them hence on the 24th of March, and pursued them to the foot of the Brenner, which they crossed in haste and in a state of complete disorder. Having no longer any immediate danger to fear in the Tyrol, and believing that Bonaparte regarded whatever could afterwards happen in that quarter as of secondary importance, Joubert collected his troops again at Brixen, and there took the right road which leads from the Tyrol into Carinthia.

After the army left Italy, those events took place in the Venetian states which we had rendered inevitable, and which it was easy for us to have prevented. The spirit of revolt, which had been fermenting before we left, necessarily increased after our departure. To all the causes of agitation which we had brought into this unhappy country, the occupation of her fortresses, the disarming of her garrisons, the pillage of her arsenals, the distress produced by our requisitions, the destruction of those of her castles which the proximity of a fortification condemned to be destroyed, a tyrannical system of espionage which violated the secret of letters, and did not even respect the despatches of the Government—there had been added a system of political proselytism which, though it found few echoes with the mass of the people, in general attached to the government of the nobility, had met with ardent partisans in the aristocratic families of the inland provinces, who were shut out from all participation in public affairs, and were jealous of the nobility of the Golden Book. This exclusion was assuredly a legitimate cause for discontent; but any change wrought by foreign interference was a death-blow to Venetian independence.

Two parties then confronted one another in Venice: one, which comprised the immense majority of the population, hated us for all the calamities we had already brought upon them, and for what they feared we might yet bring; the other was composed of a smaller number, but their courage was high, for they had placed all their hopes in us. In spite of the ostensible instructions left by Bonaparte to General Kilmaine, in spite of his repeated and solemn declarations of impartiality, he evidently encouraged the latter party; for at the point to which he had brought affairs it would have been impossible for him to remain neutral, even if he had desired it sincerely. Bonaparte considered this minority as his natural centre in case of a rupture with Venice; he reckoned on the pretexts and facilities which their agitations would afford him; he lost no opportunity of complaining of the precautions which the agents of the Venetian Government felt it necessary to take against this party, pretending to regard them as directed against the French; and at length openly announced that he meant to allow neither arrests nor persecutions, which was the most effective form of connivance, since it was to authorise attack and to forbid defence. To these indirect encouragements was added the provocation of the Lombard patriots, to whom Bonaparte had skilfully insinuated that Lombardy had no chance of independence after the war, unless, by adding to her territory, she could form a state strong enough and compact enough to stand alone. We had thus made their liberty depend on the destruction of the liberty of their countrymen, and they showed themselves all the more enterprising in the work, from feeling assured that they could act with impunity. But, for all that she acted through the intervention of such instruments as these, it was none the less France that brought all this about.

On the 8th of March the insurrection, predicted by the organ of the Directory, was announced as imminent by the Podesta Ottolini, in a report dated from Bergamo. He disclosed every particular of the plot, and named beforehand the authors and actors in it. At their head was to figure, as he did actually figure, the chief of the Lombard legion, Lahoy, who was in reality serving in our army, since he received his orders from Kilmaine. This information had been given to Ottolini by one of our adjutant-generals, named Landrieux, who on the one side excited the inhabitants of Brescia and Bergamo to revolt, and on the other accepted money for denouncing the conspiracy. Bonaparte, who always so confidently asserted that our officers had nothing to do with these intrigues, was however the first to accuse Landrieux of this double play, when he afterwards had occasion to complain of him to the Directory (Letter of the 14th November 1797). The explosion took place on the 12th of March. Some hundreds of the inhabitants of Bergamo, aided by the Lombard patriots, rose and proclaimed a new municipality. Ottolini, who had some troops, wished to resist, but the French commandant who occupied the citadel stopped him, assigning for a reason that his instructions were to maintain order. The Venetian patrols received notice to withdraw under pain of being fired upon, and being inferior in numbers, they obeyed. The next day Ottolini left the town, and Bergamo declared itself united to Milan.

Two days later Brescia followed the example of Bergamo. A hundred inhabitants of Brescia or Bergamo presented themselves before the gates of the town, crying that they were followed by several thousands of Cisalpines and French, which was false. Battaglia, who was proveditore of Brescia, either from credulity or connivance, allowed them to do as they pleased. They disarmed the garrison, seized the posts, and threw the magistrates into prison. From Brescia the insurgents turned towards Salo, where the insurrection was equally successful (17th March). In neither of these three towns did the French troops take any direct and open part in the movement; but it is absurd to conclude that they did not support it, since they hindered all action on the part of the Venetian Government. The French officers made louder protestation than ever of their respect for neutrality, but at the same time they encouraged and supported Lahoy and his Lombards, who were placed under their orders. Before long they ceased to be satisfied with depriving the Venetian Government of all the means of defence in the towns which they occupied, and openly attacked the party who were in favour of it. A counter-insurrection having been formed after the rising at Bergamo in the country districts where the inhabitants had unanimously remained faithful to the Republic, Kilmaine gave orders to Lahoy to march against them and disarm them, a measure which could not fail to lead to violent retaliation. Thus, of the two insurrections of the two opposite parties, to which our presence had given rise in the Venetian states, the one which was caused by a small minority was openly patronised and protected by us; the other, which comprised almost all the population, was crushed by our arms, and we condemned to a humiliating impotence the only power that could have effectually interposed between them. These two facts are evident, notwithstanding the obscurity and confusion thrown over the events by a patriotism that is narrow, unintelligent, and incompatible with the rigorous laws of history. The only way for nations, as for individuals, to avoid fresh faults, is loyally to discern and acknowledge those of the past.

When this news arrived at Venice, the senate immediately perceived what advantage their enemies would derive from it: they were filled with consternation. Convinced that everything depended on France, they addressed themselves to Lallement, our minister at Venice, seeking his advice, as an intimation that they threw themselves on our mercy, and asked him if in this danger the Republic could count on our friendship. Lallement gave an ambiguous reply; our policy prevented his doing otherwise: he promised to consult his Government, and advised the senate, in the meantime, to grant such reforms as would satisfy the insurgents of the inland provinces. This proposition was debated in the grand council. The advantage and even the necessity of making some change in the old constitution of Venice was acknowledged; but at the same time it was agreed, that to make any concession just then would have all the drawbacks of an act of weakness, and that it would be better to postpone it. They, however, decided upon consulting General Bonaparte, as a striking mark of profound deference, and they despatched two deputies to him, of whom one was François Pesaro, the same negotiator who had already been employed on a previous occasion.

The two deputies met Bonaparte at Goritz, where he had at this moment his head-quarters. They related what had taken place at Bergamo and Brescia, and represented to him that the insurrections could not be suppressed as long as these towns were occupied by French troops; and they begged him to allow the Venetian garrisons to return. The General gave a positive refusal to this request, but offered to bring the insurgents back to their allegiance himself, if Venice would only make some concessions to them. He could, in fact, have done this by a word or a sign; but before he would decide on doing so, it was necessary for the Republic to throw herself on his discretion. The only safety for Venice, according to him, lay in a strict alliance with the Directory, in throwing herself into the arms of France; and the two deputies were reminded of the case of the king of Sardinia, an example which only proved the insincerity of his advice, for in his correspondence with the Directory he never spoke of Sardinia except as a lost power, which had committed suicide by putting herself in our grasp. The Venetian deputies were too keen-sighted to mistake the meaning of such overtures. They reminded Bonaparte that the policy of Venice was neutrality. In a second interview, Bonaparte told them the senate could do what it pleased, but it would act at its own risk and peril; for his own part, he should refer the affair to the Directory. The deputies entreated him (François Pesaro's Report), as his army had entered the Austrian territory, to lighten the burden which weighed so heavily on the Venetian Government, and to repay them their advances. Whereupon the General peremptorily declared that, on the contrary, it was his intention more than ever to draw on the resources of the Venetian territory, in order to spare the Germans, and that he wished Venice to furnish a subsidy of a million francs a month, to supply the place of the system of requisitions. When the deputies exclaimed about the poverty of their treasury, Bonaparte replied that they had only to take possession of the funds which the duke of Modena, England, and Russia had stored in Venice. He then dismissed them, greatly embarrassed as to the line their Government should take, for Bonaparte, as he wrote to the Directory on the 24th of March, giving an account of the interview, had had no other end than that of 'gaining time:' in this he succeeded, as well as in rendering their situation worse than ever.

Venice, the neutral power, on whom the title of friend was so freely bestowed, was treated with a thousand times greater severity than the enemy's territory, whose inhabitants were to be spared from all contributions, in order to gain their goodwill. The General, in spite of his assurances of friendship, promised nothing, but left Venice to bear alone a responsibility which was becoming each day more embarrassing and more terrible. Bonaparte tells us in his *Mémoires*, that he said to the deputies, as they were taking their departure: 'Take care! What I might have passed over in Venice while I was in Italy, would become an unpardonable crime when I am in Germany. If my soldiers are assassinated, my convoys molested, or my communications interrupted, your Republic will cease to exist; she will have pronounced her own death-warrant.' This important sentence is not found in the very minute report of the Venetian deputies, nor in the account which Bonaparte wrote of the interview to the Directory; it even contradicts this last narrative, which represents things in a very different light, and which the General concludes with these words: 'I believe I have sent Pesaro away quite satisfied, and we have parted very good friends,' which is inconsistent with a threatening and imperious tone. But there are sometimes more scruples in the art which recounts, than in the conscience which acted. The events which were to follow stood in need of a certain preparation.

During this time the Venetian ambassador in Paris had been proceeding in a similar way with the Directory; but this body having no other policy in regard to Venice than a wish to turn to the best account events which they had rendered inevitable, referred the Venetians to Bonaparte, just as Bonaparte had referred them to the Directory. The latter alleged the impossibility of deciding on any course before they had received the General's report. And when Quirini pressed for permission for his Government to reduce Bergamo, since they thus pretended not to interfere with the affairs of the Republic, a member of the Directory told him very bluntly that the French were the strongest, and therefore it was for them to command the town as long as they remained in it. The ambassador saw clearly the end of all this temporising, and explained it to his Government. The Directory, he said, in order to make peace with Austria, want to offer her some compensation in Italy, and secretly encourage insurrection, because insurrection would render a redistribution of territory easier. And the ambassador again referred to the project, of which he had given information in his former despatches. 'He had,' he said, 'strong and well-grounded reasons for fearing that the Venetian provinces were concerned in the compensation which Austria demanded, and would be made the pledge of peace between these two powers.'

This was the state of affairs, when an incident occurred of a more significant character than any that had preceded, which hastened events, and gave its true colour to the situation. On the 27th of March a detachment of French cavalry presented itself at the gates of Crema, a place which had hitherto been left in the hands of the Venetians, as being of no importance for us. The soldiers were refused entrance, and the bridges were drawn up, but they insisted, on the pretext that they only wanted to pass through the town. They were admitted on this assurance; but instead of leaving the next day, as they had promised, they opened the gates to two fresh detachments, which rushed in, disarmed the garrison, drove out the magistrates, took possession of the magazines and public offices, and then declared the town free, like Brescia and Bergamo.

To this fresh act of hostility the mountaineers replied by pouring down upon Salo, where they took three hundred prisoners, among whom were two hundred Poles belonging to our army, and some few French. From that time the quarrel, which already existed between our soldiers who occupied the towns and the people in the mountains, became more serious, and was characterised on the one side by sudden assaults on detachments and isolated groups of soldiers, and on the other by fires and pitiless devastations. By a chance, which seemed to conspire with us for the downfall of the Republic, the Austrian troops reappeared in the Tyrol, which Joubert had left quite unprotected when he went to join Bonaparte in Carinthia. This encouraged the insurrection by giving rise to stories of reverses, which had no foundation. These false reports, skilfully spread by Austrian agents, increased the confidence of the mountaineers, while the severity of our measures raised their exasperation to its height.

Bonaparte had descended the Noric Alps in pursuit of the archduke, who could nowhere offer any serious resistance to his progress, and contented himself by yielding the ground, step by step, as he fell back upon Vienna. From Villach, Bonaparte had gained Klagenfurth, the capital of Carinthia. But the further he advanced into the enemy's country, so far from the base of his operations, the better he understood the fault he had committed in dispensing with the co-operation of the armies of the Rhine, and his entreaties to the Directory to hasten the opening of the campaign on this river became more sincere. But such was the poverty of the treasury, that Moreau could not begin his march for want of some few hundred thousand francs, and the letters from the Directory to the General could only hold out very distant hopes.

Bonaparte was thus condemned, entirely by his own fault, to be drawn deeper and deeper into the hereditary states of the emperor, without being able to count either on any effectual diversion, or any speedy succour in case of a check. If the emperor, deciding to push the war to extremities, should abandon Vienna to take refuge in Hungary, and raise an insurrection there, our army even in the midst of its triumphs would be placed in a most critical position, and Bonaparte would be forced to retire before his own success. These reflections presented themselves to his mind with additional force, from the thought of the responsibility he had voluntarily incurred, and the impression they made on his imagination was so strong, that he even suspected the Directory of wishing to sacrifice the army of Italy in order the more surely to get rid of its general. This monstrous suspicion is recorded in the dictations of St. Helena.

It was under the influence of this depression, on the 31st of March 1797, a few hours after receiving the despatch announcing that the armies of the Rhine were still unmoved, that he wrote from Klagenfurth to the Archduke Charles the celebrated letter in which the conqueror offered peace to the conquered. He spontaneously invited the prince 'to earn the title of benefactor of humanity,' declaring that as far as he was himself concerned, 'if the overtures of peace which he had the honour to make could save the life of a single man, he should feel prouder of the civic crown which would be his reward, than of all the mournful glory of military success.'

This letter, which so eloquently expresses all the usual commonplaces on the evils of war, with a profession of respect for human life, slightly hyperbolical on the lips of a man who has himself related that, at his *début* in the army of Italy, he once engaged a detachment in combat and had men killed, merely to afford a spectacle for his mistress,[1] is especially remarkable, because it contains the expression of feelings of which we find no other trace in all Bonaparte's voluminous writings. It is difficult to say whether his mind was, for once in his life, accessible to feelings of philanthropy, or whether he feigned them at the time to suit his

---

[1] The *Mémorial* of Las Cases contains an account of the circumstance in Napoleon's own words: 'Walking with her one day, in the midst of our positions near the Col di Tenda, the idea suddenly occurred to me that I would let her see something of a battle, and I ordered an attack to be made by the advance posts. We won, it is true, but the *combat could, of course, result in nothing.* The attack was a pure fancy, but for all that some few men were left on the ground. Whenever I have since recollected the affair, I have always reproached myself for my conduct.'

purpose, thus giving an additional proof of his marvellous aptitude for playing every part, and adopting every kind of language. In any case, it is certain that this extraordinary man never experienced, or at least never expressed, any scruple about the thousands of men who died to realise the plans of his ambition.

The Archduke Charles, who had no more right than General Bonaparte to offer or refuse peace, but who, notwithstanding his near relationship to the emperor, did not treat his instructions quite so cavalierly as his opponent, replied on the 2d of April, that, much as he desired peace, he had no authority to enter into negotiations, and that he would await orders from his Government. It was, however, well known in the French head-quarters that a powerful party had been formed at the court of Vienna which was in favour of peace, and that M. de Thugut himself was beginning to lean in this direction. It was to Bonaparte's interest, then, to strengthen these inclinations, by striking blows that would increase the peril of the situation, augment its confusion, and spread dismay in all minds. The pursuit was resumed with extreme energy. At Friesach, Masséna seized the enemy's magazines. The archduke, who had received reinforcements from the Rhine of four divisions, tried to make a stand in the gorges of Neumarkt, but he was driven back and lost three thousand men. Perceiving that one of his corps, which had come up from the Tyrol, was on the point of being cut off, he tried to gain time by asking for an armistice, but Bonaparte replied that a suspension of arms could only be accorded to treat for a definitive peace. The next day, the archduke encountered a fresh check at Unzmark. After that, his march was less like a retreat than a rout. The 7th of April our advance-guard reached Léoben, a place whose name hitherto obscure will retain an evil celebrity from the transaction which there had its origin.

The French army was now only twenty-five leagues from Vienna. Two Austrian officers, MM. de Bellegarde and de Merfeld, came to the head-quarters to ask for a suspension of arms, and this time it was to treat for peace. It was granted for five days, and was afterwards prolonged from the 13th to the 20th of April, in order to give the time necessary for the negotiation and the signature of the preliminaries of the treaty.

On what bases were they going to treat? Bonaparte had often asked himself this question, but at the time of signing the armistice he had come to no decision. He was resolved that the conditions should be more advantageous than the Directory had fixed with Clarke; he felt in honour bound to obtain more, since he had caused the failure of that diplomatist's mission. At the same time he knew that we should meet with great resistance from this power, unless he could offer her some suitable compensation for the loss of Lombardy. Both the Directory and himself had thought of providing this at the expense of the Venetian states; but as he was still in ignorance of what had taken place at Salo, he had not even the shadow of a complaint against Venice. He reckoned rightly that the shocks which this tottering edifice had received, would in time afford him the pretext he needed; but it might still stand firm for some time, and time pressed. He watched with impatient eye the symptoms of dissolution, which did not develop themselves quickly enough to please him; but he had prepared the elements too surely to doubt the result. As early as the 5th of April, before he had received Kilmaine's despatches relative to the collision between the insurgent mountaineers and his army, he wrote to the Directory: 'I enclose you letters, which have been sent me by the inhabitants of Brescia and Bergamo, with several of their proclamations. The Venetian Government is detested all over the mainland; *it is possible that the present crisis may achieve its overthrow.*'

But in order to render this possibility a certainty, some plausible pretext had to be found to give a colour in the eyes of Europe to this striking violation of national rights. The mere fact of war was not a sufficient excuse for such an abuse of force; for whole populations could not be wrested from Italy and delivered over to their natural enemy, for wrong done by their Government. But the maxims and usages of the right of conquest in its most brutal form had not been restored to credit in vain. Men's minds were already fully prepared for what was going to take place.

If General Bonaparte had been so skilful in keeping up with Venice what he terms 'an open quarrel,' at a time when his only aim was to get from her some millions of francs, it is easy to understand the consummate art he would display, when provinces were at stake which were to be the pledges of peace and the consolidation of his triumphs. He simply adopted the method which he had hitherto found so successful, incessantly flaming out in complaints and menaces against the Republic, now on one pretext, now on another, exaggerating beyond measure any fact he could turn to account, driving the Venetian agents to extremities by continual vexations, and feigning to consider as pure inventions all the grievances which they alleged, though they had often infinitely more cause to complain than he had himself. However, in spite of the disposition which this conduct announced, we can see from his correspondence with the Directory, that on April 8th he did not feel that he could take upon himself the responsibility of touching the Venetian provinces. He reckoned on restoring to Austria the whole of Lombardy, keeping for France '*in the heart of Italy a republic of two million souls.*' This was at that time all the good, to use his own words, that he fancied he got from his successes.

The following day, April 9th, he received Kilmaine's report of the events of Salo. He saw in an instant to what account he could turn this affair against the Republic of Venice, and before he had even made up his mind as to the line he would take, he fulminated a tremendous message to the Doge of Venice: 'All the mainland had taken up arms to the cry of Death to the French! *Several hundred soldiers* of the Italian army had already fallen victims. Venice had secretly authorised these risings while disavowing them. Did they doubt his power to make the first nation in the world respected? The senate could choose between peace and war. If the risings were not immediately put down, and the assassins punished, war should be declared, and the inland provinces delivered from Venetian tyranny.'

It is scarcely necessary to point out to those who have followed the course of the narrative, how completely this anger was feigned. The events at Salo were an almost unlooked-for chance for Bonaparte, so exactly in time did they arrive to save his plans and simplify his embarrassments. But as history ought never to abandon the severity of her method, we must compare the facts with these accusations, to show the extent of their sincerity. First of all, Venice was made responsible for entirely fortuitous events, which resulted from a popular movement, and which were by no means the work of the Government, though some of its inferior agents took part in them, in consequence of the ill-treatment of which they had been victims. She had armed, it is true; but we had given her a right to do so by driving out her garrisons, and, in spite of the feelings of hatred which we had busied ourselves in provoking among her subjects, in spite of the evident interest she had in seeing us expelled from Italy, she was too prudent to try to avenge herself at a time when she made it her aim, on the contrary, to conciliate France, and when, as we have the united testimony of Lallement and of Bonaparte himself to show, she fulfilled with the most scrupulous zeal her heavy engagements to provide supplies for the army. With regard to the collision between the inhabitants of Bergamo and our troops, the insurgents had only made use of the right of legitimate defence; their attack was a retaliation for the taking of Crema, for the exploits of the Lombard legion sent by Kilmaine to burn their villages, and the excesses of every kind committed during the previous six months by our troops in violation of all the laws of neutrality. Bonaparte was equally untruthful, when he stated 'that *several hundreds* of our soldiers had fallen victims,' and on this point we need no other testimony than his own; for the same day, April 9th, in summing up, in a letter to Lallement, his complaints against the Republic of Venice, he says, that 'more than *fifty Frenchmen*' had been assassinated,[1] and this number is an exaggeration; applying, besides, the term 'assassination' arbitrarily to partisan warfare, according to the custom of soldiers, in whose eyes murder is only lawful when committed in uniform.

General Bonaparte acted with still less good faith when he accused the senate 'of having purposely furnished pretexts in order to seem to justify a rising directed against our armies.' According to this view, the Venetian Government itself had stimulated these insurrections in Brescia and Bergamo, which had caused them so much embarrassment, and were likely to prove their ruin. The absurdity of such imputations is as evident as their injustice. They are, besides, disproved a thousand times over by the secret reports of the Venetian agents, in which they gave undisguised utterance to all their trouble and alarm. Such charges only signified one thing, that the ruin of Venice was resolved upon. The satisfaction, which the General required of her 'immediately,' was so impossible in the precarious state to which the regular force of Venice had been reduced, that he could have had no other end than to raise the perplexities of the Venetian Government to their height, by filling all minds with terror, confusion, and dismay. That this was Bonaparte's intention is evident from the pitiless instructions sent the same day to Kilmaine, in case, as was certainly inevitable, the satisfaction demanded should not be accorded in twenty-four hours. He enclosed an appeal to insurrection, to be published throughout the inland districts, which might in a few hours set the whole country in a blaze.

But all this outburst of anger, of menace, and imperious urgency, was a complete comedy, and the end he had in view was so far from being the satisfaction he demanded, that he did not even take the trouble to wait for an answer from the Venetian senate, whose absolute submission would have greatly embarrassed him, by preventing the retaliation

[1] It is needless to say that all these quotations from the letters and reports of Bonaparte are taken from his Correspondence, recently published.

on which he was reckoning. On the 15th of April, at the very same hour in which his aide-de-camp, Junot, introduced by Lallement into the senate of Venice, was presenting Bonaparte's letter with military arrogance to the Doge Manin, the General was holding a conference at Léoben with M. de Merfeld and the Marquis de Gallo, and was giving up Venice to Austria. Without waiting to enquire how his letter had been received, he drew up, in concert with these two plenipotentiaries, three different plans, and in two out of the three the Venetian territory was disposed of by way of compensation.

The dates of these events are of capital importance. The greater number of historians have paid no attention to them, imitating the example given in the *Mémoires* of Napoleon, in which the order of events is constantly confused, so that the reprisal which his policy provoked on the part of Venice has always been made to appear as the principle and motive of his conduct, instead of being merely its consequence. The preliminaries of Léoben, for example, have always appeared to have been prepared and justified by the *pâques véronaises*, whereas in reality Bonaparte had fully made up his mind to sacrifice the Venetian states long before he had the shadow of complaint against the Venetian Seigniory. The admission contained in his report to the Directory, together with incontestable facts, proves that his resolution was taken during the days which elapsed between the insignificant collision at Salo and that on which he received the answer from the senate of Venice, that is to say, between the 9th and 15th of April 1797.

But it is now time to relate the progress and bearings of the negotiations which went on at Léoben after the extension of the armistice. Bonaparte, as I have said, had no power to negotiate. Clarke alone had received this mission from the Directory, but Clarke was then at Turin; and after having despatched, for form's sake, a courier to him, who certainly used no great haste in his journey, Bonaparte proceeded to act, according to his custom. M. de Merfeld and the Marquis de Gallo, the Neapolitan ambassador, had received full powers from the court of

Vienna. They arrived at the head-quarters on the 13th of April; on the 15th the first conference took place in a little pavilion situated in the middle of a garden, which was declared neutral ground; 'a farce,' wrote Bonaparte, 'to which I yielded, giving way to the puerile vanity of these people.'

The General had the sense to banish all questions of etiquette. The Austrian plenipotentiaries stated as a concession, that by Article I. the emperor recognised the French Republic. 'Strike that out,' cried Bonaparte; 'the French Republic is like the sun in heaven; so much the worse for those who do not see it.'

The next day they completed the drawing up of the three schemes, and these were forwarded to Vienna to be submitted to the emperor. All three comprised the cession of Belgium, and the recognition of the limits of the Rhine; the difference was with regard to the compensation to be offered to Austria. The first two proposed the whole or a part of the Venetian states; the third offered Milan and Lombardy, and said nothing of Venice.

In the summary and very incomplete account which Bonaparte sent the Directory of these debates, he expressed himself thus: 'They demand the restitution of Milan; in fact, they wish for the Milanese and some portion of the Venetian states, or of the Legations. If I would have consented to this proposition, they had power to sign at once. This arrangement did not strike me as possible.

'His majesty the emperor has declared that he *does not desire any compensation in Germany.* I first offered *the evacuation of the Milanese and Lombardy, which they refused.* We then drew up the three propositions, which we have now sent to Vienna' (To the Directory, April 16th).

In order fully to understand the double part Bonaparte was playing with all the world, we must compare these last few lines with the proclamation, which only four days before, April 12th, he addressed to the same Lombards, whom he was now offering to deliver over again to Austria, not knowing whether she would take them, or seize a richer prey nearer home.

'You will ask for a guarantee of your future independence, but are not the victories, which the Italian army is gaining day after day, a sufficient guarantee? Every fresh triumph is an additional line in your constitutional charter. Facts are stronger than a declaration that is substantially puerile. You cannot doubt the interest and desire of the Government to make you free and independent.'[1]

Nor is this all. Bonaparte has formally declared that, when he wrote to his Government that 'the emperor would accept no compensation in Germany,' he deceived the Directory. This is the curious admission he has left in his *Mémoires* on this subject:—

'The Austrian plenipotentiaries agreed from our first conversations to the cession of Belgium and the line of the Rhine, but they demanded indemnities, and when it was proposed to give it them in Germany, in Bavaria for example, they immediately replied, that in that case they should require *a guarantee that the constitution of the Venetian Republic should not be changed*, and the consolidation of the aristocracy of the Golden Book, because they would not on any account allow the Italian Republic to extend from the Alps and the Apennines to the Isonzo and Julian Alps. But this would have been to consolidate the most active and constant enemy of the Republic.'

We see from this how easily the General might have avoided the great iniquity which sullied his victories. The occupation of Bavaria by Austria would not have been by any means perfectly justifiable from the point of view of law: but Bavaria had, at any rate, given us great cause of complaint, by taking up arms against us, and we should in no way have wronged her nationality by cession to a German power, on whom all the odium of the transaction would have fallen.

Bonaparte, after briefly explaining the state of the negotiations, launched out into bitter invectives on the subject of the armies of the Rhine, whose intervention, which he had so obstinately refused to wait for, would have rendered the conclusion of peace so easy.

[1] *Moniteur*, reproduced in the Correspondence.

'If Moreau wishes to cross the Rhine, he can cross it, and if he had done so before, we should have been in a position to dictate the conditions of peace as masters, and without incurring any risk. But he who fears to lose his glory is sure to lose it. I crossed the Julian and the Noric Alps in three feet of snow, and I brought my artillery by roads where not even a cart had ever been, and every one said it was impossible. If I had consulted my own interest and the comfort of the army, I should have remained on the other side of the Isonzo. I threw myself into Germany to extricate the armies of the Rhine, and hinder the enemy from assuming the offensive. I am at the gates of Vienna, and the ministers of this haughty and insolent court are at my head-quarters. The soldiers of the Rhine can have no blood in their veins. If they do not come to my assistance, I shall return to Italy. Europe shall judge between the conduct of the two armies. They will then have the whole forces of the emperor to contend with; they will be overwhelmed, and it will be their own fault.'

Nothing could be more unjust than this manner of throwing the blame of his own conduct on others. So far from trying to put off the campaign, Moreau and Hoche had submitted with impatience to the delay which had been imposed on them, and if they did not afterwards join Bonaparte while he was treating for peace, it was because they did not wish to divide with him the honours of the war. There was nothing genuine in all these recriminations, but his fear of seeing the negotiations fall to the ground, and being obliged to recommence the war alone under unfavourable circumstances, of which the issue would be very uncertain. Besides this apprehension, he wanted to forestall the reproaches with which they had a right to greet him.

Two days later, that is to say April the 18th, Clarke not having arrived, as Bonaparte had good reason to expect, the preliminaries were signed, till the treaty of peace could be concluded in a congress that was to meet at Berne. The emperor gave up all his rights over the Belgian provinces and Lombardy, and received as indemnity all the

Venetian provinces situated between the Oglio, the Po, and the Adriatic, in addition to Istria and Dalmatia.

The remaining inland provinces of Venice were given to France, who, in her turn, by the most useless of formalities, made them over to the so-called independent Republic, formed by the union of Lombardy, Mantua, Reggio, and Modena. The Venetian Republic was thus reduced to the lagoons, which had been its cradle. But in anticipation of the effect which this spoliation would produce in Europe, she was offered by way of indemnity the three legations of Ferrara, Bologna, and the Romagna, a derisive proposition, for the negotiators must have known better than any one else that Venice would neither accept these provinces, nor be able to keep them if she would.

General Bonaparte has left us his own opinion as to the value of this indemnity, which was meant to console Venice for all she had lost:—

'As for the surrender of our rights over the provinces of Ferrara, Bologna, and the Romagna, in exchange for the states of Venice, *they will always remain in our power.* If the emperor and ourselves succeed in getting the senate to consent to this exchange, it is evident that the Venetian Republic will be under the influence of the Lombard Republic, and *at our disposal.* If, on the other hand, the exchange cannot be effected and the emperor takes possession of a portion of the Venetian states, while the senate refuses *an indemnity which is disproportionate and insufficient,* the three legations still remain in our power, and we can unite Bologna and Ferrara to the Lombard Republic' (To the Directory, 19th April 1797).

In another passage of the same letter he expresses with admirable clearness the idea which had inspired all his policy. 'We have,' he said, 'in the centre of Italy a republic with which we shall have communication by Genoa and by the sea. In all future Italian wars our communications are assured. The king of Sardinia is henceforth at our disposal.'

His Italian Republic, then, was created as a conquest for France, and in his offer of an indemnity to Venice he only sought an opportunity of putting his hand on the last refuge of this republic. Such were the principles which a young general, whose glory was but of yesterday, dared openly to admit to men who were proud of the name of Republican, and such were the confidences which, without fear of contradiction, he confided to a Government newly sprung from that Revolution which had shed so much blood in honour of the rights of men!

While Bonaparte was engaged in signing the preliminaries of Léoben, the armies of the Rhine were beginning a campaign, to carry him the assistance which he had rendered useless beforehand. Hoche, who quivered with impatience at every account of fresh victories won by the armies of Italy, and to whom Fortune had always refused a task worthy of his great abilities, cursed the delays and obstacles which held him back, as if he had instinctively felt that his days were numbered, and that each hour as it passed was a day lost for his glory. Moreau, who was of a calmer temperament, had gone to Paris to beg for a miserable sum which he could not obtain, but which was indispensable to him before he could open the campaign. At last Hoche commenced operations without waiting the return of his colleague. He crossed the Rhine at Neuwied, drove back the Austrians at Heddersdorf, taking six thousand prisoners, and by a rapid movement was on the point of cutting off their retreat, when a courier brought him news of the signing of the preliminaries, and stopped him short in the midst of his success. This was the last exploit of the heroic young man, who was doomed to fall before his time. Moreau's army, led by Desaix, crossed the river with equal success, below Strasbourg, and then marched on the Austrians and drove them into the Black Mountains; but he had to retreat, like Hoche, on receiving the same news. Thus the assistance of the armies of the Rhine, which might have been so decisive in the conclusion of an advantageous peace, had Bonaparte chosen to wait, was completely lost and had no weight in the balance.

CHAPTER VIII

THE OCCUPATION OF VENICE—THE 18TH FRUCTIDOR

THE crisis, which had been so long impending in the Venetian states, thanks to the feul of every sort which our policy had thrown on the fire on pretence of extinguishing it, was now rapidly approaching. The popular passions, restrained for nearly a whole year, notwithstanding the state of exasperation to which so many humiliations and spoliatory or harassing measures had brought them, must inevitably burst forth the moment that fear became weaker than resentment.

On the 15th of April 1797 Junot had delivered Bonaparte's imperious message to the senate of Venice. The aide-de-camp read it in person, assuming the blunt and rough manner of a soldier, in order to strike consternation into those whom he addressed. The doge's reply was more humble, submissive, and resigned, than became the representative of a republic once so proud. Fallen though Venice was, her past dignity he was bound to remember. The senate identified itself with the reply of the doge by a resolution, and decided also that two envoys should be sent to meet the General. The Venetian Government knew beyond doubt that the negotiations entered into between France and Austria were about to be brought to a close, nor were they ignorant of the fact that the division of their provinces was to be a point of discussion. It was to their interest then to offend no one, and they were waiting with an anxiety bordering on terror the results of their ambassador's steps at Paris, and those of the envoys sent to Bonaparte, when the news of the insurrection of Verona arrived to put out their last hopes.

General Kilmaine, on the receipt of Bonaparte's despatch, had given orders for the immediate disarming not only of the insurgents, but of all the Venetian garrisons which remained in the inland provinces. This order was executed without opposition at Peschiera, Castel-Novo, and several other places. But at Verona, where the Venetians were more numerous than the French, and could count on the support of the population, they were forced to postpone the disarming. The two garrisons remained face to face in a state of defiant irritation, in the midst of a population which was placed since the beginning of the war at the strategical point most disputed, and was more than any other excited from the remembrance of all the evils we had brought on them.

In such a state of affairs a spark was enough to produce an explosion. On the 17th of April some French reinforcements entered Verona, and being naturally looked upon as sent to carry out the same measure which had been taken in the neighbouring towns, they were immediately surrounded by the inhabitants, and had great difficulty in joining our garrison. A fray having begun between two patrols, the whole population soon joined in it, and the cry for vengeance on the French resounded on every side. All who did not succeed in taking refuge in the fortress were massacred on that and the succeeding days by a multitude in a state of frenzy, and Verona was stained by all the horrors which accompany popular outbursts. All this time our soldiers, shut up in the citadel, bombarded the town. It was not long before they were released by troops, which surrounded Verona and quelled the insurrection. There were on our side about three hundred victims. Such was the *pâques véronaises*, the spontaneous and furious manifestation of resentment long devoured in silence. Vengeance, only half appeased in this first insurrection, burst forth in a fresh paroxysm on the 18th of April, as if popular hatred, more clear-sighted than the policy of statesmen, had divined that at that very moment Bonaparte was signing the preliminaries of Léoben, and abandoning to Austria the spoils of Venice.

Two days later France had a fresh cause of complaint. A French vessel, commanded by Captain Laugier, had moored alongside a powder magazine situated near the Lido. An old law, which the English navy itself always scrupulously observed,[1] forbade any armed vessel to enter the port. A Venetian officer ordered Laugier to set sail. The captain refused to obey, in a tone that gave reason for thinking he had entered the port out of bravado, and not merely in mistake. The forts fired on him. Some men were killed, the others taken prisoners. It was an unfortunate circumstance that precluded all idea of premeditation, so greatly did it increase the dangers of the Republic. The blame falls partly on the arrogance of the French captain, and partly on the blind and stupid precipitation of the Venetian officer. The deputation from the senate joined the General-in-Chief at Gratz. He had already heard of the events at Verona. The envoys were not long in perceiving that his mind was irrevocably made up with regard to Venice, and that he had decided on listening to nothing; but they could not penetrate the exact reason of this inflexibility, for the substance of the preliminaries of Léoben had been kept secret. No terms they could offer could satisfy him; what he wanted was to dictate the law to them, and he held the language of a conqueror. 'I have eighty thousand men and some gunboats. I will have no inquisition and no senate. I will prove an Attila to Venice. . . . I will have no alliance with you. I want none of your proposals. I mean to dictate the law to you. It is of no use trying to deceive me to gain time. The nobles of your provinces, who have hitherto been your slaves, are to have a share in the Government like the others; but your Government is already antiquated and must crumble to pieces.'

These *Je veux*, expressed in so despotic a tone, threatened something more than the mere ruin of the Venetian Republic. And yet, in spite of this imperious will, what dissimulation lay in his words! What would these nobles, whose cause he espoused so warmly, have said, if they could

[1] Botta, *Storia d' Italia*.

have known that he, who affected such indignation at seeing them the slaves of Venice, had already made them subjects of Austria?

The envoys' report of this interview concludes thus: 'We regret that we cannot give you any positive details about the treaty of peace. The secret of the conditions is impenetrable. God grant that this mystery may not hide the division of the states of this Republic!'[1]

But after all, notwithstanding the violence which his words displayed, the General had received and listened to the envoys of the senate; he had not broken with them, and therefore all hope of appeasing him did not appear to be lost. The day after the interview, however, news arrived of the death of Captain Laugier, an event which came so opportunely to furnish an excuse for our aggression, that some have gone so far as to believe it was planned. Bonaparte would listen to nothing more; he wrote to the envoys that he could not receive 'men whose hands were all dripping with French blood.' Then he published at Palma-Nova the manifesto which contained our declaration of war against the Republic of Venice.

The manifesto of Palma-Nova, drawn up with an eye to Europe and the legislative councils at Paris, contained a statement of all the wrongs the General imputed to the Republic. They were developed and classified with a great deal of skill, and presented in the light which suited his policy. Small skirmishes between our troops and the Venetian insurgents were greatly exaggerated; events which had occurred accidentally, or things done in opposition to the wishes of Government, were isolated from all the circumstances which had provoked them, and transformed into a long premeditated conspiracy.

The manifesto of Palma-Nova was immediately followed by a revolt of the whole inland provinces against the capital. The Lion of Saint Mark was pulled down in all the towns, and the Tree of Liberty set up in its stead. Scarcely any resistance was offered to this change, for the provinces felt

[1] The greater part of these reports are to be found in Daru's *Histoire de Venise*, but the history is neither impartial nor exact.

they were threatened by the return of a triumphant and irritated army, and the party whom our presence had encouraged was daily increasing, owing to our secret but active support.

General Bonaparte directed his attack on the lagoons. Intrenched behind this last refuge, which had once been the cradle of its power, the Republic could easily have held out a considerable time against an enemy who, notwithstanding his boast to the envoys, had neither gunboats nor any other means of transport, while Venice possessed ships of every description, and all the entrances were protected by innumerable batteries. The garrison, which amounted to thirteen thousand men, was composed partly of Italians and partly of Sclavonians, but the latter had only that kind of attachment to the Republic which mercenary troops have for the country that pays them.

Notwithstanding this disadvantage, such troops might have become formidable under an able and decided commander. But demoralisation was in every rank, and none of these degenerate nobles had the courage to think of defence against an army which had just conquered the Empire. Those whom dejection had not paralysed gave way to feelings that were not less dangerous. In times of great public peril hope is sometimes even more fatal than fear. The idea of disarming the General by making all the concessions he demanded possessed many credulous minds, for the majority, ever eager to embrace pleasing illusions, were a long way from suspecting the secret plans which Bonaparte concealed under an anger that was all the more difficult to appease as it was calculated. Their blind confidence discouraged the few who were disposed to take energetic measures. The members of the Government met at the doge's palace, and convoked the grand council. This assembly, composed for the most part of old men possessed by the general consternation, and finding in itself nothing better than the inspirations of weakness and senility, decided that two commissioners should be sent to the General, and should come to an understanding with him upon the modifications he wished to see introduced into the constitution of Venice, a surrender of authority which was scarcely concealed by the right they reserved themselves of ratifying Bonaparte's propositions.

The commissioners found Bonaparte at Marghera. As soon as he was informed of the resolution taken by the grand council, he exclaimed, 'that there was no possibility of a treaty, as long as the three inquisitors and the commandant of the Lido had not been given up. The lagoons would not stop him; he should be in Venice in less than a fortnight, and would drive out the Venetian nobles, as the French emigrants had been driven out.' He agreed at last, on their earnest supplication, to an armistice of six days.

On the 4th of May the commissioners appeared before the grand council, and the members yielded on every point. They agreed to the arrests demanded by Bonaparte, authorised their delegates to consent to the modifications in the constitution, and even went beyond what was required of them, by giving, in spite of the despairing protestations of several senators, authority to the commandant of the lagoons to treat for capitulation. Bonaparte had returned to Milan. It was there the commissioners were to meet him, which considerably delayed the negotiations. Meanwhile, the excitement in Venice was on the increase. The resolutions of the grand council had been made known; the Government was annihilated by the arrest of the inquisitors; and these events raised the general agitation, stupefaction, and confusion to its height. A democratic party, till then almost unperceived, but which was being rapidly recruited from all those whom the uncertain state of affairs or private interest had drawn towards France, took their watchword from Villetard, our *chargé d'affaires*, who had succeeded Lallement after the declaration of war. This party hoped, by acceding to all the General's wishes, to enlist his favour for the new organisation which was to take the place of the old Venetian aristocracy. Villetard, following out the instructions he had received in anticipation of this, encouraged them with promises, which were all the more persuasive for being, so far as he was concerned, in perfectly good faith. He became in a few days the centre and chief of the movement, and the programme prepared by him was popular at once, because it was known to be dictated by Bonaparte. The measures which Villetard advised the Venetian democrats to adopt, were the abolition of the aristocratic government and the formation of a municipal one, the discharge of the Sclavonians, the institution of a national guard, and the introduction into Venice of four thousand French. The people eagerly agreed to all, believing that to be their sole means of safety. This was the only party in Venice who had aim or will or definite programme, and though they were looked up to by some as a safeguard, they made others tremble as if they already involved collusion with the enemy. The enthusiasm of the one waxing greater by the fears of others, and the revolt in the midst of the confusion of some Sclavonians, who had been sent back to Dalmatia, giving rise to a fear that massacre and pillage would follow, the grand council met for the last time. Villetard's propositions were accepted even without discussion, and the assembly pronounced its own dissolution in the midst of an indescribable tumult. The council abdicated in favour of a provisional government, subject to the approval of the General-in-Chief, and vowed that they were only acting with a view to assure the safety of the country, of religion, and of property. Such was the last act of this government, which Bonaparte had called 'atrocious, sanguinary, and perfidious,' and which would certainly have prolonged its existence, had it merited any such reproach. History more justly will blame its want of energy, its pusillanimity, and its childish confidence in old diplomatic routine.

The news of this extraordinary resolution produced a reaction among the people in favour of the national Government. They instinctively felt that, however worn out and superannuated these institutions might be, they still represented the independence of the country. Civil war, the last throb of antique pride and expiring patriotism, burst out in Venice for an instant. As soon as this agitation was suppressed, the members of a provisional municipality were named. The Venetian flotilla was then sent to introduce the French garrison into the lagoons, and our soldiers came to take possession of Venice amidst a dull silence, only broken by the unseemly joy of a few scattered groups (16th May 1797).

While these events were taking place at Venice, with that rapidity which accompanies all popular panics, the two commissioners sent by the council to Bonaparte were signing a treaty of peace with the General at Milan, containing stipulations in every point identical with those drawn up and carried out by Villetard. Article I. provided 'that peace and friendship should be established between the Republic of Venice and the French Republic.' The succeeding articles regulated the conditions of this peace; the abdication of the aristocracy, the sovereignty of the people, French occupation until the 'new government was established and should declare that it had no further need of assistance,' and lastly, the trial of the inquisitors and the commandant of the Lido. By secret articles it was stipulated 'that the French Republic and the Republic of Venice should come to an understanding about the exchange of certain territories,' a clause which referred to the indemnity in the Papal states offered to the Venetians in the preliminaries of Léoben. The Republic of Venice also engaged to pay us several millions of francs, to give up three vessels, two frigates, supplies of every kind, and, in accordance with the custom already introduced into Italy, 'the choice of twenty pictures and five hundred manuscripts.'

This treaty was concluded and signed at Milan with the usual formalities by General Bonaparte and our minister, Lallement, on the one side, and the representatives of the Republic of Venice on the other. It was ratified, we shall see presently how, by the provisional government. In spite of the relentless cruelty of this treaty and the glaring abuse of force, of which it was an example, the name and traditions of this great Republic were still preserved; national life was not quite extinguished; the Venetians could still hope that their new institutions would give them fresh vigour, and that by remaining united to Italy they might by their own efforts aid the great revival in which the whole nation seemed summoned to participate, and that this would be the reward for the crushing sacrifices they had been called upon to make. Under the momentary influence of these feelings, the Venetians joyfully accepted a treaty which, bitter as it was, put an end to a long anguish, and at any rate guaranteed them a political existence.

These illusions did not last long. The General, writing to the Directory about this treaty, which had given rise to so many hopes, expresses himself in the following terms: 'I had several motives for concluding the treaty. 1°. To enter the town without any difficulties; to have the arsenal and all else in our possession, in order to take from it whatever we needed, under pretence of the secret articles; 2°. To give us the advantage of all the strength of the Venetian territory, in case the treaty with the emperor should not be executed; 3°. To avoid drawing on ourselves the sort of odium that may attach to the execution of the preliminaries, and at the same time better to furnish pretexts for them, and to facilitate their execution' (May 19th, 1797). He then goes on to announce his intention of annexing Venice 'as a provincial chief town' to the Cispadane Republic, to which he had also just united the same Legations he had promised to the Venetians by way of indemnity.

General Bonaparte's views are still more clearly explained in the instructions he gave to General Baraguay d'Hilliers, commandant of the corps of occupation in Venice, and especially to General Gentili, whom he ordered to go and take possession of the Venetian fleet and the Ionian Isles, till Admiral Brueys could come and occupy them definitely. History must notice with the same care the explanations that he gave the provisional government of the measure. Seeing he could no longer make use of the excuses which heretofore had served his purpose, since the Republic had yielded on every point, he now placed in front his desire to defend Venice against imaginary aggressors.

'You are to start,' he wrote to Gentili, 'as quickly and

as secretly as possible, and take possession of all the Venetian establishments in the Levant. You will take care to act as an ally of the Republic of Venice, and in concert with the commissioners sent by the new Government; and, in short, do everything in your power to win the peoples, on the condition of maintaining ourselves as masters. At Corfu or at sea you will seize, if it be possible, all the Venetian vessels that may still be uncertain which side to take. . . . *If the inhabitants of the country should be inclined for independence, you should flatter their tastes, and should not fail in your proclamations to allude to Greece, Sparta, and Athens'* (May 26th).

These last words, among the most significant that Bonaparte ever wrote, and which shed a light on the inmost depths of his soul, express the sum of all his policy with regard to Italy. In the remainder of his instructions he showed how he meant to interpret the treaty, by which he had just stipulated 'that there should be peace and friendship between the two republics.' This treaty, which he did not even then recognise as valid, was immediately carried into execution, as far as the spoliation of Venice was concerned; the only clauses that were unfulfilled were those which insured protection to the Republic. While they were laying hands on the wealth of Venice, Gentili accomplished his mission with a duplicity worthy of him whom he represented. He arrived before Corfu on the 18th of June, presented himself as an agent of the new Government, and then, once introduced within the fortress, he assumed the tone of a master, took possession of the navy, five hundred guns, and immense magazines.

The same day on which Gentili received his curious instructions, Bonaparte wrote to the municipality of Venice, entreating them to have full confidence in him. The expedition to the Levant had been undertaken merely 'to aid the Venetian commissioners in preventing the enemies of the country and liberty from taking advantage of existing circumstances to seize the islands, and put them under the yoke of a foreign power.' He even got the municipality to send forward some troops; and then, in order to deceive them still more completely, he referred to the treaty which at that very time he was so outrageously violating, and urged them to confirm it by a fresh ratification. These facts prove the value of the argument, made use of by many historians, that the treaty of Milan was not binding on Bonaparte, because it was only ratified by the municipality, and not by the grand council; as if treaties concluded with a nation could be invalidated by changes in the Government, or as if the sudden events which took place in Venice during the signature of the treaty were anything else than the anticipated execution of all its stipulations! 'The treaty,' he said, 'which has been concluded at Milan with the envoys of the grand council, can for the present be ratified by the municipality, and the secret articles by a committee of three members. And,' he added, 'under any circumstances I shall do all in my power to give you proofs of the great desire I have to guarantee you liberty, and to see this unhappy Italy free from all foreign intervention, and triumphantly placed in that rank among the great nations of the world, to which by her nature, position, and destiny she is so justly entitled.'

These last words appealed to noble sentiments which were more common in Venice than any other part of Italy, in spite of the catastrophe in which the Republic had just foundered. They were received with acclamations of joy, for they expressed a kind of personal engagement on the part of the General, which inspired far more confidence than all the declarations of a distant, abstract, and collective being, such as the French Government was. It was a thorough belief in the sincerity of these promises which induced the Venetians to give such a magnificent reception to Madame Bonaparte, whom the General sent to Venice as a sort of second self, in pledge of his hearty friendship. But the proofs of 'his great desire to see liberty consolidated among them' were ill in accordance with these assurances of protection. The fine words directed to the municipality were written May 26th, and the next day, May 27th, at one o'clock in the morning, Bonaparte wrote to the Directory: 'To-day we have had our first interview with

M. de Gallo, on the subject of the treaty of peace, and we have agreed to present the following propositions :—

'1°. The line of the Rhine for France.

'2°. Salzburg, Passau, for the emperor.

'3°. For the king of Prussia, an equivalent to the duchy of Cleves, or the restitution of the said duchy.

'4°. The maintenance of the Germanic body.

'5°. The reciprocal guarantee of the said articles.

'For Italy, 1°. *Venice for the emperor.*'

And, by way of justification of this new arrangement in the eyes of the Directory, who had only consented to the cession of the inland provinces, Bonaparte said :—

'Venice, which has been gradually decaying ever since the discovery of the Cape of Good Hope, and the rise of Trieste and Ancona, can scarcely survive the blows we have just struck. With a cowardly and helpless population, in no way fit for liberty, without territory and without rivers, it is but natural that she should go to those to whom we give the continent.

'*We will seize the vessels, despoil the arsenal, and carry off the guns; we will destroy the bank, and keep Corfu and Ancona for ourselves*' (May 27th, 1797).

Bonaparte's accusations against the Venetians were merely made to justify his own conduct, for in his correspondence at this epoch we find him expressing himself in exactly opposite terms with regard to the Venetians, affirming that they were 'the only people among all the Italians who were *worthy of liberty.*'

Thus, in the space of a few days, that is to say, between the 17th and 27th of May, during which time the Venetians had given him no cause of complaint, under the influence of no pressure, not even from the Austrian negotiators, without any reason to believe that this would be the price of peace, without even trying any other expedient which would have been less oppressive to Venice and less dishonourable to ourselves, this lawless spirit had, after the first conference, leapt over the whole space that separates the preliminaries of Léoben from the treaty of Campo-Formio. He betrayed of his own accord to Austria, without making one effort to save her, this new republic, founded according to his own counsels on the ruins of the Venetian aristocracy, guaranteed by a treaty which he had signed, and to which he added each day fresh assurances of his protection; and, not content with delivering her up, he appropriated to himself the spoils, and would not abandon her until she was ruined and annihilated.[1]

All these changes effected in so short a time by Bonaparte's all-powerful will, all these arts which displayed an unscrupulous and insatiable ambition, met with little serious opposition from the French Government. There had been some disagreement among the members of the Directory about the preliminaries of Léoben. Lareveillère and Rewbell thought Bonaparte might have obtained more advantageous conditions. Quirini, the Venetian ambassador at Paris, had even succeeded in buying the support of the venal Barras in favour of his Republic, and had signed an engagement to pay the sum of six hundred thousand francs, on condition of receiving a written assurance that orders should be sent to Bonaparte to put down the insurrection on the mainland; but the General intercepted their correspondence at Milan, with the list of the sums to be distributed, and after this all opposition ceased, and the preliminaries were ratified without difficulty. Bonaparte

[1] The Correspondence of Napoleon shows that by the 13th of June he had not succeeded in getting possession of the whole of the Venetian navy, and thought more falsehood necessary. The following were the instructions given by him to Perrée:—

'... You and General Baraguay d'Hilliers must go with our minister to the provisional government of Venice, and say that the conformity of principles which exists between the French Republic and the Republic of Venice demands that they should immediately put their naval forces on a respectable footing, in order that we may in concert be kept masters of the Adriatic and the Isles of the Levant, and to protect the commerce of the two republics, and that I have already despatched some troops *to enable the Venetian Government to keep possession of Corfu.*

'*Seize everything under this pretext; but take care to call it always the Venetian navy, and constantly have on your lips the unity of the two republics.*

'... My intention is to get possession of all the Venetian vessels and all possible supplies, to send to Toulon for the use of the Republic.'

still continued to act on his own responsibility, only consulting the Directory on affairs which had already been decided, or were so far gone that to retract would be impossible, following no other rule than his own inspirations, and presenting the unparalleled spectacle in history of a general who disclosed his most Machiavellian ideas to the very Government whose rights he was usurping, and on whom he was imposing all his own plans. The Directory yielded passive submission to this ascendency, which was daily becoming more absolute, without stopping to ask what place they would have to yield by and by to a man accustomed to exercise such authority ; or rather they avoided all reflection on the subject, in order to relieve themselves of the necessity of taking those energetic measures which might possibly have prevented the mischief.

General Bonaparte had taken up his residence at the Château de Montebello, or Mombello, a magnificent residence near Milan, and had assembled a complete court around him. Deputies from all the towns, and representatives from all the Italian powers, waited on him here, to learn from him their future destiny. In this *cortège* figured, not only his own generals, but several from the other armies of the Republic, drawn thither by the admiration and curiosity which his exploits had inspired ; and by their side were savans, men of letters, and artists, all of whom he captivated by those courteous attentions which were one day to be so useful for his reputation. Besides the envoys of the emperor of Austria, there were ministers from all the secondary princes of Germany, who foresaw that his will would be an immense force in the settlement of peace with the German Confederation. Madame Bonaparte, who had arrived from Paris, accompanied by several members of her family, softened by her gentleness and kindness what was rough and imperious in the manners of the General, and drew to the splendid *fêtes* over which she presided ladies of the highest rank in Italy. During his meals, which he took in public, like a sovereign of the ancient *régime*, the inhabitants of the surrounding country, eager to behold the features of the conqueror, were brought into the dining-hall, and he received this primitive homage with all the gravity of a man accustomed to it from childhood.[1] His power was at once more extensive and more real than that of any sovereign in Europe. He alone, in all the world, possessed at that time the privilege of making and destroying kingdoms at his will, distributing nations, modifying territories, and creating new states. Creating! that attribute of the gods, the most seductive and the most flattering form of power! And he exercised this authority after the manner of a military chief, this is to say, as an absolute master. Everything ended in him, as at the only true centre of affairs.

While he was negotiating for peace with the plenipotentiaries of the emperor, he completed the organisation of the two republics, which he considered as his own particular work, and he was already planning their union into one, notwithstanding all the obstacles which local traditions presented. The Cisalpine, comprising Lombardy, the districts of Bergamo and of Modena, did not appear to him strong enough to stand alone. Its union with the Cispadane, that is to say, with Bologna, Ferrara, the Romagna, and Treviso, would form a nucleus of four million souls, constituting, he thought, a centre of attraction for the rest of Italy. He insensibly urged the two republics towards union, preparing them for this result by giving them identical institutions, modelled on the constitution of the Year III, and by exciting, after his own fashion, the patriotism of the two populations. He flattered himself that he should thus create in the heart of Italy a powerful and vigorous republic, which should go on developing as the ancient states fell into dissolution. Such an idea shows how singularly ignorant Bonaparte was of all that constitutes the strength and vitality of free nations; for while he expected the Italians to realise a work which it implied the highest intellectual and moral energy to achieve, he treated them with a contempt they would never have borne for an instant, if they had possessed even the bare idea of qualities

---

[1] *Mémoires* of Miot de Melito, of Marmont, of Lavalette, of Bourrienne, etc.

which he assumed in them. The men, whom he now called upon to accomplish the difficult task of founding their liberty, were the same who had for so many years borne the yoke of foreign invasion without a complaint, the same whom we had trodden under foot, spoiled and degraded by our tyrannical exactions; and, at the very moment while he proclaimed their independence, he expected his slightest wish to be regarded as law, required the most servile obedience, and would unhesitatingly have followed the example of Charles XII., who threatened the Swedish parliament to send one of his boots to represent a president. Such were the future citizens of this republic, to the formation of which all his plans had for a whole year been made subordinate.

This delusion, which was perhaps more feigned than real, was in some measure caused by the increasing weakness of the few remaining ancient states of Italy. The king of Sardinia, disarmed and almost powerless since the treaty of peace with France, was tottering on his throne, ready to fall on the first outbreak, and the strength of the party which our influence had created in his states was increasing in proportion as the monarchy grew feebler. At Rome, Pius VI. was almost dying, and General Bonaparte had already consulted the Directory about allowing his successor to be elected. At Florence, the grand duke of Tuscany was only a harmless shadow. At Genoa, everything was ripe for a revolution owing to our frequent intercourse with that republic, and the considerable number of French who resided there. General Bonaparte foresaw the coming revolution with so much the more clearness, from having tried to effect it for some time, notwithstanding the recent treaty he had concluded with the Republic of Genoa. He wanted Genoa to accept a constitution similar to that of the Cisalpine, in order to interest her in the defence of his work. 'Genoa cries loud for democratic rule,' he wrote to the Directory, May 19th; 'it is very possible that within ten or twelve days the Genoese aristocracy may share the same fate as the nobles of Venice.'

The meaning of this assertion, 'that Genoa demanded

democratic rule,' was simply that the General had resolved on the change, and thought well to prepare the Directory for what was to follow.

His prediction was sure of fulfilment, because he had determined that events should take such a course, and nothing could protect Genoa against this decision. She must, in her turn, receive the reward of her neutrality. Bonaparte was not wrong in comparing the fate of this republic (for her fall dates from the day on which she lost her independence) to that of Venice; he dealt with both alike, and the additional rigour he displayed towards Venice was due to circumstances which urged him on to dispose of her territory.

Faypoult, our minister at Genoa, was the leader in this revolution, just as Lallement and Villetard had been the instigators of the insurrection in Venice. Faypoult, like the other two ministers, found a small minority of discontented men, incapable of doing anything by themselves, but strong enough to stir up confusion and give a pretext for Bonaparte's interference. About the middle of May, Faypoult thought the time for action had arrived, and had written to the General-in-Chief to say so. 'I think with you,' replied Bonaparte, 'that the fall of Venice is a death-blow to the Genoese aristocracy, but we still need *a fortnight longer*, till things at Venice are completely settled' (Letter of May 15th). The insurrection occurred rather sooner. The democratic club, composed partly of Frenchmen, and under the secret direction of Faypoult, sent to the doge, requiring him at once to declare the forfeiture of the nobles, and upon his refusal to comply with their request, they seized by a *coup-de-main* on the arsenal and port.

Their triumph was short. The whole population rose against the clubbists, drove them from all the posts they occupied, killed a certain number, threw the rest into prison, and pillaged their houses. Faypoult tried in vain to interpose his authority, to quiet the storm he had himself raised. Intimidated by the unexpected resistance his designs had met with, he had not even the courage to play his part to the end; he got confused, lost his head, and refused the assistance which Admiral Brueys offered him. The French, who had taken part in the insurrection, naturally shared the fate of the insurgent Genoese, and were imprisoned with them. Assured beforehand of General Bonaparte's support, and certain of success, the chiefs of the insurrection showed a great want of tact, and by their insolence and rashness made enemies even of those who, under other circumstances, would have remained neutral. Bonaparte made no secret with the Directory of the faults and folly of his allies. 'The so-called patriotic party had,' he wrote, 'behaved extremely ill, and by their folly and imprudence had done good to the aristocrats' (May 25th). But while he blamed them, he did not hesitate to turn to good account what they had done under his inspection. He sent his aide-de-camp, Lavalette, to Genoa with a message, which was a second edition of the letter that Junot had presented to the doge of Venice.

Lavalette had orders to deliver the letter to the doge while the senate was sitting, an unprecedented proceeding, and showing a contempt for forms that was calculated to show that the General's authority was as much above custom as it was independent of law. Lavalette replied to those who objected to his entrance, in the same imperious and peremptory tone which the envoys of the old Roman Republic used to assume. He presented himself before the senate, and, without paying any attention to the indignation and excitement which his presence called forth, he began reading his General's letter with the utmost coolness. Bonaparte declared, 'that he only interfered to protect the lives and property of his countrymen, and to secure his own communications. He required the immediate liberation of the French who had been arrested, the disarming of the people, and the arrest of all enemies of France. If these measures were not executed in twenty-four hours, the Genoese oligarchy was doomed; the heads of the senators would answer for the safety of the French, as the whole states of the Republic would answer for their property.'

In this harsh letter Bonaparte seems to exact nothing with reference to the change in institutions, of which there had been a question in Genoa. He purposely held himself aloof from the chiefs of the unsuccessful revolution, no doubt to prove that he had nothing to do with the scheme. He protested against any intention to interfere with the affairs of the Republic; but he did not mean to be taken literally on this point, for it is certain he only abstained from acting himself in the belief that events would turn out as he wished. He was mistaken, however. The senators, though at first irritated by the imperious tone of the letter, soon grew calm, and hastened to acquiesce in all the demands of the General. But when Faypoult, now recovered from his alarm, wished them to accept his democratic constitution, it was impossible to overcome their resistance. It was not till our minister threatened to leave the town that the magistrates, convinced by his resolute conduct of the influence of some stronger will than his own, consented to send three deputies to General Bonaparte to ascertain the value of his promises of respect for the institutions of the Republic. The envoys had an interview with Bonaparte at Montebello, and at once perceived that not only did the General intend to change the existing order of things, but that a new constitution was already drawn up and completed. After fruitless attempts to make him relent, they gave way, having no other choice but submission, and Genoa received the law, as her ancient rival had already done with conditions a thousand times more cruel.

Negotiations for the peace with Austria were being carried on at Montebello, but as the envoys of the emperor were anxious for delay, privately hoping in the meantime to gain something from the dissensions in the French Government, little progress was made. This tardiness among the diplomatists greatly annoyed Bonaparte, whose active and restless disposition began to crave for more excitement than the leisure of a truce afforded him. He had soon exhausted the interest which his office of legislator offered him, an office which he greatly simplified by his peculiarly military method of deciding all difficulties. To try and discover what kind of institutions would be most in accordance with the historical traditions and national spirit of the Italians, and most likely to effect their regeneration, was a task worthy of the greatest genius; but Bonaparte regarded politics not as a means of raising the people, but simply as an instrument of domination: he conducted politics like war, and, even if he had tried to cope with the difficulties in Italy, his intelligence, marvellous as it was in many respects, had neither the maturity nor the experience necessary to success. This great object once put aside, the trifling differences between the king of Sardinia and his subjects, or between the Valteline and the Grisons, were not fit to assuage the thirst that consumed this insatiable soul. With his head already full of new projects, he lived with his eyes fixed on Paris, where grave events were obviously at hand. Like every one else, he clearly foresaw that power was about to pass into new hands, and he was anxious to foresee what the change would be, and to mark his own position beforehand. Speaking to Miot, he repeated what he had once before said to Prince Pignatelli: 'Do you think that it is for the benefit of the lawyers in the Directory, the Carnots and Barras, that I triumph in Italy?' But recognising, according to his own expression, *that the pear was not yet ripe* for him in Paris, and being accustomed to look upon peace and war with a view to his own fortunes, he felt half inclined to renounce war with Austria, in order to earn augmented glory and popularity; 'for he would only leave Italy,' he said, 'to go and play a similar part in France;' a remark which contains a striking commentary on the earnest desire, so often expressed in his letters to the Directory, to live in retirement. Judging events merely with regard to the facilities and advantages they offered for his own advancement, he was never embarrassed either by considerations of conscience or by any previous determination; he never lost his time in deliberating on the moral bearing of things, a fetter often so troublesome to those who submit themselves to it; nor did he ever consider himself pledged to any one course, while the most opposite resolutions often presented themselves to his mind with equal force and weight.

Before coming to a decision he liked to try the different chances which the situation offered, and after examining each in all its bearings, then he pronounced for that which appeared most advantageous to his own interests.

Thus, for example, at the same time that he was raising his arm as if to annihilate the papacy, and keeping alive against it the democratic conspiracy that stirred the States of the Church, he wrote privately to the Pope (August 3d, 1797), urging the Holy Father to assist in reconciling the clergy to the Government, which would have the double effect of strengthening the established Government and winning back the majority of the French people to the true Church. France would thus become the ally of the Holy See, and the union would be of infinite benefit to the two states. Bonaparte does not say that it would be a benefit especially to him who proposed it.

While this first sketch of the Concordat was occupying his thoughts, other leanings and other projects, which gained a still more powerful hold on his imagination, began to reveal even then the infirmity of that immoderate spirit, which afterwards dreamt of building an indestructible edifice, when it was only assembling the materials of a gigantic ruin. The seizure of the Ionian Isles had opened up to him fresh perspectives of that magic East which he had seen in his youthful dreams, and to which he was never weary of returning. It had brought him into relations with some men of influence in provinces of the Turkish empire; and, as he never looked upon one conquest but as a means of acquiring another and a greater, from Corfu his imagination flew to Constantinople. He drew the attention of the Directory to the decrepit state of the Ottoman empire, and, compared with this magnificent booty, Italy seemed to him but a mean and narrow theatre. "The islands of Corfu, Zante, and Cephalonia are more interesting to us than the whole of Italy. If we were called upon to make a choice, it would be far better for us to restore Italy to the emperor, and keep the four islands for ourselves' (August 16th, to the Directory). From this fortified position Turkey could be protected or a portion of it taken, and England could be reached across Turkey. But, before this could be done, it was necessary first to lay hands on Egypt. *Deinde Egyptum*, as King Pyrrhus said to his confidant. 'The time is not far distant when we shall feel, that in order to destroy England we must make Egypt ours.'

The blind docility with which the Directory submitted to the decisions of the General, as if its business was simply to register the decrees of his sovereign will, was not, however, to the taste of everybody at Paris. In spite of the efforts of the Government to throw doubt and obscurity over the events which had just taken place at Venice and Genoa, they appeared presently in their true light, and roused the reprobation of all those who retained any love for liberty. Unfortunately, the bitter strife in which all parties were engaged in Paris prevented men from attaching to these events all the attention they deserved. The iniquity of what had been done struck clear-sighted observers, but they acquiesced with selfish indifference. Very few understood that the fall of these two republics threatened their own with danger, while the greater number regarded all blame on what had occurred as nothing but a manœuvre of party spirit.

On the 23d of June, Dumolard, a man who, without possessing great strength of understanding or character, still showed to the end of his career that he was actuated by generous sentiments and a sincere love of liberty, ascended the tribune of the Five Hundred, to interrogate the Directory on the affairs of Italy. Whatever may be said to the contrary, his language was extremely moderate. Not only had Dumolard no personal dislike to Bonaparte, but he had frequently spoken of him with admiration, and quite recently, at the time of the insurrection of Verona, had publicly praised his energetic measures. He wished neither to accuse nor to blame the General; he addressed the Directory, and asked of them above all accurate information.

How was it that France was at war with Venice before the Directory had consulted the Legislative Body, as the constitution required? By what authority had they dispensed with the formality of submitting to the Assembly the declaration of war? Then, coming to the acts which had followed our entrance into Venice, he said: 'Are we, then, no longer the same people who proclaimed in principle and sustained by force of arms, that under no pretence whatever ought foreign powers to interfere with the form of government of another state? Does the fact that the Venetians had insulted us give us a right to attack their institutions? Even as victors or as claimants, was it our business to take an active part in their apparently unexpected revolution? *I will not ask what is the fate reserved for Venice, especially for her inland provinces. I will not examine whether their invasion, meditated perhaps before the commission of the offences which are assigned as motives, will not figure in history as a fit pendant to the partition of Poland.*'

This speech shows how far Dumolard was from knowing the whole truth, since he scarcely ventures to mention his suspicions of facts which have since become the property of history a thousand times over. He then passed on to the revolution of Genoa, and stigmatised the grievous madness of pretending to liberate nations by beginning with the destruction of their independence. The only result of such a policy would be endless wars, and France wanted peace. At last, coming to the object of his speech, and the distrust with which the Directory treated the Councils, 'Every one,' he said, 'who reflects on the nature of our government is indignant when he thinks of the blind and silent confidence required of us in everything connected with peace or war. In England, where the constitution only gives the two Houses an indirect participation in foreign affairs, we see them demand and obtain communications on all events of importance, while we, republicans, to whom has been delegated the sovereign right of making peace or war, allow our rulers to draw the veil more and more closely over a dark and obscure policy!'

This speech contains a just and striking criticism on the constitution of the Year III, which, by dint of insisting on a complete separation of the legislative and executive powers, in order to prevent conflict, had deprived the former of all influence over the proceedings of the Government, and even of any control over its acts, though such control is a necessary condition for every free government. Dumolard concluded by demanding an exact and precise account of the facts connected with our intervention at Genoa, at Venice, and in the Valteline.

The friends of the Directory only answered by vague shifts. Doulcet Pontécoulant, who had been Bonaparte's protector, supported Dumolard's resolution. He pointed out the mischief to the Legislative Body of only receiving information on the affairs of the Republic through the medium of journals more or less worthy of belief, and of never knowing for a certainty whether we were at peace or war. He especially brought out with startling evidence how contradictory was the assertion that both Venice and Genoa had first declared war, or had at least given the signal for hostilities, as people dared to say. 'What!' he exclaimed, 'when the coalition threatened us, and held out against our soldiers, Venice and Genoa were neutral, and at the moment that vanquished Austria is asking for peace, Venice wished for war, and Genoa betrayed her plainest interests? Our faithful allies, the Swiss Cantons, wished to break the bonds of an ancient friendship? It is on, such events, so difficult to conceive, that we ask information of the Directory.'

Dumolard's proposition was referred to a commission charged to draw up a report on the rights of the Legislative Body with regard to foreign affairs. The Directory paid no attention to it. Such was the celebrated motion which it has been so long a matter of tradition to stigmatise as 'audacity and arrogance.' These wise and clear-sighted counsels fell unheeded in the midst of the fatal dissensions which were then rending the country, but they deserved a better fate, and will be more fully appreciated as we proceed. The two ends proposed, namely to put an end to the abuses which were disgracing our occupation of Italy, and to restore to the Legislative Body the control of our foreign policy, were not only legitimate but most urgently necessary.

And if the warnings already received had not been sufficient, the effect which Dumolard's motion produced on Bonaparte ought to have been enough to dissipate all illusion.

The news reached him at his court of Montebello, where he was reigning as absolute sovereign, and exercising that uncontrolled power which was so attractive to him. Insensible to the marked consideration of which his glory had been the object, he resented the criticism on his acts as an atrocious outrage. What! an obscure representative, one of those lawyers of whom he had spoken with so much contempt, had dared to discuss him, the chief of an army of eighty thousand men, the sovereign of so many nations, the distributor of states, the arbiter of princes! A member had dared to do this, and had done it amidst the applause of a majority in the Assembly! He had dared to raise doubts about the sincerity of the declarations, which had been the text of the manifesto against Venice, and the ground of our intervention; he had presumed to suspect a preconceived plan, to divine the ulterior projects which Bonaparte had explained to the Directory, but which he believed to be impenetrable! He wrote immediately to the Directory (letter, 30th June), in a fit of irritation, which for once was not feigned, and which plainly showed what might be expected of him if ever the vicissitudes of the Republic threw power into his hands. 'Although he had a right, after having concluded five treaties of peace and given the last blow to the coalition, to expect, if not civic honours, at least to be allowed to live tranquilly, he saw himself denounced, persecuted, and decried by every possible means. He might be indifferent to most things, but he could not be so to the kind of opprobrium with which the first magistrates of the Republic sought to cover him. . . . He should not have expected that this manifesto, *got up by an emigrant in the pay of England*, would have obtained more credit in the council of the Five Hundred than his own testimony and that of eighty thousand soldiers.' With this letter he sent a stiletto, similar to those used by the assassins of Verona, a melodramatic expedient which had no connection with the point at issue, but which he thought likely to work on the imaginations of the Parisians. He concluded by again offering his resignation, a proposal which was not at all seriously meant, and by declaring his intention of living tranquilly, if, he said, 'the *poniards of Clichy* will allow me to live at all.'

This expression, '*the poniards of Clichy,*' was an allusion to an association, partly composed of members of the opposition, who held their meetings at Clichy, and in which Dumolard, thus strangely transformed into a Catiline, had first announced his intention of interrogating the Directory. Between this resolution and that of poniarding General Bonaparte there was some difference. The General wrote several letters after this, designed to represent the affairs of Italy in the light which suited his own purpose. It is enough to say, in order to show the historical value of these letters, that they contain the assertion that he only entered Venice on the supplication of the deputies, 'moved by compassion, in order to hinder carnage, and to save the town of Venice from devastation, murder, and pillage.' The letters abound in threats against the members of the Club of Clichy, whom he apostrophised in the following terms: 'But I give you notice, and I speak in the name of eighty thousand soldiers, that the time when cowardly lawyers and miserable babblers guillotined soldiers is past; and if you compel them, the soldiers of Italy will come to the barrier of Clichy with their General at their head, but woe betide you if they do come!'

And Bonaparte was not a man to be satisfied with recriminations in phrases merely. He immediately began to meditate active opposition to the party in whom he discovered an obstacle to this ambition. It would be wrong, however, to believe that he was actuated by this grievance alone. Together with the men, who sincerely desired a return to legal forms and guarantees of liberty, Bonaparte with his piercing eye had discovered a group of royalist leaders, who saw in the honest efforts of this party a means of retarding the Revolution and bringing back the Bourbons. Though perfectly indifferent to all political ideas, his ambition had already gained strength enough to make him look upon the return of the Bourbons as incompatible with the realisation of the future of which he was now dreaming for himself. His antipathy to the constitutional party was almost equally deep, for its triumph would consolidate free institutions and render a military dictatorship impossible. As for the members of the Directory, the General despised and hated them profoundly; but he had them in his power, and imposed a yoke on them that no other government would have submitted to. He felt that public opinion already placed him far above them, and that sooner or later he should be called upon to succeed them. But, that he might reap the fruits of this inheritance, the Directory had to be maintained. However wrong they were in the dispute, which was daily waxing hotter between the majority of the directors and the Legislative Body, Bonaparte had long determined to side with the Government against the Legislature, unless the victorious party should offer him an important place in the new distribution of power; and he could have no illusions about this, after the manner in which they had attacked his conduct as conqueror and dictator in Italy. The opposition, which blamed at Paris the excess of power usurped by the Directory, could not, without stultifying themselves, countenance the infinitely more glaring abuses of the General's authority in Italy. His interest and his feelings, then, both led him to espouse the cause of the Directory.

The directors, on their side, after the triumph which their adversaries had just gained in the elections for the partial renewal of the Legislative Body, could not be blind to the fact that the nation was against them, and the mere thought of doing violence to the national sovereignty, by which they had been chosen, and to which in theory they rendered such magnificent homage, was a genuine crime on the part of the Directory. Their only safety lay in legality; that offered them ample protection, for the constitution of the Year III had made a kind of fortified position of the executive power; it was a position, in fact, too strongly fortified, for it had been strengthened at the expense of legislative influence. That position was very easy to defend, and would have afforded an ample safeguard; but, unfortunately, they only regarded it as an offensive arm against their adversaries, and in proportion as they appreciated the extent of the ground lost in the elections, they began to accustom themselves to the idea of a *coup-d'état*, assured as they were of the support of the armies. In their determination, however adventurous it was, there was more fear than daring. The directors were convinced that the triumph of the constitutional party would infallibly lead to a Royalist restoration, and, as Treilhard said to Mathieu Dumas, *their heads were at stake*.[1]

Of what, after all, was this party composed, who were preparing thus intrepidly to dispose of France, as if the country had been their own patrimony? It could not even count on the whole of the Directory, for, admitting that they might reckon on the not very reassuring adherence of the venal Barras, and the more sure support of Rewbell, and of that bombastic rhetorician who was the pope of theophilanthropy, there was against them the probity of Carnot, a convert to the procedure of legal government, as well as the enlightened moderation of Barthélemy. Everywhere else, in the councils, in public opinion, in the popular suffrage, throughout the entire nation, this party was in a minority. The greater part of the measures which the Legislative Body had passed in opposition to it, the liberty of public worship, now become a reality, the modification of the laws against emigrants, the repeal of the law against the nonjuring clergy, and the partial recovery of that just influence, which in all free countries belongs to the assemblies, over the administration of the finances, over the declaration of peace and war, and over all the acts of the executive power, bore the unmistakable mark of wisdom and legality. That violent passions, imprudent perorations, and untimely urgency, had been mixed with these claims, is what we have no right to wonder at, after all the storm and turmoil of the revolution. The party who opposed the Directory had none the less for this the immense majority of the nation on their side,

[1] *Souvenirs de Mathieu Dumas.*

were none the less sincerely constitutional, and the directors could not even with justice reproach them with the two or three royalist conspirators whom they unconsciously sheltered among them; for if the leader of the Club of Clichy and the constitutional circle had behind them Pichegru and Imbert Colomès, the three directors had behind them all the surviving partisans of the reign of terror, who, after having failed recently in the senseless attempt of Babeuf, as well as in all their former conspiracies, rallied round Barras, and were ready to forgive him anything, if he would only consent to lead them to the battle.

The Directory, finding its position more and more isolated, and forced to give up its policy of see-saw, which had led it to strike alternately enemies of every colour, was naturally thrown back for support on the army, in alliance with revolutionary passions. The soldiers were in general disposed to side with them. Indifferent to liberty, or rather ignorant of the very meaning of the word, they dreaded above everything a restoration of the ancient *régime*. They only saw in the constitutionalists instruments of the Bourbons, and the Bourbons themselves were especially odious to the army, because their return would necessarily compromise all the conquests of this military democracy. The younger officers, who were certain that merit would insure their promotion, generals of five-and-twenty, to whom the Republic had trusted the finest armies in Europe, were unwilling to resign their command in favour of emigrants, whom the Bourbons would bring back with them; a feeling that was thoroughly legitimate, but warped by the solidarity it established between the plots of a few traitors and a movement of public opinion full of generosity, which, if it had gone on to its end, would have definitively established free institutions in France.

None of these circumstances escaped the penetrating eye of Bonaparte, and he quickly saw what advantage he could take of the temper of the Directory. He resolved to envelop the constitutional opposition, including those whom he considered as his personal enemies, in the fate of conspirators, hitherto only suspected though not convicted.

A circumstance happened which singularly aided his plan. When he sent a corps to occupy Venice, he gave orders for the immediate arrest of the English consul, and one of the most active agents of the emigrants, Count d'Antraigues. Some papers were seized on D'Antraigues, which proved the existence of relations between Pichegru and the Prince of Condé. Instead of treating D'Antraigues with the rigour which the laws against the emigrants warranted, Bonaparte showed great leniency; he had frequent interviews with the count, and made himself acquainted with all the secret plans of the royalist conspiracy. Owing to this incident, he was able to place in the hands of the Directory the formidable weapon which it might use to strike its enemies. This was not enough for him; he wanted to give the directors an unequivocal pledge, a striking proof of his determination to act with them, and, in case of need, to urge them forward. By exciting manifestations in the army in favour of the policy of the directors, he knew he should redouble their boldness, and at the same time spread dismay among their adversaries. There was a law, it is true, which forbade such deliberations among the soldiers, but General Bonaparte was above laws, as he had abundantly proved. Taking advantage of the anniversary of the 14th of July to issue a proclamation to his soldiers, he thus addressed them: 'Soldiers! I know you are deeply stirred by the dangers which threaten the country, but the country can have no real dangers to face. The same men who made France triumph over united Europe still live. Mountains separate us from France; you would cross them with the speed of the eagle, if it were necessary, to uphold the constitution, defend liberty, protect the Government and the republicans. Soldiers! the Government watches over the laws as a sacred deposit committed to them. The royalists, the moment they show themselves, will perish. Banish disquiet. Let us swear by the shades of the heroes who have died by our sides for liberty; let us swear on our new standards: "War implacable against the enemies of the Republic and of the constitution of the Year III."'

The *fête* was followed by a banquet, at which numerous

toasts were proposed in the midst of an increasing exaltation. They drank to the Directory and the annihilation of their enemies, to the *re-emigration* of the emigrants, to the establishment of liberty by the soldiers, and the destruction of the Clichy Club. The officers and soldiers of each division then signed addresses, in which the same sentiments were reproduced in terms of unexampled violence. The soldiers of the Italian army, recruited from the population of the south, seasoned the phraseology of terrorism with the emphasis of their natural language. Foreigners to France, so to say, since the siege of Toulon, they had in some measure retained the revolutionary excitement of the crisis, and understood nothing of the political movement which had taken place since then. Augereau's division was especially remarked for the menacing tone of its language. Augereau, whose impetuous courage was incontestable, had the language, the opinions, and the leanings of a club leader. Bernadotte's division, on the other hand, which had come from the army of the Rhine, was remarked for the moderation and decency of their language, indicating a superiority of intelligence and bearing which made them hated in the army and involved them in frequent duels.

In forwarding these addresses to the Directory, Bonaparte devoted himself energetically to secure the advantage he hoped to derive from them. A fortnight had passed since he had first read Dumolard's motion, but his irritation had become sharper in the interval, or at any rate he thought fit to feign it more violently than before, if we may judge from the barely credible exaggeration of his complaints. He begins with the journalists, who had commented on the speeches made in the Five Hundred.

'The soldiers receive a great number of the Paris journals, especially those of the worst kind, but they produce an effect totally contrary to what is intended.' But if such was the case, why had he written the previous night to Berthier, enjoining him to stop all the papers which displeased him?

'Indignation is at its height in the army,' he wrote.

'The soldiers are asking whether the fatigues they have undergone, and a six years' war, are to be rewarded by assassination on their return to their homes; for this, it appears, is what patriots are to expect. The peril is increasing every day, and I believe, citizen directors, that it behoves you to decide on your course of action. . . .'

He then returned to Dumolard's motion. 'As regards myself, I am accustomed to a total disregard of my personal interests; nevertheless, I cannot but feel the *perfidy and the mass of calumnies* contained in the motion which has been printed by order of the Council of Five Hundred. I see that the Clichy Club is resolved to pass over my corpse to the destruction of the Republic. Are there no republicans left in France? After having conquered Europe, shall we be driven to some obscure corner of the earth there to end our days?'

Then, changing from complaint to advice, he proceeded to indicate the measures which, in his opinion, the Directory ought to take :—

'You can with a single blow save the Republic, and the two hundred thousand lives that are perhaps bound up with its fate, and conclude peace in twenty-four hours. Arrest the emigrants, destroy the influence of foreigners. *If force is required, recall the armies ; break up the printing-presses of all those papers which are sold to England*, and which are more sanguinary than ever Marat was.'

He concluded by again offering his resignation, and sent the Directory a second stiletto, taken from the insurgents of Verona (July 15th, 1797).

Two days later, he again proposed to the Directory this simple and expeditious means of extricating themselves from the difficulties in which they were involved, and added, in support of his counsel, that a rupture with Austria was imminent, on account of the hopes which our intestine discord gave the emperor.

'It is evident that the court of Vienna is not acting in good faith, and that it is procrastinating, in order to wait for the decision of the crisis in France, which all Europe believes to be close at hand.

'Will you not spare the lives of fifty thousand men, the flower of the nation, who would perish in this new campaign? *Break up the press of the* Thé, *the* Mémorial, *and the* Quotidienne, shut up the Clichy Club, and establish five or six good constitutional journals.

'Such a crisis, which will in truth be extremely light, will be enough to show the foreigner that he has nothing to hope. It would calm the minds of the public, and relieve the soldiers of the inquietude which is fast spreading in the army, and will end in explosions of which it is impossible to foresee the consequences.'

In subsequent letters he again referred to this subject. The Directory had already come to a decision, and had chosen for the agent of their *coup-d'état* General Hoche, whose life till then had been one of untarnished civic purity, and whose name was intended to ease the anxiety of all those who were afraid of seeing the enterprise degenerate into a military dictatorship. Hoche was a warm and sincere republican, but, like the greater part of his companions in arms, his judgment was on this occasion blinded by his abhorrence of royalist intrigues. He saw nothing in the movement, which was gradually spreading over the whole of France, but Pichegru, one of its principal leaders— Pichegru, whom he justly looked upon as a traitor to his country, and who was also his personal enemy. Hoche came to Paris, had an interview with Barras, and concerted with him the details of the *coup-d'état*. But as Article 69 of the Constitution forbade any military corps to come within a radius of fifteen leagues of the building in which the Legislative Assembly were sitting, there was great difficulty in having soldiers close at hand. It was agreed, therefore, that Hoche, under pretext of sending on a portion of his army towards the coast, for an expedition into Ireland, should concentrate his troops round Paris, and place them within reach of the Directory. In order to facilitate these operations, he was made Minister of War.

But Hoche soon learned to his cost for what kind of men he was about to risk his life and reputation. The movement agreed upon was effected by his troops (July

8th), but by some misunderstanding or imprudence one of the detachments crossed the constitutional limit. The councils, already made alive to the projects of the Directory, by their very transparent threats and by measures which they took very little trouble to dissemble, denounced the march of the troops upon Paris, and appealed to the violated constitution. To the questions put to Carnot by the Legislative Body he replied that the general had acted without orders, which was, as far as he knew, the truth, though Barras had made Hoche believe that he was acting in concert with all his colleagues. The young general was summoned before the Directory, and most bitterly reproached by Carnot. Barras was present, but not daring to set his colleague at defiance by acknowledging the order he had given, he kept silence. Hoche might easily have cleared himself by implicating Barras, but he kept the secret. He was, however, deeply wounded, and left Paris to rejoin his army a few days later (July 26th), after having sent in his resignation as Minister of War, a post which he could not retain, being under the age, thirty years, required by the constitution for a minister.

The alarm having thus been given peremptorily, and Hoche being discontented and compromised, the *coup-d'état* was put off for a time, and the three directors resolved to apply to the man who had so warmly encouraged them in their undertaking, and who had procured the powerful adhesion of the army of Italy. Bonaparte had some time before sent to Paris his aide-de-camp, Lavalette, a moderate, judicious, and clear-headed man, to observe what was going on, and to act as a medium between himself and Barras and Carnot. 'See every one,' he had said to him; 'keep clear of party spirit, give me the truth, and give it me free of all passion.' A little later, he charged him to offer Barras three millions of francs, to facilitate the execution of the *coup-d'état*, a proposition which Barras closed with eagerly. Barras wrote several times to Bonaparte, to remind him of his promise, which had probably some influence in the decision of the Directory, though it was not fulfilled till after the 18th Fructidor.

Lavalette obeyed his instructions, and saw men of all parties. To a mind so just and enlightened as Lavalette's, a few interviews with Barras were sufficient to convince him of all that was mischievous in the plot of the triumvirs. He wrote to his general in this sense; he warned him 'that he would tarnish his reputation if he gave his support to measures of such unjust violence, which the position of the Government in no way justified; that he would not be forgiven for uniting with the Directory to overthrow the constitution and liberty; that the proscriptions proposed were directed against the national representation and against citizens of tried virtue, who were to be punished without trial; that the odium of such tyranny would fall not only on the Directory, but upon the whole system of republican government; and that, in short, there was no adequate proof that the party whom they were going to proscribe intended the return of the Bourbons.'[1]

These warnings, together with a more attentive examination of the situation of France, convinced Bonaparte that the victory of the directors, even if they should be triumphant, would be inevitably followed by a reaction; and, without taking any steps to hinder a fatal struggle in the Republic, and which he thought must profit his own interests, he withdrew by degrees from the affair, not to be found implicated in it. He sent General Augereau to the Directory, as the fittest man to execute a *coup-de-main*, and to draw the directors on into that demagogic path, where it was to his interest that they should incur disgrace and lose all consideration; but at the same time he wrote to Lavalette: 'Don't trust Augereau; he is a seditious man.' He recommended his aide-de-camp to treat all parties with consideration, to feel his way, and especially to curry favour with Carnot, who, hitherto his constant protector, was now becoming suspicious of him. He ceased to write to Barras, and said nothing more to the Directory of the *coup-d'état;* his communications with them became more and more rare, and soon came to an end altogether.

General Bonaparte had now two agents in Paris:

[1] *Mémoires de Lavalette.*

Augereau, who said publicly, '*I am sent to kill the royalists*' (Letter from Lavalette to Bonaparte, August 8th, 1797), and Lavalette, a man of moderate opinions and amiable manners, who was himself an ancient royalist, and who was openly connected with all the chiefs of the Council's party. Both sent him frequent accounts of the state of affairs. Augereau had received the command of the 17th Military Division, in which Paris was situated. No one was better calculated for the part he had to play. 'He has decidedly the air of sedition,' said Rewbell of him, the day of his presentation to the Directory. 'What a haughty brigand!' He frequented all popular meetings and public *fêtes*, dressed in a brilliant uniform covered with gold and diamonds, with rings on every finger,[1] joining the language of a demagogue with military attractions, claiming for himself all the merit of our victories in Italy, speaking of his general in a tone of patronage, and received all ovations with that braggadocio which never fails to produce an effect on the vulgar. He prepared his measures without taking the trouble to conceal their aim; but he was stopped for want of money, and wrote letter after letter to Bonaparte, to press him to send the funds he had promised. To these letters the General did not reply. He meant to keep aloof from the party, in whose future he had no longer any faith, and he was also perfectly aware that the state of uncertainty in which he was keeping every one, by leaving room both for hope and fear, was the surest way of increasing his own importance. Bernadotte, a third observer, was soon added to the two already in Paris; and the advice of this cautious man, who confirmed the testimony of Lavalette, decided Bonaparte more than ever to withdraw from all participation in the plot, and to await the event. The mystery in which his plans were at this time enveloped gave rise to the most extraordinary rumours. It was reported in Paris that he was thinking of making himself king of Italy. Madame de Staël relates[2] that, having asked Augereau if this were the case, he replied:

[1] Carnot, *Mémoire sur le 18th Fructidor*.
[2] *Considérations sur la Révolution française*.

'Certainly not; he is a young man of far too good principles for that.'

While these plots were preparing for their destruction, the Councils were much agitated, a prey to that irresolution and vacillation of which assemblies have given so many examples in similar circumstances. They constantly denounced the plans of their enemies, without taking any effective measures to frustrate them. They complained bitterly of the presence of the troops and the threatening addresses of the army, sure omens of the reign of force. The Directory, instead of offering a defence, turned accusers, and threw all the blame of these demonstrations, which they recognised as illegal, on those who, according to them, had provoked them by their plots. The Councils dared go no further. Their language became more aggressive and irritated than ever; but the moment they began to discuss means of action, their incapacity became overwhelmingly evident. Neither Pichegru nor Carnot, the two men of action of this party, regarded resistance as possible. They had not even succeeded in organising the National Guard. They had nothing to rely on but the weak guard of the Legislative Assembly, with a few *affidés* who had come up from the provinces, and chance, the great resource of all those who cannot count upon themselves. The very few generals who, like Bernadotte, sympathised with them in feeling, soon rallied round the Directory. Kléber alone, whose republican convictions were above suspicion, persisted to the last in offering his services to the constitutionals. If, he said, they could guarantee him the fidelity of the Legislative Guard, and some of the battalions of the National Guard, he would undertake to resist Augereau and his division. Mathieu Dumas, through whom this offer was transmitted, was the first to dissuade him from carrying out his project. In discouraging him thus, he was influenced less by reason than by a strong conviction of the uselessness of these efforts. They expected nothing more of a nation wearied and blunted by so many revolutions, and become so prodigiously sceptical. All the prestige and popularity which formerly belonged to the cause of liberty were now on the side of military force.

The imminence of the danger did not alter this inactivity. The taciturn Pichegru waited events with the impassiveness of a fatalist, presenting an impenetrable countenance to those who suspected his treason, and believing that none would dare to assail the conqueror of Holland. Carnot, bewildered between his old and his new friends, having everything to fear from the one, and nothing to hope from the others, persevered obstinately in a neutrality which resulted in nothing; he talked of resigning, but still kept his post in the Directory, and continued his old habit of countersigning such acts of his colleagues as displeased him most—such as the nomination of Augereau. He had, however, an open rupture with Barras, who had conceived an implacable hatred to him, of which the preliminaries of Léoben were the pretext rather than the origin. A scene of unheard-of violence took place between them, in which Barras loaded Carnot with the grossest abuse. 'Thou hast sold the Republic,' cried Barras, 'and now wouldst fain strangle those who defend it. Infamous brigand! there is not a louse on thy body that has not a right to spit in thy face.' 'I despise your provocations,' coldly replied Carnot, 'but a day will come when you shall answer for this insult' (Lavalette to Bonaparte, August 16th). When his friends proposed however that the so-called triumvirs, viz. his three colleagues, Barras, Rewbell, and Lareveillère, should be outlawed by the Councils, he strenuously opposed the measure, alleging that it would be the ruin of the constitution. At times he even hoped to effect a reconciliation between the Directory and the Councils. In this attempt he was supported by several friends of the Directory, who, in spite of their partiality for him, were afraid of the consequences of such a struggle. Among these were Talleyrand, who had just been called to the ministry, Madame de Staël, whose salon was a power, and whom Talleyrand had drawn into the camp of the Directory, and Benjamin Constant, just entering upon life, and whose errors were excused by his youth. They soon recognised the uselessness of their efforts, which were too late to produce any effect. While Carnot was offering his hand to Barras' friends, they were openly declaring: 'We will kill him.'

This extreme and desperate step, the sure sign of the weakness of parties, was not, however, discussed by the friends of the Directory only. A young officer proposed to Carnot himself to assassinate Barras; another made a similar proposition to Dumas, who was known to be one of the most influential leaders of the Councils. It is unnecessary to add that both rejected the offer with indignation. Several years later Dumas told Napoleon of his refusal. 'You were a fool then,' said the emperor; 'you understand nothing about revolutions.'[1]

At last, after long hesitation, the Directory resolved on action. About one o'clock in the morning of the 18th Fructidor (September 4th, 1797), Augereau with twelve thousand men invested the Tuileries, where the Legislative Body held their sittings, and occupied all the outlets. The palace was only guarded by a troop of a thousand men, part of whom had been won over beforehand, while the rest were irresolute and incapable of offering any serious resistance. At three o'clock, the signal was given by the firing of a cannon, which broke all the windows in the neighbourhood, and roused the population from sleep. Augereau took possession of the palace without firing a single shot, in spite of the courageous protest of Ramel, who commanded the guard of the Legislative Body, and a few of the members who were conducted to the Temple. At the same time, at the Luxembourg another troop entered Barthélemy's apartments, and arrested him. Carnot, whose rooms were also invaded, had been warned in time and was able to escape. At eight o'clock all was over.

The citizens came out of their houses, the people filled the streets, learned that a revolution had taken place and the nation had thus been summarily disposed of in their absence, and remained perfectly quiet. The firmer of the members of the two Councils assembled, resolved to ascertain whether the national representatives had not retained

[1] *Souvenirs de Mathieu Dumas.*

some of their old prestige; they marched through the streets with their presidents at their head; they passed, however, through an indifferent crowd, and were greeted with no signs but those of curiosity. At the gates of the palace they were met with bayonets, the soldiers drove them back and dispersed them, only retaining those whose names were on the lists of proscription.

The remains of the national representation, thus mutilated and degraded, were then convoked in the Odéon and the School of Medicine, to ratify the will of the triumvirs, and sign decrees which sealed their own political annihilation and the enslavement of France. After listening to the reading of an act, which implicated in Pichegru's conspiracy all the adversaries of the Directory, they voted successively the transportation of a great number of their colleagues, including the most irreproachable citizens of the time, and only three royalists, the transportation of all the 'writers, proprietors, managers, conductors, and editors' of forty-two journals, the cancelling of the elections in the forty-eight departments which had dared to name deputies opposed to the Directory, and the renewal of the laws against priests and emigrants, which had been repealed by the Councils. They destroyed all liberty of the press, by giving the Directory the right to suppress journals at pleasure; and they abolished all judicial power in the forty-eight departments declared to be seditious, by dismissing the judges and municipal magistrates in a body, and assigning the nomination of new ones to the Directory. They also gave this body power to organise and dissolve at will all political societies, to proclaim a state of siege, to delay to an indefinite period the organisation of the National Guard, and they gave the triumvirs two new colleagues, indicated to them beforehand, François of Neufchâteau and Merlin of Douai. The nomination of these two was a great disappointment to Augereau, who had himself hoped to get a seat in the Directory. The chiefs of the Fructidorian dictatorship intended to accept help from the soldiers, but not to share power with them—a childish and gross illusion. In politics, power goes where the real action and influence are. The 18th Fructidor was the work of soldiers; all was ready for military dictatorship.

'No blood has been shed,' said the Directory in its proclamations; 'all effusion of blood has been avoided,' were the words of the address of the Legislative Body. 'It has not cost a drop of blood,' repeated Augereau in his account to Bonaparte; and the philanthropic Lareveillère employed the same expression, adding 'that this was a point of view most sweet to contemplate.' Nevertheless, every one knew that banishment to Cayenne was equivalent to a death-warrant. But, with an hypocrisy which was even more odious than the cruelties of the preceding epoch, they tried to maintain all the honours of virtue and all the profits of crime. Never was the pastoral style more in vogue. Even the proclamations, in which the Directory assailed its adversaries, were filled with sentimental effusions to the French nation; they were exhorted to conjugal union, parental affection, filial piety, 'and every domestic virtue.' 'Let taste and cleanliness mark your dress; never let a sweet simplicity disappear from them; and may gentle beauty, decked in modesty, ever give a preference to ornaments made by French hands,' etc.[1] In the meantime the men condemned to banishment, whose number had happily been reduced, owing to the active measures of their friends, were thrown into iron cages and conveyed to Rochefort, from whence they embarked for the pestilential shores of Guyano. Among them were honest Barthélemy, one of the two directors whose places had just been filled, Lafon-Ladebat, president of the Five Hundred, and several other members known for the purity of their lives, whose only crime had been the unpardonable offence of opposing Barras. Pichegru, Rovère, and Lavilleheurnois were the only acknowledged conspirators. Half of them died speedily at Synamary, the rest succeeded in escaping. It was in this sense that the 18th Fructidor had not cost a single drop of blood.

A few days after the *coup-d'état*, the Directory received

[1] Bulletin des Lois.

a letter from Moreau, containing fresh proofs of Pichegru's treason. Moreau had had these proofs in his hands for some time, but, though warmly attached to the Republic, had abstained from making use of them, either out of consideration for an old friendship, or from a dislike to aid a policy which he disapproved of, or perhaps because he believed Pichegru could do no harm since he had no longer a command. Bonaparte, who has imputed it as a crime to Moreau that he should have kept back this famous correspondence, which he took in General Klinglin's baggage-waggons, acted in precisely the same manner himself with regard to Antraigues' revelations. He only communicated them to the Directory a short time previous to the *coup-d'état* when Bernadotte went to Paris, and through Bernadotte's agency. Moreau's error was in making his revelation after he had heard officially of the imminence of the *coup-d'état*; for the motives which had induced him to keep it back before ought to have given way before the impossibility of keeping a secret that was known to all his staff. He was punished for his tardy complaisance by being deprived of his command; and he was succeeded by Hoche, who had under his command the two armies of Sambre-et-Meuse and the Rhine. Hoche did not however long enjoy a position which would have given him a preponderating influence in the affairs of the Republic. He died shortly after of an unknown illness, which gave rise to suspicions of poisoning that have neither been confirmed nor disproved since. He was the only man of the time who, by his lofty intelligence and an ambition free from any vulgar taint, his military skill and remarkable talent for politics, displayed in the difficult task of pacifying La Vendée, as well as by the popularity of his name, would have been at all able at a given moment to counterbalance the fortunes of Bonaparte.

Although he supported the 18th Fructidor, he was sincerely attached to the great principles of the Revolution, and had he lived would quickly have recognised his error; for under an air of impatience he had a mind that was master of its own impulses. An inevitable rivalry would have led him to oppose Bonaparte's projects ; and by one of them thus restraining and neutralising the other, perhaps France might have been spared the terrible trials she has undergone.

Such was the celebrated *coup-d'état*, which destroyed the independence of a nation already wearied of changes, and of the various parties by whom it had been so often deceived. Those who look in the history of human circumstances for the too rare spectacle of the triumph of justice, may here allow themselves to behold it. The 18th Fructidor was the immediate contre-coup of the violation of law that we had just committed at Venice. Legislative protests led to the menaces from Bonaparte and his soldiers ; the irritation of the army furnished the Directory with an arm, without which it would never have triumphed over the Councils ; and by a righteous expiation France was deprived of liberty by the same blow which had just destroyed the independence of Venice.

The principal strength of the Republican Government had lain hitherto in the sincerity of even its fanaticism. The moment they let it be seen that they no longer believed in themselves, and turned their own maxims into derision by openly trampling the national will under foot, they lost all value as the representatives of a principle, and their power was gone. The Republic only continued to exist from the interests their *régime* represented and protected. Any power which should bring an adequate safeguard to these interests was sure to be well received.

If, instead of proscribing so many innocent people, and placing themselves above the law, the Directors had only struck at the royalist conspiracy, and thrown upon that the odium of complicity with the foreigner, and at the same time had shown a disposition to adopt, as far as conformable with the constitution, a policy which was evidently desired by the majority of the citizens, their moral authority as well as public liberty would have been fortified in the crisis, instead of perishing in it.

CHAPTER IX

CAMPO-FORMIO

BONAPARTE did not immediately congratulate the Government on the success of the *coup-d'état*, of which he had been the first instigator. His enigmatical attitude disquieted the Directory. Barras wrote to him, 'Your silence is very singular, my dear General.' Augereau too expressed the same astonishment and the same anxiety. The General's first reply contained only a lukewarm approbation of their conduct; he either did not believe in the duration of their success, or else he felt the awkwardness of suddenly espousing their cause with enthusiasm, after the long reserve he had maintained. 'This victory avails us little,' he wrote, 'if we are in disgrace with our countrymen. One may say of Paris what Cassius once said of Rome, of what value is her title of queen, when she is on the banks of the Seine slave of Pitt's gold?' The same day he wrote to Talleyrand: 'I tell you again that the Republic must not waver; let that swarm of journals which corrupt the minds of the public, and lower us in the eyes of foreigners, be stifled; let the Legislative Body keep pure and free from ambition; let the emigrants be expelled from France; and let all the friends of Louis XVIII., who are paid by gold from England, be compelled to resign their appointments; then will the great nation have peace. Till all that is done, reckon on nothing.'

In a proclamation, addressed by him to the 8th Military Division formed from the Southern departments, and just placed under his command, he attacked in the same manner 'the agents of Louis XVIII., and the men covered with crimes, who had delivered Toulon to the English,' without making any allusion to the 18th Fructidor.

He could not, however, always stop at these purely general terms, and soon saw the necessity of pronouncing more clearly. Accordingly, in an address to his soldiers, September 22d, 1797, he publicly proclaimed his adhesion to a cause which his private feelings belied; but it was by claiming for them the victory which the Directory had just gained, and by leaving the excesses, the disgraces, and the embarrassments of it to the Government.

'While you are triumphing over united Europe, in a distant country, chains were being prepared for you at home; you discovered this; you spoke; the people rose, transfixed the traitors, and they are already in prison. You will see by the proclamations of the Directory what the enemies of the country, the special enemies of the soldiers, and above all of the Italian army, were plotting. To be thus singled out does us honour. Hatred of traitors and tyrants will ever be our noblest title to glory and immortal renown. Let us render homage to the courage displayed by the first magistrates of the Republic, to the armies of Sambre-et-Meuse and of the interior, to the patriots, and the representatives who remained faithful to the destinies of France. They have repaid us at a stroke for six years' service to our country.' He wrote, at the same time, to the two new directors, Merlin and Neufchâteau, to congratulate them on their election, and then to Augereau, praising him for the 'wisdom and energy' he had displayed in the *coup-d'état*. In all three of these letters he dwelt on the necessity for moderation on the part of the Directory if they wished to gain the respect of the nation, and give France the stable government which she so much needed, —advice which plainly indicated the line of conduct he himself intended henceforth to adopt. 'It is to be devoutly hoped,' he wrote to Augereau, 'that there is to be no seesaw nor variation.' If he had consented for a time to adopt the tone and language of Jacobinism, he was anxious to make them understand that for the future this attitude did not suit him.

His coldness and slowness in expressing his opinion had not escaped the notice of the directors, in whom for this time interest served instead of penetration. They also knew beyond a doubt, that in private conversations the General avenged himself for the self-restraint of his public declarations, and that he condemned in bitter terms the violence and severity which he had previously recommended them to display, as well as the condemnation without trial of men conspicuous for the purity of their lives. They resolved to make him feel their dissatisfaction. In some letters written by Clarke to Carnot they discovered several passages which showed on the part of the former disapprobation of the party who had made the revolution of Fructidor. Knowing that Bonaparte depended on Clarke, a docile and devoted instrument, they sent through one of Augereau's aides-de-camp an order to the General for his dismissal. At the same time, they pointed out several measures to be taken that were incompatible with the unlimited authority which he had arrogated to himself in Italy. The blow was indirect, but it was sufficient to make Bonaparte feel that he was suspected by the Directory.

He replied at once, by complaining of the 'horrible ingratitude of the Government,' and again sent in his resignation. Once more he alleged his bad health, and 'the state of his mind, and the need he felt of invigorating his spirits by mixing with the mass of the citizens;' he assumed, in fact, the tone of outraged virtue. 'He had used his powers under all circumstances for the good of the country; so much the worse for those who had no faith in virtue, and were capable of suspecting his! His reward was the possession of a clear conscience, and the approval of posterity. Now that the country was tranquil and free from the dangers which had threatened her, he could safely quit his post; but they might be sure that were there to come a moment of peril, he would be in the front rank to defend liberty and the constitution of the Year III' (September 25th).

No one understood better than Bonaparte the deadly perplexity which his resignation would cause the Government at a time when the whole country had just been shaken to its very foundations, and when all negotiations depended on himself alone. The directors felt this also, and decided to disavow an anger which they had neither the dignity to maintain nor the tact to conceal, till a more favourable moment, though all the while they cursed an ascendency which was every day becoming more and more absolute. They decided to apologise. They humbled themselves before Bonaparte, and entreated him to continue in a post which he had never intended to quit; there had been, they said, a misunderstanding, from orders having been wrongly interpreted. 'Take care,' they said, 'lest the royalist conspirators, who poisoned Hoche, sow in your heart seeds of distrust that may deprive the country of the achievements of your genius.' They thanked him for his goodness in cautioning them against the temptation to *military government*, and for having reminded them of the sacred maxim, *cedant arma togæ*, a recommendation which was certainly remarkable from his lips and worthy of all praise, if it had been disinterested (October 22d). In short, they satisfied all his claims, and got Bottot, Barras' secretary, to write him a letter full of caresses and flattery. 'With what touching anxiety,' he wrote, 'they inquired for your health, and about everything that concerns you. What a contrast these affectionate expressions presented to the cruel letter with which you entrusted me! I am frank and sincere; citizen general, you are wrong about the Directory. They may commit faults, they may not always see so clearly as you do, but with what *republican docility* they received your suggestions!'

Republican docility was a fresh expression in the vocabulary of the time, but its application to a government in relations with a general was particularly novel. How was it possible not to feel sooner or later a temptation to make courtiers again of men who had so imperfectly unlearned the language of courtiers? What could Bonaparte desire more? Did not this moral dictatorship, which they accepted voluntarily, contain a secret charm far above that of the delights which in later times he was to exhaust?

Up to the 18th Fructidor the negotiations for peace, of

which we have seen the commencement in the conditions drawn up in the month of May by Bonaparte on the one hand, and MM. de Gallo and de Merfeldt on the other, had been carried on with a deliberate tardiness. The revolution preparing in Paris was known at Vienna, where they believed in the possible defeat of the Directory, or at any rate they hoped that the precarious situation in which the Government would be placed after the conflict would allow them to demand more favourable terms than those consented to by General Bonaparte, and perhaps even to recommence a war which had been terminated without honour just at a time when it might have become perilous to the conquerors.

They accordingly refused to accept the stipulations by which we were to give Venice to the emperor, and required in addition Mantua and Brescia. They also insisted on the necessity of a congress, which would have given them the double advantage of gaining time, as well as an opportunity of re-opening everything which had been settled. The directors, notwithstanding the General's advice, refused their consent to this arrangement. With the exception of Carnot and Barthélemy, who thought peace so necessary to France that they were willing to have it at almost any price, they would not agree to give up Venice. 'If your terms are too hard for the emperor,' said Carnot, 'you had better declare at once that you mean a war of extermination.' A dilemma of a not very strict kind, which might more justly have been stated in favour of the rights of a friendly people, and which was indignantly rejected by his colleagues, especially by Barras, whose soul, steeped as it was in infamies, still retained a spark of patriotism. They energetically opposed the proposition of a congress, alleging, not without reason, that England had consented to treat with France privately in a conference at Lille (July 1st). This conference, which came to such an untimely issue owing to an impolitic-exactingness, was in fact just about to open. All this first phase of the negotiations between France and Austria, fettered as they were by obstacles raised at pleasure, and governed by questions to which diplomacy was necessarily subordinate, resulted in nothing more than the liberation of Lafayette and his companions, who for several years had, in defiance of the law of nations, been detained prisoners in Olmutz.

Towards the end of August, Bonaparte left Montebello to go and reside at Passariano or Passeriano in Friuli, in a villa belonging to the Doge Manin. The negotiations, which both sides had begun to abandon to prepare for war, were now resumed at Udine, in the neighbourhood of the General's residence. The directors, desirous at any rate of getting rid of part of their difficulties, had ended by coming to an understanding, after discussions that were mingled with warm invectives. But the crisis of Fructidor was then imminent, and the emperor, who was discerning the precursory signs of the conflict, felt less disposed than ever to sign the peace. The brilliant success of the Fructidorians suddenly changed the aspect of affairs. The directors, elated by a victory which had rid them so cheaply of their enemies at home, were again filled with repugnance for a treaty of peace, which had always been far from answering their hopes, and which would release a man whose ambition and popularity were so alarming. The emperor's fears were again roused. Bonaparte, who at one time had almost decided to recommence hostilities, seeing Augereau, whom he despised, in command of the army of the Rhine, and Bernadotte, whom he disliked, about to be made Minister of War, so much influence thus passing into the hands of two men whom he knew to have no very kindly feeling towards himself, and who were determined to act on their own judgment, being assured besides that peace was becoming increasingly popular in France, and desiring more than ever to have the entire credit of it, so that he alone might gather its fruit, now resolved to do all in his power to hasten the conclusion.

Taking no notice whatever of what Barras styled 'the wish of the purified Directory' (September 8th) that the Rhine should be our limit, that Mantua should form part of the Cisalpine, and that Venice should not be given to the house of Austria—conditions honourable enough, notwithstanding the polluted lips that uttered them, and which Bonaparte, with the aid of the armies of the Rhine, could easily have made the emperor accept, had not his ambition again interfered as it did at Léoben—he drew up in concert with M. de Gallo a draft of articles, which M. de Merfeldt took to Vienna, and which the General on his side communicated to the Directory in these terms :—

'It is possible that before the 1st of October M. de Merfeldt may return with instructions to sign a treaty of peace on the following conditions :—

'1°. The line of the Adige, including the city of Venice, for the emperor.

'2°. The line of the Adige and Mantua, for the Cisalpine.'

France was to have the line of the Rhine, Belgium, Mayence, Corfu, and the Ionian Islands (September 19th).

In the event of the Directory refusing to accept this ultimatum, the General declared that he considered another war inevitable, and he enumerated with a view to this, and with evident exaggeration, the dangers, disadvantages, and difficulties in which a fresh war with Austria would involve them; he added a calculation of the reinforcements in men and horses which would be necessary to renew it with success. This explanation, on the part of a general whose words had so much weight, was tantamount to a refusal to act if all his requests were not instantly complied with, and he knew perfectly well how little the Directory was in a position to furnish the forces he had named.

But this is not the most important nor significant part of the memorable letter of September 9th, 1797. It contains an admission of immense historical interest, and a piece of irrefragable testimony. This ray, which can only be attributed to the force of truth, throws an unexpected light on Bonaparte's policy towards Venice, and shows what value we ought to set on all the accusations he had accumulated against the unfortunate republic which he was on the eve of finally sacrificing. 'I must know,' he wrote to the Directory, 'if it is your intention, or not, to accept these propositions. If your ultimatum is not to include Venice in the emperor's portion, I doubt whether peace will be concluded (*for that matter, Venice is the city most worthy of liberty of any in Italy*), and hostilities will recommence in the course of October.' The declaration contained in this short parenthesis has more value in the eyes of history than all the recriminations without number which Bonaparte thought it necessary to make in order to justify a policy that without these false appearances would have excited universal reprobation. By the side of evidence of every description, which rises to condemn his conduct with regard to Venice, we can henceforth add his own admission, which speaks more loudly than all the rest.

Just at this time there broke out that dissatisfaction which the Directory felt at Bonaparte's mysterious behaviour with respect to the 18th Fructidor. He knew both by Lavalette, and from Bottot, Barras' secretary, that he was an object of decided suspicion, and that the Government was less disposed than ever to make peace with Austria. While, then, he was tendering his resignation, as we have described, with feigned indignation at the ingratitude of the Directory, he wrote to Talleyrand, of whose skill and influence he was perfectly aware, and tried to gain him to his own views. He insisted afresh on the difficulties which would attend a new war with Austria, on the necessity of making the armies of the Rhine open the campaign at least a fortnight beforehand, in order to draw away a portion of the overwhelming forces which were opposed to him; he dwelt especially on the advantages of a treaty with Sardinia, and declared himself wholly unable to understand the scruples of the Directory. 'Are they held back by a desire to revolutionise Piedmont, and unite it to the Cisalpine? The way to effect this without a collision, *and without violating the treaty*, and even without violating good behaviour, would be to join a corps of ten thousand Piedmontese to our troops, and let them share our victories. Six months later, the king of Piedmont would be dethroned. It is a giant embracing a pigmy, and clasping it in his arms; he stifles it, without anybody being able to accuse him of the crime. It is the result of the extreme difference in their organisation' (September 26th).

No one was better able than Talleyrand to comprehend political morality like this. The General next alluded to the delusions of the Directory with regard to the stability of our work in Italy—delusions which he had both created, and done more than any one else to keep up while it suited his purpose to do so, but which he was anxious to dispel, now that his ambition had caught a glimpse of a more brilliant scene of action in Paris than he had ever dreamed of in Milan. 'They greatly exaggerate,' he wrote, 'the influence of these Piedmontese, Cisalpine, and Genoese patriots; the moment we withdraw by a blast of the trumpet our moral and military influence, these pretended patriots will be murdered by the people.' What! was this, then, the work of which he was so proud? Was this the result of so much diplomacy and skill? Where could we find a more crushing commentary on the system he had adopted? He finished his letter by interceding on behalf of Clarke, whose complaisance had been so useful to him, and who had fallen into disgrace with the Directory, since his correspondence with Carnot had come into their hands.

Events shortly afterwards proved that the sombre picture Bonaparte had just drawn of the situation of Italy was much nearer the truth than his first brilliant accounts, dictated by an interested optimism. But could he have passed upon himself a severer condemnation for having entailed on France the responsibility of maintaining such a work, whatever it was, conquest or emancipation? He had, in fact, no sooner founded the Cisalpine Republic than, recognising the evident incapacity of the Italians to adopt French institutions, he was compelled to write to Talleyrand for a commission of publicists, who would reorganise his Italian Republic on a new plan. This letter, which contains his own ideas on Government expressed with the greatest confidence, is extremely curious, and shows how early he had adopted in theory the system which he was afterwards to carry into practice. It is a singular proof of the fixedness of purpose of his absolute disposition. We find in it the essence of the Imperial constitution. All the reality of power is placed in the hands of the executive, which he considers as 'the true representative of the nation.' Besides this body, and subject to its control, is a Council of State, which inherits the most effective attributes of legislative authority. As for the Legislative Body, it only retains a shadow of power, 'without rank in the Republic, impassible, with neither ears nor eyes for what is going on around it; it will cease to be ambitious, and cease to inundate us with laws of the hour.' Is not this a picture of that assembly of mutes which the First Consul afterwards brought into being?

Such were Bonaparte's first views on government, and such, with very slight modification, they were to remain. His conception of politics was a sort of amalgam of crude recollections of classic antiquity, and experience gained in revolutionary transactions or in the habits of military command. It is strange that a mind in many respects so powerful could never rise above this inadequate type, conceived between two battles, at a time when he lacked both the experience and the knowledge necessary for the solution of so difficult a problem. We are amazed that he should not have understood its sterility. He persisted to the end in introducing geometrical precision into an order of ideas that could not bear it. In this he may justly be said to have been despotic both in character and in the natural turn of his mind. He was, besides, perfectly ignorant of modern political science, and looked upon the system of checks and balances as a useless complication. He knew nothing, or next to nothing, of those institutions for the protection of liberty which had birth in England and were perfected in the United States—institutions which the Constituent Assembly sketched out under a monarchy, and the Girondists dreamed of under the forms of a republic. This inexhaustible store of ideas that were destined to regenerate the world remained for ever unexplored by Bonaparte.

His letter finished by asking Talleyrand to communicate his plan to Sieyès, whom he wished eagerly to see in this commission. If he could persuade our most eminent publicists to accept his theory, he cherished the secret hope of one day seeing it transported from Italy into France.

The court of Vienna, having lost all hope of seeing the royalist conspiracy succeed in Paris, was disposed to listen to the conditions proposed by M. de Merfeldt. Still the emperor resolved, if possible, to obtain more advantageous terms, and with this view sent to Bonaparte M. de Cobentzel, a diplomatist of the old school and a pupil of Kaunitz. His departure was announced to the General in an imperial letter, couched in the most flattering terms. The negotiations were thus reopened under sufficiently unfavourable circumstances, M. de Cobentzel expecting to find in the General the same wish to conciliate which he had before displayed, while Bonaparte felt fettered by the strong opposition made by the Directory to his concessions of the 19th of September. Long discussions were entered into, in which the wily diplomatist used his subtle and insinuating eloquence, and some few graces that were slightly superannuated, and the imperious soldier all his abrupt logic. Each asked for more than he expected to obtain. Cobentzel, who was more exacting than his predecessors, now demanded the States of the Church, while Bonaparte, withdrawing his first concessions, pretended that he should not give up Venice, alleging that his Government, which had just recognised this republic, had strictly forbidden him to do so. Even to Talleyrand, to whom he did sometimes express himself sincerely, he wrote that he had resolved not to improve the conditions he had offered, without the consent of the Directory.

It was not so, however. He had long made up his mind to sacrifice Venice, and his hesitation arose simply from his inability to get the French Government to accept the idea. He did not try to overcome their scruples or to combat their objections; his plan was to make the cession of Venice an absolute necessity by accessory considerations, or at any rate to prepare them insensibly for such an issue, so that when once done, it should appear perfectly natural. His letters to the Directory were full of the difficulties that were on the point of arising in Italy, the expected death of the Pope, the hostile disposition of the king of Naples, the discontent of Sardinia, and his own unfitness to remain any longer at his post. 'He could scarcely mount his horse; he needed two years' rest.' He asked for some one to take his place, both as negotiator and as legislator for the Cisalpine Republic. He would furnish his successors with all the necessary instructions. Thus, at the same time that, to use a vulgar expression, *il faisait le mort*, and pretended to have no choice in the matter beyond the wishes of the Directory, he was binding up as in a single parcel all the reasons for imposing his wishes upon them. How was it possible to be imperative with a man so profoundly depressed? How could they send him positive and categorical orders? And who could surmise that a man, so anxious to resign his office, was on the eve of acting on his own authority with more boldness than ever, and had made all preparations for doing so?

What Bonaparte most desired to avoid was the receipt of a formal and absolute prohibition from his Government to give up Venice; for this would have tied his hands, and he warded it off by this dejected attitude and feigned prostration. On the 29th of September the Directory sent him their ultimatum, which though not firm enough to restrain a man to whom they had so often yielded, yet by its generosity redeems many wrongs. This ultimatum was, Italy free as far as the Isonzo. In it they pointed out the danger of allowing Austria to extend her frontier to the Adige, and thus introduce 'this voracious power' into the heart of Italy. They spoke of the 'shame of abandoning Venice,' and refused all connivance with 'a perfidy for which no excuse could be found,' since the effects would be far more disastrous than the most unfavourable chances of war. This despatch, though the Directory had not the courage to maintain the views it contains, against the universal explosion of joy which saluted the conclusion of peace, is the most honourable they ever signed, and suffices to throw on the General the whole responsibility of the transaction of Campo-Formio. It had no effect on Bonaparte, whose determination had been so decisively taken since the 7th of October. Feeling that further dissimulation was useless, he wrote to Talleyrand: 'In two or three days everything will be settled; we shall either have peace or war. I tell you plainly that *I will do anything for peace*, for the season is too far advanced to leave much hope of doing great things.'

Talleyrand tried to convince the General that the Directory was in the right. He pleaded the cause of the freedom of Italy with more warmth than could have been expected of him; but Bonaparte refuted all his arguments. Talleyrand, he said, knew nothing of this 'indolent, superstitious, buffoonish, cowardly population.' The army had not found 'a single Italian recruit, except some fifteen hundred rascals picked up in the streets of different towns, who are thieves and good-for-nothings. The French were the dupes of a few Italian adventurers. The Italian people had neither courage nor energy, nor any desire whatever for liberty. Such was their real state. *As for what was good to say in proclamations and printed speeches, that was mere romance.*' And who knew this better than himself? It was time to exchange the chimeras of revolutionary policy 'for true policy, which is nothing else than a calculation of chances and combinations.'

On the 10th of October he informed the Directory of his intention to sign a treaty of peace. The motives he gave for this decision were the lateness of the year, Hoche's death, the weakness of his army and the distance between it and the armies of the Rhine, the nullity of the Italians, the breaking-off of the conference of Lille, the strong desire of the French for peace, and lastly, 'the folly of risking certain advantages and more French blood for a people so unworthy of the sacrifice, who care so little for liberty, and who, from character, habits, and religion, have so deep a hatred of us.' All these reasons were more or less specious: not one was sincere. It was not later in the season than when, at the commencement of the campaign, he had, to use his own expression, crossed the Alps over three feet of ice. He could have been at the gates of Vienna before the middle of November. His army had never been in a better condition. Hoche's death had rid him of an embarrassing rivalry; and as regards the wish of the people for peace, which was true, he had never taken it into consideration till it suited his purpose to do so. The peace would only be the more solid for resting on a more complete triumph. Never did success appear more certain, more fruitful in great results, more evidently marked by the force of things, than that which seemed to deliver up to him beforehand this tottering and terror-stricken monarchy; never could he have dreamt of a more magnificent opportunity of repairing the evil he had done to Italy. Our army of the Rhine, relieved in consequence of the changes which the Austrians had been forced to operate in their own movements, had nobody in front, and nothing could stop Augereau on this side of the Danube. But how share such glory with Augereau?

His mind was too exclusively filled by his own interests to listen to the suggestions of a nobler and more generous ambition. He wished to be the only mediator, as he was already the only victor. His intimate friends, Marmont, Miot, Lavalette, and Bourrienne, however much they may differ in other respects, all agree in their testimony to the immense influence which this thought exercised over his determination. He wound up his letter to the Directory with expressions of respect and submission, which were all the more derisory at the moment when he was treating their instructions with contempt, and carrying out his own plans. 'England,' he said, 'offers a far more magnificent field for action. The English are worth more than the Venetians, and their *liberation* would consolidate for ever the liberty and happiness of France.' To show how far he was serious in this strange idea of liberating England, we may add that he had already planned his expedition to Egypt; that he was studying with Monge the means of executing it; and that he was on the point of sending Poussielgue to Malta to ascertain how it would be received by the French knights.[1] With regard to himself, he added

[1] *Mémoires de Lavalette.*

that 'his heart was pure, and his intentions upright; he had silenced the interests of his glory, his ambition, his vanity; he had only had in view the country and its Government. . . . It now remained for him to retire into the crowd; like Cincinnatus, to return to the plough, and give an example to the world of respect for civil authority and aversion to *military rule, which had destroyed so many states, and been the ruin of so many republics*' (October 10th, 1797). 'The 13th of October,' says Bourrienne, who was then Bonaparte's secretary, 'on opening the window at sunrise, I perceived the mountains covered with snow. The weather had till then been remarkably warm, and *everything had seemed to promise a fine and long autumn.* At seven o'clock I entered the General's room, awoke him, and told him of the change. He pretended at first not to believe me, then jumping out of bed, he ran to the window, and seeing for himself the sudden change of temperature, said very calmly, "Snow before the middle of October. What a country! Well! we must have peace."'

He then examined the state of his army, which amounted to eighty thousand men, and made a minute calculation of his chances of success, if he opened a campaign under such circumstances; as if his decision had not already been made several days before, and as if he wished to deceive even his secretary as to his true motive; but in reality because he saw that this change in the weather would give additional weight to his representations with the Directory. 'It is all over,' he exclaimed; 'I shall conclude peace; Venice shall pay the expenses of the war and the Rhine boundary. The Directory and the lawyers shall say what they please.'

But now that he wished to settle terms of peace with M. de Cobentzel with the briefest possible delay, he followed his usual custom, in which nobody has ever been his equal, and feigned a transport of anger and a firm desire to recommence hostilities. Orders were given to the different corps to commence a movement; preparations for a fresh campaign were carried on with extraordinary activity; and the General assumed a haughtier and more abrupt tone with the imperial diplomatists. M. de Cobentzel at first suspected that these demonstrations were only feigned, and kept strictly to his programme—Italy to the Adda. He spoke of departure, and had his carriages prepared with much haste. He threatened Bonaparte with an Austro-Russian alliance in Europe, and with the reproaches of his own countrymen. This obstinacy on the part of his adversary might at any moment change the General's feigned irritation into real anger, and in such a game the weakest was evidently he to whom peace was of most consequence. However much reluctance Bonaparte might feel to a renewal of hostilities, he had every reason to believe that what was only an object of reluctance with him was a matter of real dread to Austria. This fear, on which he speculated with so much boldness, shows clearly the slight foundation of all the pretences he alleged in justification of his policy. On the 16th of October, seeing he could gain nothing from M. de Cobentzel, and desiring to come to some definite conclusion before he received fresh instructions from the Directory, he rose suddenly in the middle of a conference, seized from a side-table an ornamental piece of china, which had been given to the count by the Empress Catherine, and dashed it to the ground, exclaiming: 'That is the way in which, before another month has passed, I will break your monarchy to pieces.' He then declared the truce ended, bowed to the negotiators, and went out.

Bonaparte had scarcely left Udine, where this tragi-comical scene took place, when M. de Cobentzel, who was at last seriously alarmed, followed him to Passeriano, and offered him the adhesion of the Austrian plenipotentiaries to the ultimatum proposed in the name of France.

The day following, October 17th, 1797, the articles were drawn up, copies were made, and at ten at night the signatures were affixed. It was dated from Campo-Formio, a little village close by, which had been declared neutral, but it was really written and signed at Passeriano. The General was in an unusually good humour all day. They passed a great part of the evening in cracking jokes and telling ghost stories. At midnight, Monge and Berthier started for Paris, to carry the treaty to the Directory.¹ Twelve hours later, a courier from the Directory arrived at Passeriano. The instructions he brought not only strictly forbade the cession to Austria of the line of the Adige, but also announced the speedy arrival of Bonaparte's successor as negotiator with Austria. 'We feel the necessity,' wrote the directors, 'of naming some diplomatist, *who will ease you of the work of negotiating*, and leave you free for military arrangements.' It was the reception of this order before the signature of the treaty which Bonaparte had tried so hard to avoid, and he succeeded.

In the first moment of irritation, the directors felt inclined to refuse to ratify the treaty; but, as the General had foreseen, this feeble protest was soon drowned in the enthusiastic explosion of joy which burst from all France at the news of peace. Instead of expressing discontent, the Government had to offer congratulations, which were as insincere as all the manœuvres which had prepared the successful issue of this work of falsehood and deception.

The emperor gave up Belgium to us; he renounced his claims to Lombardy in favour of the Cisalpine Republic, which comprised besides the provinces of Bergamo, Cremona, Brescia, Mantua, Modena, Bologna, Ferrara, and the Romagna. We gave him Venice, Istria, and Dalmatia, and all the Venetian territory beyond the Adige. We kept for ourselves Corfu and the Ionian Isles. A congress was to be held at Rastadt, to treat for peace between France and the German empire. The emperor further engaged by a secret convention to use his efforts in obtaining for us the line of the Rhine.

Talleyrand lost no time in offering his congratulations. 'Adieu! general, mediator. Accept my friendship, admiration, respect, gratitude.' . . . There is no knowing where to stop in this list. 'We shall perhaps have some *squalling among the Italians*, but that is no matter.'

General Bonaparte wished, however, to do something for the people at whom he had struck so cruel a blow. He wrote to Villetard, our representative at Venice, to

¹ Lavalette.

offer a refuge in the Cisalpine Republic to all the Venetian patriots who cared to leave their country. He proposed that everything in the shape of stores, ammunition, and supplies which remained in the Republic should be transported from Venice to Ferrara, and there sold for the benefit of the emigrants. Villetard, who had been the sincere and honest agent of a perfidious policy, had wished to revolutionise Venice, but not to sacrifice her. The new Republic had become to him a second country, and when he had to inform the Venetian Government of the treaty of Campo-Formio, and saw the utter dismay which the news produced, his own emotion was so great that he broke down in his speech and burst into sobs. He afterwards spoke of the General's offer, but it was rejected with indignation. 'I rejoice,' he wrote, 'to find the Venetians have too much pride to accept the proposition which you have made them through me. They will go elsewhere to seek a free country, for they prefer poverty to infamy. . . . The reading of your order was followed by curses and groans for the French nation, and an unanimous refusal to be accomplices in the ruin of their country.' The General replied with bitter irony to the man whom he had made his tool, 'We were bound by no treaty to the municipality of Venice. France was not called upon to make war for the benefit of other peoples. As for the chattering declaimers who talked of an universal republic, let them come and try a winter campaign. The Venetian Republic existed no longer. The people were corrupted, hypocritical, and effeminate. If they had spirit enough to appreciate liberty, they could stand up for it. France had not given the Venetians to Austria; she did not claim the right to do so; they had only to defend themselves as soon as we evacuated their territory.'

What a contrast between these insults so gratuitously heaped upon a people whom he had ruined and deprived of all means of resistance, and the motives which he afterwards, when at St. Helena, assigned for his policy towards Venice. There, where the magic of an obliging memory without conscience so often changed events to suit his purposes, he speaks of the cession of Venice to Austria as a trial to which he wished to expose the Venetians for a while, in order to renovate their patriotism. 'The years which the Venetians would have to pass in subjection to the House of Austria would fit them to receive with enthusiasm a national form of government, whatever it might be, whether more or less aristocratic. . . . There was little reason to fear that a people of such gentle manners would conceive much affection for a German government. . . .' These excuses are as insincere as his accusations against a people whose doom he had settled simply because they interfered with the execution of his plans, and they are even worse, because they are used to attach a sort of merit to one of his acts which has been most justly branded with shame.

It was adding insult to misery to tell a fettered and downcast people to defend themselves, and Bonaparte intended it. The Venetians, however, did send two envoys from the municipality, one to Bonaparte, and the other to the Directory, to solicit permission to sustain the combat alone, after the departure of our troops. The General replied to this demand by throwing the envoys into prison. Shortly after the French troops were withdrawn from Venice. Sérurier carried off all that remained in the magazines, sank all the vessels that he could not take with him, and lastly, set fire to the Bucentaur, that antique monument of the most flourishing days of the Republic. This done, he handed over the place to the Austrians. A profound consternation and mute despair reigned in the town, and this death-like silence was only interrupted by the acclamations of a hired populace. The imperial commissioner who was sent to receive the oath of allegiance from the Venetians was the same François Pesaro who had so often treated with General Bonaparte. The ex-doge Manin was forced to take the oath in the name of his countrymen, and with a broken heart prepared to submit to the painful ordeal. But, at the moment when he rose to pronounce the fatal formula, he was seen suddenly to totter, and he fell senseless to the ground, struck down by shame and grief. Thus vanished the Republic of Venice, after a long and glorious existence. The Venetian people did not die with her; they still suffer, and still protest. They have been again and again avenged since then by the endless dangers and complications that the iniquities of Campo-Formio bequeathed to Europe, but the crime committed by French hands still waits for reparation.[1]

[1] Written in 1865. Reparation has since been made, but not by French hands.

CHAPTER X

THE EXPEDITION TO EGYPT

GENERAL BONAPARTE remained in Italy till the middle of November, in order to put the last stroke to the organisation of the Cisalpine Republic. His final arrangements made, he quitted Milan, November 17th, 1797, bidding farewell to the Italians in a proclamation that abounded in the most magnificent promises. To these he added warm congratulations, the insincerity of which is proved by his correspondence with the Directory. 'The Cisalpines were the first example in history of a people recovering liberty without violence, without civil ruptures, and without revolution. They would be called upon to play a great part in the affairs of Europe; they would soon be too strong for any power in the world to rob them of their freedom. Until then the great nation would protect them from the attacks of their neighbours. He should hasten to be by their side on the first signal of danger.' This was the last encouragement he gave to an illusion that he had never shared; the useless commendation of a work incapable of standing alone for a single instant; and which, after having afforded us all the profits of conquest, was about to entail on us all their cost in the shape of a burdensome protectorate.

Bonaparte first proceeded to Turin, but did not see the king of Sardinia, to avoid all engagements with a power already tottering. From thence he proceeded by Mount Cenis to Geneva, where his first act was to imprison the banker Bontemps, who was suspected of having aided in the escape of Carnot, whose services and old friendship were now only a tiresome reminiscence. At Lausanne he received an ovation from the democratic party, who were preparing an insurrection in the Canton of Vaud against Bernese supremacy. At Morat he visited the field of battle where we had once been beaten; he criticised the plans of Charles the Bold, and deplored his faults with as much interest as if he had been one of his immediate predecessors; he then crossed the Rhine, and at last arrived at Rastadt. Here he found the plenipotentiaries already assembled, but he had no intention of taking any part in their negotiations; he had had enough at Campo-Formio, and he foresaw that the present treaty would involve still more perplexing complications. He only wished to make his appearance at Rastadt, to take possession, so to speak, of the diplomatic debate, in such a way that if it came to a successful issue, all the credit would be his, and if not, he could disown the responsibility. He resolved that people should remember that he had passed that way; for he took care to make himself conspicuous by a violent though not unjustifiable outburst against Count de Fersen, the Swedish envoy, who throughout the Revolution had been marked by his intimacy with the queen and his active participation in all the plots of the court. In a few warm and haughty words, Bonaparte made the count understand the impropriety of his conduct in presenting himself to negotiate with the French Republic; and M. de Fersen, thus denounced as an obstacle to the success of the negotiations, left Rastadt the very next day. The General next exchanged with M. de Cobentzel ratifications of the treaty of Campo-Formio, and then set off for Paris, after having signed the military convention which gave us Mayence and Manheim.

He arrived at Paris on December 5th, and went straight to his little house in the Rue Chantereine, which on this occasion received the name of Rue de la Victoire, the ingenious and spontaneous compliment of the municipality. He was the object of an immense and universal curiosity, and he was acute enough never to allow it more than a half satisfaction, which was the surest means of prolonging it, and stimulated instead of discouraging. Full of reserve and of the apparent modesty of those who escape vanity by pride, indifferent rather than simple, artificial and studied even in his negligence, he shunned alike the acclamations of the crowd and the splendour of official receptions; he replied to eager congratulations with strict politeness, but without familiarity; he scarcely went out, talked but little, and displayed in his whole bearing and manner a plainness which formed a striking contrast to the glory of his name and the rather theatrical tone of his proclamations.

The Directory, seeing how useless it would be to complain against a man who enjoyed such universal popularity, forgot their own private griefs, and gave the General a magnificent reception. An altar to the country, covered with trophies and surmounted with allegorical statues, was raised in the court of the Luxembourg; the walls were hung with flags, and a vast amphitheatre was raised around it. Here the Directory, the authorities, and the diplomatic body, all arrayed in robes of state, received General Bonaparte. An immense crowd, anxious to catch a glimpse of his features, filled the enclosure and the adjacent streets. When he appeared, all eyes were fixed on him, and endless acclamations resounded on every side. His short stature, the pallor of his face, his feverish sickly aspect, his profile —the type of a foreign race—and his spare frame, which seemed consumed by the ardour of genius, everything about his person, was unexpected, extraordinary, and calculated to strike every imagination.

Talleyrand was the first to speak. His eloquence on this occasion had neither the taste nor moderation which usually characterised it; either he was led away by the general enthusiasm, or else he was anxious to win and attract the conqueror. While claiming for France and the Republic a portion of the glory of the General, he went on to praise him in terms that can hardly be used with decency except of the dead, and the fulsomeness of which had never been surpassed by Bossuet himself in addressing Louis XIV. He expended infinite, but, alas, superfluous art in demonstrating that this day was 'the triumph of equality.' Then, taking up the suggestions which could not fail to present themselves to every thoughtful mind, he transformed Bonaparte into a kind of Stoic hero, weaned from all worldly grandeur, with no other taste than for simplicity, obscurity, and the study of abstract science, and for 'that sublime Ossian, who appeared to detach him from the earth.' Not only was there no reason, according to the orator, to fear his ambition, but 'the day might even come when they would have to entreat him to tear himself away from the leisure of studious retreat.'

Those who knew Bonaparte easily recognised in the tone of his reply his contempt for the extravagant and childish eulogy of which he had been the inappropriate object. When he spoke, a profound silence reigned; the people listened eagerly for his words, without being able to catch them. His voice betrayed a sort of annoyance and irritation, the only protest permissible against the singular burlesque which had just been imposed on him. His discourse was made up of a few generalities devoid of any specific significance, especially when contrasted with the fiercer eloquence of his proclamations; but there was a tone in his curt and abrupt manner that revealed the man born to command. The only striking point was in the conclusion. 'When the happiness of the French nation is based on the *best organic laws*, all Europe will have liberty.' These words, which it would be well to remember, pronounced under such solemn circumstances, and by a man as calculating as Bonaparte, were not without a clear meaning. It was his announcement for the future that he saw more than one change to be made in our political system. The phrase deserved to be remembered and weighed maturely.

Barras followed, and spoke amidst general inattention, and with an emphasis that far surpasses anything that this declamatory epoch offers us in that kind. He compared the General successively to Socrates, Cæsar, and Pompey; he addressed to him the most fulsome adulation in reference to the treaty of Campo-Formio, of which, however, he had often spoken as a disgrace to the Republic and an infamy for the man who had signed it; then, inviting the pacificator of Europe to crown a glorious life by new conquests, and pointing to England, he exclaimed: 'Go there and capture the giant corsair that infests the seas; go punish in London outrages that have too long gone unpunished. Many an adorer of liberty awaits you; you are the liberator to whom mankind appeals with plaintive cries.'[1] Barras then embraced Bonaparte. The orchestra sang a hymn composed by Chénier and Méhul, after which Joubert and Andréossy were presented to the Directory.

For several succeeding days *fêtes* were given in honour of the young General, but he did not often join in these festivities. He was very cautious in his behaviour to men of different parties, and always skilful in dealing with all varieties of opinion, escaping from declaring himself on thorny questions, showing a decided preference for the society of artists and savants, men without any particular political views, and whom he henceforth patronised, after the fashion of a sovereign who delights to encourage a taste for the fine arts. The vacant place which Carnot's proscription left in the Institute was offered him by the unanimous vote of the members, and he felt no scruple in accepting the seat of his former protector, who was then expiating in exile the crime of his conscientious opposition to the *coup-d'état* of Fructidor. He thanked the Institute in a letter, in which he extols 'the only true conquests, those gained over ignorance.' The idea is very fine, and the only fault to be found with the expression is the entire contrast it offers to his acts. From that time he assumed with some ostentation the title and dress of a member of the Institute, pretending to place the palm of the savant far above the honours of Commander-in-Chief, and delighting on all public occasions to show himself as conqueror of Europe clothed in this modest and peaceful uniform.

In his intercourse with the Directory he concealed, under a certain freedom of exterior, an extreme mistrust, and on one or two occasions even took precautions which

[1] *Moniteur*.

were an insult to the members, but which he justified by Hoche's premature death. He was most suspicious of Barras, the director with whom he was most closely connected. He regarded him as a man who would shrink from no extremity. We have no proof that he had grounds for such apprehension, though the corrupt Barras may be said to have united all the vices of the old *régime* with all those of the new. But, even supposing the directors capable of the crime of wishing to get rid of him by foul means, their case was not desperate enough to drive them to such a point. They were aware that a great many people were already pressing the General to seize the reins of power, but they knew also that nothing was ready for the dictatorship, and that the elements on which he would have to rely were as yet without any coherence. They constantly showed him police reports upon this subject, not so much to testify their confidence, as to show him that they kept their eyes upon him. His increasing popularity did, however, cause them serious alarm, and while they pretended to rejoice with him, they secretly did all they could to diminish it. They made the Council of the Five Hundred reject the proposition to present him with Chambord as a national gift. On the other hand, they warmly urged him to undertake the adventurous enterprise which was to crown his glory, and which was announced to Europe through the title he received of General-in-Chief of the army of England.

Preparations for this expedition were being made in all the ports of the Republic, but they were carried on with more ostentation than real activity. Meanwhile Bonaparte was consulted on all occasions, and called to take part in every important deliberation. They wished apparently to make amends for the severity of an improvident law, by associating him beforehand in a power in which his twenty-nine years prevented him from taking open part. The first use he made of this influence was to withdraw the command of the armies of the Rhine from Augereau, who had become his declared enemy since the dupery of which he had been the object in Fructidor. Augereau, with the penetration of hatred, had long suspected Bonaparte's designs, and had incessantly cautioned the Directory. Bonaparte, in return, accused him of having retarded by his Jacobin demonstrations the progress of the negotiations with Germany; and in disgrace that was thinly disguised, he was confined in an obscure post at Perpignan, without any prospect of advancement.

General Bonaparte had never seriously thought of invading England. Not only were the means at his disposal insufficient for such an undertaking, but even supposing an invasion could be effected, which was very improbable, he knew that he would meet with a race of men totally different from those whom he had fought in Italy; and that if it was no easy matter to penetrate this famous island, the scene of so many unsuccessful attempts, it would be still more difficult to retire from it; and he was unwilling to stake all the glory he had won on so hazardous a game. He had for a long time cherished another project, which was not, perhaps, less hazardous than the conquest of England, but which would offer abundant opportunities of astonishing the world, that is ever more struck by brilliant execution than by solid results. It was this that he cared for more than all else. An expedition to Egypt did not involve the long and perilous labour which the thankless task of vanquishing the haughty England would require, and the feeble, decrepit state of the East offered a field in which brilliant if not lasting success was certain.

The General, however, feigned to enter entirely into the views of the Directory. When at Passeriano, in the first ardour of his passion for the enterprise, he had called the attention of the Government to the facilities which our establishment in the Ionian Isles would afford us of founding a new state on the ruins of the Turkish empire, and particularly of taking possession of Malta and Egypt, his proposals had been met only by objections; and though the directors afterwards gave their adhesion to the project, it was done in a vague and indefinite manner. Before he again preferred this demand, he wished to convince them that he had made every effort for the realisation of their own plans. He set out accordingly to make in person a complete inspection of the preparations directed against England (February 10th, 1798). He questioned the pilots and sailors, and made his examinations with that minute care for detail which he carried into all his undertakings, but with his mind fixed on a totally different enterprise from that which this journey implied; for he had with him in his carriage all the books, plans, and notes, relative to the expedition into Egypt, to which he intended to direct the material now preparing for the invasion of England. On his return to Paris, he declared that nothing would be ready for a long time, 'and that he would not stake the fate of France for a throw so full of risk; and the preparations for the English expedition received a new destination, that was carefully concealed from the public. The idea of conducting into a distant and unknown country, from which our communications must of necessity be cut in a given time, the flower of our soldiers, generals, and men of science, at a time when peace was not signed, when Europe was still in arms against us, when such a conquest could not fail to aggravate the general discontent, and was certain to revive enmities that were fading but were not destroyed, was almost as impolitic as the policy which afterwards led to the war in Russia, though not of a kind to bring about such disastrous results. The chimeras which Bonaparte mixed with his views of conquest, and which are almost the only part of the conception peculiarly his own, were not less hazardous than those which were afterwards to cause his fall; but, fortunately for him, he had only a small army to work with, instead of the forces of several nations, and at the very outset he met with insurmountable obstacles.

In the occupation of Egypt there was nothing impracticable. With wise and skilful management, in a time of peace it might have offered some useful results. The plan had been more than once discussed in the councils of the ancient *régime*. Leibnitz had submitted to Louis XIV. a project for the colonisation of Egypt. It had been taken up again under Louis XVI., and Bonaparte had in his hands he plans made with that object. Still more recently, too,

Magalon, our consul at Alexandria, had presented a memorial on this subject to Charles Delacroix, the minister who had given him authority to come to Paris and explain his views to the Government (August, 1796). But in Bonaparte's plan the project had assumed quite different proportions. He proposed, not merely to colonise Egypt, itself a formidable undertaking, with a race so unlikely to assimilate with others, and with such colonists as the French, but completely to revolutionise the whole of the Eastern dominions, where the elements of regeneration were supposed to exist, waiting but a spark to kindle them; an hypothesis warranted by no serious grounds. To ruin the English settlements in India, to chase the Turks from Constantinople and drive them into Asia by means of an immense rising of the Greek and Christian populations, and then return to Europe *la prenant à revers*, to use the picturesque expression of the author of these gigantic plans,— such was the conception which haunted an imagination that knew no rein, and of which the occupation of Egypt was only the moderate preliminary.

It would be difficult to explain the ease with which Bonaparte obtained the consent of the Directory to undertake this expedition, at a time when the unsettled state of the French Government and the prospect of a fresh coalition rendered it so perilous, did we not remember not only the intoxication of prodigious success, but also how eager the Directory were to rid themselves of a man whose ambition increased with his fortune, and the devouring and insatiable need which Bonaparte himself felt of escaping from this inglorious leisure, and of once more fixing the eyes of Europe upon him. General Bonaparte had too much penetration not to perceive that the Directory could not without his assistance maintain France at the perilous height to which his victories had now raised her. But this knowledge, far from interfering with his plans, in a sense actually formed a part of them. It was his interest to prove by a striking evidence that they could do nothing without him, that all our military successes depended on his genius, that he was in fact the single indispensable man;

and since Hoche's death this had become the conviction of a great many people. They believed, as he wrote of himself with ingenuous Machiavelism, that, 'in order to be master of France, it was necessary for *the Directory to experience reverses during his absence*, and for his return to restore victory to our flag.'[1]

Besides which, he had a horror of repose, and all his faculties turned to the side of action. He dreaded still more the inevitable analysis to which he would be subjected by the witty and penetrating scepticism of the *salons* of Paris, those intellectual laboratories where everything is decomposed and tested. He thoroughly understood the character of this fickle and satirical people, which avenges its infatuations by indifference, and so quickly grows familiar with the idols to whom it has offered most incense. 'They recollect nothing at Paris,' he said to one of his intimate friends. 'If I remain long without doing something else, I am lost. On my third appearance at the theatre they will cease to look at me.' He must create new food, then, for curiosity, for emotion, for that thirst for the marvellous which in the mind of the nation had taken the place of revolutionary passions. He must keep up his character; complete by fresh strokes the conqueror and hero that the popular imagination had erected. From this point of view 'little Europe was a mere mole-hill, and afforded no scope for glory; he would go and seek it in the East, in that land of miracles where great empires had risen and fallen, and which contained six hundred millions of inhabitants.'

How could a mind ruled by such reflections as these be deterred by any scruple about violating the right of nations from seizing Malta, though it had given us no cause of complaint; or from breaking our relations with Turkey, our ally for centuries—with our 'good friends the Turks,' as Bonaparte himself called them (Letter of December 23d, 1797), in return for the money and supplies of all sorts which they had voluntarily furnished to our garrison at Corfu?

[1] *Mémoires de Napoleon.*

One thing only retarded the execution of these projects, and that was want of money. Since the treasury was no longer nourished by the millions from Italy, our finances had fallen into their old confusion, and this penury paralysed everything. The Government met the want by the occupation of Rome and the invasion of Switzerland.

Bonaparte, in his Memoirs, severely blames these two acts, and claims for himself the honour of having offered to both a strenuous opposition. His correspondence, however, contains the clearest evidence that from beginning to end he had the chief direction of the transaction. All the instructions addressed to Brune and Berthier are in his own handwriting. The consequences of this twofold invasion in the precarious state of European peace were only too easy to foresee; but it was not he who would have to answer for it. And were not these two invasions, which were to furnish him with means for his expedition, also the events which, to use his own striking expression, were necessary in order that *the Directory might experience reverses during his absence?* However this may be, no trace of his opposition remains, the evidence of his connivance is ample and conclusive; and if, as he affirms, he disapproved of these hazardous undertakings, was it not clearly his duty, seeing the preponderating political influence he possessed, to refuse to associate himself in their accomplishment?

The motive assigned for the occupation of Rome was the assassination of General Duphot. This murder no doubt called for severe punishment; but if it was to be followed by a measure so pregnant with complications as the destruction of the papal power, the moment ought at any rate to have been chosen when the blow could be struck with advantage. It was madness to go to Rome, if they persisted in going to Egypt; one or the other of these great adventures ought to have been sacrificed. As regards the invasion of Switzerland, nothing could justify it; and the Vaudois democrats, who, in order to free themselves from the detested yoke of Berne, did not hesitate to subject their country to the thousand times worse scourge of a foreign invasion, were cruelly punished for their blindness, when the pillage of the treasures, slowly amassed by the toil and economy of their fathers, opened their eyes to the motives which had actuated their pretended liberators. This motive, which is so clearly proved by the conduct of the French authorities in Switzerland, and by the documents which are left concerning that sad enterprise, has been represented as an invention to which the 'whimperings of this miserly little nation' have given rise.[1] The best authority on this point is perhaps Napoleon himself, who had the direction of the expedition. 'Another motive,' he said, 'which influenced the Directory was *the millions they hoped to get from Berne.*'[2]

The expedition to Rome was conducted by Berthier, chief of Bonaparte's staff. The General had named him his successor in Italy, partly because he knew his incapacity as a Commander-in-Chief, and was sure that of all his lieutenants Berthier was the most likely to make his own absence regretted, and partly to refute the ridiculous assertions of those who attributed his own victories to the counsels of this officer. The invasion of Switzerland was entrusted to Brune, a general who had distinguished himself in Italy, where he arrived towards the end of the campaign, and whom Bonaparte wished to conciliate on account of his well-known influence over the extreme section of the republican party. Both received their instructions from him, submitted their plans to him, and reported their operations to him, of which the aim, as Berthier naïvely wrote to his General, was more fiscal than political. 'In sending me to Rome,' he wrote, '*you appoint me treasurer to the English expedition.* I will endeavour to fill the chest.' Very soon the pillage of this museum of the world, the revolt of the troops, who were left in a state of absolute want that the treasury might be all the better filled, and the relentless requisitions of Haller, contractor for the expedition to Egypt, were sufficient evidence that

[1] Thiers' *History of the French Revolution.*
[2] Letter of January 19th, 1798, quoted by M. Barante in his instructive *History of the Directory.*

Berthier had kept his word. As for Brune, in Berne alone he took possession of more than sixteen millions in specie, seven millions in arms and ammunition, and eighteen millions in stores and supplies. The use to which this money was to be applied had been so clearly stated beforehand, that several millions were sent direct from Berne to Toulon. Such was now the employment of these Republican armies, so renowned at their first appearance for their disinterestedness, their nobility, and their purity. Two years of war in Italy had sufficed to effect the change.

On the 12th of April the Directory signed the papers relative to the expedition to Egypt; but the secret was kept, lest the English should take alarm. These decrees placed at the General's disposal considerable naval and military forces, with a discretionary power in their employment. He had authority to take with him 'what troops he thought fit,' to withdraw from Italy the divisions which had been left at Genoa and at Civita Vecchia as well as those in Corfu, to seize Malta and Egypt, to drive the English from all their possessions in the East, and to 'pierce the Isthmus of Suez.' They gave him, in fact, a foreign kingdom, to avoid letting him take possession of the sovereignty of France. Bonaparte availed himself freely of the license thus accorded him. He enlisted in his service all the most distinguished artists, savants, and men of letters: Monge, Berthollet, Geoffroy Saint Hilaire, Fourier, Denon, Larrey, Desgenettes, Dolomieu, etc. He did not confine himself in his choice of generals to his old companions in arms of the army of Italy, but made a choice from among all the armies of the Republic, thus depriving them of all nerve and muscle. He seemed unwilling to leave any one of any worth behind. He took Desaix, Kléber, Davoust, Reynier, Caffarelli, and Belliard, and with them his old lieutenants Murat, Lannes, Marmont, Berthier, Andréossy, Junot, and every one who had youth, energy, and daring. The Directory, in their eagerness to rid themselves of his presence, allowed him to carry off the strength and flower of the nation; and the motives which induced them to aid the General were as little avowable as those which led him to embark so many precious lives in the rashest of enterprises.

An incident calculated to make a government jealous for the honour and security of their country hesitate, retarded for a fortnight the departure of the expedition. Bernadotte, our ambassador at Vienna, having been reprimanded by the Directory for his lukewarm republicanism and his consideration for the aristocracy of Vienna, hoisted the republican flag at the embassy in obedience to the orders he had received, but contrary to diplomatic custom. This demonstration irritated the population of Vienna, who insulted the national standard and broke the windows of the embassy. The riot, which was quelled with some difficulty, was especially grave because it indicated the real feelings of a people whom we had believed, if not subdued, at any rate demoralised and terror-stricken. It showed us that if the court of Vienna wished to renew hostilities, the people would give a hearty response, instead of opposition or reluctance, as we had amused ourselves by supposing.

In their first alarm the Directory looked upon this event as an unhoped-for opportunity for recommencing war and retracting the stipulations of Campo-Formio. They offered Bonaparte the title of General-in-Chief of the army of Germany, but his mind was too full of his own projects to enter very warmly into their views. He knew too well how embarrassed Austria still was, to believe that the scene in Vienna was intended as a signal for a rupture. Still, as he was always ready to modify his plans according to circumstances, if profitable to his own interests, he determined to try what new chances were open to him, and wrote to M. de Cobentzel to arrange the affair, offering even to return to Rastadt; and his offer was accepted. But the dictatorial tone he assumed on this occasion, the mystery in which he enveloped his proceedings, and the portentous activity with which he drew everything to himself, made the Directory very quickly repent of their first movement. The court of Vienna, wishing to gain time, concealed the irritation which the invasion of Switzerland and Rome had caused, and offered the most satisfactory assurances. But in proportion as the Directory cooled towards a rupture with Austria, Bonaparte seemed on his side suddenly to have conceived conscientious scruples, and he was all at once seized with dismay at the idea of the responsibility which would devolve on him if he withdrew such an army while the Republic was in so perilous a situation; and although he wrote to Kléber, Caffarelli, and Brueys, 'that some disturbances which had just happened at Vienna would render his presence at Paris necessary for a few days, but *that it would in no way affect the expedition*,' his hesitation appeared to increase each day. He either wished the Directory to compel him by a formal order to set sail for Egypt, and so relieve him of responsibility in case of failure, or else, and this is more probable, the state of affairs suggested to him the possibility of realising a project dearer than any other to his ambition owing to the forces then at his disposal. Mathieu Dumas declares in his Memoirs that he was told in confidence by General Desaix, that the night previous to his departure for Egypt Bonaparte had prepared everything for the overthrow of the Directory, and was on the point of executing his *coup-de-main*. This evidence confirms the information which the directors received about the intrigues of the General. Hence the significant energy of the order for him to start. The scene which took place was extremely violent. At the first words of opposition Bonaparte flew into a passion and offered to resign, but this offer had lost its effect. Rewbell quietly offered him a pen, saying, 'Write it down then, General; the Republic has other sons who will not abandon her.' The General took the pen, but allowed it to be snatched from his hand by Merlin, and said nothing more about resignation.

He quitted Paris May 3d, leaving for General Brune, who had received the command of the army of Italy, instructions for the military operations in that country, so imminent did a rupture with Austria appear. The position which Brune was to defend at all costs as the key to Italy was the same line of the Adige, from Lake Garda to Porto-Legnago, upon which Bonaparte had successfully borne so many terrible shocks. The pivot of resistance was to be Castel-Novo, whence he could at once defend the passage of the river and command the passes that debouch upon Rivoli. He reminded him especially of the original manœuvre which had succeeded so well at Ronco, when he threw himself at a bound upon the enemy's rear,—vain recommendations which never supply the place of genius. Besides, the gravest danger to Italy did not lie there, but in the weakness of the governments which he had founded. Bonaparte's work crumbled away of itself. The day that Berthier ignominiously drove from the Council of the Cisalpine those deputies who refused to ratify a measure which he had submitted to them for deliberation, the last mask which disguised conquest fell off. The disgraceful anarchy which reigned among the conquerors, wearied of their own excesses, foretold with equal force the speedy ruin of this ephemeral erection. But Bonaparte had grown indifferent and a foreigner to that Italy which he had so often promised to regenerate. He had never loved her for anything else than his own glory. As soon as she ceased to contribute to his revenue she had lost all interest for him. What mattered to him the destiny of a country in which he no longer was present? The phantom of his future grandeur henceforth appeared to him through the mirages of the East; and the memory of the brilliant landscapes of Italy was effaced by the frightful deserts of Africa.

One of his last acts before leaving France was to make an energetic and eloquent protest against a sanguinary execution which, on his arrival at Toulon, he found had been perpetrated in the name of the law against emigrants. An old man of eighty years of age had been shot. Bonaparte severely reprimanded the military commission who passed this iniquitous though legal sentence. 'The soldier,' he wrote, 'who signs a sentence of death against a man incapable of bearing arms is a coward.' Happy and blessed his memory, if he had never placed himself above the laws of his country, except by acts of this kind!

The day before he embarked he reviewed his army, and

addressed them in a harangue which has remained famous for the disclaimer of which it was the object, and which is at once more significant and more consistent with the character of its author than the proclamation which was afterwards substituted for it. Although every line of this harangue bears traces of Napoleon's diction, its authenticity has again been recently contested, though on no very substantial grounds, for it is established in an irrefragable manner in one of the numerous conversations collected by Las Cases. Bonaparte made a fresh appeal to those passions which he had found so effectual in Italy. But it was necessary that the language should be plainer still, because of the uncertainty attending so speculative an enterprise. Hence what is so revolting in its phrases.

'Soldiers,' he said, 'it is two years since I came to take command of you. You were then in the Riviera in the greatest misery. You had disposed of everything you possessed, down to your watches; and you were in need of everything. I promised to put an end to your distresses: I led you into Italy. There all was given you. Did I not keep my word? Learn now, then, that you have not yet done enough for the country, and that the country has not yet done enough for you. I am going to lead you into a land where your future exploits will eclipse those which have already astonished your admirers, and where you will have an opportunity of rendering to your country the services she has a right to expect from an invincible army. *I promise each soldier on his return from this expedition a sum sufficient to purchase six acres of land.*'

This language, the crudeness of which so revolted the delicacy of the directors, was perfectly appropriate to the passion which Bonaparte had developed in the Republican armies. Its only fault was that it expressed too plainly sentiments which, in his former harangues, he had veiled by rhetorical commonplaces. It was acknowledging too freely that the object of the war was booty; and such an avowal was hardly calculated to calm Europe at a time already alarmed by our enterprise in Switzerland. The oration was relieved towards its close by the inevitable appeal to the recollections of Roman antiquity : ' Accustom yourselves to manœuvres on the coast, and make yourself a terror to your enemies by sea as well as by land. In this take the Roman soldiers for your pattern, who vanquished both Carthage on the plain and the Carthaginians in their fleets.'

This harangue, which excited the soldiers to the highest degree, had not the same success with the public, whose enthusiasm was pitched in a nobler key. It is probable that Bonaparte himself felt the impolicy of his language, for two days later he published a proclamation in which all appeal to the cupidity of the soldiers was carefully suppressed. The Journal of the Directory reproduced this, declaring the first to be apocryphal, and assuring the world ' that it did not contain enough depth of thought nor sufficient nobleness of sentiment to be the work of the conqueror of Italy.'

The expedition set sail on the 19th of May. The English, fully persuaded that the object of all these preparations was the invasion of England, had contented themselves with guarding the entrance to the Mediterranean at Gibraltar, and had only left at Toulon a small blockading squadron under the command of Nelson. A storm had forced it back to the south-west of Sardinia, and our fleet was thus able to set sail without any notice being given to the English forces. On the 9th of June it was reinforced at Malta by the divisions which had been sent from Ajaccio and Civita Vecchia. This magnificent armament now comprised thirteen ships of the line, fourteen frigates, seventy-two corvettes; the total number amounting to nearly five hundred vessels of all kinds, conveying twenty-five thousand soldiers and ten thousand sailors. It was an imposing spectacle, but it did not conceal from professional men the dangers attending such enormous incumbrances. According to Brueys himself, who was Commander-in-Chief of the naval forces, ten English men-of-war would have thrown this immense convoy into disorder and sufficed to destroy it. The whole success of so many combinations and designs depended on the uncertain chance of the fleet crossing the Mediterranean without a hostile encounter.

But fortune seemed to watch over her favourite with a kind of maternal solicitude and foresight. She began by giving him Malta. The feeblest resistance would have forced us to abandon this island, for it was of the utmost importance to get away before the English had time to surprise us there, which would have been an irreparable misfortune. Bonaparte could only try a *coup-de-main* on Malta; there were a thousand impossibilities in the way of a regular siege, and the place was so strong that the smallest demonstration, if only a little sustained, would have obliged him to proceed past it. But instead of meeting in the Knights of Malta with the intrepidity that might have been expected from the Order, he only found adversaries divided and demoralised—younger sons who, having had no enemy to fight but weariness, consumed in ignoble leisure an aimless strength, and passed their lives in giving and receiving entertainments in the towns on the Italian coast. It was the moral degeneration into which the Order of Malta was sunk, far more than the intrigues of Poussielgue among the French knights, which enabled Bonaparte to take possession of this impregnable place.

Count de Hompesch, then Grand Master of the Order, displayed a blind incredulity at this critical moment: he would not believe in the danger; and when the forces were really landed, a deep despondency was followed by a disgraceful inactivity. He paralysed the efforts of those knights who wished to defend their posts, encouraged by his cowardice the Maltese to mutiny, and capitulated after an insignificant defence, showing no other anxiety than that of securing for himself a handsome pension, which Bonaparte fixed at three hundred thousand francs. Caffarelli's witty saying sets a right value on this feat of arms: 'It was lucky,' he says, 'that there was somebody within to open the gates for us, or we should never have got in.' Thus perished this ancient institution, which, if it did not merit a longer existence, deserved at least a nobler end. If the knights had retained a spark of their chivalrous spirit, they would not have lost the opportunity of honouring their downfall by resisting, if only for a moment, a man who was a greater enemy to the enthusiasm of chivalry than any of the former adversaries of their Order.

Bonaparte found in Malta twelve hundred pieces of cannon, ten thousand pounds of powder, two ships of war, a frigate, four galleys, and forty thousand muskets. He seized all this booty, which had become our property by virtue of the new principle of law which he had established. The only complaint we could possibly allege against the knights was the asylum they had offered some emigrants, which was rather an honour to the Order than a reason for our seizing all that it possessed. The General sent as a trophy to the Directory a silver model of the first galley the knights had ever had. He left Malta on the 19th of June, after organising his conquest and leaving a garrison in the island.

Meanwhile Nelson, reinforced by a squadron of ten ships of the line, had re-appeared before Toulon, and heard of the departure of the French fleet. With only vague and incomplete indications to guide him, he had touched at Naples at the moment we were leaving Malta. Arrived at Naples, he divined that Egypt was our destination, passed us without knowing it in the night before Candia, where our army escaped certain destruction by a miracle, was one day in advance of us at Alexandria, and being unable to obtain any information there, and supposing us to be on our way to Syria, he turned with all haste in this direction, and thus saved us a second time without our own knowledge. This marvellous fortune, which the best-combined plans are not often favoured with, seemed accorded to us by the fickle goddess to hide more effectually the snare into which these kindnesses were to make us fall later on.

On the 28th of June, while the fleet was still in the open sea, Bonaparte informed his soldiers of the country to which he was conducting them, and the aim of the expedition: they were going to strike a death-blow at England, and undertake a conquest of which the effects on civilisation would be incalculable. But they were to conciliate the inhabitants of the country by respecting their religion, their manners, and their customs. 'Behave towards them as you did towards the Jews and the Italians. Treat their muftis and their imaums with respect, as you did the rabbis and the bishops. You must show the same spirit of toleration towards the ceremonies prescribed by the Koran that you did to the synagogues and the convents, to the religions of Moses and of Jesus Christ. The Roman legions protected all religions.' At the same time he issued an order against pillage, a very necessary precaution for the maintenance of discipline in an army so well prepared to take advantage of all the rights of war, that is to say of all the abuses of force, by the profitable use they had previously made of them in the Italian campaign.

On the 30th of June the French fleet appeared before Alexandria. The English had only left the day but one before, and were believed still to be not far off; in consequence of which the landing was effected with so much precipitation that it resembled a rout more than a capture. The place of disembarkation was the creek of Marabout, whence the troops immediately marched to Alexandria, which they took without difficulty. There Bonaparte halted for a week.

Egypt was at that time regarded as a dependency of the Ottoman Empire, but the Sultan was only represented by a Pacha, who resided at Cairo, holding an honorary office without any substantial authority. The real power rested with the Mamelukes, a service dating from the time of Saladin, and resembling no other military body in history. Recruited by slaves, purchased when children in Georgia and Circassia, and governed by twenty-four chiefs under the name of Beys, this force formed a strange kind of Order, which recognised no other religion than that of military fraternity, and no other law than the will of their masters. The right of sovereignty which the Porte maintained over the Mamelukes had long been nominal, and the Sultan was fortunate not to have even that disputed. Under the rule of this singularly constituted body there existed a population of which the various strata, differing widely from each other in manners and condition, bore witness to the successive invasions to which Egypt had been subjected. In the lowest rank the Cophts, a miserable degraded remnant of the primitive Egyptian race, filled certain offices and furnished agents and tax-gatherers to the Mamelukes. The class next above them were the first conquerors—the Arabs—of whom part, called Bedouins, still led the wandering pastoral life of Biblical times, while the rest cultivated the ground under the name of Fellahs, or possessed large tracts of land and were called Sheiks. And lastly there were the Turks, whose sovereignty had preceded that of the Mamelukes, and still received a purely formal homage in the person of the Pacha.

In any other country it would have been easy to excite a rising of the population against such rulers, but in Egypt nothing but passive and fatalist inertia could be expected from a people enfeebled for ages by the enervating influence of their religious faith, and brutalised by the abuses of despotism.

Bonaparte addressed himself first of all to the Pacha, and assured him of his respect for the Koran and the Sultan; he was only come to deliver Egypt from the oppression of the Mamelukes, and invited him to unite with him, and with him to 'curse the impious race of the Beys.' He next drew up some proclamations, which were translated into Arabic, and in which he appealed to all the passions he thought likely to act on the minds of the people. He enumerated all the evils which the tyranny of the Mamelukes had brought on them, all the privations it caused them; he promised to restore to them *their rights*, a word which was wholly incomprehensible to them, and which contrasts strangely with the oriental turn of the manifesto; then, assuring them of his respect for their religious faith, he said—

'We also are true Mussulmans. Is it not we who have destroyed the Pope, who said that it was necessary to make war on the Mussulmans? Is it not we who have destroyed the Knights of Malta, because those madmen believed that it was God's will that they should make war on Mussulmans? Thrice happy those who shall be with us! They shall prosper in their fortune and in their rank. Happy those who shall be neutral! they will have time to know us, and they will range themselves on our side! But woe to those who shall take up arms in favour of the Mamelukes and fight against us! There shall be no hope for them, they shall all perish!' (July 2d, 1798).

A great deal of admiration has been expressed for Bonaparte's political sagacity in these lavish flatteries of the Mussulman faith. But they were too immoderate and overdone to be really clever. They provoked the mirth of the soldiers, and produced no effect on the minds of the people to whom they were addressed. Our language was too much out of harmony with our situation to appear sincere. With the simple, instinct supplies the place of reasoning, and saves them from falling into snares so gross as these. It would have been both politic and just to respect the faith of the country, and honour it by constant consideration; but to pretend to adopt it, to sacrifice to it what passed for our own religious belief, and to shower contempt on what in Italy Bonaparte had treated with an exaggerated veneration, was too open a display of a spirit of charlatanry for which no artifice would be too base. The General might have spared himself a piece of dissimulation which was as useless as it was dishonourable to his dignity.

After having put Alexandria in a state of defence, the army plunged into the desert, to march upon Cairo by the most direct road, while a flotilla ascended the Nile in the same direction. The first few days' march under a fiery sun, across immense plains of sand, whose undulations formed here and there little hillocks behind which Arab horsemen lay in ambush to assassinate our stragglers, was extremely trying to the soldiers, and depressed them in an alarming manner. Harassed and fatigued, without bread, and without water to quench their tormenting thirst, they began to ask aloud if this miserable and barren country was going to realise the magnificent promises on the faith of which they had started. The 'Intercepted Correspondence,' partly written under this first impression, which was soon after published by the English, is one long cry of anger and disappointment.

Several officers remarkable for their bravery, but of quick and excitable imagination, shared this dejection and broke out in bitter complaints. But on the 10th of July the sight of the Nile revived their spirits, and on the 13th the first engagement with the brilliant horsemen of Murad-Bey, the principal chief of the Mamelukes, stimulated the army by proving that it would soon have to deal with enemies more worthy of resistance than the savage hordes whom only they had encountered hitherto. It is melancholy to have to acknowledge that it was cupidity which worked most powerfully on our soldiers. They stripped the dead Mamelukes; their arms were remarkably fine, and as each carried about him his whole fortune, considerable sums in gold were often found in their clothes. They now only thought of reaching Cairo, supposed to be the centre of immense riches. This first encounter, which took place near Chébreïss, had the additional effect of relieving our flotilla, which incurred the greatest dangers from the attacks of the Turkish gunboats. Bonaparte on this occasion made the experiment of the tactics most likely to be successful against cavalry which was so intrepid, but so incapable of discipline and combined action. The Mamelukes dashed themselves everywhere on our immovable squares, and retired without succeeding in breaking them at a single point.

On the 20th of July the army came in sight of the Pyramids. The following day they perceived the minarets of Cairo, from which they were only separated by the intrenched camp of Embabeh, where the Mamelukes had concentrated all their forces. They consisted of eight or ten thousand horsemen, who were to strive to surprise our battalions on march, while the infantry, troops of no value, but supported by cannon, were to wait for our encounter with the cavalry sheltered behind the intrenchments of Embabeh. Bonaparte adopted the same order of battle as at Chébreïss. He disposed his squares in alternate rows, with express orders only to halt to receive charges. He directed his movement in such a manner as to cut off from the enemy all retreat on the side of Upper Egypt. This battle, which, seen at a distance in the imposing framework furnished by the Pyramids, which had looked on the earliest ages of humanity, was destined to produce so powerful an effect on the minds of his contemporaries, was from inequality in arms rather than in bravery much more like a massacre than a serious contest. The comparative numbers of the killed and wounded in the two armies speak more plainly on this point than the most learned dissertation. According to Bonaparte's own account, we only had in this famous battle of the Pyramids 'from twenty to thirty killed, and a hundred and twenty wounded' (to the Directory, July 24th, 1798). On the other hand, the enemy lost two thousand men, of whom a portion were driven into the Nile and drowned.

In their regret at seeing such rich spoils swallowed up by the stream, some of the soldiers conceived the idea of bending their bayonets and fastening them to a piece of cord to fish for the dead bodies. There was scarcely one on which they did not find a sum of five or six hundred louis in gold, and 'for several days,' Napoleon's Memoirs inform us, 'the army was occupied in nothing but fishing up the corpses of Mamelukes.' He adds, 'that from that time the soldiers began to be reconciled to Egypt.' It is necessary to be acquainted with and to weigh all these details, in order to know exactly in what the glory of a conqueror consists.

Our soldiers waited for some days in the beautiful gardens of Giseh till the arrival of the flotilla; they then marched on Cairo, which surrendered without resistance. Bonaparte established his head-quarters in this rich and populous city; he laid himself out to captivate the inhabitants by that mixture of persuasion and severity which he had already learnt how to assume in Italy. He assembled the Sheiks, congratulated them on having got rid of their enemies the Mamelukes, and raised their expectations with regard to the re-establishment of Arab domination in Egypt. At the same time he assured the Pacha that he was only working to re-establish Turkish supremacy. As a pledge of his intentions to the Sheiks he formed them into a kind of central municipality, under the name of Divan. A local Divan was to be established in each province, and to send deputies to that at Cairo. He left the administration of justice in the hands of the Cadis, proclaimed more loudly than ever an unbounded attachment and respect for the religion of Mahomet, showed himself in all religious *fêtes* and public ceremonies, treated the women with the greatest consideration, and by this prudent and skilful, but ineffectual, conduct he obtained from the populace a semblance of adhesion, in which, however, he was not long in discovering the entire want of reality.

The General left Cairo at the end of a fortnight to pursue the scattered remnants of the Mamelukes, who had united under the command of Ibrahim-Bey and still annoyed our army. It was at Saleyeh, just as he was preparing to return from this expedition, that he received news of a disaster which cut off from his army all communication with Europe. Nelson had annihilated our fleet at Aboukir.

At the time when our army was leaving Alexandria, General Bonaparte gave Admiral Brueys instructions to move his squadron for shelter into the harbour of Alexandria, if he found sufficient depth of water; or else to ride in the Bay of Aboukir, if he thought that he could defend himself there against a superior force; and if both these courses were found impossible he was to set sail for Corfu. But this order left him only a choice between three impossibilities. On one side, the entry of the harbour of Alexandria was closed to his vessels of deep draught, and the channel, which was only discovered after a long search, was too shallow; on the second, the Bay of Aboukir only offered him a shelter which was worthless; and lastly, he could not sail for Corfu, which would have been the most advisable step to take, for want of provisions and stores. Independently of this necessity, which prevented his departure, he had other motives which made it a duty to remain. No news had for some time been received from the army; all communications were intercepted, and the most sinister reports were in circulation with regard to the fate of our soldiers. The squadron, which afforded their only hope of return, could not leave them in this uncertainty; the admiral wished to take news to France that the army which had just plunged into the desert had not encountered insurmountable obstacles, or else secure its retreat in case it had experienced reverses. Finding it impossible then either to enter the harbour of Alexandria or to set sail for Corfu, Brueys waited at Aboukir for provisions and for news of the army. It was there that Nelson surprised him on the evening of the 1st of August. Our fleet, boldly attacked in a position where it was thought the enemy would not venture to approach it, and placed between two fires, while its rear line was unable to take a share in the combat, was set on fire and destroyed, after a resistance in which our sailors attracted more admiration by their heroism than by their skill or their experience.

Bonaparte sent the Directory a long report on this disaster, throwing all the blame on the admiral, who was unable to answer him, for he had left as his only justification a sublime death. The General repeated the orders he had given, but said nothing about the impossibilities which opposed their execution. The only excuse he offered for Brueys was, that apparently 'the admiral did not wish to take the fleet to Corfu till he was sure of not being able to enter the harbour of Alexandria, and had ascertained that the army, of which he had received no news for some time, was in a position not to need a means of retreat' (to the Directory, August 29th, 1798). General Bonaparte could not, however, have been ignorant that Brueys was unable to sail for Corfu for want of the provisions which he had promised him, for in all his letters the admiral dwells on the need of stores, which was so paralysing that he could not even send two cruisers to watch for and signal the approach of the enemy. 'If I had only provisions,' he wrote to Bonaparte (July 26th), 'I should have sent out two large frigates on this mission, and I would keep all spies away from the coast; but without provisions or any means of repairing the tackle, one is paralysed: this inaction makes one ill.'[1] Bonaparte wrote to Brueys, the 30th of

[1] Correspondence of Brueys, quoted by Admiral Jurien de la Gravière in his *Histoire des Guerres Maritimes:* appendix.

July, the day before the disaster at Aboukir : 'I imagine that the fifty vessels laden with provisions have already arrived;' and he added, 'I am about to send off another thirty vessels laden with corn for your squadron.' It is evident that he only intended Brueys to sail for Corfu after the arrival of these vessels, for in every letter he repeats, 'You must get into port at Alexandria, *where you will take in as quickly as possible the stores of rice and corn* which I send you, *and then sail for Corfu.*'

Admiral Gantheaume's report of this disastrous event also attributes Brueys' protracted stay to Bonaparte's instructions, though, it is true, without dwelling on the necessity of waiting for the arrival of provisions : 'Considering the orders of the Commander-in-Chief, and the incalculable strength afforded to the land army by the presence of the squadron, the admiral thought it was his duty not to quit these waters.'

But, fearing that the responsibility of so great a disaster would bring discredit on his name, Bonaparte suppressed these explanations, that were due to the memory of the brave sailor who had been his friend. In their stead he substituted commonplace observations about destiny and fortune, to prove that even on this occasion they had exhausted their favours on our behalf, and only withdrawn them because we had shown by our improvidence that we were unworthy.

'This reverse, great as it may appear, cannot be attributed to the fickleness of Fortune; far from having abandoned us, she has favoured us more in this expedition than in any other. When I arrived before Alexandria . . . I recollect that while the troops were landing, the sail of a man-of-war was seen in the distance. It was the *Justice* coming from Malta. I exclaimed : "Fortune, wilt thou abandon me? What! I ask but five days!" And in five days I was master of Egypt. It was only when Fortune perceived that all her favours were useless, that she abandoned our fleet to its destiny.'

What singular pride, or rather what penetration and knowledge of human nature, Bonaparte displayed in thus attributing his success to the fidelity of fortune, and not to the skilfulness of his own arrangements! He knew that there was more to be gained by proving the fidelity of his star than by giving evidence of his genius or his virtue. The true cause of the destruction of our fleet lay neither in any want of forethought on the part of Brueys nor in the fickleness of exhausted fortune, but in the essence of the enterprise itself, full as it was of insurmountable difficulties. This destruction was an inevitable fact under the circumstances. Before arriving at Alexandria the French fleet had twice escaped certain ruin by a miracle. When once the alarm was given to the English, seeing the great importance they were sure to attach to its destruction, the hope of keeping open communications with Europe by means of the squadron was the most foolish delusion. Our fleet was doomed either to destruction or to be so effectively blockaded as to be perfectly useless.

The news of the disaster of Aboukir caused a profound explosion of despair and exasperation in the army. Bonaparte, however, set the leaders an example of calm and firmness. He depicted Egypt as a sort of island shut in on all sides by the desert, which they could easily render impregnable, and in which they would soon create all the resources they needed. 'If the English relieve this squadron by another,' he wrote to Kléber, 'they may perhaps oblige us to do greater things than we intended doing' (August 21st). These words only prove that the writer's confidence was already shaken, and were not likely to delude the sceptical good sense and keenness of Kléber.

In the present state of nearly complete isolation, and depending entirely on such resources as they might extract from the country, the scientific men who had joined the expedition were of the greatest assistance to Bonaparte. He had associated them with his administrators and some of his most distinguished officers, and had thus formed that Institute of Egypt which he intended to be as much an instrument of colonisation as a scientific body. He first employed them to make a report on the economical resources of Egypt. Before they studied her ancient monuments or geological structure, they were to examine the products of the soil and the industrial processes of the country. The General assigned them their task in a series of practical questions, in which his great and clear-sighted administrative ability reveals itself. They were to find out the best methods of constructing mills, of cultivating the vine, of making powder, to discover a substitute for hops in brewing beer, and a means of purifying the waters of the Nile. They were to find a solution to these problems, propounded by necessity, before they entered on those of a purely speculative nature; but Science had her turn, and it may be said that the only conquest of Egypt was hers. From this point of view, at any rate, our sacrifices were not made in vain. Bonaparte opened a French and Arab printing-press at Cairo, which enabled the army to have its journal. He also constructed manufactories and established a mint, which yielded considerable profits by increasing the means of exchange in a country in which money was almost unknown, and where the inhabitants preferred brass buttons from uniforms to European coins.

These peaceful occupations did not, however, make him forget the necessity of completing the destruction of the Mamelukes, of whom a portion, after the battle of the Pyramids, had united under Murad-Bey and taken refuge in Upper Egypt. This task was entrusted to Desaix, who after two or three days' march came on Murad-Bey at Sédiman, where the Mamelukes, as if blinded by an unconquerable love of routine, employed the same tactics as in the battle of the Pyramids. They had formed another intrenched camp, guarded by a body of infantry and flanked by five or six thousand horsemen who were drawn into the plain, where they broke on our squares without finding any advantage in their own foot-soldiers. But this time they fought with a desperate impetuosity, which was shared by the Arabs, who had joined their army in great numbers, thus proving how little we had obtained the favour of this part of the population. The revolt of Cairo came to confirm this demonstration, throwing the most sinister light upon it.

This insurrection, which was prepared with a secrecy

and an amount of union rarely exhibited in enterprises of the kind, was especially remarkable from the fact that it had not been provoked by any of the acts of excess which generally accompany foreign occupation, and render the presence of invaders hateful and intolerable. It had no other cause than the incompatibility of two civilisations diametrically opposed to one another. Bonaparte had displayed infinite skill in trying to make his government in Egypt a real benefit to the country, and the recollection of the Mamelukes, harshest of oppressors, might be supposed to render this task easy; he endeavoured daily more and more by every possible means to conciliate the population by lightening their burdens, and showed the greatest respect for their customs and prejudices, especially for their religious doctrines, which fixed a gulf between them and us. Still, he felt that in spite of all his efforts an invincible barrier existed; and as it was hopeless to think of making the Arabs Christians, he would gladly have seen his army embrace Mahometanism, to bring this difficulty to an end. But the initiative taken in this respect by General Menou only excited ridicule, and he found very few imitators, for if the soldiers had no religious convictions, they had, at any rate, a proud feeling of their moral superiority. This obstacle made Bonaparte regret that he had not lived in ancient times when conquerors had no such scruples, and speaking of Alexander the Great, he said he envied him his power of proclaiming himself the son of Jupiter Ammon, which had been worth more to him in his subjugation of Egypt than twenty battles gained. All he could do amid the meanness of an age of reason and reflection was to have recourse to artifice and trick. He adopted the sententious and imaginative language of the East, and never spoke to the Sheiks or Muftis without quoting on every occasion verses of the Koran, and continually boasted to them of 'having destroyed the Pope and overthrown the Cross.' He tried hard to strike the fatalist imagination by asserting that human efforts could not prevail against him, and by attributing to himself a kind of divine commission to complete the work of Mahomet. All this was clearly seen through by those barbarian intelligences, which, to escape being made the dupes of such a game, only needed the instincts of self-preservation and hatred of the foreigner.

The revolt of Cairo broke out on the 21st of October, and lasted three days. It was repressed with a rigour which proved that we had already borrowed something else from the Orientals as well as their sentences. The blood of our soldiers, assassinated in the streets, no doubt cried for vengeance, and as we had placed ourselves where such an insurrection was inevitable, it was necessary to stifle it. But the calamity ought to have reminded the author of so much evil, that these events were caused by his own desire to find in Egypt fresh means of exciting the admiration of the world, and have made him hesitate to sign the merciless orders which changed repression into butchery. 'The General-in-Chief orders,' he wrote to General Bon, 'that all persons found in the streets with arms in their hands be put to the sword' (October 22d). And, as if the execution of this order was not sufficient, he wrote the following day to Berthier: 'Order the commandant of the place, citizen-general, to cut off the heads of all the prisoners who were taken with arms in their hands. Let them be taken to-night to the borders of the Nile, between Boulak and Old Cairo; their headless corpses will be thrown into the river.' Some days after, writing to Regnier, he said, 'Every night we have about thirty heads cut off, and a great many chiefs': this, I fancy, will be a lesson to them.' As the peasants in the neighbourhood of Cairo had taken part in the revolt, a great number were seized and beheaded. One morning a troop of asses, laden with sacks and escorted by soldiers, arrived in the place Ez-Bekieh, the most populous quarter in Cairo; the inhabitants, attracted by curiosity, crowded round the convoy, and when the soldiers opened the sacks, the heads of peasants, with which they were filled, rolled on to the ground before the eyes of the terror-stricken multitude.

We lost on our side about fifty men, the insurgents from two thousand to two thousand five hundred. Such was the reality of those dazzling dreams which fixed the eyes of the world. If, as was asserted, our security required such hecatombs, what plea can be urged in favour of the enterprise which had rendered such conduct necessary? Of these poor Fellahs who lost their lives in driving out the foreigners whom they considered the enemies of their country and their faith, and the ambitious youth from whom they learned civilisation through forms of violence and fraud, and who, to raise himself one step higher on his pedestal, had brought death and ruin to such multitudes,—who of the two was nearest to the traditions of ancient barbarism?

CHAPTER XI

CAMPAIGN IN SYRIA

1798

THANKS to this terrible execution, the winter passed without much disturbance. No news from Europe had reached the army, and General Bonaparte was not only in total ignorance of the state of the Continent, but he did not suspect that Turkey had declared war against France, though she might naturally have been expected to do so, after our conduct in return for her kind offices and constant friendship. The disposition of the Porte was indicated by the arrest of a great number of French in Syria, as well as by the conduct of Djezzar, Pacha of Acre, who treated the General's flattering letters with disdainful silence, while he beheaded his envoys. Finding he could obtain no answer from Djezzar, he determined towards the middle of December to send M. de Beauchamp to Constantinople. His mission was to represent to the Porte that 'our intentions were friendly, and that our only aim in invading Egypt was to punish the Mamelukes and the English, and to hinder the two emperors (the emperor of Russia and the emperor of Austria) from dividing the Ottoman empire between them.' He was also imperiously to require the release of the French prisoners, and promise that we would 'evacuate Egypt as soon as the two emperors had abandoned their project of dividing Turkey.' These instructions (dated December 11th, 1798), which were based on the supposition that the statesmen of the Porte were utterly devoid of intelligence, resulted in the imprisonment of Beauchamp in the castle of the Seven Towers. Meanwhile

Bonaparte wrote the same explanations in a letter addressed to 'Citizen Talleyrand, Ambassador at Constantinople.' Talleyrand had in fact promised to accept this embassy, for the purpose of preventing any interruption in our friendly relations with the Porte; but, like a man of caution, he had been in no hurry to fulfil a mission so evidently useless.

The General, however, soon received information which left him in no doubt with regard to the real intentions of the Porte. He soon knew that one Turkish army was forming in Syria, and another at Rhodes, with the purpose of recovering Egypt. He determined, in consequence, to anticipate the attempts of the enemy by invading Syria. He would thus avoid the danger of a popular effervescence that would inevitably arise from the presence of a Turkish army in Egypt; he would disconcert his enemy's plans and destroy his magazines. To take possession of Syria had always formed part of his scheme; this country being not only the necessary highroad of every invasion directed against us, but also the indispensable basis of our future operations against the English possessions in India. Syria once conquered, what would be Bonaparte's sequel to the expedition? Here this mind, at once so positive and yet so addicted to chimera, delighted to give free room to those gigantic illusions which were always mixed up with his best-conceived plans. He only half surrendered himself to these plans, and reserved to himself the chance of deciding, according to circumstances. At one time he studied the map of the deserts which separated Syria from Persia, fought over again the campaigns of Alexander, and wrote to Tippoo-Saïb that he was preparing 'to deliver him from the iron yoke of England' (January 25th, 1799). At another, he pictured himself as raising an insurrection of the Druses and Greek Christians against the Turks, and marching with this immense army upon Constantinople, and then, to use his own expression, *taking Europe in the rear*, and overthrowing the Austrian monarchy on his way, and finally making the most marvellous triumphal entry into France recorded in the history of men.

Putting aside from the second plan these magic perspectives, of which he only gave glimpses to his most confidential intimates, he spent the winter in making active preparations for the expedition. Repeated raids on the tribes of the desert had procured him the necessary camels; he formed a new kind of cavalry mounted on dromedaries; he placed little forts round the principal springs on the march, and embarked the ammunition and siege artillery in three frigates. With a view to insure tranquillity during his absence, he restored the general council or Divan of Cairo, which had been suppressed after the insurrection. In a curious proclamation, addressed on this occasion to the sheriffs and ulemas, he said: 'Make the people understand that since the world was a world, it was written that having destroyed the enemies of Islamism and beaten down the Cross, I should come from the farthest West to accomplish the task appointed for me. Show the people that in more than twenty passages of the holy book of the Koran what has happened and what is about to happen is foretold. I could demand a reckoning from each of you for the most secret feelings of his heart, since I know everything, even what you have never told to any one. But the day will come in which you all will recognise that I have received my commission from on high, and that human efforts cannot prevail against me. Happy they who first take part with me' (December 21st, 1798).

He next made an exploring expedition on the shores of the Red Sea, recognised traces of the canal of Sesostris, studied on the spot the problem of uniting the two seas, and then went on to Sinai to sign his name by the side of that of Mahomet, on the register kept by the monks—a species of homage which he had sought an opportunity of paying, for Mahomet was one of the historical figures he admired the most; and he often lamented that the poverty of imagination in his contemporaries prevented him from playing, like this great man, the double character of political and religious reformer.

Finally, he set off at the beginning of February 1799,

leaving Desaix in Upper Egypt, Dugua at Cairo, and Marmont at Alexandria. The force was composed of the divisions of Kléber, Bon, Murat, Lannes, and Reynier, and amounted to about twelve thousand men. The Pachas, whose troops were assembled in Syria, had sent an advanced guard on to Egyptian territory, as far as El Arish; it was in possession of this fort and the surrounding country when our army arrived there, after a long and troublesome march in the desert. The fort of El Arish was taken after a resistance of two days; the garrison, consisting of about twelve hundred men, surrendered, and the forces which held the country were beaten and dispersed (February 20th). The French army rested, and a few days after entered Asia. At Gaza it again routed the cavalry of Djezzar-Pacha, and on the 3d of March was before Jaffa.

This little town of Palestine, so often disputed during the time of the Crusades, and whose ancient celebrity was about to be renewed by fresh scenes of bloodshed, possessed fortifications in a tolerably good state of defence, and a garrison of about four thousand men. When the governor, who was one of Djezzar's lieutenants, was summoned to surrender, he replied by the favourite measure of his master —he ordered the messenger to be beheaded. But Bonaparte's dispositions were so skilfully made, that after a few hours' cannonade a breach was effected. He immediately ordered the assault. Our soldiers forced an entrance into the place, and committed frightful carnage among the inhabitants as well as the garrison. They killed about two thousand persons. Some officers having checked the massacre, a part of the garrison, estimated at two thousand or two thousand five hundred men, who had taken refuge in the mosques and a sort of citadel, surrendered unconditionally, according to some historians; on condition of their lives being saved, according to others.

Nearly a thousand inhabitants of the neighbouring provinces, who happened to be in the town, were sent either to Damascus or into Egypt. But what was to be done with the two thousand five hundred prisoners? To dismiss them was to furnish the enemy with certain recruits; and to detain them was to keep useless mouths. For two days their fate was in suspense; on the third, March 9th, 1799, they were formed into columns and placed in the centre of a large square battalion, commanded by General Bon, who ordered them to take the road to the sea. They foresaw the doom that awaited them, and marched on in silence with the dull resignation of fatalism. When they arrived at the sand-piles they were divided into small platoons, and put to death by the musket and the bayonet. The original copy of the order for this execution, in which General Bonaparte recommends that in shooting these poor wretches 'care should be taken that *not one of them should escape*,' still exists. Happily for the honour of human nature, this order was not executed without protests and murmurs, and several chiefs of brigades, Colonel Royer [1] among others, positively refused to undertake the execution of it.

It is easy to understand that the friends of Napoleon's memory should be anxious to find excuses for this horrible massacre. They have given three principal reasons, founded on his affirmations at Saint Helena, in justification of the deed: first, the danger of furnishing the enemy with reinforcements; secondly, the impossibility of keeping the prisoners, since he had no food for them; and, lastly, that these soldiers formed part of the garrison of El Arish, which he had spared.

But these allegations unfortunately do not bear a strict examination. The danger of reinforcing the enemy by dismissing the prisoners was perhaps real; but there was nothing very redoubtable in a struggle in which in fighting armies of fifteen to twenty thousand we lost on an average thirty or forty men. Bonaparte himself states in his report to the Directory (March 13th, 1799), that in the two sieges of Jaffa and El Arish—and the sieges were by far the most murderous affairs—and in all the battles in which the army had been engaged since it entered Syria, including that of Gaza, we had lost but *fifty men*. He might easily have dismissed enemies from whom he had so little to fear. The wretches were, moreover, sufficiently demoral-

[1] *Mémoires of Prince Eugène.*

ised by the massacre they had witnessed at the taking of the town.

But the same report shows that he was not driven to get rid of them for want of food. We had found abundant provisions both at Gaza and El Arish. 'At Jaffa,' wrote Bonaparte, 'we took more than four hundred thousand rations of biscuits, and two hundred thousand hundredweight of rice.' To detain the prisoners, therefore, though difficult and inconvenient, was by no means impossible. The pretended identity of the prisoners of Jaffa with those of El Arish is one of the numerous fables invented by Bonaparte at Saint Helena to influence the judgment of history. There is not a trace of this assertion in the numberless letters and pieces of various kinds in which Bonaparte gives an account of the event; there is not a word of it in Berthier's report, not a word of it in the narrative of Miot, the historiographer of the Egyptian expedition.[1] It is evident that if these prisoners had formed part of the garrison of El Arish, the General would have taken advantage of such a pretext to lighten the odious effect of his order. In writing to the Directory he merely said, 'I have treated with severity the garrison who allowed themselves to be taken with arms in their hand.' This was the single crime which, according to his construction of 'the rules of war,' authorised the dreadful massacre. It was at Elba, in a conversation with Lord Ebrington, that it occurred to him to plead this striking circumstance: 'What you say of this massacre is true,' he said; 'I did order nearly two thousand Turks to be shot. You look upon this as rather strong; but I had allowed them to capitulate at El Arish, on condition that they should return to their homes. They broke it, and threw themselves into Jaffa. *I could not take them with me, for I was short of bread, and they were too dangerous to be set at liberty a second time.* I had no alternative but to put them to death.' Admitting the possibility that the defenders of Jaffa were some of the fugitives of El Arish, which is not unlikely,

[1] This Miot was the brother of the Miot who afterwards took the name of Melito.

they must have been there in a very small number, for Bonaparte had incorporated in his army nearly half of the twelve hundred men who formed the garrison of El Arish. 'We found at El Arish,' he wrote to the Directory, 'five hundred Albanians, five hundred Moghrebins, and two hundred Anatolians. The Moghrebins have entered our service. I have made them an auxiliary corps.' Supposing that all the Albanians and all the Anatolians had fled to Jaffa, which is not admissible, and which it was impossible to verify, that would only have made seven hundred men, dispersed among a garrison of four thousand, the half of which had been already massacred. But admitting the truth of all the conditions of this hypothesis, the number of El Arish soldiers among the prisoners of Jaffa could not have been more than two or three hundred men. Referring to the taking of Jaffa, Bonaparte said that 'war had never appeared to him more hideous,' a remark he felt it necessary to make after the recital of so many horrible tales; but it was more declamatory than sincere, if we refer to what he wrote on the same subject, and at the same moment, to those with whom he spoke more freely. '*The taking of Jaffa*,' he wrote to Marmont, '*was very brilliant*. Four thousand of the best troops of Djezzar, and the best gunners of Constantinople, were put to the sword' (March 9th, 1799).

On the 14th of March the army advanced to Saint Jean-d'Acre, carrying with it the infection of the plague, which had been caught at Jaffa. It was here that the terrible Djezzar resided, whose unrelenting cruelties, as his name indicated,[1] had rendered him as formidable to Syrians as to Europeans. Here he had collected his treasures, his best troops, and immense military stores. The ancient fortifications of the town had been strengthened by all the resources of modern art, through the efforts of Sidney Smith, commander of the English cruisers, who had furnished him with engineers and gunners. Sidney Smith, of adventurous and chivalrous character, an able and enterprising officer, full of an indefatigable activity, animated by all the ardour of the national hatred to the French and

[1] Djezzar in Arabic signifies 'butcher.'

their chief, had understood the importance of the preservation of Acre, and had stimulated incessantly the energy of the Pacha and his garrison by promise of reinforcements, and by supporting with the fire of his vessels the defence of the place.

He had already seized the vessels which were transporting our siege artillery, and with it had armed the ramparts of the town. In consequence of this misfortune, when the French arrived before the fortifications they found themselves reduced to batter a breach with field artillery, and so in want of balls as to be obliged to make use of those discharged from the enemy's cannon. Colonel Sanson, who had reconnoitred the place at night and very superficially, and was wounded in the attempt, had made sure that there was neither ditch nor counterscarp. In the first assault we paid dearly for this error. It was necessary to mine, which was only partially effective, and a second assault was made on the 28th of May, in which we suffered still more severe losses than in the first. The garrison defended the town with a vigour which astonished our troops, who had not been accustomed to meet with strong resistance from the Turks, and the greater part of our soldiers who penetrated into the town were slain. The firing from the citadel, directed partly by Europeans, was marked by formidable accuracy; the works which we attacked were speedily and systematically repaired. The plan had been traced by Philippeaux, a French officer of engineers, who had been a companion of Bonaparte's at the Ecole Militaire, and who quite recently had assisted in the escape of Sidney Smith from the Temple, in which he had been confined as a prisoner of war.

This success, and the arrival of the promised reinforcements, with a quantity of provisions, kept up the courage of the garrison. Bonaparte had hoped that he could raise the inhabitants of the country, who were in part favourable to us. But he obtained no effective help from them; they remained in a state of uncertainty between their old and their new oppressors. To the proclamation, full of magnificent promises, issued by Bonaparte, Sidney Smith replied by a manifesto, in which he besought them 'to trust the faith of a Christian knight, rather than that of a renegade without honour,' alluding to the profession of Mahometanism which the General had published in Egypt. Sidney Smith tried the same arguments with our soldiers, whom he openly persuaded to desert; and after an exchange of personal insults between himself and the General, he went so far as to send him a challenge. Bonaparte answered him by ironically proposing to neutralise a piece of ground on the shore, and to send as his representative one of his grenadiers; perhaps the only answer that was deserved by so puerile a thing as a challenge to such a man.

Meanwhile, it was soon ascertained that an army of twenty-five thousand men, composed partly of troops from Damascus under the orders of Abdallah-Pacha, and partly of recruits from among the warlike inhabitants of Naplouse, was marching to aid Djezzar. Kléber, with his division, was despatched to meet the enemy, and the two advanced guards came into collision at Nazareth. Kléber's, commanded by Junot, and composed of a few hundred men, resisted for eight hours forces ten times their number, and then fell back in good order on the division to which they belonged. Kléber's division was now threatened by the whole Turkish army; it became urgent to relieve him. Bonaparte, leaving the rest of his troops to keep the trenches before Acre, advanced with Bon's division and eight pieces of artillery. On his arrival on the heights overlooking the valley, which is shut in on one side by Mount Tabor, he perceived in the distance on the plains below Kléber's weak squares of infantry assailed on all sides by large bodies of cavalry. At one moment they appeared completely overwhelmed, and were almost lost sight of; then again, amidst clouds of smoke and fire, the enemy was seen to retire a short distance, only to rush forward with increased fury to make a fresh charge. Bonaparte made his dispositions in such a way as to turn the Turks and mask his march; he threw his cavalry on their flanks, and when he was within a mile and a half of Kléber, he gave notice of his approach by firing a cannon. The columns immediately moved forward, and charged the enemy, who was surprised and disconcerted by this unexpected succour. The Turkish army, enclosed in a kind of triangle of iron, and overwhelmed by the cross-fire, finding with difficulty an outlet on the side of the mountains and the river Jordan, precipitated themselves in that direction in utter confusion, leaving in their flight the field of battle covered with their dead (April 16th).

In the meantime the operations of the siege had been carried on with more perseverance than success; harassed as they were by incessant sorties, and by skilfully constructed counter-works, which made all our mines ineffectual. Rear-Admiral Perrée had, however, succeeded in escaping the vigilance of the English fleet, and had brought several pieces of cannon, by means of which they had effected a new breach and blown up a part of the tower which protected the principal point of attack. A handful of brave men forced their way into this tower, and held it for two days; but they were nearly all killed, and the remainder were forced to evacuate it, unable even to hinder the enemy from repairing the breach by new works. The army, exasperated by this resistance, delivered several consecutive assaults during the first days of May, and, carried on with irresistible impetuosity, our men more than once penetrated to the heart of the town. Kléber's division was recalled to the camp on the 7th of May to join in a general assault, and all the soldiers went out to meet him, predicting that he would have the honour of taking the town.[1] Kléber's grenadiers passed the first enceinte, under the double fire from the ramparts and Sidney Smith's ships; they then forced their way through the second, and even penetrated into the town; but here, before Djezzar's palace, where every house was converted into a fortress, their intrepid courage failed them. They returned to the trenches, while the garrison, reinforced every hour by fresh troops, made sorties by every gate, and came to harass our camp. On the 10th of May a fresh assault was made, more to satisfy the irritated soldiers than in the hope of taking the place.

[1] *Mémoires de Lavalette.*

This was the fourteenth attack, and it was more unsuccessful than any of the preceding ones. The siege of Acre had now continued sixty days, during which time the garrison had made twenty-six sorties; we had lost several generals, besides a host of officers of the greatest merit; Caffarelli, a man of distinguished intelligence as well as an excellent soldier, Rambeaud, Croisier, and Bon : Lannes and Duroc were dangerously wounded. More than four thousand men were disabled, and the plague, which we had brought from Jaffa, was raging in the camp. At the same time news was received that the Turks were preparing to embark an army at Rhodes for Lower Egypt. Nothing but a prompt retreat could deliver us from greater evils. Even Bonaparte's obstinacy was forced to bend before these inexorable facts. Many times during the deadly delays of this fatal siege, in which he experienced his first check, he was heard to inveigh against 'this miserable little hole which came between him and his destiny.' And many times later, when dwelling on the vicissitudes of his past life, and the different chances which had been open to him, he repeated 'that if Saint Jean-d'Acre had fallen, he would have changed the face of the world, and been Emperor of the East.' And he generally added, that it was *a grain of sand that had undone all his projects*. But what more striking criticism could he make to show their inanity? His own remark contains a condemnation of the speculative enterprises, which were more worthy of the inspirations of a gambler than the combinations of a truly political mind.

On the 17th of May it was decided to retreat, and a long convoy of sick and wounded preceded the rest of the army on the road to Jaffa, whence they were to gain Lower Egypt. But however bitter his disappointment, and however humiliating to his pride, Bonaparte was by no means inclined to acknowledge his defeat. In his bulletins, in his letters, in his reports to the Directory and to the generals who remained in Egypt, and even in his proclamations to the army, which was retreating from Acre, mutilated, dejected, and amazed at a reverse so novel for them, he assumed the tone and airs of a conqueror.

He had battered down the palace of Djezzar, burned the town, and left the fortifications a heap of ruins; not a stone was left on stone. We were retreating, not before the enemy but before the plague; our purpose in going into Syria was amply accomplished. The untruthfulness of such an assertion was demonstrated by the sight of such misfortunes, and the evacuation of a country, the occupation of which had been represented as necessary for the security of our possessions in Egypt. He was resolved to re-enter Egypt with all the appearances of a triumphal return. The Adjutant-General Boyer, who commanded the vanguard, received orders to take with him the Turkish standards, 'and to display them in all the villages through which he passed, as trophies of victory.' He was also to make a great parade of his prisoners; in short, added the despatch, 'he is to write, say, and do all in his power to make the entry triumphal' (to Berthier, May 24th, 1799).

The rear-guard, commanded by Kléber, received instructions to destroy everything before it, as if to enlarge the natural limits of the desert. The General enjoined him to burn all houses, to set fire to villages, and to destroy the mills, so that if a pursuing army followed us, it should find nothing but smoking ashes (Orders to Kléber and Junot). At Tantourah, the soldiers, whose sufferings, which were only beginning, exasperated by the distress of marching under a scorching sun along a road strewed with those who were left to die, and who with outstretched hands reproached them with their desertion, mutinied. General Bonaparte abstained from employing any rigorous measures to put down this sedition of despair. He contented himself with reprimanding the generals, ordered all the cavalry on foot, except the rear-guard, and set the example to his officers by giving up his own horses to convey the sick and wounded. This unexpected trial, stronger than his own will, produced in him a sombre irritation, but his indomitable courage did not forsake him; and when his equerry came to ask which horse he wished to have reserved for his use, he angrily struck him with a riding whip, exclaiming, 'Every one on foot! Did you not hear the order?'

At Jaffa the army halted for a few days. The plague was at its height. The hospitals were crowded, and it was attempted to keep up the spirits of the poor wretches by persuading them that the disease was not contagious. It was then that Desgenettes, under the impulse of heroic self-sacrifice, is said to have inoculated himself in the presence of the soldiers to give proof of a belief which he did not hold, but which he thought necessary for the safety of the army. This anecdote, though so long admitted as true, appears as contestable as the one which gave rise to Gros's admirable picture. This illustrious physician was often heard to say by friends still living, that had he been inoculated he would as certainly have died of the plague, like the two English doctors who on the strength of the report tried to imitate his example.

When the army left Jaffa, there remained a certain number of plague-stricken men in the hospital, variously estimated from twenty to sixty men, for whom they had no means of transport. Their too probable fate was to be murdered by the Turks, like the wounded whom we left behind us. Bonaparte, wishing to put an end to their sufferings, proposed to Desgenettes to give them a dose of opium. 'My art teaches me to cure men, and not to kill them,' was the physician's noble reply, which history has preserved. The rumour of the General's proposal soon spread in the army, and the belief was current that the deed was actually carried into execution. Many years later, in a conversation at Saint Helena, Grand Marshal Bertrand told Napoleon that he had always thought the opium was given, and that the belief was general throughout the army. Robert Wilson, the historian of the British expedition into Egypt, repeats the story with a great deal of exaggeration, giving the number of sick who were poisoned at more than five hundred. Napoleon, in trying to clear himself from this grave imputation, only strengthened the evidence against him by the inaccuracies of his allegations. In the *Memorial* he attributes to a subaltern the proposal to administer opium to the sick; but even M. de Las Cases is obliged to admit that the proposal came from Bonaparte himself. Then he asserts that his rear-guard was left behind at Jaffa *for three days* to protect the dying, whereas all the orders and documents prove that the rear-guard left Jaffa the *day following* the one in which the army evacuated the place. Besides, while he denies ever having ordered that recourse should be had to so horrible an experiment, he by no means recoils from the idea as 'an atrocious calumny,' to use the expression of the Duke de Rovigo,[1] but maintains its lawfulness, affirming to O'Meara and dictating to Bertrand, 'that it would have been to obey the voice of reason; that he would have held the propriety of such a step, if his own son had been in that situation.'

After so weak a defence, it is not astonishing that the fact, though indignantly denied by Bonaparte's friends with an indignation that is misplaced after such a profession of faith, should continue to have found credit for so long among his adversaries. The story would never have been credited for such a length of time, had it not been in conformity with all that is known of his principles and opinions. But history demands direct evidence for whatever it affirms, and we are compelled to state, that not only was this accusation founded only on presumptions more or less plausible, but that two circumstances tend definitively to end the controversy: first, the retractation of Sir Robert Wilson, who afterwards admitted that he had asserted the fact on the strength of rumours that were insufficient to constitute a certainty; and the second and more conclusive is the absence of any allusion to it in the official reports sent to the English Government by Commodore Sidney Smith, who, arriving at Jaffa just after our rear-guard had left, found some of the sick men still alive in the hospital, and who, though he mentions with complacency various complaints which they made against their General, does not say a word about poisoning. The most probable version of the story is that dictated to Bertrand in the Memoirs.

[1] *Mémoires du Duc de Rovigo.* Savary concludes his defence by adding that the opium could not have been given, since the army had none. If it were so, we are led to ask why Napoleon did not make use of so conclusive an argument?

'Napoleon,' he says, 'gave orders to the surgeon who remained with the sick to place opium within their reach, and explain to them that it was the only means left them of escaping from the cruelty of the Turks.' There is nothing very clear about this famous accusation beyond the characteristic opinion which Napoleon expressed with regard to it. There may be some bravado in the cold assurance with which he settled the question, but we cannot fail to recognise also a heart inaccessible to the scruples which make most men hesitate.

In Egypt, after a long and wearisome march across the desert, the army was able to take some rest, and recruit after the fatigues of the campaign. Two risings, which had been promptly quelled, had taken place during General Bonaparte's absence: one was that of Emir Hadji; the other that of an obscure fanatic, who represented himself as the Angel El'mody, promised in the Koran to the faithful in time of persecution. His only food was milk, in which he merely dipped his fingers and passed them over his lips; and his only weapon was a handful of dust, which he threw in the air, assuring his followers that this alone would disperse our army. Several thousands of men rose at his call; and though the insurrection was insignificant in itself, it proved how very little had been done in the way of that assimilation which it was our object to effect. General Lanusse, a skilful and energetic officer, who had already subdued the Emir, marched rapidly on Damanhour, dispersed the army of fanatics, and put fifteen hundred to death. The Angel himself was among the dead.

Upper Egypt, which had been placed under the command of Desaix, had remained undisturbed since the disappearance of Mourad-Bey, who had been forced to take refuge in Nubia. But Bonaparte had no sooner returned to Cairo, than this intrepid chief, learning that a Turkish army was preparing to embark at Rhodes, reappeared; and at the same time Ibrahim-Bey threatened Egypt on the side of the Syrian desert. Followed by a few hundred Mamelukes, the remnant of his splendid cavalry, and hunted down by Murat, Desaix, Junot, and Friant, Mourad-Bey appeared first at one point and then at another, and kept all his enemies in check. At the moment when they believed his forces completely destroyed, he was suddenly seen in the neighbourhood of Cairo. Bonaparte, irritated at an enemy who was always escaping his reach, and understanding nothing of his march towards Lower Egypt, because he was in ignorance of the appearance of the Turkish fleet, gave way to transports of anger against him, that were far from being worthy of a loyal and generous enemy. 'I am very anxious,' he wrote to Friant, 'that you should add to the many services you have rendered us, the *still greater one of either killing Mourad-Bey or wearing him to death by fatigue.* He must die somehow or other, and in whatever way his death occurs I shall be equally your debtor' (July 5th, 1799). He gave the same directions to his other lieutenants.

On the 13th of July, Mourad-Bey was at the Pyramids; he ascended the highest, and from the summit contemplated the splendid country over which he had once ruled as sovereign, and in which he was now a fugitive. He spent the greater part of the day in trying to catch sight of the palace in which he had left his family at Cairo, and his beautiful gardens at Giseh, all of which were now the prey of the conqueror. Bonaparte, who had gone in pursuit of the chief, understood his movements as soon as he learned that a hundred Turkish vessels and two English ships of the line had disembarked from fifteen to eighteen thousand men at Aboukir, near Alexandria, and that their first exploit on landing had been to possess themselves of the fort and bribe or take prisoners the four hundred French who had occupied it. The General immediately assembled the divisions of Lannes, Murat, and Bon, and without waiting for further reinforcements marched to Aboukir, to prevent the enemy from penetrating into the interior of the country. But the Turkish army had no cavalry, and while reckoning on the horsemen of Mourad-Bey had fortified themselves in the peninsula of Aboukir, which they had protected with a double line of intrenchments. It was here that Bonaparte attacked them on the 25th of July, after having ascertained that the works which Colonel Cretin, a particularly dis tinguished officer of engineers, had been carrying on at Alexandria had placed the town in a state of defence. He had not more than six thousand men with him, but seeing that the Turks had no cavalry, the only arm that would have rendered them formidable, he did not hesitate to attack them.

The first line of intrenchments was separated from the second by a small plain, about three-quarters of a league wide, which formed a kind of isthmus, with the sea on one side and the Lake of Madieh on the other. Bonaparte's plan was to commence an attack on this first line of intrenchments, drive the Turks into this narrow space, and keep them blocked up there till our reinforcements arrived. Accordingly, Destaing attacked them on the right and Lannes on the left. The Turks sustained the first attack with great intrepidity; but as soon as Murat succeeded in breaking through their centre with his cavalry, and penetrated into the plain between the two lines of intrenchments, they found themselves charged on both sides before they had time to gain their second line. Here they were seized by an indescribable panic, and throwing away their arms they rushed into the sea on one side and into the lake on the other, in hopes of reaching the Turkish boats. Our cavalry pursued them till the horses were up to their breasts in water. Several thousands of Turks perished in the waves in sight of our soldiers, who watched them from the shore, stupefied at their own work. This formidable triumph encouraged the army to force the second line of intrenchments. But that presented stronger obstacles than the first, and our loss was much greater. Several excellent officers, Leturcq, Cretin, Duvivier, Guibert, among others, were mortally wounded; but when the Turks left their intrenchments to cut off the heads of our wounded and dead, Murat made a fresh charge, drove them back into the works, scaled the ramparts along with them, and decided the victory. All who did not yield were massacred or thrown into the sea. Three thousand men who had barricaded themselves in the village and fort were taken prisoners the following day. Such was the second disaster of Aboukir; it was perhaps more sanguinary than the first, but it could neither blot out the remembrance of the former, nor above all could it neutralise its effects.[1]

When, after this battle, negotiations were entered into between the French camp and the English fleet for the exchange of prisoners, Sidney Smith, actuated either by motives of revenge or by a desire to discourage the French army, gave the bearer of the flag of truce a packet of newspapers addressed to Bonaparte. The General had only received one despatch from the Directory during the previous ten months.

He knew nothing of the affairs of Europe, and had only an indistinct idea of the state of France, through a letter which his brother Joseph had secretly sent him by a Greek named Bourbaki, pressing him to return.[2] He spent the night in eagerly devouring the newspapers. He read the sad history of reverses, of Italy lost, of France threatened; but the intelligence respecting the Directory was of far more importance to him. He saw power passing out of the hands of the directors, and that they were in mortal conflict with an assembly eager to avenge themselves for their past humiliations. Ever since the reception of his brother Joseph's letter, he had resolved to return to Europe; the victory of Aboukir now enabled him to quit the command of his army. This secret determination to leave Egypt explains his singular declaration before the battle of Aboukir, which so astonished Murat: 'This battle will decide the fate of the world.' The information he had derived from the newspapers decided him to realise his resolution on the spot.

[1] We may here remark that Bonaparte's account of the victory of Aboukir differs in many important points from that of Berthier. In the report sent to Mustafa-Pacha, after the disembarkation, dated 7 Sefir (July 11th), the Turkish army is estimated at only seven thousand men. A copy of the report may be found in Capefigue, *L'Europe pendant le Consulat*, tom. i.

[2] The existence of this letter, affirmed first by Miot and the anonymous author of the *Mémoires de Fouché*, and afterwards denied by Bourrienne and other historians, has since been proved by the *Mémoires* of Joseph himself.

His purpose was not for an instant shaken by any regret he may have felt at abandoning his brothers in arms. He communicated his project to Berthier and Gantheaume, and gave them orders, with the greatest secrecy, to make ready the frigates *Carrère* and *Muiron*. When this was done he returned to Cairo, to take the necessary measures preparatory to his departure. Reports soon began to be circulated with regard to his determination, but he caused them to be contradicted, and gave out a proposed visit to Upper Egypt as the pretext of his journey. At length, having assembled those whom he wished to take with him, he left the town, but instead of ascending the Nile, he took the contrary direction and went rapidly down towards Alexandria. It was not till he arrived at the sea-shore, on an unfrequented part of the beach, and had ascertained that the frigates were ready, that he openly spoke of his project. Turning to Eugène de Beauharnais, he said, 'Eugène, you will soon see your mother again.'

Prince Eugène assures us in his *Mémoires* that these words did not give him so much pleasure as might have been expected. The circumstances attending this furtive departure explain the feelings of a young and generous heart. General Bonaparte may have believed that his presence was necessary in France, but it was unquestionably more so to the army, which had trusted to his genius, which was already considerably weakened even by its victories, and which was on the point of having to engage with enemies far more formidable than the Turks, the English and Russian armies.

Since he had involved it in this hazardous enterprise on his own responsibility, he was in honour bound to share its perils to the end. He could not believe in the possibility of sending effective reinforcements, nor could he be ignorant of the state of discouragement into which the army would be thrown by his desertion of it. The flower of the army had perished in the disastrous campaign of Syria, and he ended by robbing it of the few good officers who survived, and who constituted its real strength. He took with him Lannes, Murat, Berthier, Marmont, Andréossy, Duroc,

Bessières, Lavalette; not to speak of Monge, Berthollet, Denon, men who were equally useful in another way.

He left Kléber in command of a diminished and prostrated army. Wishing to avoid the reproaches which he knew he might expect from this general's manly frankness, he assigned him a rendezvous which he knew he could not possibly attend. Many times during the campaign in Syria, the strong common sense and independence of Kléber had been displayed in pointing out to Bonaparte the hazardous and chimerical nature of his projects. The instructions which the General-in-Chief left to be placed in Kléber's hands contained the very significant recommendation to treat for the evacuation of Egypt, 'if he should lose fifteen hundred men by the plague.' In a proclamation addressed to the Divan of Cairo, Bonaparte explained that the object of his departure was to 'put himself at the head of his squadron;' and he promised to return in two or three months.

Kléber felt great indignation at the treatment he received at the hands of his General-in-Chief, who by a skilful manœuvre had thrust upon him the burden of a responsibility, the glory of which could never compensate for its danger. He showed, with all the clearsightedness of his high reason, and with the natural pain of a patriotic character, what would be the inevitable issue of the situation in which he had been left. But his letter, which was addressed to the Directory, and which might have thrown a light on the romance of the expedition into Egypt of which it is impossible to calculate the effects, was intercepted by the English, and arrived in Paris too late; it was received by Bonaparte, First Consul. Fortune, which had in the meantime changed the accused into a judge, had prepared for each his recompense: for one the poniard of a fanatic, for the other the first throne of the world.[1]

---

[1] Bonaparte was all the more annoyed at Kléber's complaints, as they were for the most part irrefutably just. He published the letter together with a detailed refutation of the charges brought against him, founded chiefly on statistics, in which numbers lend themselves complacently to the violence of his logic. A single example will serve to

show the untruthfulness of his assertions. His principal efforts are to prove that Kléber had exaggerated the weakness of the army, in order to induce the Directory to consent to a peace. Now three months before this, June 28, 1799, Bonaparte wrote himself to the Directory to press for reinforcements, and said: '*If you cannot possibly send us all this aid, we must make peace.*' In his reply to Kléber, he asserts that up to the 26th of September 1799, the date of that general's letter, the army had only lost four thousand five hundred men. Now in this same letter of the 28th of June, which he wrote to the Directory, he says: '*The enclosed statement will show you that the French army has lost, from our arrival up to the present time, five thousand three hundred and forty-four men.*' Between the month of June and the day on which Kléber wrote, the army had been diminished several times; they had lost the four hundred men who were in the peninsula of Aboukir at the time of the Turks' landing; according to most of the reports, from a thousand to fifteen hundred had been disabled in the battle of Aboukir; and they had lost the four or five hundred men who had accompanied Bonaparte to France, besides a considerable number who had died of the plague during these three months. Bonaparte then enters into long calculations, to prove that '*in the month of September* 1799, *the army of Egypt, including sick and wounded, must have reached twenty-eight thousand five hundred men.*' In his letter of the 28th of June, before the losses we have just enumerated had occurred, making a calculation of the probable number of his troops founded on his past losses, he says: '*Next season we shall be reduced to fifteen thousand men: from this number deduct two thousand sick, five hundred disabled, five hundred workmen, who do not fight, and we shall have twelve thousand men, including cavalry, artillery, sappers, staff officers, etc.; with such forces we cannot resist an attack by sea combined with one by the desert.*'

Kléber's statements are strikingly confirmed by several papers of unquestionable authenticity, published at the same time as his letter, in the *Intercepted Correspondence*. Among others, 1°. The Report of Damas, Chief of the Staff, to the Minister of War, dated October 10, 1799, which states that the army was reduced to twenty-two thousand men, of whom six thousand were disabled; 2°. A Report of Poussielgue, Controller-General of Finance, which gives a deplorable account of the distress of the army; 3°. A letter from General Dugua to the Directors, in which he says: 'Bonaparte has left us without money, without powder, without ball, and part of the troops without arms.'

Historians, who on this occasion have felt no scruples in defaming the memory of Kléber, have contented themselves with servilely copying the recriminations of Napoleon.

CHAPTER XII

THE EIGHTEENTH BRUMAIRE

DURING General Bonaparte's absence in Egypt great changes had taken place in the situation of France. At home, a policy of conspiracy and *coups-d'état*, inaugurated by the 18th Fructidor, had been continued by different parties, but henceforth with less violence than intrigue, and without producing the same effect on the minds of the people; a plain proof of the state of lassitude into which the nation had sunk. The fear which the ill-sustained tyranny of the Fructidorians had at first inspired had given way to contempt, and a perpetual instability in the government as well as in public opinion had been the natural consequence. Abroad, the ephemeral governments which we had established in neighbouring countries, decorating with some tatters of republican legality the insolence and brutality of military rule, had everywhere crumbled to pieces as soon as a fresh coalition was announced. The people, whom we had boasted of liberating, and who by an abusive and vexatious administration had been brought to regret their former masters, raised no arm in defence of institutions which had been dishonoured by all the pillage, violence, and excess of military domination.

The double invasion of Switzerland and the Papal States, which had been executed under Bonaparte's direction a few weeks previous to his departure for Egypt, had already gravely compromised the success of the negotiations commenced at Rastadt; and the departure of the finest army and best generals of the Republic, at a time when their presence was most necessary to intimidate our enemies, had caused the complete failure of all attempts at reconciliation. England had no difficulty in rallying our ancient adversaries; Austria was burning to exact vengeance for her former humiliations, and joyfully took advantage of the opportunity; Germany joined the allies to reconquer the Rhenish Provinces; the king of Naples to drive the Revolution from his frontiers; and two new allies followed their example—Turkey, whom our own policy had deliberately driven into the camp of our enemies; and Russia, who espoused their cause from the keen interest she had in Turkey.

The renewal of hostilities was notified by the assassination of our plenipotentiaries at Rastadt; an atrocity which still leaves a dark stain on the house of Austria. War had already commenced in Italy, where the king of Naples, carried away by a long-pent-up hatred, anticipated the signal, and lost his throne by his precipitation. Championnet entered Naples after a campaign as rapid as a military review, and added the Parthenopean to their list of short-lived republics which we had founded in Italy. Almost at the same time, the king of Sardinia and the grand duke of Tuscany were dethroned, and Piedmont was united to France.

Owing to these conquests, which were more disastrous than defeats, the line we had to defend with our reduced army, when the allied troops advanced on us, extended from Amsterdam to Naples. We were attacked at the same time in Switzerland, in Holland, in Italy, and on the Rhine. To occupy Naples with a considerable part of our forces, whilst the Austrians and Russians were pouring in from every direction on the Adige, was a fault all the more unpardonable, because Bonaparte had often pointed it out as certain to involve the loss of our conquests. He was himself so fully convinced of the fatal consequences of such a plan, that he had not hesitated to disobey the Directory rather than carry it out, and yet it was afterwards undertaken with Schérer for Commander-in-Chief. The defeats which followed were so disastrous that Moreau himself could not repair them, when Schérer, overwhelmed by a sense of his own incapacity, abandoned the command of the army and retired amidst the hooting of the soldiers. All that he could do was to save the rest of the army by one of those incomparable retreats in which skilfulness of dispositions, variety of resource, self-possession, and invincible steadiness rose to the height of genius; but he did not succeed in joining Championnet's army which Macdonald was marching back into North Italy, and which was crushed on the Trebia by Souvarow. Moreau, however, rallied the scattered remnants, and was obliged to confine his operations to keeping the line of the Apennines. Italy was lost for us, and the Italians remained to the end passive and almost indifferent spectators of a conflict which only left them a choice between their old and their new oppressors.

Our armies had not been more successful on the Rhine, where Jourdan had been beaten by the archduke and compelled to cross the river. In Holland and in Belgium our situation was also serious. The Duke of York had landed at the head of an army of forty thousand English and Russians, and was threatening our provinces in the north. At home, civil war, kindled by the royalists, had broken out again in Brittany and Vendée, and was contributing its efforts to hasten our ruin. France was on the eve of an invasion.

It was in the midst of these troubles that the elections of May 1799 took place. Public opinion in France was almost unanimous in imputing these misfortunes to faults committed by the Government, and to a certain extent it was so; though the Directory was by no means wholly, nor even principally, responsible for the state of affairs. The result of the elections testified to this feeling in the minds of the people, and the Councils, vanquished and subdued since the 18th Fructidor, suddenly found their powerless opposition changed into a large majority, to which the confusion and stupefaction of the Government, and the irritation of the nation against it, gave an irresistible strength in circumstances so critical. The Directory, feeling themselves arraigned as it were by this unmistakable expression of public feeling, dared not again have recourse to the cynical prevarications by which they had falsified the previous elections, and substituted their own nominees for the people's candidates, by the *coup-d'état* of the 22d Floréal. The Councils, encouraged by the public cry which charged all our reverses to the incapacity of the Directory, seized this opportunity of revenge for the outrages of Fructidor.

Their first care was to give Sieyès a seat in the Directory, in the place of Rewbell, whose term of office had just legally expired. Sieyès, who had only lately returned from Berlin, where he had displayed both tact and skill as an ambassador, was notoriously hostile to the policy of the Government, and was known to aim at something higher than a mere change of individuals, and to have a system which, if carried out, would establish a new order of things. Rewbell had become unpopular from his friendship for Schérer and his connection with the famous Rapinat, whose exactions had too amply justified his name. This friendship gave rise to unjust suspicions of Rewbell's honesty; suspicions without foundation, for he lived and died poor, but the instinct of the public had rightly attributed to him the principal influence in the Directory since the 18th Fructidor, and he justly paid the penalty of his unintelligent administration. Like all men whose understanding is inferior to their character, firmness with Rewbell degenerated into blind obstinacy, and attachment to principles into views so rigidly exclusive in their narrowness that they were more fit for a sect than a political party.

By the nomination of Sieyès a breach was made in the Directory. The Councils followed up their success by turning out Treilhard, the validity of whose election had been questioned; and they consummated their victory by forcing Merlin and Lareveillère to resign. Barras, who was spared from his insignificance and because he was always found on the side of the majority, was the only member of the ancient Directory who remained; and Gohier, Moulins, and Roger-Ducos, obscure men whose mediocrity could alarm no one, took the places of the retiring members. Such was the result of the day known as the 30th Prairial, which was a retaliation for the 18th

Fructidor and the *coup-d'état* of the Legislative Body against the Directory.

The revival of national feeling gave to the measures of defence all the energy and spirit which were needed to save France. Bernadotte, an intelligent politician as well as a distinguished soldier, was named Minister of War; he reorganised all the services with admirable activity, and roused the patriotic zeal of both generals and soldiers. The conscription which had just been voted had filled up the ranks of our armies. Bernadotte reviewed these recruits, and electrified them by his exhortations. 'Young men,' he said, addressing them, 'there will surely be found some great captains among you!' These simple words were still enough to create heroes. The exhausted treasury found fresh funds in a forced loan, which had the defect of consecrating the principle of progressive taxation, that is to say, the introduction of arbitrary imposts. The Chouannerie, or royalist insurrection, was struck to the very heart by the law of hostages, an iniquitous measure which made the whole class of persons responsible for the excesses committed by the insurgents. Popular societies were again formed, as in other times of great national danger; the surviving members of the old Jacobin Club met at the Manége, in the same room in which our great assemblies formerly held their sittings. Our armies were again preparing to resume the offensive on all sides.

But the victory of the Councils, instead of appeasing party spirit, had only raised new hopes. The Constitution of the Year III had been regarded as an arm which each party in turn had seized in order to strike the others. Finding that they were being constantly deprived of this weapon, they attributed to the imperfections of the system the bad use they had made of it, and began to meditate its overthrow. The two principal defects of the Constitution of the Year III struck all keen-sighted men; sufficient light had been thrown upon them both, one by the permanent antagonism of the Councils and the Directory, the other in the ever-recurring conspiracy of one-half of the Directory against the other half. These defects might easily have been remedied by a more exact definition of parliamentary prerogatives on the one hand, and by the introduction of unity in the executive power on the other; but as each faction only wanted power to make it their fortress, they found it easier to proceed by making a clean sweep of all existing institutions. The republicans of the Manége aimed at the re-establishment of the Jacobin Directorship. Their two leaders were the Generals Jourdan and Augereau, the former an austere and rigid republican, the other the turbulent hero of military demagogism. Sieyès, a representative of the moderate party, by whom he had been sent to the Directory after his embassy to Berlin, to which was attributed the maintenance of Prussian neutrality, always carried about in his pocket his famous plan of a constitution, of which everybody was talking, but which no one had ever seen. He had never been able to pardon the Constitution of the Year III for having supplanted this unappreciated masterpiece, the last outcome of his revolutionary experience. His position at the head of a government which he was bent on overthrowing, his reputation, consecrated by a flattery of Mirabeau, and which he cleverly increased by the mystery in which he enveloped himself, his undoubted superiority over his colleagues, and his knowledge of men and parties, all gave him immense advantages as the chief of a conspiracy, and gathered around him not only the ambitious and the able, but all those who were weary of agitation and wished for a change that would insure more stability to the Government and more tranquillity to themselves. The oracular tone which he assumed, his haughty and sarcastic spirit, and his celebrity, due to a few telling phrases which, uttered at the commencement of the Revolution, had been re-echoed like axioms, had misled the public with regard to the poverty of his political conceptions, in the same way as the apparent simplicity of his habits and the reputed loftiness of his ambition had deceived them as to the motives which ruled this grasping priest. Sieyès had no difficulty in gaining an ascendency over the feeble and wavering mind of his colleague Roger-Ducos, nor in winning over to his views a large majority in the Council of the Ancients, composed in a great measure of those members of the Convention belonging to the Plain who, like himself, during the storm of '93 had bowed their heads in order to be forgotten, contenting themselves with the simple glory of *living*. His intentions were no sooner perceived and made known than that large class of society whose interest it is to insure security and order placed their hopes in him, and turned conspirators in the name of conservative ideas. Such elements made this faction the strongest if not the most enterprising party, and all those who best knew how to judge from which quarter the wind was blowing, all those who, either from ambition, disappointment, or experience, expected nothing more from the institutions of the Year III, Talleyrand, Rœderer, Cambacérès, Regnault de Saint Jean d'Angély, Cabanis, Sémonville, Benjamin Constant, and even Daunou, naturally gave in their adhesion to it.

The name of Barras had lost all political prestige. After having betrayed each party in turn, having adopted and abandoned every opinion, he now represented only one thing, and that was immorality; but such was the state of public and private corruption that even this was still a force. Surrounded by a court of stock-jobbers and women of lost character, despised and worn out, but still enjoying a certain popularity from his easy manners, he thought of nothing but his personal safety, and went about from one to another full of anxiety and astonishment at finding that he was no longer feared, desperately trying intrigue, artifice and insinuations, making advances and offering pledges which no one believed in, and floating like foam on the surface of all parties. He had entered into negotiations with Louis XVIII. through Fauche-Borel and David Monnier, and with his usual care for his own safety had obtained from him a guarantee of security, and magnificent promises; but afterwards, fearing to be discovered, he informed his colleagues of the whole intrigue under pretext of enlightening them on the dangers of the Republic, though in reality to deceive them more easily and to turn his treachery to the best account by betraying every one at once. He had gradually retired from public work, only keeping in his own hands the direction of the police, which he used as a shield, through the medium of Fouché, a minister worthy of such a master, and Réal his confidential friend.

The Constitution of the Year III had now but two champions left in the Directory, Gohier, ex-Minister of Justice, an honest and inoffensive man and a learned and upright judge, but devoid of penetration and completely ignorant of men and affairs, and one whom only the irony of fate could have led into politics. The second was General Moulins, a warm republican, but as inexperienced in politics as Gohier; and he was unknown to the armies, and had no influence over the soldiers. The most melancholy feature of this history of the last days of the Republic is the sight of so much unavailing uprightness and almost ludicrous virtue. Never was there a better example of the fact that in certain situations good intentions avail nothing when they are not united to greatness of character, for the French Republic might perhaps have avoided Cæsar had she but possessed a Cato.

In the Ministry these two men were principally supported by Bernadotte, the Minister of War, a man of great political ability and military skill, of a firm, active, and enterprising mind, and one who, ambitious himself, had long since discovered the ambition of Bonaparte. But Bernadotte, who besides was soon removed from power by the suspicious Sieyès, could not alone make up for the insufficiency of a. party from which Daunou himself, the principal author of the Constitution, had separated, witnessing with silent and melancholy resignation the efforts which were being made to destroy his work.

In order to carry out his plans and consolidate the Government that he proposed to establish, Sieyès needed a practical man, an arm of which he should be the life and mover. While he was ambassador in Prussia he had thought of applying to one of the princes of the house of Brunswick, a choice which sufficiently proves the chimerical character of this singular man's mind. The name of Brunswick was indissolubly associated with a manifesto which made them unpopular for ever in France. Later, he is said to have addressed a letter to Bonaparte, under cover of one from the chargé d'affaires of Prussia at Constantinople, pressing him to return to France; but there is no proof that this letter ever reached its destination. He next tried Bernadotte, whom he found in no humour to be his instrument. Lastly, his thoughts turned on Joubert, whose firm and moderate opinions and noble character had gained him the respect of all parties. But Joubert, who in spite of his great services had not yet conquered a position which placed him on the highest level, had just been put in command of the Italian army, in order to furnish him with an opportunity of speedily achieving brilliant exploits. At the same time, in the hope of silencing his scruples and binding him more closely to a party whose intrigues were so distasteful to him that he had not hesitated to denounce Sieyès' projects to Gohier, they brought about a marriage between him and a daughter of M. de Sémonville.

While waiting till Joubert's reputation had become sufficiently great to entitle him to a place at the head of the Government, Sieyès resolved to strike a blow at the only party whose energy appeared to him to be dangerous. This was the old Jacobin party, which had begun to revive again since the 30th Prairial, and the agitation of the clubs, principally that of the Manége, was regaining something of its old influence over the people. This party and the Constitutionalists, headed by Gohier and Moulins, were about to unite, when Sieyès perceived the danger and averted it by a series of arbitrary measures against the press and the clubs. His two colleagues thus found themselves compromised and the Jacobins disarmed. The principal journalists of the party were transported to Oléron by virtue of a simple decree (12 Fructidor), and the Manége was closed as well as all other places where popular societies held meetings. Nobody was moved by this. Owing to the terrible recollections left by the Reign of Terror, any law could be infringed without exciting indignation in France, by merely invoking the phantom of Terrorism. Jourdan did his best to obtain from the

Councils a declaration that 'the country was in danger;' but this motion, which would have led to the substitution of a dictatorship of the Assemblies for the government of the Directory, was lost, and the faction of the Manége was left broken up and subdued.

The Sieyès party continued to increase in numbers and strength; but the premature death of Joubert, killed at Novi at the head of his soldiers on the first day of the campaign, gave it a check. Sieyès tried to win Moreau but could not succeed, for, weak and irresolute as he was, he had an honesty of purpose which saved him from this temptation, though his want of initiative and decision rendered him useless.[1] After this refusal Sieyès was obliged to put off the execution of his projects.

Meanwhile our armies, owing to the warlike spirit which Bernadotte had aroused, and to the genius and intrepidity of their chiefs, had again been victorious at all points except in Italy, where we were reduced to the defensive. Masséna, in a fortnight's remarkable campaign known under the summary name of the battle of Zurich, had completely routed the Austrians and Russians; and General Brune, after having defeated the Duke of York at Berghen and at Castricum, had forced him to capitulate. Holland and Switzerland were both freed; and though we were not successful in Italy, at least our frontier of the Alps was still intact, and Championnet had made it an impenetrable barrier.

A few days after the announcement of these victories a messenger of state, sent to the Councils by the Directory, was introduced with some solemnity into the room where the Five Hundred were sitting. In the midst of a profound silence the President read to the Assembly the bulletin of the victory of Aboukir, which the Government had just received from General Bonaparte. The news was welcomed with three rounds of applause. It was a long time since the Directory had received despatches from him.

---

[1] 'It is well known that they offered to make me Dictator of France before Bonaparte, and that I refused.' Declaration taken from Moreau's trial.

Nothing was known of the situation of our army in Egypt, except from foreign countries; and the mystery which hung over the fate of this adventurous expedition, far from diminishing the interest felt in the soldiers and their chief, created an inexpressible anxiety in all minds. Their names, which were repeated in connection with monuments of this antique and mysterious country, had gathered round them a halo of poetry, which was increased by the distance, the peril, and the vague uncertainty which enveloped them like the smoke of battles. The army of Egypt was only seen through the twofold mirage of the desert and history. Popular imagination, which transforms all that occurs at the will of a fancy which is far from being always equitable, had already created a legend out of this great enterprise, in which Bonaparte and the army of Italy were said to have been *deported*[1] into Egypt by a Government jealous of their glory. The *exile of Bonaparte* was a consecrated expression for all popular orators. They extolled his disinterestedness and patriotism, and they pitied him for having escaped the fate of Hoche only to end his days in a still more miserable manner.

This explains the extraordinary effect produced by the news of the victory of Aboukir, the real importance of which was greatly exaggerated. The following day the *Moniteur* published Bonaparte's accounts of his previous exploits: the campaign of Syria, the battle of Mount Thabor, and the pretended destruction of Acre, with all the clever artifice and theatrical exaggerations with which the report was coloured. The Directory, who in the course of the preceding season had had to announce more defeats than victories, purposely gave great publicity to this report. The *Moniteur* was still publishing Berthier's more minute accounts of these events, when on the 15th of October it gave a piece of intelligence by the side of which everything else appeared insignificant. Bonaparte had landed at Fréjus; he had been welcomed with transports of joy by

[1] This expression is found in the greater number of the petitions sent to the Five Hundred after the 30th Prairial.—See the *Moniteur* of the 8th of July 1799.

the inhabitants of the town; they had allowed him to dispense with the observation of the sanitary laws, and he was already on his way to Paris, saluted everywhere by the enthusiasm of the people.

The General was in truth in France again, after a long and painful voyage during which he had escaped the English cruisers with that surprising and miraculous fortune which never seemed to forsake him in circumstances where success depended on chance only. He had been obliged to put in for two or three days at Corsica, and while there he had quickly made himself acquainted with the state of affairs and the situation of the different political parties. His determination had been taken on the day he resolved to leave Egypt. He came back more than ever possessed by the secret thought, which had followed him for two years, and had never left him even in the depths of the desert. He was resolved to resort to any means in order to seize the reins of power. But whom to choose for auxiliaries in such a chaos of factions? On whom to rely? However low the Republic had fallen, and however much the country was rent by party spirit, would men be found capable of renouncing the generous aims of the Revolution to attach themselves to the fortunes of a soldier? Or, would he be obliged to join some particular party, serve its interests, espouse its aims, submit to its terms?

The different political parties were at that time so completely broken up, that his isolation was a strength rather than a disadvantage to him, for it gave him an appearance of disinterestedness and impartiality which promised him supporters in all camps. He was in fact perfectly disinterested in all party quarrels, in the sense that he only thought of himself. Independently of partisans of every shade of opinion whom his position insured him, he could count on the support of all those who like himself pursued only personal ends, and on the soldiers, the great majority of whom were his beforehand, because his rise was a pledge of their own influence in the state. During his absence his brothers Joseph and Lucien, either in obedience to his instructions, or else only following the suggestions of self-interest, had done everything to prepare the way,—Joseph, by managing all in authority with great diplomatic skill, and making himself agreeable even to the most opposite characters by the optimism of his apparent good nature; and Lucien, by throwing himself into the conflict, and using all his efforts to multiply discords and the general disorganisation. He had been elected Deputy to the Five Hundred, and had there acquired, from his passionate and florid eloquence and incessant activity, as well as his brother's name, an influence which could not be overlooked. Josephine herself had formed certain friendships which were useful to the ambitious General. With a truly feminine calculation, and to shield herself from the accusations of her enemies, she had formed an intimacy with honest Madame Gohier, whose virtuous reputation was proverbial. This precaution was not unnecessary with a view to her irritated husband, whose pride and jealousy had suffered severely from the scandalous reports which had pursued him into Egypt. Josephine had thus acquired for Bonaparte the confiding good-will of Gohier, who had just been named President of the Directory.

It was to him that the General paid his first visit in Paris. Notwithstanding his enthusiastic welcome in his triumphal march through France, he felt some uneasiness about the way in which he would be received after having abandoned his army without permission; for the final success of his projects depended to a certain extent on the way in which this was to be taken. 'President,' he said to Gohier, 'the news I received in Egypt was so alarming that I did not hesitate to leave the army and come and share your perils.' 'The danger was great, General,' replied Gohier, 'but we have gloriously surmounted it. You have come in time to join us in celebrating the triumph of your companions-in-arms.' The next day (October 17) the Directory received him in state. The General repeated his explanation, and added, as he placed his hand on his sword, 'that he would never draw it for any other cause *than the defence of the Republic and its Government.*'[1] The Directory

[1] *Memoir of Gohier.*

replied by words of welcome which only half concealed the feelings of uneasiness and distrust to which his sudden and unexpected return had given rise.

The Paris public, however, far from participating in these suspicions, was, like the rest of France, carried away by the impulse of enthusiasm to such an extent that those who witnessed it were never able to forget it. At Lyons, a piece entitled *The Return of the Hero* was written in honour of him. It was the phrase of the moment. He was the general subject of conversation, the object of all hopes. The newspapers talked of nothing else, and repeated his least words. There was only one man left in the Republic, and it was he. His absence had been the single cause of our misfortunes, and his return was to put an end to them all. All trouble was over; his presence would re-establish order at home and assure victory abroad. This nation of artists and soldiers, who with a vivid imagination possessed the unbounded ambition of young democrats, humiliated and disgusted by the paltry intrigues and mediocrity of the men who had governed for the two previous years, were determined to have a hero, and eagerly made one out of the man who presented himself to them, liberally ascribing to him every merit and every virtue, without considering the considerable share he had in the errors with which they most bitterly reproached the Directory. And yet, who had drawn the Directory into this system of conquest? Who had urged it, at the 18th Fructidor, into the fatal path of *coups-d'état*? Who had inaugurated the usurpation of civil power by the military? Who had undertaken the hazardous enterprise of founding those ephemeral Republics which had been the first cause of our reverses? Who had taken away the best of our armies at a time when they were most needed? A moment's reflection would have led them to recognise Bonaparte's share in the work. But experience is of little use to a people as infatuated in their admiration as in their execration. What in reality they could not pardon in the members of the Directory was, not their imprudent and iniquitous policy, but their want of success. It was not Bonaparte's genius, but his fortune that they admired; it was his lucky audacity, and a sword counted invincible. Men of intelligence, as well as the masses, shared the influence of this enthusiasm. From the time of his arrival he had a sort of court around him composed of the principal men of all the different parties. He seldom appeared in public, and carefully abstained from showing himself to the masses, who were eager to catch a glimpse of his features: his box at the theatre had a grating before it, and by these efforts to render himself invisible he was all the more present to their curiosity. He changed his military uniform for the costume of the Institute, as if to render homage to learning and throw a cloak over the projects imputed to him. Distinguished men, however, were received by him with studied affability; he encouraged them to talk freely and explain their plans, feigning a readiness to adopt them. With them he sometimes expressed his real views, and sometimes those he wished them to attribute to him. His modest house in the Rue de la Victoire was thronged with visitors of every rank, attracted thither by the same motive which induced him to seek their society,—the desire to penetrate his intentions and designs. There were seen there the friends of Sieyès by the side of those of Gohier and Bernadotte, the men of the Manége by the side of the adherents of Barras,' besides men of letters, savants, artists, and all the most distinguished generals of the army.

The far-seeing Talleyrand was among the first to join the crowd, and Bonaparte was far too clever a diplomatist to refer to his treachery with respect to the projected embassy to Constantinople, and gave him a most friendly reception. Régnault de Saint Jean d'Angély, whom Bonaparte had employed and appreciated in Italy and Malta; Rœderer, a politician of marked subtlety and dexterity, whose experience had led to scepticism, and who, to use an expression of the time, had wound himself snakelike through all parties; Réal, a witty man of the world, whose talents as an orator and a writer, and especially his place as a Commissioner of the Directory in the administration of the Department of the Seine, gave him an importance which might be turned to good account; Cabanis, Mirabeau's old friend, who must have repented later of his co-operation in a work of which he did not foresee all the consequences; Volney, an illustrious savant, who afterwards tried in vain to escape the forced honours of the Imperial Senate; and lastly, Admiral Bruix, ex-Minister of the Navy, one of the shrewdest of men, were, with Talleyrand, Bonaparte's most intimate counsellors. But even these were not much in his confidence, for such a man might have familiars, but no real confidants. The members of the Directory, Gohier, Roger-Ducos, and especially Moulins, who was at the head of the War Office, were among his most assiduous visitors, and constantly consulted him, as also did Cambacérès, the Minister of Justice, who had the same weakness for him that jurists of all ages have had for power, and Dubois de Crancé, Bernadotte's successor. As for Fouché, the favourite minister of Barras, suspecting a conspiracy with the subtle keenness of a detective, restless at seeing an intrigue formed from which he was excluded, but not daring to oppose a plot which appeared so sure of a speedy success, he overwhelmed the General with protests of his devotion, though with the clear intention of betraying him later, should events turn out ill. All the best soldiers of the Republic flocked round Bonaparte, independent of political opinions; some because they regarded him as the best representative of their interests and their fame; others because they wanted to penetrate his plans as a guide for their own conduct. This class included men who were almost openly hostile to him, such as Augereau, Jourdan, and Bernadotte; and among the first were not only the generals such as Lannes, Marmont, Berthier, and Murat, who had accompanied him from Egypt, but also many other officers who, like Macdonald and Beurnonville, had made their reputation under other chiefs.

But a more illustrious name than any of these was soon after added to the list of his visitors; Moreau, who had once been regarded as his rival, and who now, exasperated against the Directory for deliberately exposing him after a long disgrace to inevitable reverses, began to pay his court to Bonaparte. The first time they met was at Gohier's. Until then the two great captains had never seen each other. Bonaparte made the first advances, with a courteousness of manner which would probably have been less cordial had Moreau lost nothing of his former renown. It was noticed that before they spoke each looked at the other in silence, as if to complete by that rapid glance the idea which they had respectively formed of one another. Bonaparte was the first to speak: he expressed in the most flattering terms the impatience he had felt to make Moreau's acquaintance. The latter received these advances with his accustomed simplicity, and they talked together for some time on the military art and its chances. A few days later Bonaparte called on him, taking him as a present a magnificent piece of damask which he had brought from the East; and, owing to Moreau's rancour towards the Directory, he easily gained an ascendency over the mind of a man who, though eminent as an officer, was a perfect stranger to politics. But with his characteristic scruples Moreau, while he placed himself at Bonaparte's disposal, refused to listen to an explanation of his plans.

General Bonaparte thus saw himself surrounded by men who could give him information on all points, and from whom he could choose his agents. But things could not long remain stationary, without risking the success of the enterprise. It was necessary to prepare for action. Before making the necessarily hazardous attempt of forcibly attacking existing institutions, Bonaparte tried to ascertain whether it would be possible for him to get into the government by legal and regular ways. He felt an intense antipathy to Sieyès. Madame Bonaparte openly spoke of him as her husband's *bête-noire*. Sieyès was in fact the only man who by his character and position was able to place an obstacle in the way of the realisation of his projects. Nor was the director's aversion to the General less strong, for their respective situations rendered them natural enemies. They had both too much penetration not to understand one another, and each felt that the difficulty lay not so much in overcoming their mutual antipathy, as in reconciling their respective aims. Sieyès met Bonaparte at a dinner where the General pretended not to see him. 'Do observe,' cried Sieyès, in anger, 'that insolent little fellow's behaviour towards a member of a government which ought to have had him shot.' Bonaparte's first idea was to get himself named a member of the Directory in the place of Sieyès, by allying himself to the Constitutional party, and finding one pretext or another for disputing the legality of his adversary's election. He openly proposed this to Gohier and Moulins; but as he was not forty years old, the age required by the Constitution for all members of the Directory, neither of them would listen to the proposal.

But neither this proposition nor the significant persistence with which he urged it seemed sufficient to give them an effectual warning against the General's projects. The only precaution suggested to them by what he had done was to remove him from Paris by offering him a command from the Directory, in the vain hope that he would accept it and thus rid them of his presence. This middle course was adopted in spite of the opposition of Sieyès, and especially that of Barras, who exclaimed when he heard it, 'that the little Corporal had made a large enough fortune in Italy not to care about returning,' alluding to the profits the General had received from the mines of Hydria. This remark was repeated to Bonaparte, and when the Government made him the offer he replied, with a defiant glance at Barras, 'that if he had made a fortune in Italy, it was not at the expense of the Republic.' He refused the appointment, assigning as a reason the shattered state of his health and his need of rest.

After the failure of this attempt Bonaparte applied to the members of the Manége, the party in favour of a republican dictatorship; Bernadotte had allied himself more closely to this party ever since Sieyès, to get rid of so keen an observer, had driven him out of the ministry. He formed with Augereau and Jourdan a sort of military triumvirate, round which were gathered the scattered remnants of Jacobinism. This party represented as nearly as possible the former opinions of Bonaparte; it suited his despotic disposition, which could not bear the restraint of constitutional scruples; it possessed immense energy and traditions of government, and a rare discipline; its members knew how to act, to organise, and to command; and if they were hated by a very considerable portion of the nation, they were still popular with the lower orders, whom they had enriched with the spoils of the nobility. They were in favour too with the soldiers, who were certain of their influence to prevent the return of the emigrants. But Joseph tried in vain to seduce Bernadotte, who was both his friend and his brother-in-law. Bernadotte remained inflexible, though more from rivalry of ambition than from any hostility of principle. Between the collective dictatorship which was Bernadotte's dream, and a dictatorship of one which Bonaparte was aiming at, there was little difference beyond a question of time, for the first necessarily leads to the second, and is often more fatal in its consequences.

Bonaparte tried a new combination. Fouché, more and more uneasy at seeing that his patron Barras was not on good terms with a party whose power was in the ascendant, resolved to effect a reconciliation between the two former friends. Bonaparte owed a great deal to Barras. It was through him that he had obtained his command at the 13th Vendémiaire, and afterwards his nomination as General-in-Chief of the army of Italy. Their intimacy had commenced at the siege of Toulon; they had risen together, and experienced the same trials. Though Fouché was not exactly a credulous man in matters of sentiment, he somehow hoped that the close connection established between these two by common antecedents, the recollection of mutual services, and perhaps also the revival of an old affection, would enable them to forget their more recent grievances and to work together. Barras consented to take the first step, and invited Bonaparte to dine at the Luxembourg. But the result of the interview was by no means what Fouché had hoped for. Neither Bonaparte nor Barras showed the least cordiality, but each treated the other with caution and reserve, and kept on the defensive, as if better to view his antagonist. At length Barras introduced the subject which was uppermost in the thoughts of both, though they had carefully abstained from all allusion to it; but he touched it in a vague and indirect manner, speaking in general terms, as if to force Bonaparte to make the first advances, before he committed himself. 'The Republic,' he said, 'is falling to pieces, it cannot long continue in this state. We must make a great change, and name Hédouville President. You will join the army. For my part, I am ill, unpopular, and worn out. I am only fit for private life.' Hédouville was an obscure general, though not without merit, who in later life displayed the qualities of an excellent administrator; he was then the *protégé* of Barras, as he had previously been of Hoche, and his name was merely mentioned by the speaker to draw out his interlocutor. Bonaparte, who felt by no means inclined to yield confidence in one who reposed so little in himself, fixed his eyes on Barras, who remained utterly disconcerted. The conversation dropped there. A few minutes after the General left his host and went to call on Sieyès, to tell him he would work with no one but him.

Talleyrand, Rœderer, and Cabanis, who were common friends of Sieyès and Bonaparte, struck with the advantages to be gained by a union between these two men, the strength each would give to the other, and the facility they would have in the realisation of their projects, had often deplored the distance and mistrust which kept them apart. They regretted their mutual aversion all the more deeply from not understanding its true cause. With a perfect indifference to the conflicting ambition of the two rivals, they only thought of the success of the common enterprise, and so long as one succeeded, their own end being gained, they cared very little which of the two was sacrificed. They had tried several times to conquer the mutual prejudices of these two men, and make them understand that neither could do anything without the other. But the incompatibility was between their pretensions, and not their persons. Besides, it was only a few days since Sieyès had talked of having Bonaparte shot for an infringement of military law, and that Bonaparte had proposed that Sieyès should be dismissed from office because he was sold to Prussia; from this to a close alliance the transition was not easy. However marked the tact and skill of the peacemakers, the intractable pride and ambition of the two men would probably have caused them to fail, had not necessity spoken more powerfully than their counsels. The risk of being anticipated made it urgent to take some course of action. Joseph and Cabanis at last obtained Sieyès' consent to meet the General. It was, however, unwillingly given, for Sieyès had a presentiment that Bonaparte would only accept him as a tool, and would get rid of him as soon as possible after the victory. 'I know,' he said, 'the fate that awaits me; after he has succeeded he will separate from his colleagues and stand in front of them, as I am doing now.' And, suiting the action to the word, he suddenly passed between his two interlocutors and pushed them behind him.[1]

A presentiment that was perfectly justified, for the consent he had just given involved his political doom. As soon as the *coup-d'état* had taken place, it was evident that the lion's share would fall to the most popular man, and the General was so infinitely more so than the director, that he would never be able to force a division of authority, which would besides have been incompatible with such a character as his. Bonaparte had then every interest in overcoming his aversion for an alliance with a rival who sooner or later would be at his mercy. To the evident advantages which this alliance offered him was added another which was not without value in his eyes; he found a conspiracy all ready; it had been long organised, and counted a considerable number of disciplined adherents, possessed powerful means of action, and a watch-cry known to the public; to which in short nothing was wanting but a man of action. He was all the better prepared to appreciate a machine thus wound up, from his repeated failures with others, for, notwithstanding his later assertions that he had rejected offers on all sides, his unsuccessful attempts menaced him with an isolation that would have condemned him to complete

[1] *Memoir of King Joseph.*

impotence. Actuated by these motives the General no longer hesitated to make the first advances to Sieyès, and the director, accepting his overtures in spite of the usurpation which he foresaw, deserved all the contempt and oblivion into which he was destined to fall after his miserable victory. The conspiracy was already so well organised, that the very evening on which Bonaparte called to make his proposals to Sieyès it was agreed between the two that in eight or ten days the decisive blow should be struck.

The next day, when Barras was rebuked by his friends Réal and Fouché, whom Bonaparte had informed of their interview, he perceived that in trying to be over skilful he had mismanaged the affair, and immediately sought out the General and tried to appease him and regain the old footing. But it was too late. Bonaparte only replied to his protests by observations as little serious as those which Barras had himself made the day before, and maintained an impenetrable reserve.

He was already occupied in preparations for the execution of the plot. Through the two directors who were his accomplices he had the aid of a portion of the Government, and he was assured of non-interference from that quarter; through Sieyès he could count on a majority in the Council of Ancients; through his brother Lucien, whom his triumphal return had been the means of raising to the Presidency of the Five Hundred, he could insure an understanding with a few devoted men in that Council; through Réal, admitted into the conspiracy notwithstanding his intimacy with Barras, he had the municipalities and the administration of the Department of Paris; through Fouché, who was in the secret without having been openly taken into the confidence of the conspirators, and who worked with all the zeal of a volunteer, taking care however not to commit himself irrevocably till he was sure of victory, he had the connivance of the police, shown in a determination to hear nothing and see nothing of his proceedings. Lastly, through the contractors, who were the financial aristocracy of the time, he had, it is said, two millions of francs to meet his first requirements. He undertook the military force himself, and had very little difficulty in winning over the officers and generals. In the garrison of Paris there were two regiments of dragoons that had belonged to the army of Italy, and who were passionately attached to his person. A third regiment was gained over by Murat, who had come out of its ranks. They were also sure of the forty adjutants of the National Guard who had all been appointed by Bonaparte himself after the 13th Vendémiaire, as well as the greater part of the officers of the Guards of the Council and Directory. Here were elements of great force already prepared.

The greater part of the generals were already in the conspiracy. Moreau had not formally joined in the plot, but he was not less implicated in it, and in fact implicated in the worst possible way, for he knew nothing of the work in which he was taking part. When Bonaparte wished to explain his plans, Moreau interrupted him by saying 'that he did not want to be let into the secret, but that, like others, he was tired of the yoke of lawyers, and put himself and his aides-de-camp at the General's service.' Macdonald and Sérurier made the same engagement. There was no need to enroll the generals who had accompanied Bonaparte from Egypt. Lefebvre remained, an excellent soldier with a very poor head, two things which are by no means incompatible. Lefebvre commanded the division of Paris, and swore on every occasion that he would die for the Republic and exterminate its enemies, and Moulins and Gohier blindly believed in him. Bonaparte, who had a better knowledge of such men, saw no necessity for speaking to Lefebvre long beforehand, but waited for an opportunity of making propositions to him suddenly at the last moment, without giving him any time for reflection. Less explicit proposals, couched in language sufficiently vague to be denied in case of need, were made to the officers of lower rank. Murat undertook this work with the officers of the cavalry, and Lannes was entrusted with the same mission in the foot regiments. Marmont directed his attention to the artillery, which he had once commanded with honour, and Berthier was charged with the superior officers.[1]

[1] *Memoirs of Marmont.*

In the meantime Bonaparte spared no pains to lull the minds of the only two directors who were likely to embarrass him. He was even skilful enough to increase their sense of security as the decisive moment approached; and this he did so successfully, that the day before the 18th Brumaire their confidence in him was unlimited. They had not the slightest suspicion of what was preparing, though all Paris knew of the conspiracy, and it was openly spoken of in public meetings. If any allusion was made to it before them, they replied by a smile of pity and a shrug of the shoulders. They laughed immoderately at poor Sieyès, who had been spending his time in learning to ride on horseback. Moulins continued to come every morning to consult with the General, and the latter took a pleasure in explaining military affairs to him, while Gohier's society seemed to have become one of the necessities of his life. He was lavish in his expressions of friendship and attachment, which were all the more flattering because he was usually so sparing of them. Gohier was continually receiving little notes from Josephine, and Bonaparte often came to dine with him without an invitation; he had even engaged to do so without ceremony the very day on which the blow was to be struck.[1]

On the 15th Brumaire (Nov. 6, 1799) a banquet was given by the Councils in the Church of St. Sulpice, in honour of the General's return. This banquet, which was proposed by the Council of Ancients, was violently opposed by that of the Five Hundred, on account of the current reports with regard to Bonaparte's intentions, and they were obliged to defray the expenses by private subscriptions, in order to avoid discussion that would have been inconvenient for the fame which they intended to honour. Gohier took the head of the table. Moreau sat close to his rival, but he appeared to be there rather to add to his triumph than to share in it. The banquet was mortally solemn and silent. A cloud seemed to hang over the festival, and there was very little conversation. A few commonplace remarks were coldly exchanged between the guests, amongst whom were found the plotters of the conspiracy and those who were to

[1] *Memoirs of Gohier.*

be its victims; all were full of anxiety, uneasiness, and mistrust, and their minds were wholly engrossed by an event which might have such terrible consequences. Bonaparte had a small loaf and half a bottle of wine brought to him by his aide-de-camp, Duroc; an insulting and pusillanimous precaution which, to any close observer, would have betrayed the thoughts that occupied his mind.[1] It was under the influence of the same suspicions that, on leaving Lyons for Paris, he took the Bourbonnais road, knowing that he was expected through Burgundy. The conspirator is always in fear of plots and snares. He talked very little during the banquet and ate scarcely anything. At the end of half an hour he rose, walked slowly round the table with Berthier, stopping now and then to say a few words to a guest, and then escaped by a side door.

From thence he hastened to Sieyès, to arrange with him the last preliminaries of the plot. They agreed that the Councils should be removed from Paris, so as to deprive them of all means of influencing the mob, and also in the hope of more easily intimidating them. The framers of the Constitution of the Year III, remembering the frequent attacks of the people on the Assemblies, had invested the Council of Ancients with power to pass such a measure. It was accordingly decided that the Ancients, through Sieyès, should issue a decree transferring the seat of the Councils to St. Cloud. The reason alleged for the measure was the existence of a Jacobin conspiracy, of which Sieyès had openly spoken for several months past; a pretext infallibly successful even in the present day, thanks to the recollections left by the Terror. The same decree was to give Bonaparte command of the Paris division of the National Guard and the guard of the Legislative Assembly, thus placing all the military force in his hands. As soon as the Councils were assembled at St. Cloud, the resignations of Sieyès and Roger-Ducos were to be sent in, then those of Barras, Gohier, and Moulins, which were to be obtained by fair means or foul. The Directory being thus dissolved, they would compel the Councils to name a Provisional

[1] *Memoirs of Lavalette.*

Consulate, composed of Bonaparte, Sieyès, and Roger-Ducos, to form a sort of dictatorship, charged with the framing of a new Constitution.

What was this Constitution to be, which was to embody the policy of the immense change about to be accomplished? This question remained vague: except that the power was to be divided between the three Provisional Consuls, who reserved to themselves the right of establishing the basis of the new *régime*, there is no evidence that anything was settled. Neither Sieyès, nor Rœderer, whom he had persuaded to undertake the difficult task of indoctrinating the General, and who had every evening long political conversations with Bonaparte on the subject of the future government,[1] seemed to think of taking any guarantee against his flagrant ambition. Each stipulated for his own interest and his own advantage; none thought of stipulating for liberty. Sieyès contented himself with general promises; perhaps he was vain enough to imagine that he should be able to impose his famous plan of a Constitution on the General, or perhaps he felt that any precaution would be useless with such a colleague, and was resigned to yield all to him without resistance. The question of what the Constitution should be was only discussed in theory. Bonaparte, whose interest it was to avoid all allusion to it till after victory, easily eluded it by affecting to be guided on this point entirely by his learned colleague.

These resolutions having been passed by the heads of the conspiracy, the Commission of the Council of Ancients, presided over by Cornet, one of the conspirators, spent the whole night between the 8th and 9th of November, with shutters and curtains closely drawn,[2] in drawing up the Articles, in order that the Council might have nothing to do but to vote them. The Council of Ancients was to meet at seven o'clock in the morning, that of the Five Hundred at eleven o'clock, and care was taken that no notices should be sent to those members whose independence or hostility they had reason to fear. Bonaparte, on

---

[1] Rœderer, *Notice de ma Vie, pour mes enfants.*
[2] Cornet, *Notice sur le 18 brumaire.*

his side, was preparing for the part he had to play. In anticipation of a command which he had not yet received, and giving as a pretext a review, he invited the generals and superior officers, whose services he required, to come to his house, Rue de la Victoire, at six o'clock the next morning, on the 18th Brumaire (Nov. 9, 1799).

The following morning, at the appointed hour, a crowd of officers of every grade, in full uniform, thronged the streets leading to the General's house. Among them were seen the forty adjutants of the National Guard, assembled as if for the performance of some civic duty. Moreau figured in the first ranks, and with him were Macdonald, Sérurier, Murat, Lannes, Andréossy, and Berthier. Lefebvre had only been informed of the orders at midnight. Meeting with a large number of cavalry, and being astonished to find so many troops abroad without orders from himself, he stopped Colonel Sébastiani and asked for an explanation; the colonel replied by referring him to Bonaparte. He was in a state of irritation when he met the latter. 'Well, Lefebvre,' said Bonaparte, 'you, one of the supports of the Republic; will you leave it to perish at the hands of these lawyers? Here is the sword I wore at the Pyramids, I give it to you as a pledge of my esteem and confidence.' 'Let us throw the lawyers into the river,' replied Lefebvre.

Bonaparte tried the same means with Bernadotte, whom Joseph had just brought in, and whose plain clothes appeared like a protest in the midst of such brilliant uniforms. But Bernadotte was a different man from Lefebvre, and was not to be moved either by entreaties or intimidation. The General could not even succeed in obtaining from him a promise to remain neutral. Bernadotte engaged to take no steps against the conspiracy on his own account, but if he received an order from the Government he should obey it. This was all he would promise. The absence of Jourdan and Augereau was remarked; neither of them had received an invitation.

While the generals were thus flocking to the rendezvous given them by Bonaparte, the Council of Ancients was assembling in the accustomed chamber. Cornet, one of the principal members of the conspiracy, a ridiculous personage, afterwards known as Count Cornet, ascended the tribune, and denounced in plaintive terms the dangers which threatened the Councils; he represented the conspirators 'as waiting only for the signal to draw their poniards on the representatives of the nation;' at the same time he carefully abstained from mentioning any name or stating any precise fact. 'You have but a moment,' he said, 'to save France. If you let it slip, the Republic will be lost, and *its carcase will be the prey of vultures*, who will quarrel over its stripped members.'[1]

When he sat down, Régnier, another of the conspirators, rose, and proposed to the Assembly the adoption of the decrees drawn up in the midst of the commission of inspectors. Owing to the absence of the independent members the decrees were adopted and passed almost without discussion. They voted successively the removal of the Councils to St. Cloud, the unconstitutional decree which gave Bonaparte the command of all the military forces, and issued a proclamation addressed to the people recommending them to remain calm. An article of the decree invited the General to come and take an oath of allegiance in the midst of the Council.

Cornet, who was deputed to present a copy of this decree to Bonaparte, gave it to him about ten o'clock in the morning, in the presence of a large company. The General descended the steps of his house and read it to his fellow officers, who were so soon to become his subjects, and asked them if he could count on them in this hour of danger. They replied by brandishing their swords. Bonaparte then got on his horse and rode off at the head of his escort.

Everywhere on his way he saw that the orders he had given were being executed. He was saluted on the Boulevard by a regiment of soldiers placed there by his command, and who already recognised no other authority. Another regiment in accordance with his orders occupied the Tuileries, and every moment fresh troops arrived either by the garden or the Place Louis XV., to take part in the review; the

[1] *Moniteur*.

intention being to work on the minds of the people by a great military demonstration. Paris was quiet. The inhabitants were astonished, but not at all uneasy or excited. The generals and soldiers were exceedingly popular just then, and their movements were regarded with perfect confidence. At nine o'clock in the morning a small pamphlet was distributed in the streets of Paris; it was written by Rœderer in the form of a dialogue between an Ancient and a member of the Five Hundred, on the legality of the removal of the Councils of St. Cloud, and demonstrated the necessity of a *restoration* of the Constitution. The public was thus informed of the measure, and deceived with regard to its import, even before the decree had been promulgated. To the fears expressed by the members of the Five Hundred, with regard to Bonaparte's supposed ambition, the Ancient was made to reply: 'A Cæsar, a Cromwell! . . . bad parts to play, worn out parts, unworthy of any sensible man, even if he were not a good man. This is what Bonaparte has often said. It would be a sacrilegious thought, he said on one occasion, to dream of attacking a representative government in a century of light and liberty. Nobody but a madman would throw away the stake of the Republic against the thrones of Europe, after having supported it with some peril and some glory.'

Rœderer, speaking by the mouth of the Ancient, continued to express a fear lest Bonaparte should refuse the command which the Legislative Assembly had offered him, and said that in that case, and in that alone, he should not hesitate to call down upon him the poniard of Brutus.[1]

The General with his staff was introduced into the hall where the Council of the Ancients was sitting, to take the oath of allegiance to the Constitution he was about to destroy. 'Citizen Representatives,' he said, 'the Republic was in danger; you were informed of it, and your decree has saved it. Woe to those who seek to bring trouble and disorder into it! General Lefebvre, General Berthier, and all my comrades in arms will aid me to stop them. Do not look to the past for a clue to guide your onward

[1] *Moniteur du* 19 *brumaire.*

march; nothing in history ever resembled the end of the eighteenth century; nothing in the end of the eighteenth century ever resembled the present moment. We want a Republic founded on *true liberty*, civil liberty, and national representation. . . . We will have it, I swear; I swear it in my own name and that of my companions in arms.'

Bonaparte took the oath, but it was not legally done; he had not sworn fidelity to the Constitution of the Year III. Garat rose to speak, to point out the fact; but the President stopped him, giving as a reason that since the decree for the removal of the Councils, there could be no discussion except at St. Cloud. The same reply was given at about the same hour (eleven o'clock in the morning) by the President of the Five Hundred to a member of the Council who asked for an explanation respecting the decree of removal. The Constitution was thus made the means of its own destruction; Lucien adjourned the meeting till noon the following day, in the Commune of St. Cloud; and the Five Hundred broke up, a prey to the most lively agitation, amidst the cry of 'Long live the Constitution of the Year III.'

This cry was answered by a very different one from the gardens of the Tuileries and the Place Louis XV. Bonaparte on horseback was reviewing the troops, and the soldiers were receiving him everywhere with the cry of 'Long live Bonaparte!'—Bonaparte who was already everything to them. From thence he went to the Tuileries and joined the commission of inspectors, which was now become the centre of the movement, the rallying point to which all hastened, either to receive the watchword or to learn what was being done. This sort of permanent delegation from the legislative power gave the military force additional strength, without which it would perhaps scarcely have acted with so much decision. All the chiefs of the conspiracy met in the hall of the Commission, where those who were taking an active part in the events came in and went out pell-mell with others who were merely spectators. Fouché was there; the undoubted success of the morning's work had decided him in its favour. He began to display great zeal in the cause. He had, on his own authority, ordered the city gates to be closed; but Bonaparte thought the precaution unnecessary, and had them reopened. Everything hitherto had gone so smoothly that Bonaparte assumed an air of great assurance, and he would not have it supposed for a moment that he doubted the issue of the enterprise. Augereau, notwithstanding his secret hostility, was still alarmed at seeing that they were dispensing with his services, and went to Bonaparte. 'Well,' he said, 'so you no longer reckon on your old friend Augereau (*ton petit Augereau*)?' Bonaparte told him that he and Jourdan had better keep quiet.

The generals who had accompanied Bonaparte had each his post assigned, and had received his orders. Lannes had the command of the Tuileries, Marmont that of the Ecole Militaire, Sérurier was sent to Point-du-Jour, Macdonald to Versailles, and Murat to St. Cloud. The most perilous and compromising post of all still remained; this was the Luxembourg, where the Directory held its sittings. Here was no question of occupying a military post, but an act of open revolt against a legal government; it was taking men by surprise who formed part of it, and to be their jailer was a mission more worthy of a police officer than a general; it was dangerous in case of failure, dishonourable if the conspiracy succeeded. Bonaparte entrusted this post to Moreau, who fell into the snare, and accepted it without a murmur; he either did not fully understand its importance, or he thought he had committed himself too far to draw back. By this master stroke, Bonaparte got rid of the only rival whom he dreaded. Like all weak men, when once the crime was perpetrated, Moreau repented of it; he afterwards tried to exculpate himself, but for the rest of his life he remained bowed down under the weight of the remembrance of Brumaire. From this moment he counted for nothing.

But while these important events were taking place, where were the directors, whom they were preparing to imprison in their own palace? Every one was asking this question. Barras was taking a bath; Sieyès and Roger-

Ducos were with the conspirators; Gohier and Moulins were beginning to open their eyes, and ask what they could, or should, or would do. At twelve o'clock the previous night Gohier had received an invitation from Madame Bonaparte to breakfast with them the next morning, and his suspicions were aroused by the very early hour named in the note; suspicions which were confirmed by the opinion of his wife, who went alone to the General's house. It was not long before he heard of the decree which had been issued by the Council of Ancients, and hastened to Barras, whom he found in his bath, and who told him to trust to him, and promised to join Moulins and himself as soon as possible, in the hall of the Directory. He had scarcely left Barras' house, when Talleyrand and Bruix entered it; they were come to ask him to resign his office, and offer in return a promise of safety for his life and property. Talleyrand drew from his pocket a paper containing the letter of resignation, drawn up in readiness, which plainly showed Barras how determined they were to obtain it. He signed it, and thus cynically abandoning his colleagues, crowned by an act of cowardice a long career of treachery.

The letter was written by Rœderer, to whom Bonaparte had entrusted the affair.[1] There was nothing remarkable in it except the passage in which Barras declared that as liberty was no longer in peril, 'since the return of the illustrious warrior to whom he had had *the happiness of opening the road to glory*,' he joyfully returned to the rank of a simple citizen. This was the only time that Bonaparte ever mentioned the services that Barras had rendered him, and he only alluded to them now to complete his ruin and to obtain one more advantage from his recommendation. He did not perceive that in thus evoking the remembrance of the benefit he was making his own ingratitude eternal.

Owing to this resignation, which had already been preceded by that of Sieyès and Ducos, the Directory was in a state of disorganisation, for the minority could not even enter on a debate. Gohier and Moulins innocently waited for their colleague, till a copy of his resignation was brought

---

[1] Rœderer, *Notice de ma Vie, pour mes enfants.*

them in explanation of his prolonged absence. They decided to go at once to the hall of the commission of Inspectors, to see at any rate whom they could depend upon, and if possible to bring back with them Sieyès or Ducos. Bottot, Barras' secretary, had come in just before to see what was going on, and Bonaparte had greeted him by his celebrated attack on the whole Directory. 'What have you done with that France which I left in such glory? I left peace, I found war; I left victories, I find reverses; I left millions from Italy, I find despoiling laws and misery. Where are the hundred thousand men who have disappeared from French soil? They are dead, and they were my companions in arms. This state of things cannot last; *before three years it would lead us to despotism.*'

Poor Bottot, confounded and stupefied by this violent tirade, hurried away as fast as possible, wondering no doubt what he had done to merit such an honour; but it was not to him that the discourse was addressed, for while the General was delivering his fine burst of rhetoric, Bottot might have seen the poet Arnault taking it down for the Paris newspapers. Everything was a matter of calculation with Bonaparte, even anger. His manner towards Moulins and Gohier, whom he hoped to win, was very different. 'I see with pleasure,' he said, 'that you yield to our wishes and those of your colleagues. It is because you are attached to your country that you are willing to join us in saving the Republic.' And when Gohier claimed this honour for the Directory: 'With what means?' cried Bonaparte; 'with those which your Constitution gives you?—See how it is crumbling to pieces. The Constitution can last no longer!' 'Who told you so?' asked Gohier; 'traitors, who have neither the will nor the courage to work with it.' And then the honest man represented to him in words of touching simplicity the great danger of violating legality; he reminded him of the oath of allegiance so often repeated by the Legislative Assembly, and of the arms of the Republic victorious again after a short period of defeat, and the picture was certainly more truthful than the one which the General had just traced with so entire a forgetfulness of the extent to which he was responsible for our reverses; but now it was a question of victory, not of argumentation.

There was a puerile ingenuousness in trying to persuade such an adversary, when things had already gone so far. Finding that he could do nothing with Gohier by gentleness, Bonaparte tried to intimidate Moulins by threatening to shoot his friend Santerre if he attempted any resistance, and finished by demanding from both a resignation of office. To this they gave a flat refusal, notwithstanding the indirect menaces which were made use of to induce them to yield; they returned to the Luxembourg, where they were made prisoners by Moreau, and by their firmness on this fatal day saved the Republican Government from succumbing without honour.

The day closed without any difficulty encountering the conspiracy. Every public authority seemed to give way at the approach of the plotters, and one man remained master of all. Bonaparte was so assured of the same success on the morrow, that he disdainfully rejected Sieyès' proposition to arrest during the night the most independent members of the two councils. Certain of victory, he wished to avoid all appearance of disquiet. He however allowed Fouché to suspend the twelve municipalities of Paris, and to delegate all their authority to their commissaries, whose support Réal had already secured beforehand. The minister of the police, who knew well how thoroughly weary the people were of agitation, and how much they were under the dominion of selfish fear, placarded a proclamation, in which he warned the citizens of vague plots and entreated them to remain quiet: 'Let not the weak be uneasy,' he added, '*they are with the strong!*' The night passed in perfect tranquillity. There were a few secret meetings between the men of the Manége and the most courageous members of the Five Hundred, but called together suddenly, and meeting only in small numbers, without concert or communication, and without a general understanding, their efforts were lost in contradictory and impracticable resolutions. Much astonishment has often been expressed that no serious resistance was organised either before the 18th Brumaire or during the days which immediately followed it. But nothing of the kind could be expected of a nation that was decapitated. All the men of mark in France for the previous ten years, either by character, genius, or virtue, had been mown down, first by scaffolds and proscriptions, next by war. Of those who survived, there was no one of sufficient strength and authority to oppose Bonaparte. This was the principal, though not the last, expiation of the terrorist delirium. In one of these meetings, however, a project was developed, which had it been successful might have had some influence on events. A dozen deputies, among whom was Bernadotte, met at Salicetti's, and decided that on the morrow they would proceed to St. Cloud at the hour appointed for the assembling of the councils, and pass a decree giving Bernadotte the command of the guard of the Council of Five Hundred. But Salicetti the very same evening betrayed the project to Bonaparte, and Fouché took measures to prevent the deputies reaching St. Cloud.

Bonaparte spent the greater part of the night with the inspectors and principal members of the Council of Ancients, in arranging a plan of operation for the morrow. Several of the deputies began to show great uneasiness about the conspiracy, contested the necessity of a dictatorship, and expressed a strong wish that Bonaparte would be satisfied with a place in a renewed Directory. But the General took their proposition very ill. 'There was no Directory! It was not a revolution of the seraglio that France expected of them, but a change in the Constitution. A kind of momentary dictatorship, or if the word alarmed them, a concentration of the executive power, was the only reasonable and effective expedient.' The protesting faction gave way, and it was decided that they should propose to the councils the institution of a Consulate, and the adjournment of the Legislative Session till the 1st Ventôse, with no provision in case the expediency of the measures should be questioned or rejected by those called upon to vote them.

The following day, a little before two o'clock, the councils opened their sittings at St. Cloud. The town had been crowded since the morning with soldiers and persons curious to see what would take place. As nothing was in readiness for the installation of the Legislative Body, a delay took place which was detrimental to the conspirators, who had built all their plans on a surprise, and their chance of success was greatly diminished by allowing their adversaries time to reflect and devise measures. They took advantage of it to excite and encourage one another. The Council of Ancients met in one of the rooms of the palace, that of the Five Hundred in the orangery, while Bonaparte and his staff occupied one of the apartments; with him was Sieyès, for whom a carriage and six horses was in readiness at the gate in case of failure.

In the Chamber of Five Hundred, Gaudin, who had received his instructions, opened the proceedings by calling the attention of the assembly to the dangers of the Republic, and the necessity of prompt measures to insure public safety. He proposed the nomination of a commission of enquiry into the best means of saving the Republic. They hoped thus to avoid a discussion, and to evade the most thorny side of the question; but as Gaudin's proposition was made to an assembly who had just reasons for distrust, and who were irritated by the precautions, menaces, and snares, by which they felt themselves surrounded the last two days, it gave rise to an appalling storm.

A large majority of the Five Hundred were sincere republicans, and wished to maintain existing institutions. The cries of 'Down with the Dictatorship, Long live the Constitution,' drowned every voice, till Grandmaison proposed that the oath of allegiance to the constitution should be taken; this resolution was passed unanimously. But as each member had to swear separately, the taking of the oath occupied several hours, which was so much time gained by the conspirators, a fresh proof of the utter incapacity of large assemblies in circumstances where promptitude and decision are required.

The scene which had just taken place showed the chiefs of

the plot how very little they could hope to obtain by means of persuasion, and for some minutes they were disconcerted: 'Now you are in a nice position,' said Augereau to Bonaparte, with an ironical smile and a satisfaction which he no longer took the trouble to hide. But by what right could Fructidor rally or reproach Brumaire? In the Council of Ancients, where there was much less excitement, things took a different turn, but one which was scarcely less discouraging for the conspirators. The members, who had received no notice of the sitting of the previous evening, complained loudly of this irregularity, and insisted on an explanation with regard to the danger which had caused the removal of the councils to St. Cloud; but Fargues, Cornudet, and other friends of Sieyès succeeded after a warm discussion in closing the debate, till an official notice had been received of the sitting of the Five Hundred in the Commune of St. Cloud. At half-past three a letter was read from the Secretary-General of the Directory, announcing that as four of the members had resigned and the fifth been placed under the supervision of the police by orders of General Bonaparte, there was no longer a Directory, whereupon it was agreed that the letter should be sent to the Council of Five Hundred, for them to present a list of candidates, and the proceedings were again stopped. This letter was a falsehood, for neither Gohier nor Moulins had resigned. At four o'clock a general movement was made in the Assembly; the deputies hurriedly went back to their places, and General Bonaparte was announced.

He had an anxious, troubled, and irritated look, and his whole demeanour betrayed secret agitation. He had expected to meet with the same success as on the day before, and for some hours everything had gone contrary to his anticipation. The enterprise he was engaged in was in fact one of those that will bear neither the scrutiny nor the control of an adverse debate. It might be enforced by one party and submitted to by the other, but to discuss was to annihilate it. It is surprising that a mind of such perspicacity could for a moment have yielded to the delusion of wishing to proceed by the semblance of legal forms in carrying out a plan, of which neither the motives, pretext, nor end, would bear the test of examination. The whole conspiracy rested on the supposition of the existence of a great Jacobin plot, and there was so little foundation for belief in the existence of this plot, that even those who asserted it most resolutely, and were determined to aid the General to their utmost, felt that their lips were closed as soon as they were required to state a syllable of fact. They had not even that shadow of evidence which for appearance sake is always wanted in large assemblies, for men met together in a body are under a reserve which they do not feel as individuals. Such was the feeling that had hitherto paralysed the partisans of Bonaparte, and he was at once surprised and troubled to find himself under its influence. Accustomed as he was to military command, never to have his word questioned nor his wishes disputed, but to be able to say on all occasions, *Je veux*, he was disconcerted at finding himself obliged to have recourse to persuasion.

He entered, followed by his aides-de-camp, after having drawn up a regiment in order of battle in the court, and openly announced to his officers that he *was going to make an end of it.* But the moment he was in presence of the Assembly he felt ill at ease, though at the same time irritated at not being able to surmount impressions so new to him, and his speech gave evidence of his inward struggle. It has been admitted by all who were present at this singular scene that the speech which afterwards appeared in the *Moniteur*, notwithstanding its incoherence, gives no idea of his confused and disconnected language.

After having begun by saying, 'that the Republic was on a volcano,' instead of giving proofs of this assertion which had been reiterated for the last two days, he abruptly passed on to the 'calumnies which had been showered upon him in return for his pure and disinterested intentions. They talked of Cæsar and Cromwell, and they had dared to impute to him the project of establishing a military government. If he had really wished to usurp such an authority, he had no need to ask permission of the Council of Ancients; he had only to yield to the wishes of his comrades and of the soldiers, who offered it to him immediately after his return from Italy.' The evident meaning of this warning was to make the Assembly understand that, if he chose, he could act independently of its sanction. After this he went back again to the dangers of the Republic, but without stating any other fact than the 'horrible war of La Vendée, and the news that the Chouans were in possession of several places,' which was not true, and even if it had been was no good reason for the alarm he was trying to create. As he was adjuring the Ancients to save liberty and equality, Linglet asked: 'And the Constitution?' 'The Constitution,' exclaimed Bonaparte, 'you violated it the 18th Fructidor: you violated it the 22d Floréal, and you violated it the 30th Prairial. The Constitution! The Constitution is invoked by all factions, and has been violated by all; it is despised by all; the country cannot be saved by the Constitution, because no one any longer respects it.' This criticism of the system of *coups-d'état* was perfectly just, though Bonaparte more than any other man was responsible for them, and this was the only portion of his speech in which he was eloquent. But if it was necessary to introduce some reforms into the institutions of the Year III, it by no means followed that all power should be concentrated in the hands of General Bonaparte; and when he spoke of his determination, assuring his hearers that he should resign as soon as the danger was past, every one felt that the premises were too weak to justify such a conclusion. The General was again asked to explain what the danger to which he referred was. 'If I must give an explanation,' he said, 'and if I must name men, I will name them. I will tell you that Barras and Moulins proposed to me to be the leader of a party, whose aim was the overthrow of all men holding liberal opinions.'

This denunciation, which implicated in the same conspiracy two men so notoriously at variance, only testified to the confusion and embarrassment of the speaker. It was a false step, for what had become of the bugbear of the Jacobin conspiracy, about which there had hitherto been so much noise made? Cornudet, who had always used this last argument with the commission of Inspectors, feeling that Bonaparte's assertion had placed him in an awkward position, insisted on his giving some proof. The President himself pressed Bonaparte to express himself more clearly. But instead of making the revelations he was asked for, he began to complain of the inadequacy of the Constitution to save the country, and to accuse in vague terms the different factions, 'of having come to ring at his door, and offer him power which he would only accept at the hands of the French people.' At length forgetting completely all the caution which his situation required of him, and carried away by his temper, which he could no longer control, he commenced an inconceivably violent attack on the Council of Five Hundred. 'He did not reckon,' he said, 'on the support of the Five Hundred, among whom were men who wished to re-establish the scaffolds and the revolutionary committees,—on the Five Hundred, where the chiefs of this party had just been sitting,—on the Five Hundred, who had despatched emissaries to Paris to organise a rising.'

Such violent and incautious language could only be uttered by a man who had lost self-control. The accusation had fallen on a fresh party; after having invoked the old phantom of Jacobinism, then accused Barras and Moulins, he tried to extricate himself from the difficulty of giving any precise facts by attacking the Legislative power itself. The General's friends were in torture, and his fellow-conspirators were in perfect consternation. He was addressing an Assembly in which three-fourths of his hearers were in favour of him, and he had said everything that was likely to prejudice them against him and excite suspicion. He wound up his speech with almost open threats: 'And if any orator in foreign pay talks of outlawry, let him beware of levelling such a decree against himself. At the first sign, I should appeal to you, my brave companions in arms: to you, grenadiers, whose caps I perceive yonder: to you, brave soldiers, whose bayonets are in sight! Remember that I go forward accompanied by the God of fortune and the God of war!'

This pompous and unseemly language, which would

have roused the indignation of less complaisant hearers, produced so painful an impression that the president would not allow the General to close with these words. He hoped every minute that Bonaparte would gain his presence of mind, and speak in such a way as to give the Assembly a pretext for granting all his requests. Trying for a third time to bring him back to the point, he said, 'General, the Council invites you to reveal all you know of the plot by which the Republic is threatened.' Bonaparte, in reply, returned to the pretended proposition of Barras and Moulins, adding 'that these two directors would be no more guilty than many others, if they had only set forth a fact known throughout France.' This was all they could draw from him. As soon as he had said this he withdrew.

Though this memorable scene has so often been described, the striking and salient feature does not appear to us ever to have been sufficiently brought to light, namely, that this speech shows, even in the disfigured report of it in the *Moniteur*, the utter and absolute powerlessness of Bonaparte to give, not well-grounded motives, but even plausible reasons, for the revolution he was meditating. In presence of an assembly of accomplices, who entreated him to bring forward, if not a proof, at any rate an accusation in excuse for his proceedings, he hesitated, stammered, and wandered from the point, and was unable to recall any one of the numerous pretexts which his partizans had so unscrupulously and lavishly invented. What better proof that no adequate reason existed, and that there was not the necessity for this revolution which writers have chosen to believe? Its authors had nothing to allege in support of their projects, not even pretexts. They saw clearly that the need of more or less general reform was not a sufficient excuse for forming a dictatorship, and, feeling that only great peril could justify this sacrifice of the guarantees of the citizen, they invented the story of the existence of this peril, but when the time for action came the proofs were wanting, and the truth comes out with irresistible force from the long and laborious efforts thus made to deceive public opinion. It has vainly been obscured by sophists more ingenious in their apologies for despotism than the despot himself. The state of affairs at the time demanded reform, but not absolute power, and it was only by speculating on the one that they succeeded in realising the other.

As soon as the taking of the oath was over in the Council of Five Hundred, the discussion inevitably took the same turn as in the Council of Ancients, but it was carried on with more warmth and urgency. The members were more impatient than any one to fathom the plot which had caused the removal of the Councils to St. Cloud. They decided on sending an address to the Council of Ancients to ask for an explanation. A letter from Barras was then read, in which he resigned his office, a step which appeared to them the effect of duress, as in fact it was. The question was then raised, as to whether it would be well to name his successor then and there, when the door opened and Bonaparte entered, surrounded by armed grenadiers. At this sight a cry of universal indignation burst from the Assembly. Every one rose: 'What is this?' they cried. 'Swords here! Armed men!' Some of the deputies who had more courage than the others left their places, pressed round Bonaparte and overwhelmed him with invectives: 'Away,' they cried, 'we will have no dictator here!' 'What are you dreaming of, rash man?' exclaimed Bigonnet, 'you are violating the sanctuary of the laws.' 'Is it for this that you have conquered?' said Destrem, advancing towards him. Others seized him by the collar of his coat, and, shaking him violently, reproached him with his treason. The General, who had come with the intention of intimidating them, turned pale, and fell fainting into the arms of the grenadiers, who drew him out of the hall.

It was asserted at the time, and has often been repeated since, that poniards were drawn upon him. This story has always been contradicted by all trustworthy authorities.[1]

---

[1] 'I saw no poniards drawn,' says Prince Eugène in his Memoirs. Of those friends of Bonaparte's who believe the fact not one affirms that he saw it. All other eye-witnesses or historians of the time, from

Not a word of such an accusation appears in the minute account which the *Moniteur* published of the affair on the 20th Brumaire, which was written, too, by partizans of the *coup-d'état*. It is only mentioned in a sort of postscript. It was not till the day following that the idea of ascribing to Thomas Thomé, grenadier, the honour of having saved the General from a poniard-thrust was imagined by Lucien, as an expedient for heaping odium on those whom he had not been able to bend. If they had really wished to stab Bonaparte, nothing would have been easier in such a scuffle, from which he escaped with his clothes torn. But just as those who had conspired against the Republic were the first to denounce the existence of a plot, so those who had recourse to arms were the first to accuse their adversaries of having wished to make use of them.

When Lucien left the President's chair, Chazal took his place. A number of resolutions were proposed from all parts of the Assembly, but before he could put one of them to the vote a member rose and exclaimed: 'The first step to take is to declare that Bonaparte has not the command of your guard.' Another added: 'You are surrounded by six thousand men; declare that they form part of the guard of the Legislative Body.' Lucien, who understood the meaning of these measures, rose to defend his brother; he reminded them of his services, and entreated them not to pass a hasty judgment. But the tempest, calmed for a moment, rose more violently than ever, and the cry of *Outlaw* resounded on all sides. If this resolution had been passed at once, no one can say what the consequences might have been. Lucien saw this, and obstinately refused to put it to the vote. He vehemently protested against it, made a great display of his brotherly despair, and then resigned his office, laying the Presidential insignia on the table, in the midst of indescribable uproar, during which nothing could be heard but the cry, the terrible cry, of *hors la loi!* the cry which had destroyed Robespierre himself, and had still preserved

Thibeaudeau to Dupont de l'Eure, deny it, and when the accusation was brought against Arena, no witness could be found against him.

much of its ancient prestige. It was heard by those outside, in the group where Bonaparte was standing, and every one turned pale. 'Since they talk of outlawing,' said Sieyès, who alone had preserved a perfect coolness in the critical changes of this day, 'let them be outlawed.'[1] The General, who understood all the advantages of having the President in the midst of the troops, sent a platoon of grenadiers to fetch his brother, and they returned with him in a few minutes. Bonaparte resolved to break up the Council by armed force, but the soldiers to whom he gave the order formed part of the guard of the Legislative Body, and a degree of hesitation on their part made him fear that their scruples would be a cause of failure. Lucien, who was known to them as President of the Assembly, was at that moment master of the occasion, and the saviour of the conspiracy. He mounted on horseback, harangued the soldiers, and depicted the Council of Five Hundred as crushed by representatives of the stiletto, by brigands paid by England; the question was how to deliver the Assembly from this minority of assassins. Then taking a sword, and turning towards his brother, 'For my part,' he said, 'I swear to run this through my own brother if ever he strike a blow at the liberties of the French!'

This oratorical movement roused the soldiers, who replied by crying, 'Long live Bonaparte.' Taking advantage of their excitement, Murat led them forward at quick march to the rolling of the drum. When they arrived at the door of the hall where the Assembly was sitting, they stopped on the threshold as if seized by a feeling of involuntary respect. The colonel who commanded them asked the members to retire. They refused, appealing to the legislative inviolability, and remained in their places, but their protestations were drowned by the roll of drums. The officer then gave orders to the grenadiers to advance. The last cry of *Vive la République* was heard; it was the despairing cry of expiring liberty. A few minutes more and the hall was emptied, and the crime of the conspirators consummated.

[1] Rœderer, *Notice de ma Vie;* Lavalette, *Mémoires.*

Towards nine o'clock in the evening Lucien assembled about *thirty*[1] members of the Council of Five Hundred, some of whom he had gained, while others had been accomplices in the conspiracy: they assumed the title of Majority of the Council, and decreed that Bonaparte and his lieutenants had deserved well of the country. Boulay de la Meurthe, reporter of the law of 19th Fructidor, a precedent which gave him the right to present that of 19th Brumaire, rose to propose the measures which had been previously agreed upon by the conspirators: the institution of a Provisional Consulate composed of Bonaparte, Sieyès, and Roger-Ducos; the adjournment of the sitting of the Legislative Body till the 1st Ventôse; the nomination of two Commissioners chosen from the two Councils and charged with aiding the Consuls in their work of reorganisation; and lastly, the exclusion of the fifty-seven members who had been most prominent in their opposition, a measure which was quickly complemented by a list of proscriptions. The complaisant assembly spent a great part of the night in passing in quick succession all the measures proposed. The members voted with such haste that they might have been said to dread the light of day, and at one o'clock in the morning the decree was presented to the Council of Ancients to be ratified. When this was done, the three Consuls came to take the oath before this phantom of an assembly composed of their creatures. Bonaparte first swore inviolable fidelity 'to legality, liberty, and the representative system!' Then Lucien rose to congratulate his colleagues on the work they had just accomplished. He did not shrink from comparing this nocturnal meeting to the pure and glorious dawn of the Revolution! 'Representatives of the people,' he said, 'the meeting in the Tennis-Court at Versailles gave birth to liberty in France. Since the memorable scene of that day its life has been a struggle, a prey alternately to inconsistency and weakness; it has been subject to the convulsive diseases of infancy. To-day it puts on the garb of manhood. It stands firmly on the confidence and love of the French people, and

[1] This is the number given by Cornet himself.

already the smile of peace and abundance greets you on every side! Representatives of the people, listen to the sublime cry of posterity! If liberty was born in the Tennis-Court at Versailles, it was consolidated in the Orangery of St. Cloud!'

History has recorded many a solemn falsehood, but it would be difficult to cite one in which truth has been outraged with more cynicism and shamelessness. When the advocates of a cause are reduced in the very midst of their triumph to have recourse to such palpable falsehoods in order to make it prevail, the cause itself may be said to have disowned its own principle, and there is nothing to add to the judgment that it has thus passed on itself.

The next day Bonaparte published a proclamation addressed to the French people. He again referred to the proposals which he said had been made to him by all parties, but which he had rejected. He represented himself as a docile and devoted instrument in the hands of the Ancients, as the executor of a plan of general restoration which they had conceived. 'He believed that his duty to his fellow citizens, to the soldiers perishing in our armies, to our national glory acquired at the price of their blood, required him to accept the task.' Then, passing on to the events of St. Cloud, he said: 'In my grief and indignation I went into the Council of Ancients; I asked them to carry out their generous projects, I represented the woes of the country, which had also suggested to them the plan they had conceived, and they assured me that their wishes were still the same. I presented myself before the Five Hundred, alone, *unarmed*, and bareheaded, just as the Ancients had received and applauded me. *I came to remind the majority of its will and its power.* The daggers, which had threatened the Deputies, were raised against their liberator; *twenty assassins rushed upon me and tried to pierce my breast.* The grenadiers of the Legislative Body, whom I had left outside, ran in and thrust themselves between me and the assassins. One of these brave men (Thomé) was struck by a dagger which pierced his clothes. They carried me out. . . . Frenchmen,' he added at the close, 'will you not recognise in this conduct the zeal of a soldier of liberty, and of a citizen devoted to the cause of the Republic?' And the *Moniteur* of the 23d Brumaire contained the following paragraph:

"Thomas Thomé, grenadier of the Legislative Body, who had the sleeve of his coat torn in shielding Bonaparte from the dagger stroke, dined with him on the 20th and breakfasted with him on the 21st. The Citizeness Bonaparte embraced Thomas Thomé, and placed on his finger a diamond ring valued at 2000 crowns.'

This was only an additional fact borrowed from the history of the Pretorians. While these things were taking place, Paris displayed some amount of curiosity, but remained neutral; the events seemed foreign to the people; the army applauded, public opinion was silent.

Such was the *début* of the new Government, and such was the man for whom the public liberties had been sacrificed.

CHAPTER XIII

THE CONSTITUTION OF THE YEAR VIII

NAPOLEON relates, that at the close of the first meeting which the Provisional Consuls held in the Luxembourg a few hours after their return to Paris, and while the scenes of violence at St. Cloud were still fresh in their memory, Sieyès said to the principal authors of the *coup-d'état*, 'Gentlemen, you have a Master! Bonaparte means to do everything, knows how to do everything, and has power to do everything.' It was too late to think of this. That Bonaparte would wish to do everything was beyond doubt; he had given assured proofs of this, both before and after the crimes committed against the National Representatives, and the impatience of his ambition shone out in all his being. That he knew how to do everything was much less certain, and it is scarcely probable that Sieyès seriously intended to pay him a homage to which neither his intelligence nor his own pretensions could subscribe. But what neither Sieyès nor any one else could deny was that he had the power to do everything. Never had new authority established itself with less difficulty, or met with less opposition. Either the Government which had just fallen had left no regrets, or else the people, weary of agitation and change, and disgusted with parties by whom they had so often been deceived, had become indifferent to the realisation of principles, ever pursued, never reached, for which they had paid so dearly, and preferred placing their fate in the bold hands of a despotic saviour to dictating conditions to him at the cost of fresh struggles.

Having taken no part in the establishment of the new

Government, the nation could exercise no control over its acts. This was the punishment for an ignoble apathy. No share in the fight, no share in the spoil. The men who conquered without the people gave them no portion of the fruits of victory. This nullity, though humiliating to the national spirit, was submitted to with resignation. With the enlightened classes, this incredible inertness was the result of scepticism and discouragement; while, with the multitude, it was the effect of unbounded confidence in the name of Bonaparte. The first, accustomed to political influence, and to participation in public affairs, did not deceive themselves as to the sacrifices they were making for the promised stability of government; but the rest, who understood nothing of political guarantees, though passionately attached to their social conquests, did not see the fatal consequences of ratifying acts which had been accomplished without the sanction of the people. In the eyes of the majority of the nation General Bonaparte was the representative of the Revolution; they fully believed in his determination to maintain the rights of equality, the only interest, except the glory of our arms, which was still dear to this military democracy. In their eagerness to identify themselves with him, to recognise in him the soldier tribune, in his authority a consecration of their own influence, and more anxious for power than for liberty, they made light of the highest principles of the Revolution, without perceiving, in their inexperience, that in abandoning the one they were necessarily compromising the others also. The sceptical resignation of the upper classes, and the enthusiastic confidence among the lower, made Bonaparte's situation one of incomparable strength. France had placed herself in his hands. After the dispersion of the Council of the Five Hundred, all opposition instantly ceased; the different parties were silent, and held themselves in an attitude of expectation, in the presence of a mediator imposed on them by the universal adhesion of the people. There appeared to be a tacit agreement between them to accept without discussion the illegal origin of the new Government, and to judge it only by its future acts. This feeling was so universal, that the only protest against the 18th Brumaire of which we have any record, was made not in the name of a party, but in the name of the law. Barnabé, president of the criminal tribunal of the Yonne, a man who emerged that day from the bosom of his obscurity, and immediately afterwards returned to it, never again to quit it, as if he thought such an act sufficient to honour a life, alone raised his voice amidst the general silence, and opposed, in the name of the Constitution, the registration of the law of the 19th Brumaire. Arrested by order of the Consuls, dragged from his office, this courageous citizen was exiled to Orleans, and only escaped a more rigorous chastisement by the singularity of his action, which was to find no imitators.

To the advantages which this uncontested omnipotence gave Bonaparte, he joined that of inspiring no one with that irreconcilable enmity which is the lot of most men who rise to power after civil dissensions. He had for some time past represented himself as above all disputes of faction; and such a man was so much needed that they took him at his word, without examining whether this pretended abnegation was not a cloak for exclusively personal designs. Although at different epochs of his life he had taken an active part in several contests, his intervention had been so cleverly concealed that he had not committed himself with any one party; and his long absence in Egypt had greatly tended to make him appear a stranger to divisions which were partly of his own making. He had left time for all parties to exhaust themselves; then, when their strength was spent and their credit gone, he had suddenly appeared in the midst of them, and he seemed to reap the fruits of their defeat, without having done anything himself to bring it about. Hence the kind of neutrality with which after the first moments of stupor and irritation they regarded him. He had therefore no factions to fight, no vengeance to appease, no hatreds to restrain; necessities which, like so many Nemeses, are imposed on those who seize the reins of power under similar circumstances, and force them to continue usurpation in order to retain what they usurped first, and to destroy in order not to be destroyed.

Having nothing of this kind to fear, after the unanimous sanction which his first acts received, General Bonaparte found, in the very elements of this situation, the clearest indication of the grand part which was offered to him. In a position to defy all competition, armed with a power which none could resist, he had only to accept the mission of moderator and sovereign arbitrator which seemed to devolve upon him by the consent even of his enemies. To repair the evils produced by long-continued strife, to subject to common law parties accustomed to struggle by *coups de dictature*, to carry out the great principles and the large interests of the French Revolution, and guarantee them by solid and durable institutions, such was the work to which everything invited him; and never was there a task more worthy of the ambition of a man of genius. The pre-eminent position which he had been allowed to take, the need they had of his sword, the admiration that was felt for his person, the almost universal approval which his acts received, were sufficient at once to insure order and to maintain his own authority; was it not natural that to the glory of a great captain he should wish to join that of the founder of liberty? This task was comparatively easy, since the whole nation acquiesced in desiring its realisation. Whatever may be said to the contrary, France was thirsting for a firm and regular order of things, but not for despotism. Even among those who had co-operated most actively in the revolution of Brumaire, no one wished to prolong the dictatorship beyond the time necessary for realising the changes agreed upon in the Constitution.

But it is the vainest delusion to imagine that a government which is inaugurated by fraud and violence can return to the paths of justice at its own pleasure. If it had the love for the public weal which such a return supposes, it would have recoiled from the adoption of such means. Popular credulity easily admits these sudden conversions, by virtue of which good is supposed to come out of evil, and usurpation to change to a *régime* of benevolence. History gives a flat contradiction to this common opinion, and it is doubtless well that it does not sanction such a filiation of good to evil, such promiscuousness of crime and virtue. A nation, that carries love of ease so far as to thrust the whole burden of duties and responsibility on a single man, is always punished for it; for even supposing by a miracle that his ambition rises to the height of disinterestedness, his faculties, however fine they may be, will always need in some measure to be guided or checked, if not by the initiative, at any rate by the resistance, of the people. With regard to General Bonaparte, it is impossible to deny that the inexhaustible compliance which he met with, whether in the men who surrounded him or in the people themselves, renders them greatly responsible for the exorbitant authority which he assumed, and for the faults for which history justly reproaches him. This abdication by a whole people was the less excusable that, setting aside Bonaparte's opinions and character, about which illusion was possible, his career, which up to that time had been in camps, in the midst of all the abuses of force and conquest, indicated clearly enough what ideas and what proceedings might be expected of him in matters of government. He could only bring into the exercise of power the tastes, inclinations, and manner of judging and acting, which his previous life had developed in him, that is to say, the habits of military command, the forms of discipline and the organisation of camps.

And though Bonaparte, especially at the commencement, often sought opportunities of paying homage to the principles of civil government, in order to answer the objection which he felt would arise in the mind of every sensible person, it is certain that this conception of power was ineradicable with him, and was part of his very nature. Even the lessons of adversity were to teach him nothing in this respect. Many years later, in his conversations at Saint Helena, in spite of that comedy of converted despot which he was then playing in sight of posterity, alluding to the slight obstacles which Sieyès had put in his way at this epoch, he said, with a stronger conviction than ever: 'After all, it comes to this at bottom, that a man must be a soldier to govern. You can only govern in boots and spurs.'[1]

[1] Las Cases' *Mémorial*.

However, notwithstanding the kind of fatality to which his past life seemed to devote him, and tendencies against which they could not take too many precautionary measures, many of Bonaparte's first acts seemed to announce a higher idea of duty than the circumstances imposed on him. We cannot doubt that this part of pacificator of the Republic and supreme mediator of parties struck his imagination, that he felt the grandeur of it, and, before he yielded to the dizzy temptations of his ambition, was tempted by the intuition of a higher destiny, and a glory less fatal to himself and his country. The fame of Washington had made noise enough to assure him that he would neither be despised nor misunderstood, if even at a distance he followed in his footsteps. The *début* of the Consulate proves that if Bonaparte had not sufficient disinterestedness and generosity resolutely to take this path, it was not for want of having understood that his true historic mission lay there, nor without having several times tried to assume the appearance of a part he did not wish to play. The last anxiety appears in every word of his at this epoch. The watchword that was given and incessantly repeated was: 'No more divisions, no more factions, no more hatreds! We are creating a new era. There are no more Jacobins, nor Moderates, nor Terrorists; there are only Frenchmen. The Eighteenth Brumaire was not the day of a party: it was for the Republic and for republicans.' These promises were not only every instant on the lips of Bonaparte, they were daily repeated by his principal representatives, by Fouché at Paris, by Lannes at Toulouse, where they were afraid of an insurrection. At the same time, many of his measures appeared to be inspired by these sentiments; they unquestionably bore a character of reparation and impartiality. He repealed the Law of Hostages, a cruel and rapacious measure, voted by the Directory in despair, which had filled the State prisons with thousands of innocent persons, who were made responsible by their goods and liberty for an insurrection by which it was supposed that they were going to find profit or delight. Bonaparte repaired to the Temple himself, announced to the prisoners their release, and ordered the doors of the prison to be opened. He repealed the decree of a forced and progressive loan, a measure not only unjust but contrary to all the principles of political economy, which was the complement to the law of hostages, being engendered by the same spirit, and which permitted the Government to strike, by means of taxation, classes or individuals whose leanings were suspected.

Gaudin, who contributed greatly to the abrogation of this last measure, applied himself at once to the task of reorganising the finances. Another decree[1] authorised the return to their country of the greater part of the men proscribed after the fatal day of the 18th Fructidor, of which Bonaparte had been the principal promoter; a tardy and insufficient reparation, for it could not bring back from the tomb the number of upright citizens whose lives had been sacrificed to the climate of Guiana. Besides, exceptions were made, which tarnished the purity of this act of justice; if the maintenance of the sentence can be justified in the case of Pichegru, it can only be explained with regard to Aubry by feelings of personal animosity, the persistency of which, after so many years of unmerited punishment inflicted on the one, and marvellous success achieved by the other, is of itself enough to prove a cruel and mean nature. Apart, however, from the Draconian legislation against the emigrants, during these first essays of their barely established authority by the Provisional Consulate, Bonaparte displayed a spirit of clemency: he instructed his agents to shut their eyes on the return to France of all those who were disposed to remain tranquil; he formally struck off the list the names of those who had formed part of the Constituent Assembly, and declared that the law did not apply to those who had only re-appeared on French territory against their will and from inevitable necessity, as in the case of the men thrown on the coast of Calais by shipwreck, whom public pity had so long been trying to save from the rigours of an inexorable law. With respect to the clergy, Bonaparte had had a plan of his own, ever since his sojourn in Italy, which was about to be developed in a very unforeseen manner. The prelude

[1] Dated December 23d, 1799.

to this was the immediate enlargement of a great number of nonjuring priests, who were still prisoners in the islands of Ré and Oléron. These acts, of which we cannot fail to recognise the wisdom and equity, seemed to promise a government that should be superior to the passions of party spirit, and so much the stronger that, in making its private interests subordinate to those of the people, it identified itself in some sort with them. But this illusion was quickly dissipated with all but those who were determined to preserve it.

When on every occasion he spoke of reconciliation, pacification, oblivion, when he preached the surrender of personal enmities and party creeds to the country, it was in his own favour that Bonaparte intended the surrender to be made; and this purely selfish motive is betrayed, not only in measures of which there could be no doubt, but even in acts of such apparent disinterestedness as we have just noticed. It is not difficult to discover in them the invariable calculation of a man aiming at nothing beyond his own private interest. They assumed discretional forms incompatible with the conditions of breadth and generality, which alone give to law its august character. In the decree for recalling the exiles of Fructidor, Bonaparte reserved to himself the power of designating them, which changed the right into a favour, and permitted him to exclude all those who did not offer him a sufficient guarantee for their tractability. In encouraging the return of the emigrants, he took the same precautionary measures with respect to them also. In delivering the priests from prison, he required of them, not like his predecessors, an adherence to certain abstract principles hallowed by an oath to the Civil Constitution of the clergy, but a simple promise of fidelity. It mattered little to him what principles they secretly held, so long as they bowed to him and his authority.

The classes to whom these measures were more particularly directed were those who had suffered the most in the turmoil of the Revolution; and it was on account of their sufferings that Bonaparte believed them to be the most disposed to accept his government. But the blow which he dealt to the republican party, at the same time that he made these advances to the vanquished of the Revolution, proved how little he possessed of that spirit of moderation and impartiality by which he declared himself to be inspired, and how little he cared about being just towards those whom he could not hope to win for his own. Three days after the repeal of the law of hostages, the 25th of Brumaire (November 16th, 1799), there appeared a decree of proscription. What had taken place? Nothing. There had not been the shadow of a movement in Paris. Not even the murmur of opinion was heard. Under pretence of maintaining public tranquillity, which since the *coup-d'état* had not for an instant been disturbed, the Provisional Consuls passed a sentence of transportation to Guiana on thirty-seven persons. Twenty-two others were condemned to imprisonment in the island of Ré. Among these men were some who had been conspicuous in the Revolution for their exaggerated opinions; others were known for their terrible exploits; but the greater number had committed no other crime than that of disclosing their hostility to the projects of Bonaparte in the two days of Brumaire. Against some of them they had not even pretexts to allege, for they were absent, or employed in different services, like Adjutant-General Jorry, or Audoin, the magistrate, whom private hatred hastened to point out for public vengeance. In order to throw discredit and ruin more effectually on the courageous Deputies who in the Council of the Five Hundred had protested against his violation of the law, Bonaparte mixed these unstained names with those which belonged to the lowest demagogues, and which excited both horror and disgust. The names of men covered with just opprobrium, like the American Fournier, Jourdeuil, Maignet, were perfidiously associated with those of Grandmaison, Destrem, Poullain-Grandprey, Delbrel, Talot, honourable citizens, of whose attachment to liberty and integrity of character there was no doubt. But no matter what their previous lives had been, innocent or guilty, if History has not absolved them all, they were all equally absolved by Justice. A long proscription placed them under the safeguard of public good faith. There was nothing to reproach them with, since the establishment of the new Government. What was charged against them was their supposed intentions, and no one here below has a right to punish for an intention.

On this list was a name which eclipsed all the others, and whose reputation for civic and military reputation gave the measure of the scruples of those who tried to blast it; it was that of General Jourdan, the victor of Fleurus, and the companion of Moreau, the illustrious veteran who, from the commencement of the Revolution, had borne the weight of the war on the Meuse and the Rhine. Jourdan's only fault had been that of refusing to receive Bonaparte's overtures on his return from Egypt, and that fault had appeared a sufficient reason for proscribing one of his most glorious companions in arms. But this iniquity raised such a cry of reprobation, even among those who supported the decree, that the next day the name of Jourdan was struck off the list. Bonaparte wrote 'to beg him not to doubt his friendship, and to express his desire to see the conqueror of Fleurus in the path which leads to order, to true liberty, and to happiness;' but this hypocritical protestation did not blot out the premeditated perfidy, which had coupled the name of General Jourdan with that of the American Fournier. The measure itself was received by the public with significant coldness; for they had not yet sufficient energy to censure the Government openly and aloud. Nevertheless, their reprobation, mute as it was, gave weight to the exceptions demanded in favour of individuals. Bonaparte had still sufficient need of his popularity to study the current of public opinion, and treat it with respect. He was struck with the lesson contained in the stupor or timid censure of some, and the disapproving silence of others: he mitigated the sentence to surveillance by the police. He has left, on the subject of the withdrawal of this measure, as on other circumstances of his life, two absolutely contradictory accounts; asserting in one[1] that the commutation was a homage on his part rendered to the

[1] *Mémorial* of Las Cases.

power of public opinion; affirming in the other[1] that the sentence of transportation was only a feint, designed to frighten his enemies, and was never to have been executed. But these two different versions of the same act, which he adopted by turns, according as he most desired to prove his infallibility or his aptitude to turn circumstances to the best account, only show how much less he cared for truth than he cared to strike the imagination of his contemporaries, and dress himself up in the sight of History.

Bonaparte's first thoughts on seizing the reins of power had been for the army, a very natural anxiety in a man who owed everything to his sword, and whose political system was substantially a military government. Besides, the army from having been an instrument had become the principal spring of government, and its importance was sure to grow and increase still further. He had first to make sure of the chiefs. The greater part of those who were in Paris had been his coadjutors on the Eighteenth of Brumaire. Of the three generals who had refused their co-operation, Jourdan had just received a warning which had rendered him powerless; Augereau was trying to get into favour again at the price of complete submission; Bernadotte maintained an attitude of reserve, protected from Bonaparte's anger by his relationship to Joseph. Among those who commanded abroad, Championnet at once sent in his adhesion; Brune, whose first impulse had been to march on Paris with the army of Holland,[2] and throw his sword into the scales, repented almost directly, and hastened to offer his congratulations to 'the illustrious hero.' Masséna's feelings appeared more doubtful. That great captain had just saved France by his admirable campaign of Zurich, when Bonaparte returned from Egypt. In an instant everything was forgotten. It would really seem that the masses attach more importance to superfluous than to necessary services. The heroic labours of Zurich were effaced in a day by the brilliant phantasmagoria of Aboukir; nothing more was heard of Masséna, the saviour was Bonaparte. Moreover,

---

[1] *Mémoires*, dictated to Gourgaud.
[2] *Mémoires* of Miot de Mélito.

Bonaparte did not fail to repeat in his different manifestoes, that his dictatorship was necessary to drive away the enemy who menaced our frontiers, to bring back to our humiliated arms their ancient prestige; and, false as this assertion was, it was so universally accepted that it still remains as one of the blunders of history. It was natural to suppose that Masséna was so much the less insensible to this injustice of public opinion that his feelings towards Bonaparte had always savoured more of deference than of sympathy. In anticipation of ill-will on his part, he was at once withdrawn from the army of Helvetia, which he had just covered with glory in a single campaign, and placed in command of the army of Italy, which was devoted to Bonaparte, and which, reduced to the defensive, and considerably diminished, held their position with difficulty along the coast of Nice and Genoa.

The army of Helvetia united to that of the Rhine, of which it formed the right wing, was placed under the command of Moreau. Already ashamed of the part he had played in Brumaire, and dissatisfied with the issue of the *coup-d'état*, the general joyfully seized the opportunity of raising himself, by appearing afresh on a field more worthy of him. The army of Egypt was left under the command of Kléber. There is here more than one ground of astonishment. Bonaparte was fully aware of Kléber's feelings towards himself, for the General's correspondence with the Directory had just fallen into his hands. He there read, with an irritation which many years later was as lively as on the first day, the bitter and justifiable complaints to which his hasty departure had given rise, the vivid description of the deplorable state in which he had left his companions in arms, in short, evidence of every kind, that confirmed an accusation of which the just severity was far from giving an idea of the exasperation of the army. It was almost immediately after having read this unflinching and overwhelming statement, that the accused, transformed into judge, wrote a proclamation to the army of the East to inform them that in thought he was ever with them. 'Soldiers,' he added, '*repose the same unlimited confidence in*

Kléber that you had in me; he merits it' (December 2d, 1799). A fortnight later he wrote to Kléber himself to encourage him, and to announce to him the approaching commencement of the campaign in Europe. 'Why is it,' he wrote to him, 'that men like yourself cannot be in several places at once?'

At the sight of this spirit of abnegation in so proud and violent a nature, our first impulse is one of admiration. Bonaparte knew, in fact, better than any one, how well founded Kléber's reproaches were; and it might have seemed as if his heart, appeased by the grand results obtained by the Consul at the price of the already forgotten wrongs of the General, did on this occasion rise to the height of antique virtue in sacrificing personal grievances to the justice and esteem which the noble character of Kléber merited. But a more attentive examination shows that in these, as in all other circumstances of his life, he was actuated, not by motives of generosity, but by calculation.

The most important fact contained in Kléber's despatch to the Directory was the obligation which pressed upon him to treat for the evacuation of Egypt. Bonaparte afterwards denied with incredible acrimony the necessity alleged by Kléber. He taxed him with making false statements in support of it, and most historians have admitted his assertions without criticism. If such was his opinion, if he believed in the possibility of keeping this conquest, it rested with him to save it, either by intimating his wish to Kléber or by removing him. Now, how can we explain the fact, that while he possessed supreme power, he not only maintained Kléber at his post, where it would have been so easy to replace him by Desaix; that he lavished praise on that general, he who was so grudging of it; but that, in the different communications which he sent him, he does not say a word to dissuade him from that determination, in his eyes so fatal and inopportune, of evacuating Egypt, when a sign would have sufficed to have prevented it? We look in vain, in lack of an order, for even a hint or a remonstrance calculated to enlighten Kléber on the real intentions of the Consul, or to give him a presentiment of the disapproval which awaited him. Still further; when, after the victory of Damietta, and on the eve of that of Heliopolis, Bonaparte believed this evacuation which he detested had taken place, he had still nothing but compliments for him. He congratulated him on his glorious achievements, he expresses his feelings of joy at his return, and the efforts he had made to maintain the glory of the French name (April 19th, 1800). The explanation of this singular enigma is found in the *Mémorial:* 'If Kléber had evacuated Egypt,' says Napoleon, 'I should not have failed to bring him to trial; all the documents had already been submitted to a Council of State for examination.' This curious avowal proves that, if Kléber did not receive instructions calculated to avert a measure which was thought so disastrous, it was because Bonaparte would not declare it so till after its execution, so as to throw on him the whole responsibility. It proves still further that he only lavished on Kléber these expressions of a pretended friendship to lull him more surely into a deceitful security to the very end.

The army of La Vendée, momentarily inactive in consequence of the suspension of arms agreed upon by both parties during the negotiations between the principal chiefs of the insurrection and the Government, remained provisionally under the orders of General Hédouville, a good officer, but whose moderation was incompatible with the character which Bonaparte was speedily about to impose on this war. Lefebvre continued in command of the army of Paris. This post, which had been entrusted to him by the Directory, and which he continued to occupy under the new government, as if there had been no change either in men or circumstances, was an evident proof of the services he had rendered to the conspiracy, and his adhesion to the acts which followed it.

However, on account of Lefebvre's well-known opinions, and his former connection with the most zealous republicans, Bonaparte considered that he was not sufficiently compromised with those who had made him desert the cause of his old friends. He demanded of him a public declaration of his sentiments in favour of the new *régime*. Lefebvre thought it was enough to insert an article in the papers, containing a very unequivocal profession of faith; but he received a notice more peremptory than the first, informing him that he was required to give proofs more categorical and direct.[1] It was under the influence of this summons that, losing all calmness, and availing himself of the opportunity when the new Consular Constitution was submitted for vote to the people and the army, the General issued the following proclamation, in which a strained violence tries to blind men to its servility:—

'Soldiers,—The glorious days of the Revolution have returned; offices will no longer be filled by brigands. The Constitution puts an end to all our divisions. Only the seditious can reject it: let us swear by our bayonets to exterminate them!'

What a difference between the hard requirements imposed on an old soldier, brave and honourable in spite of his faults, but incapable of defending himself, and whose head had never been very strong, and the infinite consideration which Bonaparte still thought necessary to express for a Moreau or a Kléber! But the spirit of the new *régime* lay here, and not in the phraseological precautions in which he clothed his thoughts when speaking to men to whom he paid the compliment of fearing them. The army was to be everything, but on condition of receiving the yoke itself; and the chiefs were only to be raised above citizens to become the first servants of the most imperious and jealous of masters. Disguised by artful flattery in the eyes of the soldier, on whom, for that matter, it weighed lightly, this dependence was painfully felt by generals accustomed to republican equality. Bonaparte had divined, with the peculiar insight he had into passions that could be of service to him, that to humiliate the chiefs was an infallible means of pleasing those in inferior places; and he affected from that time as much familiarity with the common soldiers as reserve and coldness with the officers. If he had no

[1] Order to General Lefebvre (December 17th, 1799), Correspondence of Napoleon.

difficulty in writing to Grenadier Léon Aune: 'My brave comrade, I love you as my son' (January 15th, 1800), it was because that was an easy way of purchasing popularity at the price of a still easier formula; he knew very well that this language meant nothing, and that the grenadier would never take advantage of such familiarity. He took good care not to speak thus to those who just before had been his equals. On the contrary, he studied to keep them at a distance, and usually made a display before them of this preference for the common soldiers, which gave him popularity in the ranks, in order to make their officers feel that they were now nothing but what they were through him.

This tendency to make everything centre in one all-absorbing personality, half concealed for a time under favourable appearances, was to a certain extent explicable in military institutions, which naturally tolerate an excess of concentration, though in the end they are corrupted by it. But it was the whole State that Bonaparte intended to bring under the narrow and inflexible discipline of the camp. His intentions on this point were only too clearly seen in the debates relative to the Constitution of the Year VIII.

The two commissions appointed on the 19th Brumaire by the Ancients and Five Hundred had received instructions to prepare the changes recognised as necessary in the Constitution of the Year III. These changes, when once settled, were to be ratified by the two councils, which had been adjourned for three months. But they did not for an instant entertain the idea of keeping an engagement which was only one of the numerous lies of that famous day. What they intended to do was to remodel the Constitution in all its parts. This difficult task seemed by general consent to devolve on Sieyès. His name, illustrious from the dawn of the Revolution, and before which Mirabeau himself had bowed with an irony which was still a homage, his participation in the great work of the Constituent, his experience enlightened by the practice of Government, and lastly, his long connection with all the influential men of the day, and his active and powerful co-operation in the *coup-d'état* of Brumaire, gave him a title to the office of legislator which no one could dispute.

Besides, every one knew that Sieyès had long been secretly preparing for it. At the end of the Convention he had disputed with Daunou the honour, which they would willingly have accorded him afterwards, of giving a Constitution to France. But because some of his ideas had been unfavourably received, this dogmatic and absolute spirit shut itself up in complete silence. From that time forward, through all the vicissitudes of his life, he had never ceased to correct and improve his political system, that was designed to put a definitive end to all revolutions; but it was only known by vague rumours, for its author had never written a single article of it, and was moreover of very uncommunicative habit and temper. More than once Sieyès believed that he was on the point of bringing his grand project to light; but at the decisive moment the men he had counted on invariably failed him.

At last the long-looked-for hour had arrived; at least so he might think. The members of the two Commissions all vied with one another in deference to his authority, and Bonaparte, apparently quite absorbed in the affairs of the Government, seldom attended their sittings. Persuaded that this abstention would leave him free to reorganise everything after his own fashion, and to regain in the legislative sphere the influence which he could not dispute with his colleague in that of action, Sieyès first communicated the ideas of his plan to Boulay de la Meurthe, who wrote it down under his dictation, and then produced and explained it before the Commission itself, where his scheme had great success.

This singular system, one of the most complicated and the most chimerical which the mania for constitution-mongering ever devised, would scarcely deserve the attention of the historian if we considered only its value as a political conception. Its mechanism, more whimsical than it is ingenious, is far from meriting the reputation it has acquired. If it had been honoured by being put into practice, a proof which lucubrations of this kind seldom bear, and which alone gives them any value, its defects would very quickly have become visible to every eye. One thing, however, will always preserve its interest in the eyes of those who desire to have a thorough acquaintance with the spirit of this epoch ; that is, the designs and feelings of which it is the expression and the proof. It is one of the most significant of historical documents, for one who knows how to scrutinise it aright. By means of this curious fragment, were it the only testimony left, the historian would be able to find, under the dust of so many ruins, an expressive image of the passions of the time. He can read in it the secret anxieties of the numerous and eminent adherents who approved of Sieyès' plan ; he can, in some sort, recover the object of their fears and of their hopes, as surely as if they had left us the most candid and detailed communications on the subject.

The principal aim of Sieyès and his friends is revealed first of all in the provisions which form the basis of his plan of a Constitution, that is to say, in the system which was to replace the ancient electoral legislation. The whole system was comprised in the formation and working of the *electoral lists*. The five million electors in France were called upon to choose one-tenth of their number, and this tenth, comprising five hundred thousand citizens, formed a first list of notability called *communal*, because the members of the municipal administrations were to be taken from it. These five hundred thousand notables were again to choose one-tenth from among themselves, which list, comprehending fifty thousand citizens, formed a second degree of notability called *departmental*, because all the functionaries of the departments were to be taken from this body. Lastly, the fifty thousand notables of the departments, proceeding to a third selection, composed a last list, reduced to five thousand persons, and called list of the *national* notability, from which were to be chosen all the great functionaries of the State, from the Representative and the Minister to the Judge of the Court of Appeal.

But to whom was to be assigned the formidable right of choosing from these long lists of candidates? Sometimes the legislative power, sometimes the executive, according to the nature of the functions to be provided for. They were thus called upon themselves to recruit their own numbers, instead of inviting the nation to choose them by vote. Add to this, that by virtue of an extremely important and significant arrangement, all the men who from the commencement of the Revolution had formed part of any political or municipal assemblies, or had held any public office, were placed of right on the lists of notability. These lists were not to be meddled with for ten years. Who does not recognise in this phantom of an electoral system, in which after all nothing was left to popular initiative, the same old anxiety, under the influence of which the Conventionals had lengthened out their power beyond the legal term, and which afterwards had annulled the elections for the Departments at the 18th Fructidor and the 22d Floréal? On these three occasions a party attempted, in the name of the Revolution, to annul the national sovereignty, which they knew to be opposed to them; the nation had, however, always finished by getting the upper hand again, owing to the elections, which had gradually changed the majorities. It was these inconvenient elections that Sieyès wished definitively to abolish. Yielding to an exaggerated fear of seeing power fall into the hands of a generation hostile to new ideas, he did not ask whether in preserving it from them he was not sacrificing the principal conquest. In substituting for the suffrage these lists of notability, by means of which the privileged party, inscribed on it of right, could in some sort make its power eternal, he believed he was working for the men who, after all, had made and sustained the Revolution. But what would happen if this privilege, already so dangerous in the hands of a class, should fall into the power of a single man?

This is what Sieyès had not foreseen, and in this he furnished despotism with the most treacherous arm that could ever have been imagined; for by it the nation could be absolutely annihilated, and yet maintain all the appearances of sovereignty. The remainder of Sieyès' system was a curious amalgam of forms, borrowed from different epochs and different nations. Alarmed at the evils which the concentration of power in a single Assembly had entailed, he fell into a contrary error of parcelling out functions, which was not any less fatal. Forgetting that the problem was not to paralyse the action of the legislative power, but to favour the regularity and maturity of their deliberations, he had, so to speak, decomposed all the operations which are necessary before any result can be obtained, and had personified them in so many different Assemblies; the initiative in a Council of State, entrusted with the office of presenting and supporting the proposed laws; criticism in a Tribunate, whose mission it was to oppose in debate the Council of State, condemned to the work of vindication; the decision and vote in a Legislative Body, silent as a tribunal of judges; lastly, the conservative spirit in a Senate, which he called the *grand national jury*, guardian of the Constitution, invested with the right of repealing every law which was hostile to that, and with the care of electing not only their own members but those of all the Legislative Assemblies as well.

The executive power, divided into two principal departments, one for peace and the other for war, was assigned to two Consuls, who each nominated the ministers for the offices corresponding with his department; and these in their turn selected not only all the functionaries of Government, but all the members of the Administrative Assemblies. Above the two Consuls, a Great Elector, faint image of a Constitutional king, was to reign without governing, and without any other attributes than foreign representation, the right of signing treaties and of designating the Consuls. In order to prevent any attempt at usurpation on his part, Sieyès had armed the Senate with power to remove the Great Elector from his functions, like any other officer of the State, by *absorbing* him in its own bosom.

This last prerogative of the Senate, together with the power of repealing every unconstitutional law or measure, and the not less formidable one of electing the Legislative Assemblies as well as its own members, gave it the only real authority which existed in such an organisation. All the other powers were only empty appearances. Their sphere was so limited, their influence so circumscribed and diminished, their action so subdivided and indirect, that they were nothing more than insignificant wheels depending on a main-spring, which, receiving itself no impulse from the nation, could only make use of its power to paralyse all the rest, so that, in order to escape the inconveniences of mobility, Sieyès had stopped the movement. His Senate, master of all, but isolated from all, being itself its own end and its own renewer, with everything to fear and nothing to hope, bore from its birth all the signs of decay. It was an institution condemned to inevitable stagnation.

As for the ensemble of this complicated machinery, it was a mechanism superimposed in some sense upon the nation, capable of working without the aid of the people, having the plain object of exempting it from those daily and persevering labours which in all times and all places have been necessary for the maintenance of liberty. But a nation that considers its liberty to cost too much is always sure to lose it. This inert and passive people, penned off like flocks on the lists of notability, quietly waiting the choice of their masters instead of dictating their own, watching the administration of their own affairs without power to express an opinion, deprived in fact of all the elements of political activity, was a nation of automatons unworthy of the name of citizens.

These shadows of legislators, endowed with an infinitesimal fraction of thought, will, or action, the first proposing laws without discussing them, the second discussing them without passing them, the third passing them without either proposing or discussing, and all, by an excess of precaution, placed under the power of a *veto* intended to prevent an abuse of power of which they scarcely possessed the appearance, were only different expressions of the same nullity. The whole Constitution attested a prodigious effort of the author's mind to attain stability, but such a stability would only have been the peace of tombs. France was treated as a patient, whom sickness has deprived of the use of his limbs, and to whom is dealt out with extreme parsimony a measure of motion, air, sound, and light. Hence this orthopedic Constitution, which was the inspiration of Sieyès' own lassitude, and which might have been the work of a Byzantine legislator.

Supposing, what is far from being true, that such a Constitution was all that the temperament of the French could bear after the agitations of the revolutionary epoch (and the issue of events proved only too clearly that they aimed at something very different from unbroken tranquillity), we are led to ask how, after having seen Bonaparte at work, Sieyès did not feel the necessity of modifying it, for the more active and threatening the ambition of the future head of the Government, the more important it was to set up in opposition to him a nation armed with all its rights and public authorities formally organised. Bonaparte took very little part in the sittings of the first Legislative Commission, which no doubt contributed to keep alive the delusion of his colleagues. At first he only learned Sieyès' ideas through the remarks to which they gave rise; and as they were very favourably received by men, not less tired and weary than himself, who caught a glimpse of a delightful retirement in senatorial omnipotence, the General was not over-pleased at the popularity acquired by a scheme in which he had had no hand, and by whose rapid success he was to some extent compromised.

Sieyès was evidently delighted in his inmost heart to take the General unawares on the Constitutional question, and thus skilfully to entangle him in the network of an organisation of which he did not fully understand all the bearings. The calculated abstention of Bonaparte from the conferences which had preceded the 18th Brumaire, and the kind of indifference he affected with regard to civil institutions, had tended to convince Sieyès that the occupations of a military life had left the young General little leisure to investigate the problems of political legislation. In this Sieyès was greatly deceived, for if his colleague had not busied himself with the great interests of peoples, he had studied them deeply from the point of view of his own ambition, as is testified by the curious letter which he wrote on this subject to Talleyrand at the time of the Treaty of Campo-Formio.[1] His ideas on some points were similar to those of Sieyès: we find for example the conception of a Council of State, placed under the dependence of a government and endowed with all legislative initiative; we find, again, that of a mute Legislative Body, 'without rank in the Republic, impassive, without eyes and without ears for all around it;' but, on the other hand, we look in vain for the Tribunate. One thing only is very clear in this crude sketch: that is, the resolution to make the executive power the only effective representative of the nation, to constitute a government possessor at the same time of the rights of the sovereign and those of the people, by virtue of a fiction similar to that which invested the Cæsars with the tribunitian power. Bonaparte's views coincided with those of Sieyès to a certain extent; he strove to annul the legislative authority which Sieyès contented himself with weakening; but the analogy does not extend further, for, far from dreaming of a government exempt from all control, Sieyès subordinated it completely to the authority of his Senate.

Independently of these preconceived ideas with regard to government, ideas which had since been strengthened by his contact with the people and the institutions of the East, General Bonaparte had a formidable aptitude for discerning and seizing in the views of others whatever could serve his own plans. He had in this respect a power and rapidity of intuition which can only be compared to the sure eye of a bird of prey. He saw at a single glance the advantage he could derive from these lists of notability which annihilated the national will, and from that pulverisation of legislative authority which nullified the control and the power of the representatives. When, then, after some refusals and certain expressions of disapprobation, measured by the resistance he expected to meet with, the General yielded to the entreaties of Rœderer and Boulay de la Meurthe and consented to an interview with Sieyès and the members of the Commission, these first feelings did not

[1] See page 240.

give rise on his part to any important objections. He listened with attention and deference to Sieyès' general explanation of his project, but instead of adopting or rejecting it as a whole, he had the sagacity to propose and carry the idea, that the different points of the plan should be discussed and voted on separately.

He had convoked the two Commissions, merged into one, in his own apartment at the Luxembourg, as if better to take possession of the debate which was about to open. The preparation of the new Constitution was begun at once. Anxious to calm all apprehensions, he hastened to put the work under the protection of the tried honesty of Daunou; 'Citizen Daunou, take the pen,' he said, and the liberal author of the Constitution of the Year III, not daring to refuse an honour which he had not sought, and which he had afterwards cause to regret, immediately set to work. The lists of notability were adopted, but they took care to suppress the imaginary guarantee devised by Sieyès in favour of the men who had made the Revolution, or rather it was stipulated for the benefit of the creatures of the new power. The functionaries designated by the Consuls were the only names which were to be entered as of right on these lists. The mute Legislative Body, adopting or rejecting laws, after listening to the contradictory arguments of the councillors and the tribunes, but without power to modify them; the Council of State and the Tribunate, the one having to plead for, and the other critically to examine, the laws, but both equally deprived of the right of voting on them, except to express their opinion, were successively adopted with some slight modifications. The Senate underwent much more important changes. It was first deprived of its right of *absorption*, which placed all the powers of the State under its dependence. It was agreed, it is true, that it should retain the faculty of repealing unconstitutional acts or laws, but on condition that they should be protested against as such, either by the Government or the Tribunate, a compromise which almost negatived the right, and compelled this body to play a passive and expectant part, not likely to give umbrage to the power it was supposed to check. Lastly, if they assigned to the Senate the nomination of the principal legislative and judiciary authorities, they indirectly withdrew from it that of its own members, which alone would have secured its real independence in the absence of popular elections; it was forced to choose between three candidates, one proposed by the Government, another by the Tribunate, and the third by the Legislative Body. In its first formation it was composed for the greater part by the Government. Now this first choice was everything, for such a governmental embryo was sure to seek to reproduce itself in its elections.

But it was principally against the organisation of the executive power that Bonaparte resolved to concentrate his attack. As soon as Sieyès had explained the crowning of his hierarchy by the Great Elector, the General exclaimed with vehemence: 'Such a Government was a monstrous creation, made up of heterogeneous ideas, without a spark of rationality! This Great Elector was the faint shadow of a *roi fainéant*. No one in this plan had any guarantees, for if the Elector could rule the two Consuls by threatening to deprive them of their functions, he was himself under the stroke of absorption by the Senate. As for the separation of the Ministry into two departments, one for peace and the other for war, it was sheer anarchy, for they had need above everything else of ensemble and unity. Do you know,' he continued, addressing himself to Sieyès, 'a man of mean enough character to lend himself to an apish performance like that? Can you have imagined that a man of any talent or any sense of honour could resign himself to the part of a fattened hog on a certain number of millions?'[1]

The conception of Sieyès perished under the violence of this outburst. Only one of these criticisms was justifiable, that which referred to the Consuls of peace and war, and which separated functions essentially indivisible by a distinction more metaphysical than practical. The Great Elector, irresponsible and without the power of direct action, but not without influence, was replaced by an omni-

[1] *Mémoires* dictated to Gourgaud. *Mémorial* of Las Cases.

potent First Consul, accompanied by two supernumeraries, whose only prerogative was the privilege of being consulted by their colleague, an association devised out of consideration for republican sentiment, and to give the appearance of a division of power which did not exist in reality. As soon as the ground was thus cleared, Bonaparte put his hand on all they had wished to protect. The First Consul had, besides the supreme direction of peace and war, the initiative in making laws, of which only the drawing up was confided to a Council of State, the nomination of all the administrative officers, military, judicial, and diplomatic, which put into his hands not only all the functionaries of the State, but all the local assemblies, and all the tribunals except the Court of Appeal and the magistrates, who were to be chosen by election.

What we are justly astonished at, or rather what is truly inconceivable, is that in creating this overwhelming power, to which the ancient *régime* had nothing comparable, Sieyès and his friends did not for that very reason feel the imperious necessity of changing the other bases of the Constitution. The plan of Sieyès formed in fact a whole, and one part of it could not be changed without altering the nature of all the rest. His lists of notability were nothing more than the fringe of an electoral system, his deliberative assemblies were only the shadow of a legislative power, but both of these two elements had been conceived in connection with an executive power equally feeble and powerless, and the moment that this was fortified in so formidable and unexpected a manner, it became the only reality in the midst of these shadows, and was the master of all. The other two parts of the mechanism needed strengthening to save them from being annihilated, for the equilibrium was destroyed for the benefit of a single power. A direct and solidly established electoral system, a legislative power based upon solid and efficacious guarantees, would at least have done something to hinder such a Government from devouring everything around it. Lafayette relates that Bonaparte, who frequently saw him at this epoch, and was not without some hope of gaining him over to his views, said to him one day, alluding to this subject: 'What was I to do? Sieyès put shadows on every side—shadow of legislative power, shadow of judiciary power, shadow of a Government; it required a substance somewhere, and, in faith, I put it there.'[1] Nothing could better explain the situation; but by the simple fact that the substance was placed somewhere in the midst of shadows, it acquired an irresistible force, and its presence alone sufficed to make them vanish.

It is difficult to suppose that the consequences of such a subversion of his ideas escaped the mind of Sieyès, for the result of the victory which Bonaparte had gained over him was no longer, as had hitherto been seen, the domination of one party over another; it was the complete and irremediable ruin of all that constitutes the essence of representative government; it was the annihilation for the profit of a single man of all the liberal conquests of the Revolution. Beyond this man, his will, his power, there was nothing but words and vain shadows. The only political guarantee that they judged fit to inscribe on the Constitution of the Year VIII was the responsibility of the Ministers. But then they were responsible to Assemblies nominated and paid by themselves, which made this guarantee the most veritable mockery. This was not all; their agents could be accused by a decision of the Council of State, which created in their favour a monstrous inviolability, by constituting the executive power both judge and party in its own cause. Such was the sense of the famous Article 75, which all our successive Governments have hitherto adopted for their own convenience and our shame. The ancient *régime*, so much decried, had not a more iniquitous privilege. The worst aristocracy will always be one of functionaries, because it is a servile aristocracy. Equality before the law, without which democracy is but an empty word, perished that day in France. The only recognised right left to the French was that of petition, the resource and last consolation of epochs of servitude. As for liberty of the press, the words were not even pronounced.

[1] *Mémoires of Lafayette.*

It is probable that an energetic protest at that time from Sieyès and his friends against this audacious transformation of their plan into an instrument of despotism would have succeeded in obtaining at least some more liberal provisions in the Constitution. But the friends of Sieyès, seduced by the prospect of the high favours which were promised them as the price of their connivance, had for the most part passed over to his powerful antagonist, and Sieyès himself, since the check inflicted on his Great Elector, had shut himself up in complete silence. This silence was not, however, as might be supposed, that of wounded pride. By his cowardly self-obliteration during the Reign of Terror, Sieyès had already shown what they might expect from his courage. Bent only on being forgotten under the mask of apathy and insignificance which he had adopted, he had buried himself deep in the ranks of those whom Robespierre blasted by the epithet of 'Serpents of the Marsh,' though all the while speculating on their servility. There, lost in that crowd without a name during two consecutive years, he lavished his votes and his applause on the men whom he held the most in execration. His soul, moulded by long habit to the ignominy of such a part, had for ever lost its energy of character and its dignity. Even all that was noble and elevated in his very ambition had perished there. Caring little in reality for a power, the responsibility of which alarmed him, he coveted its honours less than its enjoyments. From the first day of the Provisional Consulate, Bonaparte, whose piercing eye had almost a magical gift of penetrating to the inmost core of every heart, to discover good or bad passion which he could turn to his own advantage, had perceived at a glance the secret weakness of his colleague, and, following his usual method, he had profited by it to fetter his independence. He has himself related this singular scene. The Director had at the Luxembourg, in a private coffer, certain reserved funds to be employed by way of indemnity to the outgoing directors. 'Look at this fine piece of furniture,' said Sieyès one day to Bonaparte, pointing to the chest which contained this money, amounting to several hundred thousand francs; 'perhaps you do not suspect its value?' He then informed him of the existence of these funds, and their destination, and consulted him as to the purpose to which they should be applied. Bonaparte, struck by the expression of cupidity displayed in his features, replied : 'If I know of its existence, the sum will go into the public treasury, but if I am in ignorance, and as yet I know nothing about it, you can divide it with Ducos.' This is what Sieyès hastened to do, appropriating to himself, however, the lion's share.

The friends of Sieyès have contested the details of this anecdote, but the truth itself has never been contradicted, and it remains an historical fact. We recognise here the man of whom Bourrienne, who knew him well, wrote that 'his look seemed always to say: "Give me money."' It was thus that Sieyès placed himself at the mercy of the General. Bonaparte knew from that time forward that he had nothing to fear from the opposition of a man whom he had enriched with the spoils of his colleagues, and whose shame it only depended on him to publish. A message addressed to the Legislative Commission a few days after the completion of the Constitution (December 20th, 1799) disclosed the manner in which Sieyès' last scruples had been overcome, or at least in what way his complaisance had been rewarded. In this document, which appears the work of mockery itself, Bonaparte, rendering homage to the 'disinterested virtues' of his colleague, at the same time that he was exposing his weakness, proposed to the Commission to bestow upon him, as a testimonial of national gratitude, the gift of the estate of Crône. At the same time they insured for him the Presidency of the Senate, a post of lucrative and idle retirement, entirely conformable to his tastes. Instead of being offended at the insult of such a present, Sieyès gloried in his own abasement. He met the reproaches of his friends with a front of brass, and the sarcasm of public opinion with imperturbable coolness; but he fell at once into that political nullity from which he never afterwards rose. Bowed down under the weight of honours without glory, buried alive in silence and oblivion during the long years of a useless old age, he outlived himself. He watched from the depths of his obscurity reputations, which he had eclipsed, revive and flourish, he saw that second youth which popularity gave to Lafayette, but neither his soul nor his fame revived from this anticipation of the grave.

The Constitution of the Year VIII, the production of a sort of compromise between the subtlety of a metaphysician without conviction and the impatience of an adventurer without scruple, preserved this twofold character. It is full both of artifice and brutality, and appears now the work of cunning bent on shirking difficulties, now the work of force brandishing before all eyes a naked sword. Both these elements contribute to the same end, and give each other mutual support. The world has already witnessed more than one of these compacts between the sophist and the soldier; it was to see many more, for extreme subtlety always bows before brutal force. Subtlety corrupts intellect as well as morality. For the honour of humanity, we must acknowledge that it is only a corrupted intellect which places itself at the service of despotism. So long as it has faith in truth, it has faith in itself, and retains the glorious pride which is its safeguard. When Sieyès yielded to Bonaparte, he was nothing more than an ingenious logician, in whose eyes principles were mere formulas, which he took pleasure in varying by forming fresh combinations with a kind of dilettante curiosity. Such minds never give umbrage to despotism, for it uses or annuls them with equal ease. The Constitution of the Year VIII was presented to the French people in a proclamation which pointed out its merits and incomparable advantages: 'No other was founded on the true principles of representative government, on the sacred rights of property, of liberty, and of equality; it guaranteed the rights of the citizens and the interests of the State.' This manifesto terminated by an assertion which appeared very rash even to those who most desired to see it verified. 'Citizens,' it said, 'the Revolution is confined to the principles which commenced it. It is finished!'

The Revolution is finished! This was Barnave's expression as early as the year 1791; and every subsequent Government had repeated it in the short space of time which elapsed between rise and fall. But what had been with them a sincere and profound conviction, that in going farther the Revolution was rushing towards its ruin and attempting impossibilities, was here only an interested pretence for confiscating all its conquests for the advantage of a single man. If he were content, the nation was to dream of nothing more. But how was it possible to persuade the people that they were in possession of all the principles they had proclaimed in '89?

The more noisily the lie was promulgated, the more eloquent was the silence which accompanied it. It was resolved to submit the new Constitution to universal suffrage. Registers were opened for that purpose in each municipality, and every citizen could go and inscribe his name and his vote with perfect liberty, but at the same time with the full assurance that neither the one nor the other would be forgotten,—a circumstance which alone sufficed to make this pretended appeal to the nation the vainest of formalities. If we add to this cause of intimidation the fear always dominant on such occasions of abandoning the country to all the hazards of long uncertainty, the threatening proclamations of the generals, the absence, in short, of all control in the estimate and verification of the votes, instead of being astonished at the small number of opponents to the Constitution of the Year VIII, we are surprised that there remained any at all.

The national consent, too, was so secondary a consideration in the minds of those who asked for it, that they did not even take the trouble to wait for it. Never were any men treated more cavalierly than those who so short a time before had still been called the sovereign people. As early as the 22d of December, before even the text of the Constitution was known in the distant provinces, Bonaparte, carried away by his natural impatience, requested the Commission to make preparations for putting it immediately into force, seeing, he said, that after the reception it had met with, 'there could be no doubt that the citizens would accept unanimously this new compact of the French;' a prediction made with a certainty that reminds us of what philosophers have said about divine prescience, and which was not very encouraging for the free will of the nation.

The day on which the Constitution was published, Garat, an eloquent talker, who, in spite of his vacillating conduct in politics, had retained a certain amount of credit among republicans, delivered a speech in the body of the Commission in defence of it. His principal aim was to dispel the distrust and apprehensions to which the formidable concentration of power in the hands of Bonaparte had given rise; he recalled the proofs the General had given them in time past of his genius and his virtues, and seeking, without finding, in the Constitution limits which his power would encounter in the future, 'his glory,' he said, 'and that influence which by his name alone he exercises over all imaginations, will not only be a powerful spring the more in the action of Government, but a limit and a barrier to the executive power. And these limits will be so much the more sure, because they are not traced in a charter, but in the heart, and even the passions, of a great man!'

The heart and the passions of a great man,—this was all that remained of the guarantees so ardently demanded and so painfully acquired in 1789! France was soon to learn what such a barrier was worth.

CHAPTER XIV

ORGANISATION OF THE CONSULAR GOVERNMENT—
ITS POLICY, INTERNAL AND EXTERNAL

BONAPARTE had at first only asked for a Dictatorship of three months, time to give France a new Constitution. He had afterwards framed this Constitution, with a view to perpetuate his Dictatorship, by masking it with certain legal appearances. It was now requisite to make it take root in the country by means of the Government and a great army of functionaries, and in the institutions of the country by means of organic laws. It was necessary to choose the *personnel* of the Assemblies and of the great Bodies of the State. It was requisite to obtain peace, or else prepare for war. It was requisite to find resources to meet the most urgent needs. Lastly, it was indispensable to subdue or to pacify La Vendée. Before all else the First Consul had to think of distributing offices to the men whom he had resolved to make his co-operators or his instruments. Sieyès having disdained a post which had no effective function to disguise its nullity, Bonaparte chose for Second Consul, Cambacérès, an eminent lawyer full of resource, who had drawn up projects of Codes for all the Governments which had succeeded one another since the Committee of Public Safety. A clear-sighted counsellor, but of inexhaustible docility; a confidant of discretion, prudence, caution; always ready to bow before established authority, whether it was called Robespierre, Sieyès, or Bonaparte; skilful in dressing the most corrupt acts in the most austere and specious forms; handling the laws with the cool dexterity of a priest who no longer believes in his idol; this man was a precious servant for a despot; and he presented a perfect image of those legists who have been seen at every epoch as the consulting counsel of all forms of tyranny.

The office of Third Consul fell to Lebrun, former secretary of the Chancellor Maupeou, an elegant and ready compiler, doomed in politics as in literature to do nothing but express the thoughts of others, a living personification of the administrative traditions of the old Government, which were about in part to be restored. Below this political trinity, of which the two inferior members had only a nominal influence, was constituted the Ministry, the composition of which dated from the first days of the Provisional Consulate, and was not sensibly modified. By the vainest of fictions, the principle of ministerial responsibility had been inscribed in the Constitution of the Year VIII, as if several can be responsible when one alone has all power and all initiative. Under such a *régime*, the Ministers, whatever may have been their personal worth, could not be, and were not, anything else than simple clerks. Talleyrand received as a reward for his services the direction of foreign affairs; a gift of which it would be difficult to say whether it was reward or punishment; for, although his counsels were then listened to, Talleyrand merited something better than a subordinate post, in which he was so soon to commence that apprenticeship of servility in which his genius became corrupted. Fouché retained in the police the place he had held under the Directory, a dangerous encouragement to treason. The importance of his office was enormously increased in a few weeks, as is always the case under absolute governments. In a free country the police is only an accessory machine. Under a despotic government it is the motive power which works the whole system. Retained in spite of the repugnance inspired by his incomparable superiority in the art of deceiving, thoroughly acquainted with the springs of his profession and the *personnel* of conspiracies, admitted into the intimacy of many men belonging to the old terrorist party, whom he had betrayed and patronised at the same time, Fouché aimed at becoming the indispensable person of the situation; and Bonaparte did in fact submit to him, certain of repenting afterwards that in this he had not followed the maxims of Machiavelli.

Lucien replaced in the Ministry of the Interior the mathematician Laplace, who had first been chosen for the celebrity of his name, but who had brought into office work the scrupulous minuteness of science, ill fitted as it was for such times and such functions. Of all the brothers of the First Consul, Lucien had the most striking individuality. His stormy and tribune-like eloquence and his incessant activity resembled in a faint degree the fever of his brother's temperament; but he was dangerous from his want of conduct, and his intelligence, in other respects quick and keen, was greatly deficient at once in moderation and order. His ambition was greater than his abilities, and clashed with that of a man who could not suffer ambition in those around him. Lucien had, moreover, one thing against him far more difficult to pardon than all his faults; it was the immensity of the services he had rendered at Brumaire. In politics, claims of this kind are certain pledges of ingratitude, on account of the expectations which they create on the one side, and the inability to repay which they establish on the other.

The other members of the Ministry were special men, recommended either by their experience in business matters, by administrative abilities, or their proved integrity; like Gaudin in the department of Finance, Abrial in that of the Law, Forfait in the Admiralty, and Berthier in the War department. It has often been remarked that Bonaparte showed a decided preference for upright administration. The choice is natural in the head of a Government, whose interest it is that affairs shall be well managed, but it strikes us more particularly in despots, from the contrast it generally presents to their own personal conduct. Yet what can be more skilful than the employment of honest agents in a crooked policy? And the senselessness of men in these shameful epochs is such, that this triumph is seldom refused to the most iniquitous usurpers. Men believe in the possibility of serving them in certain kinds of public business, without becoming responsible for the rest of their arts; integrity becomes specialised like any of the intellectual faculties; it no longer continues sufficiently entire to create absolute incompatibility between master and servant, and we see the agent flattering himself that he remains pure, while contributing to an end which is not so.

Maret, a strict and indefatigable worker, filled the office of Secretary of State; and served as an intermediary between the Consuls and the Ministry. The Ministry had moreover no solidarity of thought and action, such as the word implies in free countries; each was answerable for himself, and took no heed of the proceedings collectively. The strict dependence of each on the First Consul made them all prefer to have to do with him alone. The more entirely each was obliged to sacrifice his own opinion to Bonaparte, the less he was disposed to make concessions to any one else. This feeling was so strong, that Talleyrand declared from the earliest days of his ministry that he would only work with him, even to the exclusion of the two other Consuls. The ministers had, then, no other weight than that which they derived from their individual worth. From this point of view the choice of men was skilfully made; for some gave promise of being strict and laborious administrators, the need of whom was greatly felt, while others seemed a pledge given to public opinion, which only asked to be deceived. 'What revolutionist,' said the First Consul to his brother Joseph, 'will not have confidence in an order of things where Fouché is a minister? What man of birth will not hope to find life endurable under the former bishop of Autun? The one guards my left, the other my right. I open up a highway which everybody can use.'[1]

All could use it in fact, on condition that they were content to accept these empty appearances, and give up all they had loved and honoured heretofore. He wanted to establish, under the shadow of his power, a sort of neutral ground where all parties could forget their views and offer each other the hand, and all opinions be abandoned in favour of his own. He flattered himself that he should

[1] *Mémoires du Roi Joseph.*

rally men round him without satisfying them. He supposed that his own greatness was to supply the place of everything else, and that this was sufficient to provide the cost of reconciliation, a dream which the universal lassitude seemed almost to justify, but which higher principle alone, impersonal and disinterested, could realise, because it is not in the nature of man to sacrifice his opinions, nor even his prejudices, to a mere fact. This thought, which had guided the First Consul in his choice of ministers, influenced him also in the composition of the Senate, the Legislative Body, the Council of State, the Tribunate, and afterwards in the whole administration. He delighted in filling the offices with men of various origins, between whom the only tie and common characteristic was the homage they paid to his power. He did not perceive that in surrendering themselves to him, at the price of such apostasy, they could only bring him feigned devotion, and were in reality only giving themselves to his fortune. Woe to him, the day when fortune should fail him. But he flattered himself that he should be able to transform them by his ascendency, as he had transformed the soldiers. He seemed to think that it depended upon himself to blot out the past, henceforward to make everything date from the time of his accession; a salutary anxiety when its only object is the triumph of a disinterested cause, but terribly corrupting the moment it springs from motives of personal selfishness. Bonaparte could do all things but one: he could not rise to the height of a principle.

The nomination of the *personnel* of the great bodies of the State offered immense attraction to all ambitions. Appointments were solicited with that shameless avidity which has always been displayed in crises of this kind, and which so easily deceives new governments, too often inclined to recognise the impetuosity of national feeling in what is only the impetuosity of covetousness. The Senate was only open to men whose fortunes were already made, who had already acquired a position. It became the refuge of the illustrious whom age had excluded from an active career, or the reward of certain services which could not be put to any better use. Among the first were Cabanis, Monge,

Berthollet, Serrurier, Volney, Destutt de Tracy; among the latter, Cornet, Fargues, Cornudet, Vernier, and all those deputies of the Ancients who had obeyed their instructions by calling the soldiers into the Legislative Hall. Old Ducis alone refused an honour which was to be shared with such colleagues; and his refusal was regarded as an act of heroism, a circumstance that paints the time.

The Legislative Body, an assembly of mutes called upon to vote laws in silence which others had discussed, was composed of three hundred members; an anonymous crowd, out of whose bosom it was impossible for any great reputation to emerge. The Tribunes, a sort of legislative eunuchs who had the right of discussing without voting, that is to say, the power of talking without acting, discredited beforehand by this ridiculous mutilation which reduced them to the condition of simple political virtuosi, received into their ranks all the young men among the orators and politicians who were remarkable for talent, eloquence, and generosity of sentiments.

The Tribunate being the only body to which liberty of discussion had been left, the framers of the Constitution of the Year VIII were not content with paralysing it by withdrawing from it all effective influence on affairs. They wished to weaken its moral authority, by condemning it by its very function to an apparently systematic opposition. This was done in order to deprive its most justifiable criticisms of all value in public opinion. The Tribunes having, in fact, no other mission than to oppose in debate the Councillors of State charged with proposing the laws, found themselves placed, by their very constitution, in a situation of inevitable antagonism to the Government, which the public was sure to regard as sheer party spirit. Under such conditions their censure would appear mere matter of business, the foreseen and calculated result of the part assigned to them; their eloquence would gain no hold on the understandings of the people, and all their brilliant fire would dissipate itself in smoke.

Thus to the advantage of maintaining under the eye and the hand of the Government all the active, stirring minds of different political parties, this institution joined that of forcing all opponents to waste their strength in empty words: it did more; its effect was to bring them into discredit, and to render them objects of suspicion in the eyes of the public. It condemned to struggles without end and without issue men who would have shed a lustre over a free Government; such were Daunou, Benjamin Constant, Chénier, J. B. Say; others who would have done good service by the extent of their knowledge and the firmness of their understanding; Ganilh, Sédillez, Ginguené, Thiessé, Andrieux. Care was taken moreover to add to their number a host of men, on whose devotion they could count, such as Chauvelin, Stanislas Girardin, Riouffe.

While the Tribunate was thus discredited by its position, the First Consul lavished favours and advantages on the Council of State, the object of his predilection. He had made of this body not only a sort of legislative manufactory, in which laws were to be elaborated, but a real council of government, participating in the despatch of business, and working with the Ministers. He had divided it into several sections, each section having its own work; war, marine, finance, the interior, justice. He appointed to the Council of State men of the most brilliant character and the most active ambition; he gave them salaries equal to those enjoyed by the Senators, confidential missions, extraordinary gratuities; a distinction, in short, which eclipsed that of all the other Assemblies, in order to draw upon them the universal attention. Thanks to this skilfully conferred prestige, the public would accustom themselves to forget in their obscurity the deputies and the tribune who represented the nation, and to remember only the Councillor of State who represented the Government. By degrees they would come to attribute to this shadow of a deliberative body placed by the side of the Consul all the weight of a real national representation, and thus the appearance of control would be preserved without its inconveniences. The Tribunate, that conception of Sieyès which Bonaparte had accepted with extreme repugnance, might henceforth be suppressed as a useless superfetation.

Here were found united with most of Bonaparte's fellow-conspirators in the *coup-d'état* of Brumaire, Rœderer, Regnauld de Saint Jean d'Angély, Boulay de la Meurthe, Réal, Berlier, Régnier; some of his old companions in arms, who were useful in the military administration, such as Brune and Marmont; a few royalists, who, like Devaisnes, Dufresnes, and Defermon, had rallied round the new Government; and men eminent in some particular branch, such as Ganteaume, Chaptal, and Fourcroy. These men, of unquestionable ability and long experience in affairs, were precious auxiliaries in the vast work of reorganisation which the First Consul had undertaken; and, although they received their general directions from him, they were in reality the true reconstructors. Notwithstanding, however, the vast extent of the work, for which they must bear both the blame and the praise, it was infinitely less difficult than would appear at first sight, owing to the expeditious method which their master had brought into fashion. Despotism is a universal simplifier.

What was absolutely wanting in this assemblage of brilliant and diversified talents was precisely the quality which Bonaparte desired to see attributed to them by public opinion—independence. Every member of the Council of State had either been his accomplice, his creature, or his debtor. All depended on him. All trembled before him. The relative positions spoke louder than the pretended boldness which he liked to ascribe to them, in order to create for them the popularity excited by free assemblies. He could give them every kind of power but that. He expended an infinite amount of art in enforcing the belief that, according to the definition of Rœderer, a Councillor of State was 'a tribune placed close to supreme authority.' It was to this end that he so often appeared among them, provoked their criticism, and challenged contradiction. He had the report circulated that a member had gone so far as to interrupt him in the middle of a discussion, whereupon he exclaimed with charming temper, 'Pray let me go on. I fancy that here at any rate every one has a right to express his opinions.' But all his efforts were useless. The public never believed in the independence of the Council of State. At St. Helena even, many years later, he persisted in trying to gain credence for this legend. He inadvertently mixed with it stories strangely at variance with the idea he wished to have accepted. He related, for instance, that he one day said to a member, who had tried to silence him : ' You went too far the other day ; *you drove me to scratch my forehead:* that implies a great deal with me. Take care in future not to drive me so far.'[1] This '*so far*' shows the limit beyond which they began to be factious. Like Jupiter, he wished to be obeyed when he frowned. Still, he allowed opposition to go as far as that. It is not probable that history will believe, any more than his contemporaries did, in the independence of those who regulated their conduct by such manifestations.

After all, these active and skilful fellow-workers, henceforth slaves of a fortune which had partly been their own creation, were not too many to complete the task of which General Bonaparte had assumed the responsibility when he seized the reins of power. Independently of the great work of administrative and judicial reconstruction which he had to carry out on the ruins of republican institutions, it was urgent for him to solve the threatening political complications which had greatly increased since the fall of the Directory. The war in La Vendée, in spite of the negotiations entered into with some of the chiefs such as MM. d'Andigné and Hyde de Neuville, had spread farther and farther into Brittany ; it had even extended to Normandy. It was important to crush it before recommencing hostilities with foreign powers, whose warlike intentions were not to be doubted, in spite of the check they had sustained the previous year in Holland and Zurich. The First Consul was himself anxious to commence a new campaign, for he knew better than any one that every usurper, to make himself respected, has need of brilliant success either in peace or war ; and he was naturally led to seek it in a career which had already been worth so much glory to him. But as nothing was ready for a decisive blow,

[1] Las Cases' *Mémorial.*

it was necessary to gain time; and by one of those contradictions so frequent in France, war was for the time very unpopular with the nation who had just chosen a soldier for its chief. He resolved, then, to take a formal step in favour of peace, in order to claim the merit of being anxious for its restoration, and to throw the entire odium and responsibility of a renewal of hostilities upon the foreigner.

At the same time, then, that he addressed at once energetic and persuasive proclamations to the inhabitants of the Departments of the West whose fidelity to the royalist cause was already very much shaken, he resolved to put himself in direct and personal communication with the two most important sovereigns of the Coalition, the king of England and the emperor of Austria. He wrote to them both with offers of peace, informing them at the same time of his accession to the Consulate. 'Are there, then, no means of coming to an understanding?' he wrote to the king of England. 'Is the war which for eight years has ravaged the four quarters of the globe to be eternal? How can the two most enlightened nations of Europe, stronger and more powerful than their safety and independence require, sacrifice to ideas of empty greatness *the blessings of commerce, internal prosperity, and domestic happiness?* How can they help feeling that peace is the first of wants, as it is the first of glories?' (December 25, 1799). His letter to the emperor expressed the same ideas in rather different terms, and reminded this sovereign of the relations which had formerly existed between him and General Bonaparte. These two manifestoes, which were addressed much more to the French people than to the two foreign Courts, were not only unusual in diplomatic relations and, as such, more likely to excite ill will than to satisfy those to whom they were sent, but they involved, at least as far as England was concerned, the blunder of implying a change of political arrangements and institutions at the good pleasure of General Bonaparte. In England the supreme and effective direction of foreign as well as home affairs practically belongs not to the monarch, but to the Ministers, who are the sole regulators of the national policy, under the sovereign control of Parliament, and the king could not reply in his own name to the questions which Bonaparte so familiarly put to him, without violating the British Constitution.

However ignorant the First Consul may have been of English institutions, which remained for ever an enigma to him, however unreal may have appeared to him constitutional scruples which he always considered pure comedy, it is difficult to admit that in this instance his mistake was not pointed out to him by his councillor Talleyrand, who had lived in England, and had been engaged in important negotiation with that country. But all that Bonaparte sought was to produce an effect. He did not hope for, nor did he even desire, peace; but he wished to convince the French that he had done everything to obtain it; and he knew that their minds would be more struck by this personal adjuration addressed to sovereigns than by a proposition introduced according to the discreet forms of diplomatic chanceries. His contempt for these forms, of which they could not understand the utility or the grounds, and which appeared to them nothing but the affected refinement of a superannuated etiquette, was meant to flatter them in the person of their representative. He assumed from the first a superiority to all old prejudices and useless conventionalities. He, the chosen of the people, treated with crowned heads on an equal footing. Such was the pride, full of humility, among the republicans formerly so disdainful of kings, and now so elated to see one of themselves force his way into the monarchic circle.

This step, of which the theatrical quality was so well calculated to excite the imagination, and that was his principal aim, seemed moreover likely to cause serious embarrassment in the English Ministry by reason of the arm it was to furnish to the Opposition. The English nation was not, in fact, less tired than France of an interminable and ruinous war; but Pitt, who wanted to continue it, had found an excellent argument in our refusal to treat for peace, a refusal so clearly proved at the time of the Conference of Lille. This argument fell to the ground after the proceedings of the First Consul; and, as Talleyrand had foreseen and announced, the Opposition proceeded to take advantage of it against their powerful antagonist.

Pitt, in refusing peace which was offered him with so much ostentation, had well-grounded political motives, very different from the blind passion which is usually attributed to him. The letters addressed to his colleagues and most intimate friends, which have now been given to the public, no longer permit us to contemn that convenient system which has so long substituted invective for a statement of facts. In the first place, Pitt believed France to be much more exhausted than she really was, an opinion justified to a certain extent by the weakness and disorder which characterised the latter days of the Directorial administration. In spite of the losses experienced the previous year, he thought that by persevering a few months longer the Coalition could obtain or impose peace on infinitely more advantageous terms than they could command at that moment. He believed further that Bonaparte would not succeed in consolidating his power. A military dictatorship did not appear to him likely to last long with so changeable a people, and would in all probability lead to a return to the ancient monarchy. He was, moreover, on the point of reaping the fruit of two events, which had long been expected, and of which negotiation would rob him of all the advantages. One was the evacuation of Egypt, perhaps even the capture of our army, for his expectations went as far as that. The other was the landing, then imminent, though it did not actually take place, of an English army on the shores of Brest, in order to furnish a centre to the royalist insurrection, and hold this port 'in pledge for the king,' that is to say, in the name of Monsieur, whose adhesion he had already obtained.[1] The First Consul's letter reached him just when he was directing all his attention to these various projects, and when he believed that he was on the point of realising them. The zeal and impatience of his desire warped his usually correct judgment, and caused him greatly to exaggerate the difficulties of the Con-

[1] Letter of Pitt to Dundas, December 22, 1799, in Lord Stanhope's *Life of Pitt*.

sular Government. He did not perceive that the First Consul only asked for peace in order to win popularity and to prepare for war; that the most embarrassing office he could render him would be to take him at his word and accept his overtures. What was the use of treating with an authority whose future appeared so little assured? This was the reason he gave for his determination to his friend and colleague Dundas: 'It is, however, very material, in my opinion, to speculate on the probable terms, as I think we have nothing to do but to decline all negotiation at the present moment, on the ground that the actual situation of France does not as yet hold out any solid security to be derived from negotiation; taking care at the same time to express strongly the eagerness with which we should embrace any opening for general peace, whenever such solid security shall appear attainable. This may, I think, be so expressed, as to convey to the people of France that the shortest road to peace is by effecting the restoration of royalty, and thereby to increase the chance of that most desirable of all issues to the war' (December 31st, 1799).

These last words reveal the secret of the great and memorable blunder made in his note, written a few days later, in answer to the First Consul's letter. It is surprising that a chief, so eminent in most respects, of a people in whom the national sentiment was so haughty and so susceptible, did not understand the irreparable error he was committing, what an inestimable service he was about to do to his adversary, and what a fatal blow he was dealing to the cause which it was his aim to defend, in seeming to make the re-establishment of a proscribed dynasty an almost indispensable condition of peace. This despatch was not addressed to the First Consul, but to M. de Talleyrand, and it was signed by Lord Grenville, Secretary of State for Foreign Affairs. The Minister first explained that his Majesty the king of Great Britain saw no reason for deviating from the old form of diplomatic transactions. Then, entering into a discussion of facts, and leaving unnoticed the philanthropic considerations developed in the Consular Manifesto, he endeavoured to prove that England had always desired peace, and desired it still, but that it was not for her to conclude it, so long as the original causes which brought on the war continued to exist. These causes, he said, were to be found solely in that system of encroachment and aggression which had led our armies into Holland, Switzerland, and Egypt, without any provocation on the part of the people of those countries. So long as this system was not relinquished no peace was possible, and vain protestations, such as the Directory had so often written, did not suffice to prove that such a system had been relinquished. The English Government required serious pledges based upon facts. The best security they could offer would be the recall of the ancient dynasty. His Majesty, however, had no intention of prescribing for the French the form of their government; he only asked that their internal situation should offer him sufficient security to treat.

Some of these recriminations were well founded, particularly those which expressed the distrust inspired by the man whose influence had caused a system of conquest to be substituted for the defensive wars of the first years of the French Revolution. Others were in the highest degree unjust and impolitic, both because they tended to interference with our interior affairs, and because they took no account of England's own share, through provocation and intrigue, in this deplorable demoralisation of our wars of liberty, and in the exasperation of the revolutionary spirit. The note of Lord Grenville came at the right moment for favouring Bonaparte's plans, by deeply wounding our national pride. He was not the man not to profit by such a fault, and he determined to turn it to the best possible advantage, by pressing his proposals afresh, in such a way as to make the contrast between his own pacific intentions and the ill-will of his adversaries still more striking.

A second manifesto, signed this time by Talleyrand, replied point by point to the allegations of the English note. He boldly threw on Mr. Pitt's policy, not only the responsibility of the commencement of the war, but the ulterior development which it had assumed. As for the remark relative to the re-establishment of the house of Bourbon, he reminded the house of Hanover of its own origin; that also was an elective Government, chosen in the person of its founder. It had moreover already negotiated with Governments sprung from the Revolution; and therefore had no valid reason for rejecting overtures inspired by a desire to put an end to so many calamities. This justification, addressed more to the world at large than to the British Cabinet, only drew from the English Government a declaration confirming its first objections, and when the diplomatic contest, to which great publicity was purposely given, was brought to a close, the advantages were in favour of him who had opened it. Had it been more skilfully dealt with by the English ministers, it might have become for Bonaparte a subject of grave disappointment.

The English Cabinet, it is true, retaliated in the discussion in Parliament to which the king's speech gave rise, upon the question of peace or war; and it was not an uninstructive spectacle for Europe to see this question voted on in these two free Assemblies, while in the country which still styled itself the French Republic it was summarily settled by the will of a single man. The Opposition, led in the House of Lords by the Duke of Bedford and Lord Grey, in the Commons by Fox, Erskine, Tierney, and Whitbread, skilfully took advantage of the mistake committed by the Ministry in espousing the cause of the Bourbons; but their success was far from answering the expectations of Talleyrand. They were still less successful when they reproached the Cabinet with the distrust of General Bonaparte, to which the despatches testified. Far from trying to rebut this charge, the Ministerial speakers made it one of their chief points to show how justifiable that distrust was, and made the debate turn on this single issue. Lord Grenville, who defended the Ministry in the House of Lords, first recalled the principal acts which had marked the foreign policy of the Directory; their contempt alike for the rights of nations and of individuals; their depredations; their violation of treaties which they had themselves signed; their aggressions upon weak states with whom they were at peace. And, on Lord Grey exclaiming that these were the faults of the Directory, 'What,' said he, 'Bonaparte, then, has nothing to do with the Government which preceded him? But whose are most of the acts. I have enumerated, if not Bonaparte's? Who made a treaty of peace with Sardinia, and then violated it? Bonaparte. Who concluded, and then broke, a treaty with the grand duke of Tuscany? Bonaparte. Who made, and then annulled, an armistice with Modena, and other smaller Italian states? Bonaparte. Who exacted a ransom from the grand duke of Parma, in spite of his neutrality? Bonaparte. If Venice was drawn into the war, who drew her into into it, if it was not Bonaparte? Who, after he had had made peace with Venice, and given her a Constitution, delivered her, bound hand and foot, to Austria? Bonaparte. If Genoa has been subjugated and humiliated, it is still to Bonaparte that the relics and independence of that Republic have been sacrificed. If Switzerland has been drawn on by false offers of peace and alliances to abandon her rights and her liberty, it is still by Bonaparte that she too has been despoiled.'

To this vigorous and cutting invective there was little to reply, for the participation of Bonaparte in all these acts was incontestable, and these acts contained the germ of all the causes of complaint, for which he was one day to be outlawed as 'the enemy of Europe.' Lord Grenville's glowing philippic procured the immense majority in the House of 92 against 6, in spite of the protestations of the Duke of Bedford and Lord Holland, who excited laughter in the House by offering to vouch for Bonaparte's *sincerity*. In the House of Commons, where the Opposition was much more powerful, the victory was more vigorously disputed; but by an almost irresistible current, and in spite of the efforts of Pitt's adversaries, the debate again turned on the same ground, namely, whether the degree of confidence which Bonaparte inspired was sufficient to justify dealings with him. Dundas spoke first in the name of the

Government, and asked how they could trust a man who had not only made sport of the good faith of treaties, but who in Egypt had gone so far as to abjure his God when he had thought it useful to his purposes. He reminded the House, that all those who had treated with him had been deceived by him: Genoa, Venice, the Cisalpine Republic, Tuscany, Turkey; as many treacheries as treaties. In negotiating with the previous Government, they had negotiated to a certain extent with the French nation; now it was with Bonaparte alone, for Bonaparte was everything in France. To accept his overtures was to recognise him, to consolidate his power, to become the instrument of his violence. It was not for an English Ministry to agree to play such a part![1] Whitbread tried in vain to turn the discussion upon another point, by giving Bonaparte himself up to his adversaries, and admitting all that was criminal in his usurpation. He remarked, and not without reason, that to refuse to treat from such a motive was to condemn themselves never to treat with France so long as Bonaparte remained in power,—an extremely rash engagement. He very justly reminded them that if the French Revolution had committed great excesses, it had been provoked to them by the madness, excitement, and crimes of other powers, and English policy was specially bound to take the responsibility of this.

The young Canning, then beginning his career, replied by endeavouring to show the impossibility of maintaining such a power. It was impossible that the French could long prefer the harsh and repulsive forms of military rule to the mild and gentle forms of their ancient monarchy. They could not long accept the tyranny of '*this new usurper, who, like a spectre, wears on his head a something that has a phantom resemblance to a crown.*' His elevation was itself a proof of a tendency towards the re-establishment of the ancient monarchy. Erskine took up with striking eloquence the line developed by Whitbread: 'In God's name,' said he, making use of an expression which Burke had applied to the American Government, 'In God's name, do not let us

[1] Annual Register, ann. 1800.

pay attention to the character and promises of the French Government, but let us see what we can do with it.' What had been gained by eight years of insult and invective? Had they mitigated the evils produced by the French Revolution? No, they had aggravated them. After pointing out the inevitable humiliation to which this blind obstinacy must lead, he clearly showed the service they had rendered to Bonaparte in rousing the indignation of the French people by this ill-judged apology for the cause of the Bourbons; an argument which Tierney supported, exclaiming: 'What would you say if General Bonaparte, when victorious, should declare that he would not treat except with the Stuarts?' These objections, just and politic for the most part, made a great impression on the House, but they were overruled by the fiery appeal which Pitt made to national passions.

Pitt's speech might be described as a programme of that long duel which was about to open between England and Napoleon. Rising by an astonishing power of intuition far above purely political considerations, and divining by the perspicacity of hatred, by means of his past character and conduct, the part that Bonaparte would soon play, he depicted England as the only refuge against the calamities which were about to inundate Europe, and as the rock against which this threatening fortune would one day break. England alone had remained inaccessible to the encroachments of the French Revolution. It was necessary to preserve this privilege, it was necessary to save the instrument which was later to serve for the liberation of the world. It was better to continue the war than to treat with a man of no faith. *Pacem nolo quia infida*, said he, borrowing a sentence from Cicero. He had, it is true, consented to treat with the Republic at the time of the Conference of Lille; but what had caused those negotiations to fail? The success of the Eighteenth Fructidor. And who had been the author of Fructidor? General Bonaparte. It was owing to him that this first essay at despotism had been realised, which had only been outdone by that of Brumaire. Then passing on to the reproaches which had been cast upon him for having encouraged the pretensions of the ancient dynasty, he showed what interest both England and Europe at large had in seeing it re-established, and what security for our international relations would result from it. In the state of misery and exhaustion to which France was reduced, the Government could only continue to exist by a system of theft, confiscation, and conquest. But how different things would be, if the heir of the Bourbons were replaced on the throne. Instead of thinking of troubling his neighbours, he would have occupation enough in trying to heal the wounds and repair the losses caused by ten years of civil convulsions, to raise commerce and industry, and to revive manufactures. Whatever might be the views of the restored monarch, a long time would probably elapse before he would possess sufficient power to make him formidable to Europe.

The general character of the struggles which were about to follow, and of the epoch which succeeded them, was thus portrayed with remarkable accuracy, but also with inevitable mistakes of detail, by the man whose life up to his last hour was consumed in them. He was not deceived in identifying Bonaparte with the encroaching character which the French Revolution had assumed in its foreign policy, during the last years, but he was wrong in forgetting that it had also other passions and principles, and in neglecting to make this distinction, he placed the Revolution to a certain extent under the necessity of making common cause with its chief; in denouncing the solidarity, he contributed to create it; just as, in affirming with so much violence the antagonism of his country to Bonaparte, he fortified this antagonism, and furnished fresh grounds for its existence. Add to this one more error, graver than all the others. He supposed France to be exhausted, incapable of sustaining a long struggle, and ill-disposed towards the new despotism. Now this was an utterly false hypothesis, and by the mere fact that his policy took the character of a warning given to France in the name of a detested rival, he supplied tenfold strength to the enemy whose ruin he considered imminent.

It is not the less true, however, that the principal obstacle to the success of this negotiation lay in the mistrust which the character and past conduct of Bonaparte inspired. If this was not the motive which actuated Pitt, it was unquestionably one which helped him to influence public opinion. All the discussions in Parliament turn on this one point; a circumstance which the *Moniteur* did its best to hide, by a cynical alteration in the ministerial speeches. By way of revenge, there was to be found published in it a pretended letter of the Cardinal of York to George III., reclaiming his kingdom, and ironical congratulations addressed by Louis XVIII. to the same sovereign.[1]

Better counselled by her own experience and more exposed to the blows of her adversary, in spite of her recent success in Italy, Austria replied with more moderation to the overtures of the First Consul, but she did not reject with less obstinacy a pacification offered on the basis of the treaty of Campo-Formio. She occupied at that time not only Lombardy, but Piedmont and the Papal States; she showed no inclination to give up these states to their ancient sovereigns; she had very quickly come to regard them as her property, and could not resign herself to relinquish them without a struggle. Bonaparte insisted on his proposition, and offered great compensation in Italy; the Austrian Cabinet replied that they could not treat without consulting their allies. This revealed the subsidies they were drawing from England.

All hope of peace was therefore equally lost on this side. There remained no other resource than to gain as many allies as possible from among the neutral Powers, or to detach from the Coalition those who appeared to be wavering, whether from dissatisfaction or from lassitude. At one time Bonaparte hoped to attain this twofold object by means of Prussia. In the first days of the Provisional Consulate he had sent to Berlin his aide-de-camp Duroc, the most diplomatic of all his officers. The neutrality of Prussia had been of great service to us at a time when all Europe was armed against us; Bonaparte endeavoured to

[1] *Moniteur* of the 12th and 23d of February 1800.

persuade her to accept an alliance by dazzling her with visions of the Hanseatic Towns, over which it is true we had not even the right of conquest, but this presented no difficulty. Duroc made a good impression at Berlin by his manners, his tact, and the good sense of his conduct. He failed, however, in gaining the young king to the projects of the Consul, and Beurnonville had no better success. Still, flattered by the part of arbitrator and moderator, of which she caught a glimpse in the future, and delighted to see the great Powers ruining themselves in men and money, while she was increasing in strength, Prussia willingly interposed her good offices to win to her own system of neutrality the petty States of Germany, and to induce the Emperor Paul I. to withdraw from the Coalition. It might have been hoped that an easy victory would be gained over this fantastic and changeable mind, whose native generosity had been perverted by the madness of despotism. Discontented with Austria, because he attributed to her the defeat of Suwarow, and because she refused to replace the Italian princes on their thrones, Paul was still more dissatisfied with England for her refusal to restore Malta, which was then on the point of capitulating to the Knights Hospitallers, of whom he had just had himself chosen for Grand Master.

The more inevitable war became, the more urgent it was to put an end to internal difficulties. The necessity of war, imposed upon France in the midst of the very crisis of her transformation, by the accession of the man who was the personification of the spirit of conquest, weighed heavily on the future of our country. Plans of administrative reorganisation were then being elaborated. They were all conceived in view of the desperate situation in which we were placed for the time, or at any rate they borrowed from it a convincing force, of which they had need; for, in spite of the omnipotence of their author, they would never have been accepted but for the fears to which this situation gave rise. Inspired by these apprehensions, and expressly made for a crisis, they never combined the conditions requisite for a regular and peaceful epoch. This extremity was not less disastrous to the populations whom the Vendean insurrection had excited to revolt. As the whole of France was transformed into a vast camp, the people were treated with the pitiless rigour of military usage, and the entire nation soon became nothing more than an army, led by an iron hand.

A momentary truce had been established by common consent in the revolted Departments, during the negotiations between MM. d'Andigné and Hyde de Neuville and the First Consul. But these two chiefs were not long in perceiving how vain were the hopes of restoration which had been founded on him, and it was soon known through them that the choice lay between absolute submission and war *à outrance*. A skilfully worded proclamation was published, notifying to the inhabitants of the Departments of the West the clement disposition of the First Consul. Bonaparte was determined to crush the insurgents by a single blow, but he wished first to put them in the wrong. He repudiated, therefore, as unjust and cruel, the policy which had hitherto been followed with respect to them. He reminded them that he had spontaneously repealed the law of hostages, and that of the forced loan. He promised a full amnesty for repentance, and full liberty to public worship; but he would punish without mercy whoever should dare to resist.

The most significant passage in this manifesto was an appeal made to the clergy, whom Bonaparte had already determined at any price to secure in the interests of his power:—

'The Ministers of a God of Peace will be the first promoters of reconciliation and concord. Let them speak to the hearts of their flocks in the language they have learned in the school of their Master! Let them repair to the temples which are again opened to them, and join their fellow-citizens in offering the sacrifice that shall atone for the crime of the war, and the blood which it has caused to be shed!' (Dec. 28, 1799).

This appeal had already been heard and understood. The Abbé Bernier, curé of Saint-Laud, who had contributed most to give the royalist cause in La Vendée the impulse of religious fanaticism; the same man whom, many years before, Charette had described as a traitor; a cold calculator, entirely weaned from the passions to which he had given such a terrible momentum; beholding in power a man disposed to come to terms with the clergy, and even to give them back a part of their ancient privileges, provided he received a certain reciprocity of services in return, did not hesitate to accept the bargain as far as La Vendée was concerned. He henceforward aspired to become the principal agent in a complete reconciliation between the Church and the State. In this the Abbé Bernier was no more than the true representative of what shortly afterwards became the almost unanimous sentiment of the clergy of France. Hitherto fervently royalist, the clergy now showed signs of defection, with the usual facility of their body, for whom politics is not a question of principle, but an affair of interest, in which only their own advantage is sought. In political matters, the Catholic Church recognises neither rights nor duty, the only doctrine she professes to hold being a vague precept of submission to the established powers, which would equally permit her followers to extend a hand to the Vendéan insurrection or to bow the knee before the 18th Brumaire. The clergy were as prompt to recognise the advantages they could derive from Bonaparte's schemes as he was to covet and seize so precious an instrument. At the same time that the clergy in their addresses were hailing the 18th Brumaire as a day 'for ever memorable in the annals of history, conceived by genius, executed by wisdom and heroism, a prelude to universal justice,'[1] Bonaparte was ordering his agents to distribute and placard everywhere the decree relative to the funeral honours awarded to Pius VI. From these mutual arrangements there was speedily to rise a pact, which was the Concordat.

The influence of Berthier and the exhaustion of La Vendée proper, which for several years had alone supported the whole weight of war, promptly led to the submission of this Department. The two chiefs, MM. d'Autichamp and

[1] Address of the priests of the Departments of Doubs, Haute-Saône, and the Jura.

De Chatillon, signed peace with General Hédouville, the one on the 18th and the other on the 20th of January 1800; and, on the sole condition of laying down their arms, they obtained the favour of having the names of their principal officers struck off the list of emigrants. But in Brittany and Normandy, where the country had suffered less, where the Chouans were in constant communication with English vessels, and received from them assistance of every kind; where, in short, two chiefs, full of energy and intelligence, were in command, Count Louis de Frotté and the indomitable Georges Cadoudal, the offers of the First Consul led to nothing beyond useless conferences. He had already, in anticipation of this resistance, concentrated overwhelming forces round them. Even during the negotiations he had placed at the disposition of Hédouville 60,000 men, drawn for the most part from the victorious army of Holland; and as early as the 5th of January, recognising with his usual penetration that they were trying to drag on the negotiations for the sake of gaining time, he wrote to Hédouville to act immediately, and to act as he would in an enemy's country, that is to say, to be merciless :—

"'The measure of having Military Councils with the columns is useless. The Consuls think that the generals ought to have the chief rebels shot on the spot, when taken with arms in their hands. . . . The Government will support you, but they will judge your military actions from a military point of view; they will be examined by a man who is accustomed to take rigorous and energetic measures, and to triumph on all occasions. However crafty they may be, they are less so than the Arabs of the Desert. *The First Consul thinks it would give a salutary example, if two or three of the larger Communes, chosen from among the most insurrectionary, were burned*' (Jan. 5, 1800).

It was thus that the means he used in subduing the Arabs of the Desert were now to be employed against the French who resisted his authority. And this, from his lips, was no vain menace. The *Moniteur* had anticipated it by announcing 'the abandonment to the army and to the loyal people of the country of all the property of those who had taken up arms, until the country should be entirely subdued and peopled with proprietors interested in the maintenance of the Republic' (*Moniteur* of the 24th of December),—a measure by the side of which the law of hostages, for which the Directory has been so often reproached, might pass for the inspiration of clemency. Decrees relative to outlawry, and the establishment in the Departments of a state of siege, were added to complete this pitiless repression. Similar orders were sent to the generals of every rank who commanded in Brittany and Normandy. Bonaparte stimulated and urged them on with an impatience and irritation which seemed to increase every hour. He was resolved to terrify and annihilate with fright the populations that had dared to disregard and defy his strength. The insurgents with whom he had just treated on equal terms were no longer anything but 'brigands who ought to perish by the sword. Let them find no asylum against the soldier who pursues them, and if any traitor dares to receive and defend them, let him perish with them' (Proclamation of the 11th of January).

General Hédouville, the old friend and companion in arms of Hoche, a wise and moderate man, faithful to the traditions of this great citizen, who had been able on a first occasion to pacify La Vendée while remaining just and magnanimous to the end, did not appear suited to the functions of exterminator, which they wished to impose upon him, and was replaced, as 'not possessing sufficient energy,'[1] by Brune, whose connections with the terrorist party seemed a better guarantee for inflexibility. Operations commenced simultaneously at all points, and were conducted with a harmony which superiority of numbers rendered irresistible. Whatever may have been the zeal and skill of the royalist chiefs, they were not equal to resist the forces united against them. The struggles they maintained with their undisciplined bands against tried soldiers were more like military executions than regular battles. Bourmont, who only just escaped the massacre of his peasants, was the first to submit. A few days later Georges,

[1] Bonaparte to Brune, Letter of 14th Jan. 1800.

surrounded by several columns of Brune at Grandchamp in Brittany, was beaten in two different attacks, and saw himself in his turn reduced to lay down his arms.

Of all the chiefs of the insurrection, the most enterprising, the boldest, and the most brilliant, was Count Louis de Frotté, who held the country in Lower Normandy. Endowed with an indefatigable energy, full of resources, activity, and ambition, he had shown in this struggle that he possessed the qualities of a chief of a party still more than those of a chief of partisans. Far from sharing the mad illusions of many royalists with regard to Bonaparte, he understood that no man was more dangerous to the cause of the Bourbons. He contributed more than any one else to get his overtures rejected, and attacking him in one of his proclamations, he endeavoured to make him an object of ridicule and contempt. He depicted him as growing pale before the deputies whom he wanted to drive out, and falling senseless into the arms of his grenadiers. For all these reasons the First Consul had conceived for Frotté a violent hatred, which it is useless to deny, for it appears in all his letters to his different generals. It is against Frotté that he displays the most animosity, against him that his lieutenants were to combine their most powerful means of destruction. 'Let them give themselves no rest till they have annihilated the hordes of Frotté' (to Lefebvre, January 22). 'Send off an officer who will not return without news of the death or capture of Frotté' (to the same, Feb. 10). He goes still farther with General Gardanne: 'Set your columns to the pursuit of all the brigands. *You may promise a thousand louis to those who will kill or capture Frotté,* and a hundred louis for the other individuals named above. Not one of these men must be alive after the 10th Ventôse at the latest' (Feb. 11). It is clear from these letters that in reminding Hédouville of his manner of treating the Arabs he had used no figure of speech. He put a price on the head of Frotté, just as he had put a price on that of Mourad Bey. And these barbarous proceedings, proscribed long since by civilised nations, appeared to him legitimate and natural the moment they were employed to his own advantage. It did not occur to him that he thus suggested to his adversaries the idea of turning this dangerous arm against himself. Harassed without respite by Generals Guidal and Chambarlhac, abandoned by his exhausted soldiers, and no longer able to count on assistance from the English, who had been forced to abandon their designs on Brest, Frotté asked to treat. On being apprised of his wish, the First Consul wrote to Guidal to require Frotté to surrender at discretion. 'In that case,' he said, '*he might reckon on the generosity of the Government*, who wish to forget the past and rally all Frenchmen round them' (Feb. 14). Encouraged by these assurances Frotté presented himself at the dwelling of the general, with a safe conduct signed by him. He thus voluntarily placed himself in the general's hands, but he was immediately arrested. Fresh instructions came from Paris. He was tried on the 17th of February, and shot the following day with six of his friends, who had been arrested at the same time. The commission charged with this execution had the baseness to impute to him as treachery a letter in which he advised his soldiers to surrender, but to retain their arms. This letter, which was published in the *Moniteur*, was dated Feb. 12, and is consequently anterior to Frotté's submission.

Active proceedings had gone on around the First Consul in favour of Frotté. He pretended to yield to this pressure, and accorded a suspension of the trial, which was tantamount to a pardon. But at the very moment when he appeared to be thus yielding to feelings of humanity, he wrote to Brune: '*By this time Frotté ought to be shot.*' And this same day in fact, that is to say the 18th of February 1800, the execution of that intrepid chief took place. That expression sufficiently refutes those who have attributed to Fouché the instructions which caused the fall of this head. Bonaparte granted a pardon, but in conceding this measure of clemency to the supplications of his friends, he knew that it was already too late. The man who had just refused to Josephine's tears the pardon of a youth of eighteen, the young count of Toustaint, who had been arrested and shot in Paris, was not likely to spare the life of one in whom he recognised an obstacle to his policy.

The provinces of the West were henceforth in a state to furnish fresh fuel to civil war. Bonaparte consolidated his victory by forcibly enrolling in the army all the Chouans capable of serving, and incorporating some hundreds of the most dangerous among them among the troops destined for St. Domingo, whither it was then customary to send men whom the Government wished to get rid of (Letter to Gardanne, Feb. 20).

Struck by the energy and fanaticism which some of the chiefs had displayed in this war, he conceived the idea of making use of such precious auxiliaries for his government, and sent for some of the principal among them to Paris, in the hope of drawing them along with him by the ascendency of his genius and the prestige of his fortune. This was the calculation of a mind ignorant of moral forces, for in seducing these men at the price of such an apostasy, he must inevitably destroy in them the springs of character, and dry up the source of their devotion.

It was thus that he gained Bourmont, a conquest for which he was to pay dearly on the field of Waterloo. But all his attempts proved abortive with Georges, to whom during their long interview he vainly offered the most irresistible temptations. Georges listened to his proposals with imperturbable phlegm, and when he had satisfied himself that there was nothing to hope for his cause, he brought the interview to an end, and lost no time in setting off for England.

As soon as this grave danger was removed, the First Consul was able to turn his attention to preparations for war, and the completion of the work of internal organisation. Of all his troubles, the most serious perhaps was the impoverishment of the Treasury. On the very day after the Eighteenth Brumaire he had appointed to the Ministry of Finances Gaudin, an administrator of no great ability, but of great zeal, experience, and integrity. 'We have need of your services,' he said to him, 'and I reckon on them.

Come, take the oath, the matter is urgent.'[1] Nothing could in fact be more urgent. A sum of 137,000 francs was at that time all that the Treasury possessed in coin.[2] Gaudin had the sagacity to recognise that the most useful innovation he could introduce into an administration discredited by disastrous expedients was to establish order and regularity, and in order to attain this end he did not shrink from reverting to certain methods, which experience had proved to be sound under the old Government, of which he had himself been one of the head clerks. For the cantonal municipalities who were entrusted with the preparation of the assessments necessary for the collection of direct taxes, and who performed this duty, badly suited as it was to their natural functions, extremely ill, he substituted agents, who were charged, under the surveillance of the Government, with the assessment of taxes on persons and properties; and to register changes as they took place. There was a director, an inspector, and a certain number of controllers for each department. It differed little from the ancient administration of the twentieths.

With regard to the collection of the taxes, which had been left to those who would undertake the duty at the lowest rate, and who were always in arrear on account of the facility with which the tax-payers could escape them, Gaudin insured it by means of bills from the Receivers-General. These Receivers were both made responsible for the total amount of taxes by the bills falling due at a fixed date, and were also interested in getting the taxes in, by the delay allowed them for their payments. These bills were guaranteed by bonds of security, by means of which the Sinking Fund was created, which furnished the Treasury with precious and seasonable relief. These various measures contributed powerfully to raise the public credit. Payments in cash began to be substituted for payments in paper, which now only represented extinct values. The *Octrois* were re-established under the name of *Octrois de bienfaisance*. Their former unpopularity was the reason for giving them

[1] *Mémoires de Gaudin*, duke of Gaëta.
[2] Ibid. *Notice historique sur les finances*.

the character of a municipal tax for the use of the Communes, whose revenues were insufficient; but by a clause in the law, the right of fixing the amount of this tax was reserved to the Government alone, and this allowed them to take back with one hand what they appeared to yield with the other. The creation of the Bank of France (Jan. 1800) shortly afterwards gave an impulse to commerce and industry, by facilitating discount and the circulation of cash.

In financial matters, at any rate, the system of unity and centralisation, which had been introduced everywhere, had not the same inconveniences as in the other branches of the administration; it produced favourable results. It would have led to still greater results if, together with this centralisation which had become so necessary, they had allowed legislative control—the only means of preventing abuses—to subsist in its integrity. But this branch of administration, like many others, was destined to become simply an instrument of authority, and therefore lost all its salutary effects. Good finance, used by a Government in the exclusive interest of its own supremacy, is only an additional weapon in the hands of despotism.

Another evil, graver still, corrupted from the onset the financial system of the Consulate and the Empire, and also compromised the entire future of our foreign relations; for it was only compatible with a policy of conquest. I mean the habit already contracted under the Directory, thanks to Bonaparte and to the Italian campaign, of counting on money extorted from weak States to supplement our own resources. It was not in vain that we had so long sought temporary palliatives to our deficits in the spoliation of nations, vanquished enemies, or allies. These criminal expedients of a Government reduced to the last extremity were about to become the regular and normal system. There was no longer the excuse of the old distress, but the Government wished at the expense of foreigners to spare the tax-payers, who had it in their power to give or withdraw their support. It became, therefore, customary to consider as our natural tributaries all nations who were incapable of self-defence. And this system of exaction, which had at first only been a consequence of war, began to be regarded as its principal end. In all times and in all countries people who have interests at stake are naturally partisans of peace, which alone insures them the security of which they have need. Bonaparte henceforth indulged in that chimerical and impracticable dream of keeping them content with war by giving them Europe to devour.

One of Bonaparte's first thoughts, when he tried to raise the exhausted finances, was to reckon the sum which he could under different pretexts extract from nations placed in dependence upon us, in order to relieve by so much the people among whom he needed to strengthen his popularity. Of all these nations, the weakest were the Genoese. He began with them. Still independent in name, they had just elected a Provisional Government. Bonaparte had fully decided to incorporate Genoa with France; but, desirous at the same time not to fetter the negotiations for peace, and to preserve the credit of the new Government which he wished to lay under contribution, he directed Talleyrand 'to inform them of our adhesion,' at the same time that he informed him of his intention of annexing Genoa to France in a few months. This short reprieve was rated at two millions. 'The Genoese nobles have,' he said, 'already given a great deal, but the merchants have not been overburdened. Explain to the Minister of Finance that, if this Convention did not take place, General Masséna would be authorised to levy a contribution on the principal merchants, as he did in Switzerland' (Dec. 18, 1799).

Holland came next. As long as our troops had occupied Holland, under pretext of protecting it, but in reality to fight England from it, for Holland in no way asked to be protected, the Government of this country had provided for their maintenance, notwithstanding the ruinous expense to it of so large an army. The greater part of this army had been withdrawn to go and fight in La Vendée, and only a weak corps of occupation was left behind. Bonaparte determined, however, that the Batavian Republic should continue to find the pay, maintenance, and board of all the troops which had quitted Holland; for this reason, he said, '*That in fighting on the Rhine* (which was untrue, for they were fighting in La Vendée), *they did not cease to be employed for the Batavians.* The question ought not even to be raised' (to Talleyrand, Jan. 13, 1800).

This is not all. At the time of the war between the French Republic and Holland, our armies had taken Flushing; a long alliance had since effaced the remembrance of this exploit, and the peace concluded between the two nations had led the Dutch to believe that they had regained possession of a town shut in on all sides in their territory, and which we could not dream of holding. Bonaparte proposed to sell it back to them for forty millions, as having become our property (to Talleyrand, Jan. 13).

And as he foresaw that the Legislative Assembly would oppose such a bargain, he issued a decree by which he decided, 'That no communication of this arrangement should be made to the Legislative Body, seeing that this transfer was a *consequence of the right of conquest*, and as such came exclusively under military authority' (decree of Jan. 24).

Hoping, in spite of the exhausted state of Holland, to obtain still further supplies, he addressed a letter to the leading men and municipal authorities of the town of Amsterdam, in order to induce them, by flattery or intimidation, to raise a loan of ten or twelve millions (March 8, 1800). He conceived the singular idea of sending this letter by his aide-de-camp Marmont, a brilliant soldier, but naturally absolutely ignorant of this kind of negotiation, and his embarrassment at the part assigned to him did not tend to increase his power of persuasion over the Dutch capitalists. Marmont had, however, the hardly less strange mission of offering them as a pledge of the debt a diamond —the Regent.[1] But this original expedient obtained no other success than that of exciting much laughter.

The free town of Hamburg had been on bad terms with France ever since the Senate of this city had thought it their duty to accede to the simultaneous demands of

Mémoires de Marmont.

England, Austria, and Russia, for the extradition of the Irishmen, Blackwell and Napper Tandy. The Senate of Hamburg excused themselves on the ground of the constraint to which they had been subject, and expressed their regret to the First Consul. But Bonaparte, who had already punished these magistrates by the bitterest reproaches, took care not to lose such an opportunity of making them pay ransom. In making this sort of review of his tributaries, Hamburg occurred to his mind, and he resolved at once to profit by the terror he had spread abroad. Talleyrand received orders to demand from four to six millions from the inhabitants of Hamburg, as the price of a fuller reconciliation with the French Republic. This was the moment when Duroc had just offered Hamburg to the king of Prussia as the price of an alliance with us. The desires of the king in this direction were known at Hamburg. Bonaparte directed Talleyrand to write to the Senate, 'that whatever greed Prussia might evince, and whatever offers that Power might be disposed to make us, the French Government could be reconciled with Hamburg,' thus putting a price on the friendship of France. Even then it was not sure, for while he speculated so freely on these hopes and fears, Beurnonville, the successor of Duroc at Berlin, continued none the less to offer Hamburg to Prussia.

Of all the secondary States placed within our reach, there only remained Switzerland and Portugal to be turned to account. It was useless to think of getting anything from Switzerland, so entirely had she been ruined by the depredations which had served to furnish funds for the expedition to Egypt, and more recently by the ravages of the war of which she became the theatre. As for the Portuguese, who had reluctantly followed the fortunes of England, they asked to make peace with us, and had even sent negotiations for this purpose. Indulgence might have been shown to this little State, situated in the sphere of attraction of a Power to which it was incapable of offering resistance, and unable to do us either good or harm. To grant peace was therefore the best that could be done; and it would have been concluded at once, if only the interests of the two nations had been consulted. But Bonaparte wished Portugal to buy it, and he put off the conclusion indefinitely. 'If it be possible,' he wrote to Talleyrand, 'in the present state of affairs, to obtain eight or ten millions from Portugal, it is of the greatest importance to do so. Such an addition to our means, assigned for instance to the army of Italy, would give us thirty more chances out of a hundred' (Jan. 13, 1800).

Thus all our international interests were sacrificed to the desire of coining money, and, instead of making allies of these small nations, accustomed by a policy of three centuries to look to us as their natural protectors, we forced them to become our secret enemies, by a system of extortion which was to cost us dear in the hour of danger. And these extortions were about to become more fatal to those who were supposed to profit by them than to those even whom they despoiled; for if they crushed the conquered, they depraved the conquerors.

Adopted to-day as an easy expedient, it was about to become by degrees a necessity, by accustoming the people to count on resources superior to their real revenue, and giving them eager aspirations beyond their means. To-day they satisfied this ambitious democracy by giving it, in lieu of the aims it had first pursued, the spoils of weak states. To-morrow it would require the whole of Europe to ravage.

History, moreover, will tell, that in this sad auction French democracy was not only the dupe, it was also the accomplice. It was thus that it was seen to relinquish without a murmur the little which the Eighteenth Brumaire had left of the liberties of the Revolution. A Consular decree, dated January 17, 1800, suppressed by a stroke of the pen all the political journals, with the exception of the thirteen papers known to be devoted to the new order of things. The decree said that the measure was only taken while the war lasted; but it was to remain as long as Bonaparte's power, and the number of tolerated journals was shortly after reduced by fresh suppressions. This act had not even an excuse. Historians have alleged in justification 'the indiscretions committed by the press with regard to military operations.' Not only had these journals never given any cause of complaint in this respect, but even if they had wished, it would have been difficult for them to do so, for several months had still to elapse before the commencement of those operations.

As for the attacks which they had made on foreign Cabinets, they had in publishing them not abused the strictest and most harmless right, and their violence was soon far surpassed by that of the *Moniteur*. Not one of these pretexts will bear examination. The true motive of the measure was, that Bonaparte intended there should be only one voice heard in France—his own. The friends of liberty felt the blow, but the public remained indifferent, and intimidation was already so powerful that not a single voice was raised in protest.

A sad omen for the future, silence deepened in proportion as the Government seemed to become consolidated. The activity of the First Consul, the apparent novelty of his creations, which were most often nothing but copies, more or less disguised, of the ancient *régime*, the repose that he seemed to promise France, the energy of his administration, the prestige and renown of his name, deceived everybody with regard to the real drift of his acts. They were systematically accepted with whatever meaning he chose to give them.

Never was the contrast between actions and words pushed further; never was popular phraseology more audaciously used to destroy everything which this phraseology represented. In the least important measures of Bonaparte we constantly recognise the man, who, at the time of the expulsion of the Deputies of the Five Hundred, had declared 'that he opened the era of representative governments;' the man who afterwards, in order to re-establish the State prisons, based his measure on considerations in favour of individual liberty. It was in the name of liberty and equality that he drove out the representatives of the nation, silenced the press, and transported the Jacobins without trial. The public, who wanted no more than a pretext for making the changes, adopted with avidity declarations that left a shadow of dignity to its submission; men being more willing to be supposed credulous than to own themselves cowards. Thus a tacit compact was established between them. On one side usurpation was to be cloaked under the semblance and formulas of liberty, while on the other men were to be content with a derisive homage, without looking into the substance of things.

This twofold hypocrisy, still more humiliating for the subjects than for the master, was strikingly displayed at the time of the installation of the First Consul in the Tuileries. This change of residence was an excessively perilous feat for Bonaparte. In the eyes of the people, on whom material facts make a much deeper impression than those which appeal to reason, this taking possession of the ancient palace of our kings was much more significant than any of the acts which had established the dictatorship of Bonaparte. And though this determination had been announced long before, though they had tried to lessen its importance by publishing that the Tuileries was to be 'the Palace of the Government,' they were perfectly aware that no one was the dupe of this abstract and impersonal designation; and they were not without uneasiness about the consequences of such a step. The Government was Bonaparte, and it was perhaps imprudent so quickly after the days of the Revolution to lodge a general in the Tuileries, when the representatives of the nation were installed in the midst of the harlots of the Palais Royal.

In order to quiet the apprehensions of those who saw in this measure a beginning of monarchical restoration, the First Consul conceived the idea of placing in the long gallery of the Tuileries a collection of statues, the choice of which, far from indicating his personal predilections, as was said, was evidently calculated to work on public opinion. There were assembled pell-mell great men of all times, who would have been profoundly astonished at thus meeting one another, and at finding themselves the objects of a common adoration. Demosthenes by the side of Alexander; Cicero, Cato, and Brutus by the side of Cæsar; Frederick the Great between Washington and Mirabeau. Farther on, a few republican heroes who had died for the French Revolution—Marceau, Dugommier, Joubert. Some were his sureties with the revolutionists, and triumphantly refuted those who denounced his monarchical designs. Others were intended to keep alive the hopes of such as already hailed him for the new Cæsar. The entire medley was symbolical of that fusion which he was so impatient to realise in opinions and parties. It might almost be said that things lost their natural meaning, and only kept that which he chose to give.

A grand and pompous ceremony to celebrate the presentation to the *Temple of Mars*, that is to say, to the Invalides, of the Turkish standards taken in the battle of Aboukir, was arranged to take place a few days previous to the installation of the First Consul in the Tuileries, in order that his popularity might be testified to afresh by a brilliant ovation which would silence the feeble murmur of those who dared to disapprove of this first step towards the throne.

Unfortunately the exploits of Aboukir were of rather ancient date. They had already been turned to account once on his return from the Egyptian expedition, and there was reason to fear that they would not afford sufficient fuel to the enthusiasm that was to be excited. Just then news of the death of Washington arrived in Europe. Bonaparte saw in this event a sort of unhoped-for theme for the manifestation which would be most useful to his designs. Who but he would ever have conceived the idea of using this grand name for his own glorification? He immediately caught at it with that theatrical art, and that incomparable *à propos*, which are perhaps the most striking traits of his genius. He announced it to France by an order of the day, in imitation of the famous motion by which Mirabeau announced the death of Franklin to the Constitutional Assembly: 'Washington is dead. That great man fought against tyranny. He consolidated the liberty of his country. His name will ever be dear to the French nation, as to all free men of both worlds, and especially to French soldiers, who, like him and the American soldiers, are fighting for liberty and equality. In consequence, the First Consul orders that for ten days black crape shall be suspended from all the standards and colours of the Republic!' He decided that a funeral ceremony in honour of Washington should be celebrated at the same time as the presentation of the standards.

The taking possession of the Tuileries, an act openly monarchical, would thus be lost in the midst of this sort of apotheosis of republican virtues. On the 9th of February, Lannes presented the colours to the Minister of War, seated between two centenarian soldiers, and surrounded by the principal authorities. In the temple, adorned with all the trophies of our wars, was seen the statue of the god Mars in repose, and not far from it the bust of Washington, a monstrous association, as incongruous as that which placed the *éloge* of that great man under the auspices of the Eighteenth Brumaire! After Berthier had replied to Lannes, M. de Fontanes, who that day made his *début* as a courtier, pronounced the funeral oration of the republican hero. An elegant orator, whose language was pure and classical; a writer of perfect correctness, as superior as it is possible to be in that academical style which implies mediocrity of intellect as well as of character, M. de Fontanes proved by this discourse that he could carry out the intentions of his master with a subtle tact which concealed all that was jarring. His panegyric was in reality a continuous parallel drawn between Washington and Bonaparte, and though the second term of this comparison was almost always understood, it was not the less present to every mind, thanks to the choice even of his encomiums and his contrasts.

Thus, in criticising Washington as a general, Fontanes remarked that he had more solidity than brilliance, that judgment rather than enthusiasm had marked his manner of command and of campaign. 'Moreover,' he added, 'no people can henceforth give lessons of heroism to the one which possesses in its bosom every model. The military exploits achieved by the French troops had eclipsed all that had hitherto shed a lustre over the same career. . . . His conceptions,' he repeated, 'were more sagacious than they were daring; he did not *force admiration*, but he always commanded esteem. . . . There are prodigious men who appear at intervals on the stage of the world with a character for supremacy, a kind of supernatural inspiration animates all their thoughts, an irresistible movement is given to all their enterprises. The multitude seeks them in its midst, and no longer finds them : it raises its eyes, and beholds in a sphere radiant with light and glory one who only appeared foolhardy to the ignorant and envious. Washington *had not those lofty and imposing characteristics which strike every intelligence ;* he displayed more order and regularity than strength and elevation in his ideas.'

We see by these passages for whose benefit the parallel was drawn. In the eyes of this orator 'elevation of ideas' was unscrupulous ambition, seeking before all things noisy renown and power. He depicted Washington, however, as 'repressing audacity on all sides, and restoring order in the midst of confusion. It was when he had persuaded his enemies that he had strength to govern them,' that he was able to restore peace and liberty to his country. Here the orator went beyond all bounds, and let his secret anxiety be too clearly seen. It was going a little too far to invoke the example and authority of Washington in support of the *coup-d'état* of Brumaire. He reminded his hearers that, peace once signed, Washington had resigned his power, henceforth only to employ legal arms against faction, which led them to hope that, when once the war was terminated, Bonaparte would one day do the same.

'Yes,' he exclaimed, in conclusion, 'thy counsels will be heard, O Washington, O warrior, O legislator, O citizen without reproach ! He who while yet young surpassed thee on the field of battle shall like thee close with his triumphant hands the wounds of his country.'

It was thus that the praise of true greatness served to exalt false greatness. The ambition which abases, crushes, degrades men, was placed above that which frees and raises them. The genius which destroys was preferred to that which builds up. The shadow of Washington was evoked from the tomb to escort to the dwelling of kings the son of the Revolution who had denied his mother.

A name, but recently still dear to France, naturally presented itself to men's minds on the occasion of an oration on Washington. It was that of Lafayette, his companion in arms and his friend. Fontanes had received orders to pass it over in silence: a trait of littleness which might have served as a commentary on his adulations. Bonaparte was installed in the Tuileries on the same day on which the *Moniteur* published the discourse pronounced in honour of the founder of American democracy. The public, who associated their two names, hailed with applause this monarchical ceremony, by trying to persuade themselves that they were taking part in a republican festival.

CHAPTER XV

SESSION OF THE YEAR VIII—CENTRALISATION

ONE organ of public opinion still remained. This was the Tribune: not the Tribune from which had flashed so many strokes of genius, and whence so many sovereign decrees had been issued, but the Tribune shrunken, abased, enclosed round about with silence and obscurity. In these more than modest conditions, the legislative power could scarcely give umbrage to a government as strong as that of the First Consul. It had not been judged prudent to dispense with the help of this body in the eminently legislative task of reorganising France; but in accepting the assistance of these fellow-workers as a necessary evil, Bonaparte wished to rob them of all their ancient prerogatives, except the right of approving of the plans of the Government. Of the four assemblies between whom Bonaparte had distributed a feeble portion of the functions which formerly belonged to a single body, one only was animated by a sentiment of independence; it was that which the Constitution had treated with the most distrust, because it possessed both the right of discussion and publicity, which seemed to promise it a shadow of influence on the public. This was the Tribune. But this very inoffensive disposition in a body elected and paid by the Government, and deprived of all efficacious means of making its opinion prevail, was tempered by a prudence of which it would perhaps be impossible to find another example in the history of deliberative assemblies. It is only by the most audacious of mystifications that the story of a factious Tribunate has been imposed on the ignorant.

Never was there a more scrupulous or more moderate Opposition than that of this minority of 20 or 25 members, who persisted after the 18th Brumaire in not despairing of French liberty. If a reproach can be cast upon them, it is that on more than one occasion consideration for their opponents amounted to pusillanimity. In the voluminous official reports of the sittings of the Tribunate we find no instance in which violent language was used, except the hasty expression which escaped from Duveyrier on the third sitting, and which he very soon afterwards retracted. We look in vain for a single hostile manifestation; we find, on the contrary, plenty of advances and concessions, which were to remain useless. To refuse something to him who wants everything is as certain to offend as to yield nothing.

However little there was to fear from a Tribunate which held its mandate from the Government instead of from the people, which had neither the power of proposing nor voting laws, and whose office was reduced to a sort of consultation before a mute assembly, it was still the only representative of the liberty of the Tribune in the new institutions. Hence the excessive precautions which Bonaparte took against the possible extension of its influence, and the sort of hatred he conceived for it, even before its voice had been heard. Two measures, taken at the onset, testified to his distrust and aversion. The first was the choice of the building assigned to the assembly for the place of its sittings. The second was a bill conferring on the Government itself the right of fixing the necessary time for the discussion and study of the laws which were presented to it.

The Tribunate had been installed in the Palais Royal, which was at that time the haunt of harlots and gamblers. The choice of such a locality for the only assembly where freedom of speech was permitted appeared unsuitable, and, right or wrong, it was thought to have been made intentionally, in the hope of discrediting the Tribunes. However this may be, not a single complaint was raised on the subject; but, as some citizens had been driven out of their dwellings without compensation at the time of the installation, their case was brought before the assembly. Duveyrier, a tribune well known for his talent as an advocate, and whose ardour in opposition quickly afterwards changed to zeal in a contrary direction, established their claims in a sally which has remained celebrated for its mere boldness. This speech, for which no one besides the author was responsible, is almost the only one which historians have invariably cited in the legislative career of the Tribunate, as if they were determined beforehand to justify the blows which Bonaparte afterwards dealt to this institution. While defending the interests of the proprietors, Duveyrier alluded to the remarks which had been made relative to the choice of the locality assigned to his colleagues. He declared, for his own part, he did not approve of these criticisms: 'I render homage,' he said, 'to the popular intention of those who wished that the tribunes of the people should sit amidst the people, that the defenders of the people should meet on the scene of its first triumph; I thank them for having allowed us the means of viewing from this very tribune the spot on which the generous Camille, giving the signal for a glorious movement, displayed that national cockade which gave birth to so many prodigies, to which so many heroes owe the celebrity of their arms, and which we will never lay down but with our lives. I thank them for having enabled us to see that spot, which, if people dared to talk to us of an idol of fifteen days, would remind us of the demolition of an idol of fifteen centuries.'

This speech, an imprudent but excusable retaliation for the want of respect displayed for the Tribunate, was the inspiration of a purely individual resentment. Not only was it not a general manifestation, but it forms in the collection of the Tribunitian speeches a unique exception; and, a few days after, it was retracted by the author himself, which makes it difficult to keep up the old story of the provocations of the Tribunate. The moment that liberty of speech was granted to this assembly, it could not, without gross unfairness, be held responsible for the opinions of one of its members. In the sitting of the 5th of January, Stanislas Girardin rose to repudiate all association with the sentiments expressed by Duveyrier: 'For his own part he was far from thanking those who had assigned this palace to the Tribunate for its sittings. No place was more unsuitable, alike in a political and in a moral point of view. Happily, no member was foolish enough to believe that vehement harangues would reorganise seditious groups. He hoped he should hear no more such expressions as those which had escaped one of his colleagues, and which were irrelevant, for no idols were known in France.' He then moved that each member should promise individually 'to perform with fidelity the functions which the Constitution had assigned to him.'

Duveyrier thanked Girardin for having given him an opportunity of denying the interpretation which had maliciously been given to his expressions, not reflecting that if his words had not that meaning they meant nothing at all: an ill-considered disavowal of an unseasonable sally, and which certainly did not indicate a very dangerous adversary. He then asked to be the first to make the declaration of fidelity, that was to take the place of the oath, which the First Consul had suppressed as of no use. This suppression was a homage rendered to the philosophical spirit of the age. A simple and purely personal engagement was considered more binding than one in which the Deity was introduced. But it was not long before Bonaparte repented of his determination in this respect, for he was already beginning to think of utilising God.

The discussion was opened on the bill which proposed to assign to the Government the right of fixing the time necessary for the examination of the laws in the Tribunate. The bill provided that the Government should send three copies of the proposed laws, one to the Council of State, another to the Legislative Body, and, lastly, one to the Tribunate. On a day fixed by the Government the Tribunate should be ready to discuss the law, by means of its orators, before the Legislative Body, together with the orators of the Council of State. If the time fixed did not appear sufficient, the Legislative Body could prolong it on the demand of the tribunes. If the tribunes did not present themselves at the debate, their consent was taken for granted.

This was not all: the law was to be sent to them without any statement of reasons, which deprived the Tribunate of all means of criticism; and the Government reserved to itself the right of withdrawing it, and presenting it afresh at will in the course of the session.

This bill was not only stamped with a distrust insulting to an assembly, which was, after all, the only legitimate judge of the time it required to form an opinion; it also put into the hands of the Government an assured means of rendering, whenever it pleased, all discussion impossible. Bonaparte, during the Provisional Consulate, had conducted the legislative commissions in a military manner. As these tactics had succeeded, he now wished to impose on the new assemblies the same rapid and summary mode of procedure. The appeal of the tribunes to the mutes of the Legislative Body was certainly a feeble guarantee, but this appeal was offensive to their dignity, and the guarantee would necessarily become illusory, by reason of the frequent use they would be constrained to make of it.

The unreasonableness of the measure, and the hostile intention which had inspired it, struck all sensible minds. Still, never was a more hostile law resisted with more moderation. The necessity was so generally felt of not furnishing any pretext for anger to the imperious man on whom everything depended, that the commission named by the Tribunate for the examination of the law proposed its adoption, while they acknowledged its defects.[1] Several speakers successively pointed out the danger, without receiving any satisfactory reply. The strongest argument that could be urged in support of the law was, as usual, drawn from the necessity of the situation. 'The Tribunes were to consider,' said Chauvelin, 'the critical circumstances in which they were placed: the state of several

---

[1] *Rapport de Mathieu.* Archives Parlementaires, publiées par Madival et Laurent: séance du 15 nivôse an VIII (Jan. 5, 1800).

Departments of the Republic, which called for urgent measures; calumny, which was watching them; the divisions, which such calumny took delight in supposing already to exist among them; lastly, the pressing need of union between the powers.' In order to insure this union of the powers, they had become willing to sacrifice everything to a single one of them.

There was at that time among the Tribunes a man who united generosity of sentiments to the most brilliant gifts of intelligence, and whose graceful and happy genius deserved a less tarnished epoch. The descendant of a French family exiled at the time of our religious wars, Benjamin Constant de Rebecque, had returned to France along with liberty. He adored liberty with a passion which was a truly hereditary gift. Placed, on his entrance into public life, in the first rank among politicians by writings which his intelligent and courageous hatred of terrorist despotism had inspired, he now came to dispute with military despotism the last remnants of our free institutions. He rose to speak to oppose the bill.

Benjamin Constant had understood better than any one all the disadvantages resulting from the organisation of the Tribunate, which seemed to condemn this assembly to a systematic opposition. He first tried to put his colleagues on their guard against a danger which would deprive their criticisms of all value. The Tribunate was not a body in permanent opposition, whose special vocation was to resist every bill presented to it. Neither was it an assembly of orators, who only aimed at success in debate. It was the organ of national discussion, and interested, like all the bodies of the State, in seeing that useful proposals should be adopted without delay. 'If this truth had been recognised,' he continued, 'if the constitutional mission of the Tribunate had not been misunderstood, the bill which is now before you would probably have undergone many changes. But the idea of a perpetual opposition, whatever the measure may be,—the idea that the vocation of the Tribunate can only be to delay the passing of a law,—has stamped all the clauses of this bill with a restless and uncontrollable eagerness to evade, by rapidity and haste, assumed opposition; to present propositions on the wing, as it were, in the hope that we may not be able to lay hold of them; and to hurry them away from our examination like an enemy's army, and transform them into laws before we can overtake them.'

In order to judge the bill, it was necessary, according to him, to examine the abuses to which it was exposed; and to those who objected that this was an expression of distrust, he replied that the Constitution itself was also an act of distrust. Now, the possible abuse on the part of the Government was such, with this law, that it could henceforth suppress all discussion, by shortening the delay. Its unfitness to fix the length of these delays was proved by the insufficiency even of the time assigned for the discussion of the law which was then under deliberation. The Government had given three days to the Tribunate to form its opinion, and these three days had been found quite inadequate, although the measure under discussion was extremely simple. What would it be, when it came to laws of a hundred clauses, affecting the life, property, honour, and liberty of citizens? They pleaded the necessity of laws of urgency; but it was these laws of urgency which had caused all the misfortunes and all the crimes of the Revolution; it was time to return to the slow methods of calm epochs. If danger became imminent, they might rely on the patriotism of the Tribunate.

All the provisions of the bill fell successively under the irony of an attack full of force and reason. 'Doubtless,' he said in conclusion, 'harmony is desirable between the authorities of the Republic; but the independence of the Tribunate is no less necessary to this harmony than the constitutional authority of the Government. *Without the independence of the Tribunate there would be neither harmony nor constitution; there would only be servitude and silence, silence which all Europe would hear!*'

This prophetic warning fell unheeded. In spite of the efforts of Benjamin Constant and his friends, the bill was adopted, even in the Tribunate, by a majority of 54 to 26;

an approval which the Legislative Body hastened to confirm by its vote. The criticisms of the Opposition were not, however, lost. The law had been so eloquently denunciated, and its possible abuse so vividly described, that the Government only ventured to apply it with caution, and on one point even amended it. A statement of grounds was to be presented to the Tribunate along with each proposed law.

The speech of Benjamin Constant produced a deep sensation, but the public, already weaned from the great interests of political life, was much more struck by the Voltairian gracefulness of that sparkling intelligence than by the irrefutable solidity of his arguments. In the Tribunate, Riouffe took the opportunity to signalise himself by a panegyric on the First Consul of incredible extravagance; he claimed the right 'to praise him whom the whole world praised; having hitherto eulogised proscribed virtue alone, he wished to show a new kind of courage, that of celebrating genius in the bosom of power and of victory;' and he carried, in fact, this kind of courage, which had never been perilous, so far,—he mixed with his homage of the new master so much violence and so many denunciations against his adversaries,—that the Assembly interrupted him several times, and called him to order. The zeal of Riouffe was soon after rewarded by appointment to a Prefecture.

The First Consul had been displeased at the feeble opposition which his bill had met in the Tribunate. This irritation was, however, afterwards calmed, and the article which the *Moniteur* published on this discussion only expressed a mildly acerb tone of vexation. 'After all,' it said, 'the result was rather satisfactory than otherwise; there was nothing alarming in the opposition of 26 persons out of 80. The scruples of timid minds had more to do with this vote than ill-will. In fact, everything authorised the conviction that there did not exist in the Tribunate any combined and systematic opposition,—in short, any real opposition. But everybody thirsted for glory, everybody wished to consign his name to the hundred tongues of Fame, and some men had yet to learn that they arrive with less certainty at consideration by the ambition of making fine speeches, than by perseverance in serving usefully, or even obscurely, that public which applauds and judges.'[1]

The day previous to that on which he was to deliver his speech, Benjamin Constant said to his friend Madame de Staël, whose salon was the rendezvous of all the talent, beauty, and celebrities of the day, 'Your salon is filled with persons who please you. If I speak to-morrow it will be empty; think of that.' 'Follow your conviction,' she nobly replied. The next day his prediction was fulfilled to the letter.

Madame de Staël herself relates that all her invitations were refused.[2] The First Consul publicly reproached his brother Joseph for frequenting her house. But he did not content himself with this display of ill-temper. The conqueror of Italy was not ashamed to attack a woman, for the very moderate speech of the man whom he did not yet dare to proscribe. He was, moreover, more sure of stopping a man of delicacy of feeling by first striking him through the object of his affections. Fouché sent for Madame de Staël, and told her that the First Consul suspected her of having excited Benjamin Constant. She replied that her friend was a man of too lofty a mind for his opinions to be attributed to a woman; that his speech, moreover, did not contain a word which ought to offend the First Consul. Fouché admitted this, but still ended *by advising* Madame de Staël *to go into the country*, a hypocritical euphemism, under which this officer of police was henceforth to disguise his orders for exile. Such was the commencement of those vile persecutions against women which fell successively on Mmes. de Staël, Récamier, d'Avaux, de Chevreuse, de Balbi, de Champcenetz, de Damas, and so many other persons remarkable for their intelligence, their beauty, or their virtues. The world has witnessed many despotisms, but it has not often seen one so suspicious as to fear even the power which a woman can exercise. Bonaparte was no

---

[1] *Moniteur* of Jan. 9.
[2] *Ten Years of Exile.* By Madame de Staël.

longer content with destroying liberty in institutions. He pursued it even into the bosom of private life, and the inoffensive criticism of drawing-room conversation became as insufferable to him as the contradiction of a great and free Assembly.

The Tribunate and the Legislative Body were about to examine the whole of the organic laws elaborated by the Council of State, that is to say, the plan of a complete reconstruction of the organisation, administrative and judicial. The first bill presented to them related to the organisation of the Court of Appeal. This bill only contained two important innovations on the organisation created by the Constituent Assembly. The first allowed an appeal to the supreme court against decisions given in the first instance by the *Juges de Paix;* the second assigned to the Court of Appeal the prosecution of the magistrates of all the tribunals for offences committed by them in the exercise of their functions.

The evident intention of this last clause was to withdraw the magistrates from subjection to the common law, and render their dependence more strict. The Constitution required, in all judicial proceedings implying afflictive or infamous punishment, the intervention of a jury of accusation and of a jury of judgment. Here the Court of Appeal was transformed into a jury of accusation, which was dealing a blow both at equality before the law and at the character of this supreme magistracy, created exclusively to watch over the maintenance of legal forms. In this respect more than in any other the jury was a guarantee; for judges being made for the citizens, and not for the Government, it was well to maintain them under the jurisdiction and surveillance of those who were most interested in their right administration. Judgment, it is true, was left to ordinary tribunals; but to assign prosecution to a special tribunal was to give it the power of paralysing at will the action of justice, under the influence either of anxiety for an *esprit de corps* or for the interests of the Government, which are never made secondary to those of citizens. This was centralisation applied to justice; and it was, moreover a first step in the mischievous direction of *tribunaux d'exception*.

Thiessé, one of those obscure Tribunes who then struggled against the encroachments of despotism without any other satisfaction than that of discharging a duty, demonstrated in a strikingly clear and logical speech the numerous defects of the bill. It nevertheless passed in the Tribunate by a majority of two; but the Legislative Body, forced to make a choice between a vote of adoption or one of rejection, having no right to propose an amendment by which they could have corrected the defects of the measure, shrank from the danger of making it law, and threw it out. This was the only one rejected in the course of the session, except two measures, one relative to the right of taking tolls on bridges, and another re-establishing for the benefit of the State certain ground-rents which had been suppressed as feudal. These checks do not indicate a very strong spirit of systematic opposition, especially when we consider the immense number of laws which were submitted to these two assemblies. This vote, moreover, did not hinder the Government from presenting the bill again shortly afterwards, slightly modified in some secondary points, by embodying it in the general plan of judicial organisation.

In the sitting of the 7th of February, Rœderer read to the Legislative Assembly an explanation of the grand plan which was the keystone, as it were, to the Consular establishment. It was a description and justification of the vast administrative mechanism which was about to place France under the hand of Bonaparte, by giving him power to move a nation of thirty millions like a single regiment. This mechanism was centralisation. The name was new; the thing as old as despotism. Whenever the forces and powers of a state are centred in a single hand, there is centralisation in a form more or less elementary; it exists in entire plenitude, when despotism is regularised and provided with all its organs. The great Asiatic monarchies, Rome in its decline, and, in later times, Louis XIV., had all known and practised it. Napoleon restored it, and brought it to perfection. After him the instrument was found so convenient, that it long survived the Government of which it was the mainspring. The exposition of Rœderer was written in that abrupt and peremptory style which the Councillors of State had borrowed from their master. Humble as clerks in their intercourse with Bonaparte, they assumed the most unceremonious manner when dealing with the Legislative Assembly, and would have willingly presented themselves before it whip in hand. Rœderer proceeded by absolute aphorisms, as became the representative of an authority which suffered no contradiction; but his declaration of principles was perfectly arbitrary. It does not bear examination. It is based upon this fundamental axiom, that if 'to judge is the work of many, to administer ought to be the work of a single man.' This definition is merely a confusion of words, for all administration implies two distinct operations, namely, discussion, which ought to be the work of many, and action, which gains by being the work of one.

The new administrative organisation was a simplification analogous to that which had just been accomplished in the Government itself. The deliberative bodies were systematically nullified for the benefit of executive authority. The prefects were, to use Bonaparte's own expression, so many First Consuls, that is to say, dictators on a small scale. Like the head of the executive power, they had at their side assemblies which were supposed to take part in their administration, but whose power was still more illusory than that of the Legislative Assembly, for they had only a consultative vote. It was the same with the sub-prefects and mayors, who represented the Government on the lower step of this administrative ladder. The whole system was a sort of hierarchy of dictatorships, placed one above another, and terminating in one,—that of the First Consul.

This conception had not, for that matter, even the merit of originality. It was only borrowed from the old absolutist arsenal. It was as nearly as possible the system of *intendances* of Richelieu, brought to perfection by Louis XIV.— an institution which the old *régime* had finally abandoned as oppressive and sterile. We may add, too, in support of the *régime* of *intendances*, that its abuses were partly redeemed by the protection which it offered against the usurpations of an insolent and tyrannical nobility; that the intendants had no influence in issues between the authorities and private individuals,—a jurisdiction at that time assigned to parliaments; in short, that the most prosperous part of France, the *pays d'état*, the object of envy of all the other provinces, escaped this Government, and administered their own affairs.

This *régime* had sunk under its own abuses. The provincial assemblies had triumphed with Turgot. The Constituent had again extended their functions; but it had extended them too far—a proceeding which, while it revived local life in France after it had been stifled by two centuries of centralisation, did so at the expense of the prompt despatch of the general business of the State, which was, to a certain extent, mixed up with that of the departments. The Convention governed by the iron hand of its Commissioners, but it everywhere allowed local assemblies to subsist, which rendered it great service by stimulating national patriotism against united Europe; and as soon as calmer times returned, its first care was to engraft these same principles in the Constitution of the Year III, under somewhat different forms. These facts alone suffice to clear the Revolution from the reproach of having created and adored centralisation. This restoration of a thing as old as absolutism belongs to an epoch of lassitude and discouragement which has nothing in common with those years of enthusiasm, often unruly, but full of life, of confidence in the future, and of faith in freedom.

The principal error of the administrative organisation created by the Constitution of the Year III had been to suppress the 40,000 commercial municipalities of the Constituent, and to replace them by cantonal administrations, about 5000 in number. The Canton, though an excellent circumscription, since it is founded on the nature of things, charged with the management of the municipal business of, on an average, eight or ten communes, besides its own, answered very imperfectly. This was the principal cause of the embarrassment and disorder of the Government of the Directory. Moreover, the agents of the central power had no real authority, and could do no more than urge the local authorities to press the despatch of business. Besides, as it has been truly remarked,[1] the vices produced by the troubles of the Revolution have often been imputed to the fact of the Revolution. How could the spirit of faction fail to creep in, when it had taken possession of Government itself?

Instead of keeping the Canton, and ridding it of the administration of the communes, they re-established the municipalities. These were only revived, however, to bring them into bondage, for not only the nomination of the mayors, but even that of the municipal councils, was assigned to the central power.

In addition to this, they devised the Arrondissement, a perfectly arbitrary circumscription, taking no account of manners, customs, or local requirements, sometimes even uniting populations separated by chains of mountains[2]—an excellent means of isolating them, crushing them, destroying all public life, all collective action, in order to prevent any concert or any resistance. The prefects or sub-prefects could work these disorganised masses at will, owing to the dissolution of all natural groups. The judgment of suits between officials and private persons had until then been assigned to local assemblies; the charge was now given to special councils, which are still called *Conseils de Préfecture*, an excellent institution, if they had not been placed in dependence upon the prefects. All these petty assemblies, placed by the side of the prefects, sub-prefects, and mayors, were to assemble once a year, but the duration of their session *might not exceed a fortnight*. Nothing could more clearly show that they were only convoked as a matter of form. Their mission was accomplished as soon as they had voted the necessary supplies, and replied to the questions that the Government paid them the compliment of addressing to them.

[1] Thibeaudeau, *Histoire du Consulat*.
[2] *Archives Parlementaires*, discours de Duchesnes.

The same historians who have taxed the Tribunate with systematic hostility have blamed it in a very different way with respect to this disastrous law : they complain that its objections were frivolous. In reading the numerous speeches which were made on this subject, it is true that we are surprised to see that the objections raised by the speakers, though often very just, deal more with the details of the measure than with the general spirit of the law. But there is a very simple explanation of the fact. This general spirit had been prejudged by the Constitution itself, which had laid it down as a principle, first, that the First Consul should nominate and dismiss at will the members of the local administrations (Art. 41); and, secondly, that there should be arrondissements (Art. 1). Now the germ of the whole law was contained in these two articles, and the Tribunes were forced to confine themselves to a discussion of details, on pain of seeing themselves at once inculpated in an attack on the Constitution.

Notwithstanding the constraint imposed on them by the difficulty of the situation, the speakers pointed out with a great deal of sense the imperfections which it was easy to discover in the law, even while admitting the point from which it started. Daunou, who concluded for its adoption on the ground of the urgency of the case, strongly objected to the preponderance given to the prefects in the councils of the prefecture, reminding his hearers, that if to judge ought, as Rœderer said, to be the work of many, 'to judge between the administration and the subjects of their administration ought to be the work of many, *among whom none is an administrator.*'

Duchesnes pointed out the inconvenience of the division by arrondissements. Chauvelin, though in favour of the measure, and always ready to support the Government, expressed a wish that the election of the mayors and municipal councils should be given back to the people so soon as the times were calmer. Lastly, Ganilh combated with great force a consequence of the new law, hitherto unnoticed, which would give to the prefects the right of drawing up the lists of jurymen, formerly left to local assemblies. If this first act succeeded, if the Government were to compose the jury of men chosen by its agents, the principal guarantee of citizens was gone, there was no longer a jury.

In spite of these observations, the law obtained a considerable majority in the Tribunate as well as in the Legislative Body, and for many long years the oppressive network of centralisation was thrown over France. But the work would not have been complete if the administration of justice had been left out. The Government laid hold on that, as it had on the rest of administration. Centralisation appeared so convenient, that they were bent on applying it to every department; to religion, by means of the Concordat; to public instruction, by means of the University; to the press, by means of the censorship; to industry itself, by means of close protection and the strict regulation of patents. This system required no effort of genius; Bonaparte had only to choose among the numerous models offered to him by the past. The art of confiscating all activity for the benefit of the State had been only too well known and practised in France under the old *régime*. He returned to this routine, and worked it with superior intelligence, but it is an insult to common sense to call that a creation. A system, whose effect is to destroy all individual energy in a people, is not a creation, but a destruction. He who thinks only of himself creates nothing in politics, because the interests of a single man, however high he may be placed, are never identical with those of the public. Knowledge of the needs of the time is only to be acquired by self-forgetfulness, by rising above selfish calculations; a man needs, if not complete disinterestedness, at any rate a certain participation in the general ideas and passions of his contemporaries, things of which Bonaparte was absolutely ignorant. The plan of judicial organisation had been submitted to the Tribunate; eight days were allowed for the examination and discussion of the measure, a time barely sufficient to form the most summary idea of it, especially when we consider the quantity of work this Assembly had to get through at the same time.

The anxiety and efforts of the Constituent Assembly in its judicial reform had been principally directed to one single point,—to insure the independence of the judges. What was known best in fact on leaving the old *régime* behind, was this: that it is not in general from want of intelligence that magistrates give wrong judgments, but from want of independence. This guarantee the Constituent Assembly had sought for, perhaps a little too exclusively, in the elective principle, which the revolutionary legislators, following its example, applied to judicial offices. Experience had shown that here, as in everything else, there was some room for further improvement. It was possible, under certain conditions, to deprive these elections of the influence of popular passions, but the principle did not the less remain one of the most effectual guarantees. It had also been found that the jurisdiction of the *juges de paix* had been extended too far, and that a single tribunal for each department was not sufficient. With regard to the appeal which was made from one tribunal to a neighbouring tribunal, the uselessness of such an appeal has been greatly exaggerated, for the end of appeal is to afford the party the guarantee of double proof of his case, and double authority in the decision, rather than a recourse to superior knowledge; for each tribunal ought to possess legal knowledge in its plenitude.

The framers of this Constitution had announced beforehand this intention of destroying the guarantee of independence resulting from the elective principle, by deciding that all the judges should be named by the First Consul, but they could not dispense with the necessity of providing another guarantee, that of being irremovable. But irremovability was only an unmeaning word with the perspective of favours and disgrace which the Government placed before the eyes of the magistrates by means of promotion. To give the First Consul, in addition to the faculty of choosing judges, the still more formidable one of exciting their ambition, of recompensing their docility or punishing their resistance by envied dignities or crushing discredit, was to put their future in his hands, and to make the magistrate a kind of ministerial officer, and justice an instrument. By the side of this superior interest, unique, without price, beyond all comparison—the independence of the judge—every other advantage was secondary, or rather, every other advantage disappeared. Of what avail were improvements in detail, in the absence of this supreme and vital guarantee? The new organisation brought several unquestionable ameliorations of the old. By the creation of the civil tribunals of the arrondissements, which were united to the already existing correctional tribunals, it had placed justice nearer the reach of the litigants, it had limited the jurisdiction of justices of the peace which had extended too far, it had regulated the jurisdiction of appeal by confiding it to the twenty-nine special tribunals placed in the towns where the parliaments used to sit; lastly, it had preserved the criminal tribunals in the chief town of each department. None could fail to approve of all this; but the same law arranged the judicial appointments in a progressive hierarchy, skilfully graduated to tempt the ambitious. It left all these dignities, these lay benefices, at the arbitrary disposition of the Government. It assigned to Government the nomination of all the judges, of the presidents of the civil and criminal tribunals, of the magistrates, of all the ministerial officers, even that of the jury, which had just been given to the prefects. By the re-establishment of charges and securities it gave a finishing stroke, thus putting into the hand of Government all who were connected closely or distantly with the administration of justice. By that alone it destroyed the independence of the magistrate, and the merit of some of its innovations was nothing in comparison with a public curse like this.

The principal defect of this law had been sheltered from the criticisms of the Tribunate by a precaution similar to that which had shielded against attacks the law in the administrative organisation, namely, by a provision of the Constitution which decided that all the judges should be named by the First Consul. This reservation in fact entirely prevented any member from attacking the general spirit of the law in which all the danger lay. The obstacle appeared insurmountable to the speakers who were the most opposed to the measure. Sédillez and Thiessé, who were the first to speak on the bill, confined themselves to pointing out its defects of detail. Happily for the honour of the French Tribune an article of the bill furnished one of them with indirect means of entering into the general discussion which had appeared to be prohibited, and this enthralment of our judicial institution was not accomplished without a protest worthy of the great cause at stake in this debate.

The Constitution had assigned to the Government the nomination of the judges, but had said nothing of that of the presidents and vice-presidents of the civil and criminal tribunals, nor of the ministerial officers. This gap allowed Ganilh to bring back the discussion on to its true ground, that of the independence of the judicial power. Setting aside all secondary details of the bill, he declared that he would only examine it in its relations to public liberties; then, after having analysed the hierarchy of the judicial offices, the dignities and emoluments which the bill placed at the disposition of the First Consul, 'What,' he asked, 'will be the natural, necessary, and inevitable effect of these dignities introduced into the organisation of the judicial power, and of the nomination to them by the First Consul? What will be their influence on the judges, on the tribunals, on justice? These dignities will establish relations of superiority and inferiority between men who have equal rights, since they perform the same duties; they will destroy the good feeling which ought to exist between them for the advantage and utility of the suitors, they will foment scandalous discussions fatal to the honour of the tribunals.

'Again, the favour of the First Consul alone can distribute and retain these dignities. Those to whom they have once been awarded will do all they can to retain them, or at any rate occasions will occur when they must run the risk of losing them. They will find themselves called upon to choose between interest and duty, a painful situation in which the law ought never to place its public functionaries, especially the judges who give decisions on the property, life, and honour of citizens. Lastly, these dignities, being annual and triennial, are incentives to the ambition and intrigue of the other judges. All will bustle and struggle to obtain them in turn, all will be tempted to sacrifice their duty to the authority which can dispose of them. Thus the tribunals of a free people will henceforth only vie with each other in servility before the first magistrate of the Republic, and the independence which the Constitution had insured them by making them irremovable will be destroyed and overthrown by the seduction of dignities established by the judicial organisation.'

In consequence, he claimed for the tribunals at least the right of nominating their presidents. In reply to those who denied that Government had any interest in influencing judgments, he enumerated all the causes of litigation in which it is more or less interested—the Customs, the Treasury, Stamps, Registration, indirect Taxes, National domains. But was not the independence of the judge still more necessary in criminal causes? The power of the president was here almost arbitrary; it was in this terrible office that it was most urgent he should be protected against all influence. If it were otherwise, what guarantee would there be for the accused? Not even that of the juries named by the prefect.

'Remember, Tribunes, that when the Constituent Assembly, composed of men almost all imbued with monarchical prejudices, established trial by jury, they carefully excluded all royal influence; they entrusted the choice of the jury to magistrates chosen by the people, the conduct of the accusation to a director of juries chosen by the people, the prosecution of the accusation to a public prosecutor chosen by the people, the conduct of the discussion to a president of the criminal tribunal chosen by the people; in a word, royal authority only appeared in this great act of national power by a commissioner, whose duty consisted in requiring the observation of forms in the direction and application of the law, in giving judgment.

'And we who have been brought up in republican principles, who have had such bitter experience of arbitrary power in criminal judgments, when they are under the influence of Government,—we, who shudder with horror at the remembrance of revolutionary tribunals, have already voted the passing of a law which puts the choice of juries at the disposition of Government, and to-day we have proposed to us a measure which places the director of the jury and the president of the criminal tribunal in the hands of the Government. What will the criminal tribunal become, when the jury is chosen by the Government, when the directors of the jury, the public prosecutor, the president, and the judges, are all guided by the passions of the Government? They will be simply commissioners of the Government.'[1]

Such was this well-reasoned and prophetic speech, sober in its oratorical effects, but strong as truth itself. Those who have reflected on the course which our judicial institutions have run since the day this speech was delivered will decide whether the men who were inspired by such sentiments, and who expounded such views, have merited the contempt with which our historians have treated them.[2]

Ganilh made a deep impression on the Assembly. The publication of his speech was demanded on all sides, but Stanislas Girardin opposed it, reproaching him with having attacked the Constitution. The publication was, however, voted, but the bill was nevertheless carried by the Tribunate as well as by the Legislative Body.

Together with these two laws, a number of other bills almost equally important were submitted to the Tribunate for deliberation, and all were to be discussed in as short a time as possible, otherwise the Assembly was to be denounced as an obstacle to the restoration of public order. The speakers were, to use an expression of Sédillez, drawn along in a *whirlwind of urgency*, which seemed to aim at

[1] *Archives Parlementaires.*
[2] M. Thiers alludes to this discussion in the Tribunate on the judicial organisation, in the following terms :—' As for the judicial organisation, some cried that it was a restoration of parliaments ; they complained in particular of the jurisdiction attributed to the Tribunal of Cassation over the inferior magistrates, all of them objections scarcely worth remembering.' And that is all ! *History of the Consulate and the Empire,* vol. i.

lessening their control by depriving them of the time necessary for the formation of a well-grounded opinion. But the Opposition did not fail in its duties, and we are surprised at the number and extent of its works, when we think of the short duration of the legislative session.

One of these bills furnished Benjamin Constant with an occasion of pointing out the political importance which the Tribunate might find in the right of petition, if it knew how to regulate the exercise of it. The Tribunate was specially charged by the Constitution to receive individual petitions (Art. 83). This function, combined with that which authorised it to express its opinion on laws made or to be made, on abuses to correct, on the improvements to be undertaken in all parts of the administration (Art. 29), might enormously increase the political activity of the Assembly, if it chose to regard its rights seriously. Owing to this powerful lever, which had, doubtless by inadvertence, been put into their hands, they might exercise a strong influence on public opinion. And even if they found a public very little disposed to second them in such an undertaking, which was in fact the case, still it was their duty, in the state of annihilation to which our free institutions were reduced, not to neglect a single prerogative, nor to leave one of their forces unemployed.

The motion of Benjamin Constant was intended to increase the influence of the Tribunate, to give it the work of permanently guarding the interests of the citizens and of moderating and checking the Government. He proposed, in consequence, a regulation, and a mode of classification, which would alone have constituted an encouragement to private individuals to make use of the right of petition.

He made a distinction between petitions on local interests and those whose object was the interest of an individual; between petitions for redress of wrongs and petitions for improvements. He wanted the Tribunate not to content itself with simply sending a bill back to the Government—a useless formality, of which the Government took no account—but, whenever a petition should be well founded, he asked that it should be corroborated by observation and information taken in support of it. This work would employ the Tribunate when the Legislative Body had closed its sittings, which only lasted four months. 'It will then be seen,' he said, 'that your regular business is improvement, and opposition only your exceptional work. To oppose is your right, to improve is your essence. Now man makes use of his rights but rarely, whereas he is always doing that which is conformable to his nature. Constitute yourselves, then, what you ought to be,—not a Chamber of permanent opposition, which would be absurd, and under some circumstances even culpable,—not a Chamber of eternal approbation, which would be servile and culpable too, in certain cases,—but a Chamber of opposition and of approbation, according to the measures proposed, and a Chamber of improvements. Dismiss from your minds all apprehensions as to any dread of irregular and tumultuous action, by devoting yourselves to a steady and tranquil course of beneficent energy and meditation.'

Chauvelin opposed the motion of Benjamin Constant, cleverly saying that it was a *petition for petitions*. This was true; but it was exactly that which constituted the merit of the motion, at a time when public spirit was extinguished and had lost all its organs. Chassiron denounced the proposition as 'likely to furnish a new Erostratus with the means of lighting afresh the still smouldering flame of civil discord.' Girardin awoke the recollection of petitions brought to the bar of the Convention; he reminded his hearers of the boy of twelve years of age who one day came before the assembly of representatives and said: 'I speak to you in the name of three millions of men.' The bill was thus thrown out without having encountered any serious refutation; its principal fault was that it was too bold for the majority of the Tribunes.

The law relative to the closing of the list of emigrants met with little opposition, because, whatever its defects, it was an immense improvement on the previous state of things. The law on the emigrants, the work of anger and despair, had confounded the innocent with the guilty. It put simple absence on a level with the crime of taking up arms against the country. It sufficed to have been inscribed, rightly or wrongly, on the list, to subject the emigrant to heavy penalties. After this desperate crisis, passions had calmed, and a large number of erasures had been ratified, but the law still remained, and the Directory had several times applied it against its enemies, in the course of its heedless reaction. The First Consul felt his position strong enough to abolish the law against emigrants, which a remnant of terrorist superstition still defended, and we must do him the justice to acknowledge that, in this respect, he had done what no one had dared to attempt before him. But the measure was neither as comprehensive nor as generous as is usually believed. The inscriptions on the list of emigrants, made or ordered before the Constitution was in force, were considered as judgments, and these people were excluded from the benefit of the new legislation. But those who complained of having been unjustly inscribed on the list could appeal to the Government, which was thus made the sovereign dispenser of relief, and could attach to this favour whatever conditions it pleased. Very soon, too, there arose, to use an expression of Lafayette, *an indecent stock-jobbing in erasures.* This was not all: instead of restoring *ipso facto*, that is to say with full rights, the unsold property to emigrants whose names were erased from the list, as the Directory had done, they reserved to themselves, thanks to the silence of the law on this point, the power of restoring it or keeping it at will, according to circumstances; or they gave it back by successive fractions, thus securing for themselves a powerful means of influence. In this, as in everything else, Bonaparte would have no fixed law, no settled state. Everything was to depend on his own will.

As for the Frenchmen who should henceforth be prosecuted for the crime of emigrating before the promulgation of the new law, they were to be submitted to ordinary justice, and were to be judged according to the anterior laws, but by a *special jury*, a provision which had the great defect of sanctioning the *tribunaux d'exception*. To this exception was added another. Confiscation could only take place after the claims of the creditors, the wife, and the children had been satisfied. The result was therefore that the position of emigrants convicted according to all legal form was better than that of persons presumed to be emigrants, and arrested on suspicion by an administrative decree. Two tribunes, Andrieux and De Gary, spoke in vain against this anomaly, of which the object was clear enough.

The objections raised against the privilege which the Government assumed in defiance of common law, of arbitrarily deciding upon the erasures, met with no better success. Boulay de la Meurthe replied to this objection, that the emigrants having been inscribed on the list, that is to say condemned administratively, the erasure of their names, that is to say their acquittal, ought to be made in the same way; and that to assign it to judicial authority would be 'a thing contrary to the demarcation of the powers.' This was justifying usurpation by usurpation.

The crime of emigration was thus struck out of our Code, at least prospectively. A Frenchman could freely leave his country on condition of submitting to the vexatious passport legislation. The First Consul demanded, however, that in case of absence delayed beyond the time accorded by the passport, the Government should have authority to sequestrate the property of the absentee, after three notices to return.

But this law, notwithstanding its defects, produced such a salutary improvement, that even those who opposed it would certainly have preferred it to the state of things which it superseded. Public opinion was less just towards a measure relative to the restoration of the right of disposing of property by will, though it was not less desirable nor less useful. The Revolution had abolished in an almost absolute manner the liberty of bequeathing property. The man who had children could only dispose by will of a tenth of his substance. The new bill greatly increased the disposable portion, but the right which it gave to the father, far from being unlimited, was in proportion to the number of his children. This was only a timid step towards the normal application of the true principles of property, as they were even then carried out in the United States of America. Unhappily, the theorists of our Revolution had had too great a propensity to sacrifice property, like every other individual right, to the State. Passion for equality, distorted by the remembrance of the iniquities of the feudal system, had gone so far as to dream of the destruction of individual property. Every blow dealt at this had been applauded. Not content with destroying privileges, they had struck at rights too. These prejudices were still full of life.

The public considered as a victory of the Revolution all the restrictions that had been put on the rights of property, forgetting that these restrictions were so many shackles to the liberty of individuals, already so weak and unarmed in the face of the power of the State. There is in France an inveterate tendency to dispossess citizens for the profit of society. Instead of the protector of interests, society is looked upon as their mistress, and the rights which she leaves to individuals are considered as so many favours granted. With this tendency was mingled a certain apprehension for which there were better grounds. The First Consul had already borrowed so much from the ancient *régime* that he had awakened a good deal of distrust. The new bill was looked upon as an essay of the same kind. Andrieux denounced it to the Tribunate as a disguised return to the right of primogeniture and substitutions. He demanded and obtained that the speech should be read which Mirabeau on his death-bed had left in manuscript on this subject. We know, in fact, that this great man, under the influence of resentment against parental authority, of which he had been long the victim, had voted against the right of bequeathing property; but as Regnauld St. Jean d'Angély remarked, this speech was no more than a rough sketch dictated by him to one of his numerous colleagues in whose work he was associated, and to which he had not put the finishing strokes. It is, however, not less true that on this point personal sufferings had warped that fine understanding, which could not later have failed to recognise how necessary it is that the family should be strongly constituted, in a democratic society which wishes to remain free. What, after all, are the possible abuses of the right of bequeathing property—abuses inseparable from all liberty, and which can, besides, be provided for up to a certain point—what are they, compared with the evil which results from excessive limitation of this right, destruction of all family feeling, annihilation of parental authority, periodical ruin of industries falling under the law of division, and the indefinite pulverisation of fortunes as of individuals?

The law was attacked with significant warmth by the speakers who had displayed nothing but indifference towards measures formally directed against liberty; which proves how much more attachment was then felt for what were regarded as the interests of the Revolution than for its principles. On the other hand, several of the members who voted with the Opposition, Ganilh and Benjamin Constant among others, separated on this occasion from their colleagues, and supported the bill; a fact which proves with sufficient cogency how far the Opposition of the Tribunate was removed from that systematic and foregone resolution to thwart, which has been attributed to it.

The votes on the bill relative to the finances of the Year IX (1800-1801) is an additional confirmation of this statement. The taxes gave a net revenue of 427,000,000—a sum recognised by every one as insufficient, even in times of peace. There were required about 200,000,000 more, and we were at war with the whole of Europe. In spite of this state of things, the Government, to the astonishment of every one, proposed to continue, with very slight modifications, for the Year IX the taxes fixed for the Year VIII. The commission of the Tribunate voted for the rejection of the bill, alleging with reason that it did not propose an adequate revenue.[1] They presented the singular spectacle of an Opposition, so often termed factious, offering the Government more money than it demanded. There was,

---

[1] *Rapport d'Arnoult de la Seine. Arch. Parl.*

doubtless, a cause for this strange inversion of parts which was not expressed.

Under the more or less specious pretext of the impossibility of fixing the excess of expenditure which war rendered necessary, an amount which might easily have been calculated approximately, the Government concealed their desire to maintain popularity with the exhausted population, and their hope of finding in the war itself the pay and keep of the troops. If Bonaparte displayed so much art in making allies pay a ransom, what resources would he not find in vanquished nations? At the same time the Government dispensed with the obligation of presenting the budget a year in advance, as the Constitution of the Year VIII required. They did not increase the amount of receipts; but this was done in order to remain free to fix that of expenses, about which they did not intend to give any information till much later. This twofold motive, which they could not avow, drove them to render the control of the Legislative Assembly over the finances entirely illusory, though this is a guarantee which the most despotic monarchies have often respected as a consolation in servitude. The objections of the commission against this deceptive budget, which aimed at keeping back from the Legislative Assembly all accurate knowledge of the interests of the nation, were recognised as just and well founded; but the Assembly, having no right to propose an amendment, could not reject so important and indispensable a measure. How could they, to expose themselves to the reproach of having ruined all the services? 'The Government asks 427,000,000,' said Bailleul, in the sitting of March 12; 'do you intend to refuse the 400,000,000, because you think they need 600,000,000? That would be a revolution, not in the state, but in nature. This is the first time since their existence that popular assemblies have been angry with a government for not asking enough.' This sophism changed the ground of debate: it was a question of control, not of the amount of money demanded. But a spirit of conciliation overruled principles, and the budget was voted just as the minister of finances presented it.

This law was one of the last measures of general interest voted in the course of this laborious session, which was closed on the 1st of April 1800. The Tribunate, having no more bills to discuss, decided, upon the motion of Chénier, that the members should still continue to assemble during the vacation of the Legislative Body, but only on the 1st and 16th of each month. Thus, as we have seen, the majority of this Assembly supported all the plans of the First Consul, except two or three of quite secondary interest. It was difficult to exact more entire compliance, unless the Tribunate had been declared a chamber of registration. Its only crime consisted in numbering in its body a generous and enlightened, though very calm, Opposition—an Opposition little disposed to seek applause by oratorical glitter; for these men spoke to a people who only gave a divided attention, and who freely rallied them for their want of power. Without the support of public opinion, without the prestige of a popular mandate, or the sympathy of a public that was madly enamoured of the glory of military success, this Opposition maintained with firmness, good sense, and integrity, the true principles of the Revolution, against a headlong and unbridled ambition.

Odious to their master by an unalterable moderation, which gave him no weapon to turn against them; importunate to his subjects, whom they reminded of the nullity of their republican convictions; attacked without respite by a host of servile writers; sneered at by the Government itself, who openly denounced them in the *Moniteur*, publishing their discussions in a mutilated form, sometimes even suppressing them altogether,—they remained resolutely faithful to liberty, with the certainty of failing to work any change in the desperate state of the cause. They accepted without illusion this modest and self-sacrificing part. They accomplished their task with courage and conscientiousness, and with that simplicity which sheds a lustre on the performance of a duty; and far from having failed for want of intelligence, much of their work might profitably be consulted to-day by a generation which is so proud of having far surpassed them.

The generous efforts of this minority were useless, and

historians have hitherto been more unfair towards them than their adversaries themselves. But the future will do them justice. When severe history shall have to narrate the origin and development of that administrative despotism which so quickly took the place of our free institutions, when it has to tell of the formation of that colossal figure with feet of clay, which was to devour so much substance and so many lives, it will preserve the memory of these honest and forgotten men, whose wise warnings were despised by a people in bondage to the fascinations of success.

END OF VOL. I.

Printed by R. & R. CLARK, *Edinburgh.*

www.ingramcontent.com/pod-product-compliance
Lightning Source LLC
Chambersburg PA
CBHW031955300426
44117CB00008B/769